DATE DUE

OCT 24 2001			
MAR 12 2008			
DEC 10			
GAYLORD			PRINTED IN U.S.A.

WOMEN IN AMERICAN HISTORY

Series Editors

Mari Jo Buhle
Jacquelyn D. Hall
Anne Firor Scott

*A list of books in the series appears
at the end of this volume.*

BEYOND THE TYPEWRITER

BEYOND THE TYPEWRITER

Gender, Class, and the Origins of Modern American Office Work, 1900–1930

SHARON HARTMAN STROM

UNIVERSITY OF ILLINOIS PRESS
Urbana and Chicago

This book is printed on acid-free paper.

Library of Congress Cataloging-in-Publication Data

Strom, Sharon Hartman.
    Beyond the typewriter : gender, class, and the origins of modern
American office work, 1900-1930 / Sharon Hartman Strom.
        p.   cm.—(Women in American history)
    Includes index.
    ISBN 0-252-01806-0 (alk. paper)
    1. Office practice—United States—History.   2. Secretaries—
United States—History.   3. Women—Employment—United States—
History.   4. Sexual division of labor—United States—History.
5. Office politics—United States—History.   I. Title.   II. Series.
HF5547.5.S816   1992
331.4'81653'097309043—dc20   91-19273
                                                                                    CIP

For Burt

Contents

Photographs follow page 270.

Journal and Collection Abbreviations Used in Notes

Manuscripts and Oral Histories

BVI   Bureau of Vocational Information Collection, Schlesinger Library, Radcliffe College, Cambridge, Massachusetts.

BVIWS*   Bureau of Vocational Information Woman Secretary Survey, 1924-25

RIWBP†   Rhode Island Women's Biography Project, Special Collections, University of Rhode Island Library, Kingston

RIWW†   Rhode Island Working Women Oral History Project, Special Collections, University of Rhode Island Library

SM   Scovill Manufacturing Collection, Series II, Baker Library, Harvard Business School, Cambridge, Mass.

Journals and Periodicals

AC   *American City*

AMAOES   American Management Association *Office Executive Series*

Annals   *Annals of the American Academy of Political and Social Science*

BHR	*Business History Review*
BVINB	*News Bulletin of the Bureau of Vocational Information*
HBR	*Harvard Business Review*
IM	*Industrial Management*
JPR	*Journal of Personnel Research*
MLR	*Monthly Labor Review*
OE	*Office Economist*
PJ	*Personnel Journal*
SB	*Scovill Bulletin*
TSB	*Bulletin of the Taylor Society*
WBB	*Women's Bureau Bulletin*

*The BVIWS survey of secretaries and stenographers was nation-wide, but to reflect major centers of clerical work, I looked mainly at the responses (949 in total) from New York City, Oakland, and San Francisco, Philadelphia, Chicago, Atlanta, Los Angeles, Hartford, and Washington, D.C. When a questionnaire is cited I indicate my number, followed by the BVI survey number in parentheses, followed by the state where the respondent lived. In a few instances I cite questionnaires not in the 949 I examined in detail, and in these cases, the BVI questionnaire number is given in parentheses.

†Actual names of those interviewed for RIWBP and RIWW have been changed to pseudonyms in the text.

Foreword

At the top were the big chiefs, the officers of the company, and the heads of the departments—Mr. Pemberton and his sons, the treasurer, the general manager, the purchasing-agent . . . . The Olympian council were they; divinities to whom the lesser clerks had never dared to speak . . . . And like envoys extraordinary were the efficiency experts whom Mr. Pemberton occasionally had in to speed up the work a bit more beyond the point of human endurance . . . . Just beneath the chiefs were the caste of bright young men who would some day have the chance to be beatified into chiefs . . . . They sat, in silk shirts and new ties, at shiny, flat-topped desks in rows; they answered the telephone with an air; they talked about tennis and business conditions, and were never, never bored.

Intermingled with this caste were the petty chiefs, the office-managers and bookkeepers, who were velvety to those placed in power over them, but twangily nagging to the girls and young men under them. Failures themselves, they eyed sourly the stenographers who desired two dollars more a week, and assured them that while PERSONALLY they would be VERY glad to obtain the advance for them, it would be "unfair to the other girls.". . . Their own salaries were based on "keeping-down overhead.". . . Awe-encircled as the very chiefs they appeared when they lectured stenographers, but they cowered when the chiefs spoke to them, and tremblingly fingered their frayed cuffs . . . .

Una's caste, made up of private secretaries to the chiefs, . . . was a staff corps, small and exclusive and out of the regular line. On the one hand she could not associate with the chiefs; on the other, . . . in her capacity as daily confidante to one of the gods, . . . she should not be friendly, in coat-room or rest room or elevator, with the unrecognized horde of girls who merely copied or took the bright young men's dictation of letters to drugstores . . . .

There was no caste, though there was much factional rivalry, among the slaves beneath—the stenographers, copyists, waiting room attendants, office-boys, elevator-boys . . . .

Machines were the Pemberton force, and their greatest rivals were the machines of steel and wood, at least one of which each new efficiency expert left behind him. But none of the other machines was so tyrannical as the time-clock . . . .

She knew that the machines were supposed to save work. But she was aware that the girls worked just as hard and long and hopelessly after their introduction as before . . . . She could not imagine any future for these women in business except the accidents of marriage or death—or a revolution in the attitude toward them.

—Sinclair Lewis, *The Job* (1917)

Acknowledgments

When I was growing up I liked to hear my grandmothers, my mother, and my aunts talk about the work they had done as young women. The stories of their jobs in a Los Angeles department store, a small-town drug store, and an Idaho law office first interested me in the world of working women. My grandmothers earned incomes well into their seventies. Pearl Amy McCormick managed a boardinghouse, and Nell O'Hanlon Skinner ran a farm, then a gift shop, and later sewed and played cards professionally. My mother, Ivy McCormick Hartman, and her sisters, Kathleen McCormick Hart and Mary McCormick Searby, all went to work in offices when they reentered the work force after having their children. While none had the jobs they might have secured with college educations and a discrimination-free workplace, all cared deeply about doing their work with intelligence and integrity. I hope that the respect I have for them is evident in these pages.

This book came into being at the University of Rhode Island, helped along by financial support from the College of Arts and Sciences, the URI Foundation, and the Faculty Development Program. A grant from the Radcliffe Research Scholars' Program enabled me to investigate materials in the Schlesinger Library. A fellowship year at the Bunting Institute of Radcliffe College gave me time to draft an early version of the manuscript and to share some of my ideas with helpful colleagues.

Numerous institutions and individuals eased my way in compiling materials. The staffs of the Schlesinger Library, the Baker Library of the Harvard Business School, the New York Public Library, and the Rhode Island Historical Society were all generous with their time and expertise. I am grateful to the family of the late Richard Roberts for permission to include one of his pictures. The meticulous and timely interviews conducted by Valerie Raleigh Yow and Gail Gregory Sansbury for the Rhode Island Working Women Oral History Project were indispensable to this book, as were the biographies of women written by students at the University of Rhode Island in my Women in American History class over the last fifteen years. Martha Ashness Doyle, Herbert Carey, and Bernice Reed Anderson shared their experiences in office work with me. Joan Tonn was kind enough to show me her work on Mary Parker Follett, and Maury Klein shared his research of the Pennsylvania Railroad archives. Lisa Signorelli Corey compiled data from the Bureau of Vocational Information study of stenographers and secretaries and took care of my daughter. Frances Ward, Patricia Quigley, and Adam Strom helped track down library materials.

Parts of chapters 1, 4 and 5 first appeared as "'Machines Instead of Clerks': Technology and the Feminization of Bookkeeping, 1910-1950," in *Computer Chips and Paper Clips: Technology and Women's Employment*, ed. Heidi Hartmann (Washington, D.C.: National Academy Press, 1987), 1: 63-97, and a version of chapter 5 was first published as "'Light Manufacturing': The Feminization of American Office Work, 1900-1930," *Industrial and Labor Relations Review* 43 (Oct. 1989): 53-69.

My initial ideas for this book were generated some years ago, and a number of people urged me to carry them further. The early encouragement of Heidi Hartmann, Bruce Laurie, Ruth Milkman, David Montgomery, and Louise Tilly was particularly important. I owe special thanks to the editors of the Women in American History Series of the University of Illinois Press. Anne Firor Scott first solicited the manuscript; Jacquelyn D. Hall and Mari Jo Buhle read several versions of it. They provided just the right combination of enthusiastic support and helpful criticism. My editor, Carole Appel, was unfailingly cheerful when I needed help and left me alone when I didn't, even when I took longer than expected to finish.

A number of people were generous enough to read the manuscript and provide me with helpful advice. Cindy Sondik Aron, J. Morton Briggs, Ileen DeVault, Michael Edelstein, Natalie Boymel Kampen, Barbara Melosh, Priscilla Murolo, and Judith Smith read individual chapters. Gerald Zahavi read the final draft and offered fine suggestions. I am most endebted to Susan Porter Benson, who read two versions of the entire manuscript, and whose steady friendship and constructive collaboration have meant more to me than I can say.

Finishing this book has been both delightful and bittersweet. I feel my mother's absence deeply, but am happy for the companionship of my sister, Kathy Hartman Flournoy, and for the mothering I have received from Judith Anderson, Kathleen Hart, Mary Searby, Lois Burks, Hilda Pollack, and Carol L. Winfield. My children, Erin Hartman Ehm, Kevin Hartman, and Adam and Caitlin Strom, managed to sustain remarkable interest in the project over many years and have continued to provide me with a sense of what is really important. Burt Strom supported me in ways both great and small. He wrote the program that sorted the BVI data, helped me battle the computer, and brought a nonacademic's eye and fresh perspective to each reading. He has encouraged me to do my work, made doing it possible, and cheered me on with jokes, dinners, and affection.

Introduction

IN 1932 *The Office Economist,* a trade publication for office
workers and managers, featured a photograph of Dorothy Wilson
and described her in the caption below as a "pretty eighteen year-
old" who had been "catapulted from a stenographer's desk to film
stardom." The unusual photograph was not a standard movie stu-
dio portrait, but a shot of Wilson on a small platform, surrounded
by sister clerks from the Stenographers' and Secretaries' Club of
Los Angeles. The caption claimed they were tired of "being represented in the films as 'Office Wives'" and wanted the movie studios
"to tell them how they can dress like stenographers depicted in the
films on their salaries." In the photograph club members are holding two large placards on sticks: "DOROTHY WILSON TO MAKE MOV-
IES: ENCOURAGING LONGER LUNCH HOUR," and "WILSON: THE REAL
LIFE MIRACLE GIRL OF THE MOVIES."[1]

The Dorothy Wilson photograph is an important historical document in more ways than one. It represents, for one thing, a specific moment in time: a few years after the Stock Market Crash of
1929, a year before the darkest hours of the 1930s, a moment when
office workers were just beginning to organize into unions and
make demands they had only half-articulated in the 1920s. Today
most people refer to women clerical workers as "secretaries." But in
1932 women clerks in a Los Angeles club who divided themselves
into "secretaries" and "stenographers" were indicating important
distinctions between the two occupations based on class, craft, and
age. The meaning of the term *office wife* was multiple: it implied
that women brought their sexuality to the office, where it could be

evaluated by men, but it also indicated that women were there to take care of their "office husbands," to perform domestic house-keeping and organization chores, and to remain in subservient positions. The photograph and its caption also highlight the permeable boundaries between the sexual objectification that women clerks resented (or desired) and the mundane (or important) work they performed every day. The placards epitomized opposite poles of representation of woman clerks. At one extreme, she was a potential movie star, ready, in her glamorous clothing, to go straight from desk to screen. At the other, she was an ordinary working stiff with such workplace problems as having enough time to eat her lunch. This dichotomy of cultural representation hovered over the lives of women clerical workers between 1900 and 1930. Reduced to simple questions, the placards may be said to ask whether the woman office clerk was taking advantage of new op-portunities for the working woman or whether she was just another version of exploited female labor. The premise of this book is that the answers to both questions are "yes"; a pivotal ambiguity struc-tured the self-identity of women who entered office work in the three decades before the Great Depression.

In this book I examine the early years of the modern office, which constituted the workplace backdrop for Wilson and the other stenographers of Los Angeles in 1932. The office as we know it emerged at the turn of the twentieth century. The services it began to provide were indispensable to the managing of govern-ment, the dispensing of public utilities, the distribution of retail commodities, the production of manufactured goods, the exchange of money and the insuring of property and life. Its organizational form was increasingly hierarchical and bureaucratic. Its purpose was to integrate and facilitate the management of government and businesss through efficiency, accountability, and precise record-keeping. Government reform and the growing reliance of the cor-poration on complex functions of cost accounting required the application of new systems of paperwork, computation produc-tion, and supervising techniques that came to be known loosely as "scientific management," a body of ideas first publicized by Fred-erick Winslow Taylor and other engineers in the decade before World War I.

Labor and business historians, notably Daniel Nelson, David Montgomery, and Alfred W. Chandler, Jr., have been keenly inter-ested in how these economic and organizational developments of early-twentieth-century life affected, on the one hand, foremen, craft, and industrial workers, and on the other, executive-level managers.[2] But the vast office work system and the ways in which its clerks gave the "visible hand" greater control over "managers and workers" in "the house of labor" remains largely invisible in the work of these scholars. Important studies of white-collar work, first by C. Wright Mills, and then by Margery Davies, Harry Braverman, and Robert Howard, have concluded that scientific management techniques were applied as extensively to the office as to the factory floor.[3] This book will amplify that conclusion. But it will also suggest that without an expanded army of clerks, managers, and business professionals, modern economic and government organization would have been impossible, and that an office hierarchy based on class and gender produced the paperwork, bookkeeping, and managerial expertise that propelled the machinery of scientific management and the integration of economic functions. Scientific management could be applied to office work, but without new office work systems the application of scientific management to the workplace would have been impossible.

A new class of business professionals took up the application of scientific management with missionary zeal. Perhaps because they were defensive about their relatively new claim to professional status, these professionals were particularly adamant about the masculine identity of their disciplines. Scientific management provided business professionals not only with a system of procedures but also with an ideological rationale for their own dominance. They saw the allocation of planning to managers and the rationalization of work as not only economic goals but also political goods; summarized as "efficiency," scientific management became an indisputable moral tenet of the early twentieth century.

Both male and female reformers in the Progressive period were often as attracted to Taylorism as were business professionals, and touted scientific management as a panacea for labor unrest, political corruption, and corporate irresponsibility. Women with feminist agendas saw in the even-handed execution of its methods a means of bringing sexual equality to the marketplace. Male business professionals more frequently used scientific management to promulgate what they perceived to be masculine values and modes of thought: scientific planning, an end to sentimentality, and the objectification of workers and materials. They saw themselves as forging new frontiers in a society whose old forms of male adventurism were about to end and proposed new expeditions for themselves along the corporate frontier of cost accounting, institution building, and managerial control. Conflicts between these ways of seeing and using scientific management emerged from differing positions of gender, professionalism, and reform.

A hierarchical labor system based on class and gender not only facilitated the execution of scientific management but also made its execution uneven. Faced with a shortage of educated male clerks willing to be paid low wages, managers turned to women, many of them working class, to be the "operatives" in the office workplace. There was an association between mechanization, feminization, and rationalization, but it does not explain all that women did in the office. Many labor economists have accepted the idea that the demeaning of women's labor was nearly complete in both industrial and clerical work in the early twentieth century. David Gordon, Michael Reich, and Richard Edwards, who find extensive segmentation among categories of male workers, find few differences of importance among women workers. Apparent victims of an all-encompassing women's labor market principle, female workers are depicted as an amorphous group characterized by nothing but their gender.[4] Labor historians have often dismissed white-collar work of all kinds as non-working class and non-artisanal, so office workers are generally absent from labor history. But the evidence indicates that segmentation—or the division of workers into different categories of class and status—was as acute in office work and among women workers as it was in the workplace at large. Originally more the product of larger economic and cultural forces than conspiratorial planning, segmentation among office workers nonetheless constituted a golden opportunity for managers to prevent union organizing and the development of a collective consciousness among office workers well into the 1930s, even among women and men who were working class and came from union families.

Control of the integrative functions of early modern office work rested firmly in the hands of an executive-managerial elite that was almost entirely male. By 1930 the elite was, for the most part, being trained in business professions—engineering, business administration, accounting, and personnel management—whose influence had grown with every passing year. Engineers and accountants can trace their history to the nineteenth century, but both personnel managers and business administrators are twentieth-century creations. By 1910 the interests of these professionals had found a secure niche in both universities and governing circles of corporate and government institutions. The business professionals all followed the example of doctors, lawyers, and ministers by attempting, with varying degrees of success, to exclude women from their ranks.

As far as early business professionals were concerned, women and feminine influence had to be excluded from the managerial ethos or its masculine purity would be threatened. Women's claims for equal participation in economic life were being legitimized by the suffrage movement and expanding college educations. Clear lines needed to be drawn on the basis of gender, or qualified women would soon demand to be included at the highest levels of professional life. The professions were all under siege by women by 1900.

Nothing more clearly symbolized the defensiveness of the business class to women's demands to "get in" than the footbridge over the Charles River that connects the Harvard Business School to the Cambridge campus. The graceful 1926 pathway was dedicated to John W. Weeks, a banker and former Massachusetts senator, one of two senators in the country chosen for defeat by the woman suffrage movement in 1918 because of his long-standing opposition to votes for women. The steps on either side of the bridge are guarded by double obelisks, the phallic symbolism of which could not be lost on anyone. The Harvard Business School did not admit women until 1963.

But the Harvard Business School was not guarded by castle walls or gun turrets; a footbridge was a far more ambivalent symbol, and one that might someday let women cross the moat. Scientific management had its problems by 1920. Pure Taylorism remained difficult to install. Workers found its methods to be ruthless, and they often rebelled against them. Managers found scientific management too costly to implement. As women reformers had suggested, its emphasis on statistical measurement and investigative inquiry could undermine the privileges of traditional elites. Psychologists, whose influence in academic institutions was growing rapidly, offered tempting new subjective possibilities for manipulating and organizing human beings. With roots in both the ministry and philosophy, fields many considered effeminate anyway, psychology provided new methods of manipulation for those already in control but also tended to undermine the masculine ethos of business. If women found it nearly impossible to enter engineering and the best graduate schools of business administration, they could certainly become psychologists, and psychologists could become employment experts and even personnel managers. Many men in personnel management and psychology promoted an essentially feminine point of view when they talked about paying attention to workers' instincts, needs, and capacities for internalizing discipline. The truth of the matter was that scientific management needed a feminine touch in order to survive. The "human factor" proved to be beyond the scope of pure Taylorism.

By excluding most women from the business professions and refusing to hire them as executives, the upper echelons of management remained free of women, if not of feminine influence. The office itself, however, was increasingly full of females. Women, as far as managers were concerned, made ideal candidates for clerical jobs and clerical work supervisors, but the presence of so many women also threatened the cultural dominance of men. William Leffingwell, an ex-bookkeeper turned office manager and Frederick Taylor's counterpart in the field of office management, remained nervous about the extent to which women poured into office work after 1900. He feared that slack standards might ensue, that the "Cinderella" of feminization would turn the office into a "Frankenstein" of sexual disorder. A variety of strategies were available to managers for keeping women in the office under control. Gendered categories of office work helped to maintain sexual difference and made certain that women would be confined to assisting, not directing, men. Employers sought to designate routine clerical work as "light manufacturing," to associate it with women's operative status in factories, and to suggest that while it was appropriate for most women it was not in any way similar to the skilled work of most men.

The attempt to separate clerical workers along lines of gender and class was never as successful in reality as the paradigm I have sketched out here would suggest. The office required a finely tuned range of workers from different classes with varying levels of education and left workers with some room to maneuver into new situations. Discrimination barred nearly all people of color from offices outside their own communities, and the poor English-language skills of most immigrants disqualified them as well. But English-speaking white workers of both sexes with high school, business college, or college education could be plugged into a growing hierarchy of specialized jobs. Although there was a sexual division of labor—most typists were women, most sales forces were men—occupations such as bookkeeper and general clerk were made up of large proportions of both men and women. The growing employment of women did not mean that men stopped seeking work in the office. As clerical, sales, and managerial occupations mushroomed in the years before 1930, both men and women flocked to office work. Nor were women entirely confined to "operative" work; they became secretaries, office managers, bookkeepers, and general clerks. Women and men frequently did similar kinds of work and sometimes had the same job titles.

The insatiable demand for high school-educated workers shaped the profile of American secondary education after 1900. Faced with low attendance rates at the turn of the century, educators bolstered high school attendance in the teens by promoting staying in school as a way that children could "move up" to office work. Parents, who grasped the same possibilities, demanded commercial education for their children. Working-class women and men used public education in business to train themselves for jobs that promised some upward mobility. Employers saw the public schools as places where future workers could receive training at the state's expense.

Prestigious men's colleges and coeducational universities also experimented with business curricula, and by 1910 business schools and departments were a permanent and rapidly growing component of higher education in the United States. The prestigious women's colleges were considerably more ambivalent about business education. They set up vocational bureaus to help their graduates find jobs in fields "other than teaching"—often a euphemism for office work—but resisted business courses for college credit. Their goal was to open the more prestigious professions to women, but the reality was that both high school- and college-educated women often found office work to be their only real choice of employment beyond teaching. Mostly closed out of medicine, law, engineering, and business administration by sex discrimination, middle-class women often tried to claim professional status for secretarial work and to set it off from the more "factorylike" jobs of stenography and business machine operating. Class distinction as well as gender difference was a source of tension in the office.

Both sexes enjoyed the heterosocial environment of the new office. Women welcomed the opportunity to work alongside men and to do what had been men's work, and popular culture at large endorsed the sexual objectification of women and eased their transition into the workplace; flirtation and romance among coworkers of the opposite sex was decidedly modern. The new office hierarchy created supervisory positions that many men were happy to hold. But male clerks, bookkeepers, and stenographers had something to lose with feminization. They might fear, with good reason, that management planned to lower the status of their work and give it to women. Real clerical salaries began to decline as jobs were rationalized and women entered the office in large numbers.

During the extraordinary years of growth that surrounded World War I and continued into the 1920s, the art of applying scientific management to office workers emerged as a full-fledged discipline. Office managers sought to classify and segment workers, develop tests for hiring and promotion, apply rationalization, and reduce labor costs by eliminating the higher salaries. The application of scientific management techniques to office work, which tended to appear along with more women clerks, undermined men's expectations for self-governed work and respectable wages. Dependent on the labor of both sexes, managers tried to arrange a compromise that would placate men and still allow them to rationalize and feminize clerical work. Men were allegedly given access to promotions, salary increases, and managerial positions. A different ladder of opportunity, with much smaller rungs and increments, was offered to those women who stayed in the workplace beyond their early twenties. What economists call the marriage bar—the firing of women upon marriage or the denial of promotions and more responsible positions to them because they might marry and have children—was used to justify these different labor systems, even though many women stayed on in office work for most of their adult lives.

The segmentation of office labor along lines of gender and class remained difficult to resist, and once installed, difficult to change. Some women faced segmentation along gender lines squarely. They protested barriers to promotion, attacked the marriage bar, and grumbled about their low salaries. But the segmentation of women along lines of class and age also produced conflict between groups of women and undermined an office politics based squarely on sex. Despite the assumption by popular commentators and most recent scholars that office workers were pretty much all the same in these years—young, middle class, and bent on marriage—employers of the time knew otherwise. They purposefully sought to segment women's labor in the office and capitalized on the divisions they fostered. Labor segmentation in the office reflected important differences of class, marital status, and age as well as of gender. Middle-class and middle-aged women most frequently rose to better positions in office work, including those of secretary, employment manager, and office manager, and youthful working-class women most often found themselves typing, doing machine work, and taking dictation, although none of these class and age expectations were ever absolute. The marriage bar isolated women who did not marry or did not intend to marry from those who did, even as employers increasingly allowed some married women to stay at their jobs. As more and more women stayed on in office work beyond their twenty-fifth birthdays, age became a major dividing line between women. "Younger women" (those under twenty-five) and "older women" (those over twenty-five) had different self-conceptions that influenced their responses in the workplace. All of these forms of segmentation divided women from each other, women from men, and prevented office workers from sharing common grievances.

In the years between 1900 and 1930, the discourses of both unionism and feminism were available to office workers as methods for analyzing and improving their situation. Here and there, among telephone operators and government employees, women office workers tried to combine the two. But the working-class connotations of unions, the hostility of most of the dominant unions to women, and the middle-class origins (or aspirations) of many clerical workers made unionism an unworkable strategy for the time being. With the feminist movement at its peak, the women's rights movement provided a more accessible language than the ideals of unionism for those who wanted to attack the sexual division of labor in office work. Feminism alone was limited in its usefulness for changing the conditions of office work. Without a union consciousness, mainstream feminism tended to reenforce notions of individualism even as it built a mass movement.

Liberal notions of equality of opportunity can be both class and race blind, and more often emphasize the right to compete for a place in a hierarchy than the dramatic restructuring of it. Many ambitious women office workers, the "career women" of their day, wanted the right to compete for better jobs. They criticized discrimination in employment and the marriage bar. But they took an individualist, not a collective, view of their own oppression. They often blamed the office flapper, the working-class clerk with a grammar school education, or the woman who left work to be married for the failure of business elites to take working women seriously. Because there really were expanding (but limited) opportunities for women in clerical work positions, blaming other women for their own lack of success was a predictable response of ambitious women. A different paradigm based on both feminism and unionism might have acknowledged that the marriage bar was largely a smokescreen, that women were excluded from the upper ranks on the basis of their sex, not their qualifications, and that most women would remain in the lower ranks no matter how ambitious and hardworking they were.

Office jobs were the best jobs available to most women between 1900 and 1930. Women understood this and made rational choices for the future by investing in commerical education and taking office jobs. Even though the decision to enter clerical work was usually made in the context of the family, performing clerical work often served to separate women from their families' identities and to make them more independent. Office work, despite its gendered limits, could open the door to a wider world. Even though many women languished in boring jobs from which they longed to be freed, they also experimented with downtown amusements, pursued friendships and flirtations, and sought more education. Many others did what they considered to be worthwhile and inventive work, experimented with careers, and moved on to more expansive horizons. But not all of these women were the same. Some had to support themselves and their families, others really didn't have to work. Most expected to marry, some hoped to spend the rest of their lives with women or on their own. Most were white, but some were black. Most were young, but a significant number were middle-aged.

By 1930, office work was the most likely occupation of urban working women and one of the most important occupations for men. This host of clerks, male and female, reflect, in the end, not just where many workers were—in the office—but how reliant the new organizational order was on the office and the extent to which office work made possible more visible kinds of labor.

What follows is a brief explanation of some terms used frequently in the text: The modern office encompassed three main strata of workers. At the top were the managerial executives and company officers, who were almost without exception male. I will refer to these men as "employers," "executives," or "top-level managers." Reporting to these men was a broad layer of managers, some of them lowly and others quite important. They governed departments, supervised large groups of clerical workers, or managed small office staffs. Analagous to foremen and forewomen in factories, these "mid-level" and "low-level managers," both women and men, were responsible for supervising the clerical work produced in the office. Women and men who produced the clerical work—in the form of letters, telephone calls, reports, ledgers, timecards, sales summaries, and payrolls—included bookkeepers and secretaries, typists and stenographers, machine clerks and shipping clerks. When not referring to them with a specific job description I have labeled them as "clerks" or "clerical workers."

Gender is a term which has only recently made its way into American scholarship, so I offer an explanation of how I have used the term here. While human beings have many biological traits in common, there are usually clear differences in the anatomical and reproductive characteristics of men and women that indicate their "sex." Whether these differences have any essential meaning for how we live our lives or organize our workplaces is open to debate, but thus far has not been established scientifically; these differences are the ongoing products of political and social debate. When they come up for discussion in various subjective ways ("women are more patient and better at repetitive work than men," or "men are more rational than women," or "women are naturally maternal") differences between men and women are no longer those of sex but of gender. Instead of referring to clear biological differences, as sex does, gender refers to the social construction of sex: the cultural and psychological traits different societies attribute to being male and female. In the early twentieth century, managerial elites (nearly always male) promoted nineteenth-century notions of gender to establish and maintain their own dominance of institutions, the professions, and emerging discourses such as scientific management. What is masculine and what is feminine, however, is not strictly the province of either sex; human beings internalize aspects of both genders and can call on any combination of these traits, which meanwhile are changing in the context of historical circumstance. Although powerful elites fought a constant holding action to exclude people of the "wrong" sex (and class and race) from positions of influence, both masculine and feminine traits found their way into managerial strategies. To give just two examples, scientific management would not work without a "feminine touch" (whether administered by men or women), and women could not be successful upper-level managers without adopting "masculine" personae. When I say that something is "masculine" or "feminine," to repeat, I do not imply any biological connection, but rather a culturally constructed one.

This book is divided into two parts. In the first half I examine the economic and managerial structure of the modern office, the reasons for the recruitment of a vast office labor force, the gendered construction of engineering, business administration, accounting, and personnel management, and the growing feminization, mechanization, and rationalization of office management systems.

In the second half of the book I turn to the office labor force. Here I have made the arbitrary decision to focus on women office workers. While I describe gender relationships in the workplace I do not examine men's office work culture in any detail, not because I doubt its existence or importance, but because there is not enough room to consider it in this book. If Part 1 evokes the economic and historical reasons for the evolution of the American office work structure and its dominance by business class elites, Part 2 examines more ordinary office workers as a manipulated group but also as one with potential self-consciousness.

NOTES

1. *Office Economist* 14(Sept. 1932): 13.

2. Alfred D. Chandler, Jr., *The Visible Hand: The Managerial Revolution in American Business* (Cambridge: Harvard University Press, 1977); David Montgomery, *The Fall of the House of Labor: The Workplace, the State, and American Labor Activism, 1865-1925* (Cambridge: Cambridge University Press, 1987); and Daniel Nelson, *Managers and Workers: Origins of the New Factory System in the United States, 1880-1920* (Madison: University of Wisconsin Press, 1975).

3. C. Wright Mills, *White Collar: The American Middle Classes* (New York: Oxford University Press, 1951); Harry Braverman, *Labor and Monopoly Capital: The Degradation of Work in the Twentieth Century* (New York: Monthly Review Press, 1974); Margery W. Davies, *Woman's Place Is at the Typewriter: Office Work and Office Workers, 1870-1930* (Philadelphia: Temple University Press, 1982); Robert Howard, *Brave New Workplace* (New York: Penguin Books, 1986).

4. David M. Gordon, Richard Edwards, and Michael Reich, *Segmented Work, Divided Workers: The Historical Transformation of Labor in the United States* (Cambridge: Cambridge University Press, 1982).

PART I

Economic and Cultural Origins of the New Office: Gendered Hierarchies of Management

1

Efficiency, Accountability, and the Rise of Scientific Management

W HEN JOHN H. GOSS graduated from Yale University in 1894 with a degree in liberal arts, he returned to his home town, Waterbury, and went to work as an apprentice in the tool and machine room of the button department at Scovill Manufacturing Company. Goss was no ordinary apprentice. His older brother, Edward O. Goss, had been trained as a mechanical engineer at the Massachusetts Institute of Technology and was already poised to enter the top ranks of Scovill management. The Goss brothers' father, Chauncey P. Goss, first hired as an assistant bookkeeper at Scovill during the Civil War, had forged a managerial partnership with another bookkeeper, Mark L. Sperry, and together they had steered the brass company through difficult decades. The senior Goss had risen to treasurer and then to general manager. He would become president of the Scovill corporation in 1900, and Sperry would succeed him for two years in 1918. As Chauncey Goss's eldest son, Edward O. Goss had only to wait until 1920 before becoming president. John Goss would not hold that position until 1938, after Edward died, and then for only six years. Yet his influence at Scovill, first as superintendent and then as vice president, was to be far-reaching. Inspired by the principles of "system," or scientific management, he helped to usher in new methods of management that transformed the work force at Scovill in the years between 1900 and 1930.

Goss would later say that when he first worked at Scovill he made ten cents an hour and worked sixty hours a week. He thought the value of that experience had been incalculable, and it probably had. While he assumed that his fancy college education had enabled him to "introduce a little system into the immediate area in which I was working," his three years in the tool and machine room also gave him an understanding of how the most powerful workers at manufacturing plants like Scovill, the machinists, did their work and managed their days. "I had a pretty stiff job," he recalled of his attempts to reorganize the machine room. "I met at least passive resistance from every direction."[1] Like his older colleague Frederick Winslow Taylor, Goss was part of an ambitious, self-confident group of professional managers who saw the reorganization of the workplace and the appropriation of knowledge from machinists and other largely self-governed workers as their most important task.[2]

Goss, his brothers (a third brother, Chauncey Goss, Jr., ran the rolling mills, and a fourth, A. Goss, the manufacturing department), and the three sons of M. L. Sperry, all engineers and accountants, used their expertise to make Scovill one of the most competitive companies of Connecticut's "brass valley" as well as to break the hold of the old technical experts of brass production: machinists, rollers, and casters. Disputes between management, male craftsmen, heavy-manufacturing workers, and the women who produced buttons and straight pins preceded Chancey Goss's rise to the presidency of Scovill and culminated in a strike in 1919. Efforts to impose new forms of industrial discipline and the strike of 1919 were battles in an ongoing war. A new phalanx of mid-level managers, clerical workers, and technicians had been hired by the Gosses and Sperrys to fight that war and to help work out the systems of managerial control they were installing: elaborate cost accounting methods, research and development schemes, payroll and timekeeping plans, personnel management techniques, and centralized planning.

A variety of new occupations and people to fill them were required to transform office work at Scovill. Frederick Packard had been hired as a clerk in the casting department in 1904. By 1911 he had become assistant manager of the newly created central timekeeping office and in 1919 became its head. Ella Patchen, born in Middlebury in 1871, first worked as a school teacher. After clerking at two bicycle companies, she came to work at Scovill as one of three stenographers in 1901; she "returned from her vacation one summer to find her desk moved to the president's office." Never married, she would work at Scovill for more than forty years and be private secretary to three chief executives, including John Goss. Edna Murray first joined Scovill in the button shop in 1898 as a factory worker, but in 1902 was assigned to help the foreman with his new bookkeeping. The packing room had not even contained an office; the foreman, Mr. Ashley, did his paperwork on a soapbox. But Murray's "transfer to this work meant a great change in the room, for from then on they had a desk for the timekeeper." One of the first women to do timekeeping, Murray was sent into the male world of the high finishing and rolling department to compute time records in 1913.[3]

A relatively late arrival but nonetheless an important one at Scovill was Millicent Pond. Pond graduated from Bryn Mawr in 1910, stayed on for a master's degree in mathematics in 1911, taught high school in Philadelphia, and then worked as a chemist for the Atlas Powder Company during World War I. She arrived in New Haven in 1919 to take a job at the employment department of the Winchester Repeating Company and to begin a Ph.D. in psychology at Yale. John Goss hired her in 1923 to assist in the ongoing reorganization of the employment department and to devise mental tests for machinist apprentices. Having disrupted machinists' control over themselves and their apprentices, Scovill management found it difficult to predict which of their factory workers would do well in the tool and machine department. Goss and Pond were both active in regional personnel and office management circles in the 1920s. Representatives from Scovill went to meetings of both the Office Executive Group of the American Management Association and the Personnel Research Federation, and Pond published the results of her psychological testing methods at Scovill in the *Journal of Personnel Research*. Goss continued to believe that it was the moral obligation of managers to impose efficient methods of work in industry.[4]

A college graduate turned business administrator, a department manager, a private secretary, a timekeeping clerk, and a personnel manager: these new office occupations lay at the heart of dramatic and far-reaching changes in American office work after 1900. Both government and business experienced staggering expansion. Between 1897 and 1904 more than four thousand firms merged into 257 combinations, trusts, or corporations. The net production of electricity quadrupled between 1902 and 1912 and then doubled again by 1917, spurred by consumer demand and industrial growth, leading to the nationwide growth of the public utility industry. By 1905 estimates of the total income of life insurance companies stood at $642 million a year, and four years later one of the largest of these firms, Metropolitan Life, issued more than $2 billion worth of insurance. At the turn of the century Sears and Roebuck sometimes processed a hundred thousand mail orders a day through its Chicago mail order house and in 1905 had sales of nearly $38 million. By 1919 Macy's Department Store employed as many as twenty thousand people, more than some of the largest manufacturing establishments in the country. Macy's was heavily dependent on clerical work; increased sales depended on more sophisticated inventory, pricing, payroll, and accounting records. A host of new government agencies appeared in the early twentieth century, all requiring administrators and office workers. The number of workers employed by the executive federal civil service rose from nearly 236,000 workers in 1901 to more than 476,000 by 1915.[5]

The gendered composition and size of the American office labor force was changing. Even with intense mechanization of the workplace clerical workers in the United States increased overall nearly two and a half times between 1910 and 1930. Although more and more clerical workers were women, men found expanded arenas of employment in the office too. Women were only 5.7 percent of the bookkeepers in 1880, but were 31 percent of them by 1910; by 1930 women made up 63 percent of all the bookkeepers. But there were 113,300 more male bookkeepers, more than a million more male clerks, and 638,900 more male managers and salesmen in 1930 than there had been in 1900. There were nearly a million more female stenographers and typists employed in 1930 than there had been in 1900, but there were nearly 180,000 more engineers and over 168,000 more accountants, nearly all of them men. While typing and stenography turned into "women's" jobs in these three decades, a new class of office professionals, mostly men with college degrees like the Goss and Sperry brothers, began to assume administrative responsibilities which had existed in only primitive form in smaller-scale, older organizations. These business administrators, accountants, personnel managers and engineers were part of an emergent group of middle-class experts assuming social and economic control at the turn of the century. They saw the hordes of new office workers as an army that could gather and transmit information. The army required an array of office machines to permit rapid collection, assembly, and production of the information the experts needed to interact effectively with workers, boards of directors, customers, citizens, and politicians.

The rapid feminization of jobs with the titles of *typist, stenographer,* and *telephone operator* all masked the fact that much of the new recordkeeping extended beyond the typewriter, the dictaphone, and the telephone, and that more men as well as women were performing these jobs. While more complicated organizations certainly required more letters, more memos, more reports, and more telephone calls, the new strategies that made the integration of complex organizations possible were based on cost accounting. The faith that "scientifically managed" organizations (run on the principles of cost accounting) would carry both workers and the country into a new era of prosperity and international prominence was deeply resonant in the first third of the twentieth century. The formulas and ledger sheets of the accountants and the efficiency promises of the engineers provided a more abstract language with pretenses of transcending ethnic, class, sex, and political divisions. Progressive policymakers thought accounting would provide both fairness and "accountability" as more traditional methods of governing seemed to be failing.

By 1910 the need for a new ideology was overpowering. As the United States entered the twentieth century, every sector of its society had become more complex. Rapid urbanization created unmanageable cities; the immigration of new workers and their families accelerated industrialization and resulted in badly needed but more unwieldy labor forces. Mergers and combinations created giant business entities that neither their owners nor an enraged citizenry could control. As more sophisticated technology provided a rapidly growing list of services to consumers they became more dependent on railroads, utilities, and telephone companies, which charged mysterious rates smacking of conspiratorial and monopolistic practices. Governments collected public revenues but seemed unable to provide the most basic of services. And everywhere the heroes of the nineteenth century—the practical inventor, the swashbuckling businessman, the city boss—were under attack as old-fashioned remnants of a society that needed experts to create order out of chaos. Indeed, the "search for order," as Robert Wiebe so aptly describes it, became the motivating spirit of the age. It was shared by factory owners, corporate businessmen, municipal reformers, Progressive politicians, and a rapidly growing class of college-educated professionals.[6]

The reification of both efficiency and accountability (often merged in the term *scientific management*) became a critical part of the search for order. Efficiency and accountability provided a paradigm that seemed to offer hope of managing mushrooming industrialization, a more complicated work force, the increasingly large business enterprise, and a rapidly expanding hierarchy of local, state, and national government. The paradigm was endorsed by businessmen, politicians, public reformers, and professionals. It was expected to increase profits, end corruption, solve labor unrest, give new power to the emerging professions, and provide reasonable checks on the expenditure of vast sums of money, both public and private. It bridged the gap between progressive reformers and railroad tycoons, efficiency experts and production managers, consumers and corporations, labor arbitrators and some labor unions. This is not to say that efficiency and accountability did all that their varied supporters said they would. But the belief in and ultimate reliance on them revealed both the deep contradictions of the American social and economic system and the search for a new language of interpretation. That this language—a language of balance sheets, annual reports, labor turnover sheets, and commission rate hearings—gained ascendancy over other approaches—fundamentalism, socialism, or even liberalism—revealed a great deal about the search for a moderate response to America's problems of poverty and wealth, inequity and privilege, and the postponement of their solution to a later day.

By 1900 a number of American institutions were perceived to be badly out of control or in need of acute restructuring. In large factories, corporations, and governments from the local to the federal level, the old methods of doing things seemed to be inadequate. A closer examination of the crisis in structure and administration of factories, governments, and corporations reveals how sorely a new integrating language was needed.

The Organizational Crisis

In the late nineteenth century rapid technological change enabled factory owners to create more efficient energy-driven systems and rationalized divisions of labor. Owners could make the factory do more than it had ever done before. But their new technological prowess had not been matched by progress in their relations with labor or their administrative techniques. Employers everywhere complained of high rates of labor turnover, of resistance by workers to the pace of work sought by management ("soldiering"), and time repeatedly lost to job actions, strikes, and walkouts. Two traditional management policies were clearly contributing to labor unrest: use of the drive system (constantly increasing the pace and amount of work) in order to lower wages and increase profit margins; and the factory's continued reliance on foremen to perform a variety of functions, including managing, hiring, and firing employees, production control, job pricing, and tool maintenance and development. Traditional foremen were "internal contractors," who both managed workers and determined wage rates. While factory managers could base selling prices on costs, they seemed to have no way of intervening directly in how those costs were determined. The foreman's management of workers seemed equally problematical and mysterious. Workers appeared and disappeared with alarming frequency. Hiring seemed to be more dependent on ethnic and community ties than on aptitude or reliability; what it took "to make them happy" remained eternally elusive. A dozen different rate and wage schedules were paid, with some workers on day wages and others on the piece rate. The result was a labor relations nightmare.[7]

Correlated with the problem of controlling labor was management's inability to govern itself. When manufacturing firms were relatively small in size, often owned by one family and run by a single manager, the manager was able to integrate the various functions of the firm by daily interaction with the foreman and the workers. But as the division of labor grew with the addition of more complicated mechanical systems, increased job specialization, and larger size, the business manager found it difficult to oversee and integrate all the functions of the factory process. Coordination among different parts of the factory process broke down and the result, according to one historian, "was that orders were lost or delayed, necessary parts or operations were forgotten or performed incorrectly—all of which culminated in a frustrating, wasteful, and somewhat confusing business situation." At the same time executives lost their ability to control their own representatives, like the foremen, who were supposedly acting in their interests. Managers tended to constantly increase in number as organizations grew, no one individual understood how the whole system worked, and there were no firm methods for communicating management policies through managers and on to workers. The result was a system which, as it grew larger and more specialized, also increasingly "disintegrated" or "uncoupled."[8]

A wave of mergers and combinations began to create the corporation at the turn of the century, a business form that would increasingly dominate the American economy. Loose alliances fell apart and trusts became targets of public criticism, so the corporation made more sense. The corporation magnified the problems of "uncoupling" even further and led to a desperate search for predictability: of prices, markets, reasonable inventory levels, and future economic trends. Combinations of firms into larger corporations were aimed at reducing competition, avoiding overproduction, and ending disastrous price-cutting, all of which would give their managers greater control and reliable estimates for future developments. Through vertical integration from raw material extraction to production, shipping, and distribution, corporations were often able to achieve near monopolies over the marketplace. But the elephantine size of these new combines prevented them from making the kind of predictable profits from year to year that their owners had envisioned; instead, boom and bust cycles ensued. Demand remained a mysterious variable, and executives often failed to guess properly what it would be. The tendency was to produce as much as capacity would allow, and to plow most capital into more and more goods to sell. A recession or drop in demand could bring a firm to the edge of bankruptcy.

General Motors before World War I, for example, was really a kind of holding company made up of scattered production and selling facilities assembled by entrepreneur William C. Durant. Durant, who ran GM from a tiny main office with a staff of five or six, assumed that the demand for automobiles could only increase and put away almost no cash reserves; he was nearly put out of business by the business downturn of 1910. Standard Oil of New Jersey had the opposite problem. By the end of 1918 the surplus financial holdings of the giant oil company stood at nearly half a billion dollars. Yet accounting and employment methods at Standard Oil remained casual. Foremen still did hiring and firing. Company auditors made periodic examinations of affiliates and prepared financial reports on standardized forms, but the firm's historians conclude that "accounting uniformity . . . was a hope that had not been realized."[9]

While the quest for predictable profits would eventually push some corporations toward organizational and accounting reform, public uproar over the business practices of a wide variety of large-scale institutions was creating similar pressures. In 1898 the Industrial Commission began hearings that revealed corporate abuses related to the capitalization and issue of stock. In a classic exchange the commission's lawyer John North asked how Henry O. Havemeyer of the American Sugar Refining Company could carry on a business, lose money, and still pay dividends. Havemeyer replied: "'You can carry on business and lose money, you can meet and declare dividends. One is an executive decision and the other is a business matter.' Somewhat bewildered, North asked: 'Where do you get the money?' 'We may borrow it,' said Havemeyer. Puzzled, North continued. 'How many years can the American Sugar Refining Company keep up the practice?' 'That is a problem to everyone,' conceded Havemeyer, and explained that 'we should either buy or sell[our] stock if we knew that.'"[10]

Equally perplexing statements were issued by executives of public utilities called before local and state commissions after 1900. In the rush to provide municipal services and to cash in on the enormous profits involved, many city politicians had borrowed money recklessly, accepted bribes and kickbacks, and failed to institute any safeguards for the spending of the public's money. A committee investigating electric utility companies in New York "found literally unbelievable the bookkeeping and accounting practices used by the utilities. The assistant treasurer of the Consolidated Gas Company admitted that neither he nor any other human being could account for the sale of four million dollars in convertible debenture bonds." Charles Evans Hughes, who had become a public hero during his investigation of the gas industry in New York City, took on the insurance industry in 1905 in the Armstrong Committee investigations. Hughes found that a small group of officials who ran the three largest companies in the country often spent huge sums of money without recording them properly in the books.[11]

Government at every level, from the federal to the municipal, was riddled with similar problems. In 1911 the Bureau of Municipal Research examined the financial reports of seventy-five American cities and found that "68 do not show . . . how much they have spent, including bills not paid and revenues due but not yet received . . . . Assets are not shown by 48 of the cities, which thus have no balance sheet . . . and 21 do not state their bonded debt."[12] A former legislator described the situation in California when he took office in 1909: "There was little short of chaos as far as any orderly provisions for state expenditures were concerned. There had been no audit of the state finances for over twenty years. The finance committees of the two houses were scenes of a blind scramble on the part of the various institutions and departments of the state in an endeavor to secure as large a portion as possible of whatever money might happen to be in the treasury . . . . Logrolling and trading of votes on appropriation bills was the common practice among members of the legislature."[13]

At the home office of Metropolitan Life Insurance Company in New York City, where the State Insurance Department was conducting a five-year audit requiring five examiners and twenty assistant auditors, a new addition was being completed which included a tower in the manner of the campanile of St. Mark's in Venice. The tower, then the tallest office structure in the world, held a clock by which a watch could be set a mile away.[14] Accuracy would be both the goal and the symbol of the accounting revolution.

Cost Accounting and the Organizational Solution

The attempt to find a solution to financial crisis and organizational chaos was in the wings. The overarching ideology of the solution became known after 1911 as "scientific management," and its implementation required extensive new methods and personnel for running organizations effectively. They included what Alfred Chandler, Jr., has described as new "strategies and structures" for managing large corporations; far more extensive government regulation at every level; the development of an independent accounting profession; the emergence of a hierarchy of office occupations ranging from chief executive to file clerk; and new methods for keeping workers under control. These changes all relied for their execution on each other, and the language of cost accounting tied them together into an integrated system.

Prime cost accounting—the attempt to arrive at selling prices or rates on the basis of costs for materials, labor, and fixed costs like rent and utilities—had first been developed by the nation's railroads. Intense competition for consumers' business in the 1870s in an interlocking network of lines covering huge geographical areas forced railroad administrators to assess unprofitable roads and inefficient managers. Andrew Carnegie turned to his accounting experience at the Pennsylvania Railroad when he instituted cost sheets as his major "instrument of control" at U.S. Steel in the 1880s: "Watch the costs," said Carnegie, "and the profits will take care of themselves." Carnegie in some sense presaged the future by seeming to transfer his decision making to the abstract and irrefutable "science" of cold, hard numbers, although his understanding of accounting remained elementary and his use of it arbitrary. U.S. Steel workers already perceived the cost department as the ultimate authority and a kind of living presence: "'The men felt and often remarked that the eyes of the company were always on them through the books.'" Despite their refinement of prime cost accounting, neither the railroads nor Carnegie had made much progress by the 1890s in calculating overhead, average capacity, or depreciation.[15]

When Frederick Winslow Taylor, an engineer, sought a new method of accounting for his management techniques in the late nineteenth century he turned for advice to a leading railroad accountant. Taylor began to attack managerial problems on the factory floor in ways that were heavily dependent on both cost accounting and administrative reform. He believed that both soldiering and labor unrest could be eliminated if the worker was paid "a fair day's wage for a fair day of work." But he also thought the determination of both work and wage must be made by the engineer or the manager, not the foreman or the worker. To arrive at an estimate of the most work the worker could do in a day without becoming either inefficient or overtired, Taylor proposed time and motion studies of the work process. The more work that could be subdivided into specialized tasks, mechanized, standardized, and measured, Taylor argued, the fewer skilled workers that would have to be hired, and the more efficient and less costly the factory would be. An end to inefficiency would also somehow guarantee fair wages and thus also accomplish an end to labor strife.[16]

Taylor and other advocates of what was referred to as "systematic management" at the turn of the century were attempting to gain access to what David Montgomery has called "the manager's brain under the workman's cap." But they were also attempting to "recouple" or reintegrate firms that had become unmanageable due to their increasing size. If managers could begin to understand and measure what elements went into production—labor, materials, and overhead—they could also wrest control of those variables from foremen and begin to influence directly both the pace and cost of production. If better tabs were kept on inventory and sales it might also be possible to link production more closely to demand and costs of materials. To accomplish these changes accounting would have to change. More sophisticated and detailed cost accounting could reveal most things the Taylorites wanted to know.[17]

The influential accounting theorist Henry Metcalf had recommended the use of a card system for job accounting as early as 1885 in his *Cost of Manufactures*. But he simply proposed adding this new bookkeeping duty to the foreman's work rather than creating a clerical staff to do it. Taylor and other scientific managers argued the institution of cost accounting and the paperwork it required could only work if a new administrative layer was added; both bookkeeping and labor policies had to be taken out of the hands of the foremen and placed in the hands of the engineers and their assistants.[18] The engineers would require an expanded clerical staff to handle the paperwork. As the contract system with foremen was eliminated and systematic management installed, Chandler observes, "a voucher system of accounts was introduced; times studies were carried out; route, time, cost and inspection clerks were employed; and the manager's staff was enlarged."[19]

Systematic managers like Taylor and John Goss were trying to coordinate but also separate different aspects of management that had formerly been handled by foremen and bookkeepers—purchasing, production control, inventory records, payroll, and pricing—by creating a series of administrative units or departments that had only existed in primitive forms in most businesses before 1890. These units required new kinds of office employees and records. While the engineer or administrator set up the system and gauged how well it was working, mid-level managers were needed to compile the information that would tell bosses what they wanted to know. And to keep the now far more detailed records that were required, new office staffs of clerks were essential. The coordination and management of these administrative systems was dependent upon the manufacture of paperwork, paperwork not required under the old order. By keeping better records management did two seemingly contradictory but really complementary things. It took administrative responsibilities away from the foreman and the bookkeeper ("centralizing" authority) as it delegated some of their mental responsibilities to subordinates like timekeepers and clerks ("decentralizing" authority). Management's overall purpose was to separate mental and manual work by extracting as much decision making as possible from production workers and transforming it into standardized tasks performed by clerks and managers.

Engineers installed these new methods of administration and cost accounting at the Watertown Arsenal in 1915. The arsenal was a government manufacturing complex where skilled workers had long managed their own work days and foremen and bookkeepers had performed most management functions. A series of simple but detailed mathematical and clerical operations were put into place to seize control. The key to the system was a "job card," a slim piece of light cardboard on which data could be recorded and then punched and sorted on a Hollerith card-sorting machine.

The first task was to compute direct labor costs. Each wage earner was given a number. Each worker's number and labor time was listed on the job card as the job moved through the shop: "To compute a man's total earnings over a given period, it was necesary only to add the times stamped on all the job cards which carried his code number, multiply by his wage rate, and add on premiums earned." The same cards could be used for seeing how much the job cost ("costing out") and computing the payroll by shuffling them into different accounting categories. A second set of records— attendance and time cards filled out by the men when they clocked in and out—provided a way of double-checking labor costs. Workers wrote down the code numbers of the machines and the times they were used on each job card, so by punching and then reshuffling the cards, it was easy enough to compute overhead costs. As with labor costs, total overhead costs were "checked against the total overhead charges for the shop computed from the general financial accounts of the Arsenal." The same procedure was used to compute costs for materials, balanced against total costs of materials used from stores.

All the functions of the foremen except immediate supervision of the workers and their discipline had been transferred to a higher authority. In fact, the foremen were no longer "foremen," even if the workers called them such; the engineeers had now labeled them "gang bosses." The "nerve center of . . . communication and control" had passed from the shopfloor to what engineers liked to call the "planning room." The planning room was an office. In charge was the engineer, or "master mechanic," who prepared "assembly diagrams and route sheets." He was assisted by several foremen, a route-sheet clerk, a production clerk, and a rate-setting department (a staff of six time, motion, and rate clerks). A "minor functionary" was stationed at a window and handed out and received back job cards. There were also several typists, junior clerks, and costing clerks in the planning room.[20]

Predictably, these dramatic changes in the usual way of doing things provoked resentment and sabotage among workers at Watertown. The engineering managers would never quite understand why the workers could not see it their way, and their high-handed methods would eventually have to be doctored by psychologists and personnel managers. What was entirely clear to the engineers, however, was that Taylorism and its variations could not proceed without elaborate cost accounting methods and extensive new paperwork. There were still many refinements to be made to the science of cost accounting as applied to the shopfloor, not the least of which was how to factor in the cost of the new administrative systems, depreciation, and idle plant time. But the belief that accounting told managers what they wanted to know had taken hold.[21]

Accounting Reform, Scientific Management, and the New Experts

Taylorism was one spur to the new importance of accounting and record keeping; financial and political reform was another. A rash of investigating commissions after 1900 convinced many business leaders that they would either have to have their books audited by independent accountants and present some information to their stockholders or face increased government regulation of their business practices. The accounting profession, despite much internal bickering, moved toward acceptance of state regulation of public accounting: a group of "neutral" accounting experts would be needed to verify financial records and statements. The United States Industrial Commission recommended in 1902 that "larger corporations . . . be required to publish annually a properly audited report, showing in reasonable detail their assets and liabilities, with profit and loss; such a report and audit under oath to be subject to government regulation." Although it would take the stock market crash of 1929 to actually produce such federal legislation, some states did begin to require corporations to provide annual reports (although they rarely specified what was to be in them), and the New York Stock Exchange required the issuing of annual reports before corporations could be listed on the exchange.[22]

Some corporations began, in the light of public criticism and the expectation of government regulation, to provide financial information. U.S. Steel issued an annual report in 1902. After being publicly humiliated in the Armstrong Committee investigations the Equitable Life Assurance Society announced that its accounts would be independently audited and presented in an annual report in 1906.[23] Legislation that grew out of the Stevens Committee investigation of public utilities in New York led to the creation of a state Public Service Commission in 1907, which could not only examine books and contracts but could also require annual reports, fix rates and services, and "establish a uniform system of accounts and prescribe the manner in which they must be kept." A similar commission in Wisconsin developed a "uniform system of accounting which all utilities were required to follow." Both commissions and their uniform accounting systems were widely copied by other states and cities in ensuing years.[24]

Demands for organizational and accounting reform cut across both conservative and liberal constituencies and sometimes made for interesting alliances. Depending on the level of their civic-mindedness and the size of their concerns, many businessmen found certain aspects of progressive reform to be not only palatable, but also beneficial. Regulation might drive competitors out of business, stabilize the economy, and improve the public image of big business. Even if businessmen resisted regulation of private enterprise, they were likely to see budget reform of government in a different light: as a means of bringing proper business practice to the public sphere. The most ardent critics of sloppily managed city government were likely to appear first in local chambers of commerce.[25] The influential New York Bureau of Municipal Research was funded by the comptroller of New York City, Herman Metz, in 1905, to make available to other cities New York's new accounting methods. Metz's *Handbook of Municipal Accounting*, published in 1913, was widely used by cities to reform their accounting procedures. E. H. Harriman, the railroad tycoon, had been an ardent supporter of the bureau, whose influence extended far beyond New York.[26]

A similar organization, the National Municipal League, prepared model charters that were widely used to reform city governments. The league promoted state regulation of city government, including the requirement of uniform municipal accounting procedures; by 1912 only ten states in the union did not have such laws. City managers, budget bureaus, central purchasing, and efficiency agencies all spread rapidly after 1910 in American cities.[27] Few municipal reformers would have disagreed with A. E. Buck, who came out of the New York Bureau of Municipal Research and was a leading expert on government budget reform before World War II, that "when properly instituted and administered, the budget is the most effective means yet devised for the establishment of control over the public purse. Viewed in this light it becomes a powerful factor in the maintenance of modern government; indeed, its influence extends to the very roots of organized society." Budgeting could also be a powerful molder of visionary policies: "the budget is a *plan*—a plan of action for a government looking toward the future."[28]

Accounting reform reached the national level as well. The Dockery Commission's revelations in 1893 of the "costly variety of qualities and prices" that government agencies received and paid for goods and services inspired Theodore Roosevelt to appoint the Keep Commission. The Keep Commission suggested double-entry bookkeeping for the Treasury Department and published a handbook on cost accounting for government agencies. The Dockery Act of 1894 legislated the first changes in the auditing and accounting procedures of the Treasury Department since 1817. It centralized bookkeeping and created six auditing offices for government departments. Congress created the General Supply Committee in 1910 to centralize purchasing, and in 1911 President William Howard Taft appointed a Commission on Efficiency and Economy. The commission's chair was the accountant Frederick A. Cleveland of the New York Bureau of Municipal Research, who both influenced A. E. Buck and was a friend of Frederick Winslow Taylor.[29]

Although further budget legislation at the federal level was a decade away, the recommendations of the Taft Commission had a wide-ranging impact on budget reform of state governments in the teens and increasingly became a political campaign issue. The Budgeting and Accounting Act of 1921 mandated a uniform system of accounting instituted in a new General Accounting Office directed by a comptroller general whose sole responsibility was to Congress. No longer simply to audit past financial practices, "Congress clearly intended the comptroller general to point out where expenditures could be made with greater wisdom as well as to determine issues of accuracy and legality." The budget itself was to be prepared by a Bureau of the Budget after reviewing budget requests from government departments and consultation with the president. The federal budget could now be used to shape future policies of the United States.[30]

The federal government created new financial paperwork for itself and for business when the first corporate income tax was passed in 1909 and when the Sixteenth Amendment levying personal income taxes was ratified in 1913. In 1914 the Federal Reserve Board issued new rulings for the preparation of banks' applications for loans and discount of commercial paper, which required that applicants' statements be certified by public accountants. The excess profits tax of 1918 required even more information on tax returns. Interstate Commerce Commission regulation of railroad corporations produced more independent audits, and in 1914 the Federal Trade Commission urged corporations to adopt standard systems of bookkeeping and cost accounting because to do so would be in the public interest.[31]

New financial departments to do cost accounting and control more specialized administrative functions appeared with increasing frequency in a wide variety of American businesses after 1900. Cost accounting and administrative reform were dependent upon one another, for accounting was the language that could tie vast departments or affiliates, often in completely different geographical locations, together in a common effort. For example, in 1903 the treasurer's office at Du Pont began to "develop uniform statistics essential to determining over-all costs, income, profits, and losses." By centralizing the treasurer's office, assigning it several new functions, and developing a new accounting system, Du Pont had achieved not only a language that could be "spoken" (or computed) by everyone in the corporation, but also one that could be used to determine future business decisions. Du Pont executives and their accountants began to require departments to predict costs for particular projects and how much return the company could expect on its investment. Capital expenditures were now predicated on "general forecasts of economic conditions." Du Pont constructed a new office building in the center of Wilmington to house its managerial and clerical staff.[32]

Similar accounting changes were afoot in most large business institutions before World War I. As early as 1905 the larger department stores had created a functional system that separated merchandising, advertising, personnel services, and accounting into different departments. A Standard Classification of Accounts for department stores was made available in 1916.[33] By then industries as diverse as banks, breweries, mines, utilities, foundries, hospitals, cities, and textile manufacturers had taken up cost accounting. The chain of events leading the Philadelphia Electric Company to more elaborate accounting procedures began with public questions about the utility's high rates in the early teens. To legitimize its rates, Philadelphia Electric reorganized its financial departments and gave new authority to the comptroller. More detailed accounts were also required because the utility was making loan applications to banks for expansion purposes. Having launched a "wire your home" campaign in 1916, Philadelphia Electric was selling appliances and encouraged customers to buy them on the installment plan. By 1918 Philadelphia Electric had more

than a hundred thousand customers, many of whom required periodic billing.[34]

Before 1913 Standard Oil of New Jersey, already one of the largest corporations in the country, had a relatively primitive accounting system, and almost no time was devoted to tax planning or
preparation. New federal tax law changed all that. After 1918 professional tax consultants had to "compute the well-discovery valua-
tions and the depreciation and depletion schedules on producing
property that would determine for years to come the allowable
charges which Jersey Standard and its affiliates might claim on tax
returns." By 1920 "tax accounting at Jersey Standard had become an
intensely specialized and intricate art." Tax computation and planning thus had far-reaching ramifications for both what accounting
was and how it was done: "federal tax-reporting certainly introduced greater accounting consistency and possibly introduced
greater realism into the records of the petroleum industry, but the
cost to the companies in terms of clerical expense and supervisory
effort was enormous."[35]

New tax and banking regulations helped to speed along the refinement of accounting procedures in American business. But administrative reform was equally important. When W. C. Durant
not only stocked up on inventory but also increased plant capacity
in early 1920, only to find the automobile market collapse later
that year, he was replaced by Alfred P. Sloan, an MIT graduate in
electrical engineering. Sloan ended the loose affiliation of companies that had characterized General Motors before 1920 and instead created a set of divisions overseen by a far more powerful
general office with executives, staff members, and clerical workers.
The multidivisional corporation was the result: an organizational
form that provided both autonomy to and integration of the functions of the corporation. By now cost accounting and financial
planning were inextricably intertwined at firms like General
Motors:

> Annual forecasts were prepared for each division by a collaborative
> effort between divisions and the general staff. These 'divisional indi-
> ces,' as they were called, included not only purchases and delivery
> schedules for materials and capital equipment required and labor to
> be hired, but also estimated rates of return on investment and prices
> to be charged for each product. Prices, unit costs, and rates of return
> were all closely related to the volume permitted by demand. In draw-
> ing up these divisional indices, the staff computed the size of the na-
> tional income, the state of the business cycle, normal seasonal

variations in demand, and the division's anticipated share of the total market for each of its lines.[36]

Advice on how to implement these administrative and accounting reforms came from a new class of managerial experts like Taylor, Sloan, and Goss, who wanted to place themselves at the helm of rapidly burgeoning bureaucracies. The importance of the new managerial class, its promotion of cost accounting and scientific management, and the public's faith that it could solve the problems of the industrial age, all emerged in the famous Eastern Rates case of 1910.

The eastern railroads wanted an increase in freight rates and went to the Interstate Commerce Commission with their petition. Although a variety of roads were involved, some of them small, badly managed, and clearly inefficient, the larger ones had pioneered in modern accounting techniques. They presented a detailed statistical analysis of their financial condition which relied on the latest methods of prime cost accounting. Anticipating that they might be accused of seeking rate increases simply to charge what the traffic would bear, the roads sought to demonstrate the rate increases were justified because their costs had actually risen. In attacking the rate increases, Louis Brandeis debated with railroad spokesmen on such accounting issues as fixed versus variable costs, replacement and depreciation policies, and the impact of slack or busy seasons on total performance. Ironically, none of this actually figured in the final outcome of the case. Brandeis had become intrigued with the ideas of Frederick Winslow Taylor, who was in the midst of trying to get his lectures on new management techniques published by the American Society of Mechanical Engineers. Brandeis decided to attack the management policies of the railroads as a way of preventing a rate increase. He summoned Taylor and other management engineers to New York to "choose the most suitable designation for the new philosophy of management which they were to expound and defend at the forthcoming hearings." The group decided upon *scientific management*, a term Taylor may have already formulated. The "expert" testimony of the engineers and managers changed the hearings from a request for a rate increase to a national stage for the philosophy of scientific management. Arguing that newer methods of management could save the roads a million dollars a day, Brandeis promised benefits to workers, consumers, shippers and the railroads themselves.[37] Brandeis argued that cost accounting was not an end in itself, but part of a process that would incorporate the scientific method into the economy and therefore further progressive political ideals:

> As an alternative to the railroads' practice of combining to increase rates we offer constructive policy—scientific management, under which as costs fall, wages rise . . . . Under scientific management nothing is left to chance. All is carefully prepared in advance. Every operation is to be performed according to a predetermined schedule under definite instructions, and the execution under this plan is inspected and supervised at every point. Errors are prevented instead of being corrected. The terrible waste of delays and accidents is avoided. Calculation is substituted for guess; demonstration for opinion.[38]

The ICC ruled against rate increases for the railroads, but the ruling was the least important outcome of the hearings. Brandeis emerged from the rate case as a national spokesman for scientific management and the ideals of progressive big business. Taylor's reputation as a Progressive hero was secure. Engineers presented themselves as scientific management technicians who could fine-tune both both business and government.

In Taylor's home town of Phildadelphia, where engineer Morris L. Cooke served as the director of public works from 1911 to 1915, consumers complained that the Philadelphia Electric Company was charging too much for electricity. When the company refused to lower the rates, Cooke took them to court. Without a valuation of the company's assets and the demand for such a valuation from the city council, which was controlled by the utilities and the machine bosses, no determination regarding the "fairness" of the rates could really be made. Cooke sued the company as a taxpayer, and in the ensuing case, financial probing did uncover "extensive watering" of Philadelphia Electric's securities. Defended by another engineer who was also a dean at MIT, Philadelphia Electric presented as cloudy a picture of its assets as possible to the newly established Pennsylvania Public Service Commission. The commission ordered a more accurate valuation, the company capitulated, and the general public of Philadephia was saved a utility bill of $1 million a year. The commission hearings resulted in the formation of a Public Utilities Bureau, a national watchdog agency, and Brandeis, Cooke, and Taylor all served on its board of trustees.[39] More elaborate cost accounting and administrative reform, Brandeis preached, were the keys to curing labor unrest, insurance fraud, and poorly run utilities and railroads. "Indeed," he argued, "the increased efficiency of the wage-earner is not possible until the heavy demands which scientific management makes upon those controlling and directing the business, including superintendents and foremen, are fully met. Increased efficiency must begin with those higher up. This is of the essence of scientific management."[40]

Taylor was pleased that scientific management had been linked to the ideals of Progressivism and that experts like himself were receiving such acclaim. He wrote to a friend in 1911 that Brandeis "has awakened the whole country, and the interest now taken in scientific management is almost comparable to that which was aroused in the conservation of our natural resources by Roosevelt."[41] That year Taylor's essays were printed both privately and in a popular progressive journal, *The American Magazine*. His disciples were in demand at a variety of firms hoping to institute scientific management techniques. The railroads' experience with the ICC and the public utility dispute in Philadelphia showed that cost accounting was never an end in itself; it had become a medium in which social and political ideas could find a common terminology and meeting ground. The cultural context of Progressivism structured the meaning of cost accounting, and the techniques of cost accounting gave politicians methods for producing real change.

By 1912, then, the rhetoric of the accounting revolution had been formed. The scientific management movement, the emergence of the multidivisional corporation, the appearance of a growing and articulate class of professional experts, and the rising tide of government legislation requiring financial accountability had all contributed to the molding of that rhetoric. Its implementation on a material basis, however, was far from complete. That required a staggering new array of paperwork, computations, and hierarchy of office workers. Without fundamental changes in the organization of the office work force and its composition, the accounting revolution would not have been possible.

A Case Study: Scovill Manufacturing, Management by Design, and the Rise of an Office Labor Force

The cost accounting and scientific management revolutions demanded both mechanization of clerical work and the rise of a more elaborate office hierarchy. A closer look at Scovill Manufacturing Company's history shows just how this was accomplished. Scovill, a brass-producing and fabricating firm in Waterbury, Connecticut, was founded by the Scovill brothers in the 1820s. By the 1870s the brass industry saw its profit margins drop precipitously as competition grew and overproduction ensued. Pools of companies to set prices had no real effect, and in 1899 four firms in the Naugatuck Valley formed the American Brass Company in order to survive. Rather than combining with other firms, Scovill seems to have turned to more sophisticated cost accounting techniques and reorganization in order to regulate production and cut costs. By 1917 Scovill was among the two hundred largest industrial companies in the United States.[42]

The brass companies bought copper and zinc from mining companies in the West. They sold much of their brass output in sheets, rolls, and ingots to other manufacturers, and they fabricated some items out of brass, particularly buttons, wire, and fixtures. The manufacture of brass into various shapes and alloys gave the casters enormous power over the pace of the production process. Melting and shaping was more art than science and difficult to systematize. At Scovill the casting, rolling, and shaping departments of the plant tended to be worlds unto themselves, managed by the foremen and their workers, all of whom were men. Women worked in repetitive jobs connected with the manufacture of brass products such as buttons and screws that had been far easier to rationalize and reduce to piece work.[43] Scientific management techniques had been difficult to apply in the metal-fabricating industry at firms like Scovill because of the widely differing styles of management required for the extraction of raw metals, conversion to alloys, and manufacture into usable materials and products.[44] The melting, shaping, and cutting of metals were still controlled by industrial craftsmen and their assistants. But between 1900 and 1920 Scovill managers devised new techniques for wresting more control of the foundry process from the workers who controlled it.

Scovill was the kind of corporation most likely to engage in the new managerial reform. The Scovill brothers died in the 1850s, and none of their direct family descendents assumed control. Instead, the firm was managed day to day by salaried executives who practiced hands-on supervision. [45] Profits were put back into the firm to finance expansion and capital expenditure. In 1900 Chauncey Porter Goss became president of Scovill, but his influence, and that of his colleague M. L. Sperry, had long been felt at the firm. Goss was the son of an attorney and attended public high school. He first worked as a clerk in a country store and came to Scovill as a bookkeeper in 1862. Sperry was also a bookkeeping clerk, and his corporate bookkeeping system, introduced in the 1870s, was used at

Scovill until after the turn of the century. By the late nineteenth century the two men had developed a rough functional division of responsibilities, with Goss attending to contacts with raw material suppliers and plant development, and Sperry administering finances, day-to-day operations, and supervision of the foremen. Goss was known for rewarding innovative ideas that came out of the tool room, and Sperry developed a workable cost system for determining selling prices. Like most of his contemporaries he had no real way of estimating overhead and depreciation costs, but he "conducted meticulous studies" of the cost of labor and materials. In reality the cost of materials was the only flexible variable in this equation, because labor management remained in the hands of the foremen: "Under Sperry and Goss, the foremen ran the plant; it was their job to hire and fire . . . . They paid the wages current in the neighborhood and got involved in no serious contemplation of the correctness of those rates which, so far as they were concerned, were determined by 'natural forces.'"[46]

These old-fashioned methods were about to change. Goss and Sperry were grooming their sons for modern management positions. Four of Goss's sons and three of Sperry's joined the management of the firm and continued their fathers' tradition of managing both production and accounting in a personal, hands-on way, but not as bookkeepers. Goss and Sperry encouraged their sons to obtain college degrees in such business professions as accounting and engineering. The firm would depend on these professionally trained men for its survival, because Goss's and Sperry's sons faced a more challenging economic world than had their fathers. By the mid-1890s the consumption of nearly half of all the copper in the United States for electrical wire and products destabilized the prices of copper and zinc and drove them upward. Prices went even higher with the sudden upsurge in demand for brass from the military during World War I for uniforms, munitions, and electrical products. Labor and production costs were at an all-time high, but so were profits available for capital improvement. The obvious way to reduce costs was to make casting and mill work more efficient by applying the principles of scientific management. That would mean assuming greater control over casting from the artisans who had traditionally controlled it. Control meant an increase in the pace of work, lower labor costs, and the ability to trace materials more effectively in inventory, including scrap. It also meant importing such new mechanical processes as extrusion and the hot press, mostly from Germany, finding more efficient continuous heating methods, and developing new commerial uses for brass. And it required more effective links between casting and other parts of the plant, so that integration or "coupling" of the industrial process could take place. Scovill managers wanted greater control over the ingredients that went into the brass, the casting process, and the workers who did the most mysterious work in the plant.

Edward Goss became director of the company in 1898, assistant treasurer in 1900, and general manager in 1918. His brother John apprenticed in the tool and machine room and then became assistant superintendent in 1903. In 1908 the main office took the important step of divorcing itself from day-to-day plant operations and assigned these to a new general superintendent with a separate office. John Goss was given the job in 1909. Not an engineer by formal training, Goss nonetheless pursued scientific management with fervor. While his brother oversaw the corporation and M. L. Sperry managed the accounting, John Goss launched a series of dramatic changes in the everyday functioning of the plant. Scovill rebuilt its casting plant, used oil and then electrical furnaces to improve production, researched new firing processes, and replaced the artisans who had used the old methods with unskilled workers. The new self-contained furnaces allowed for continuous production, did away with the grip of skilled casters over melts, and also saved considerable amounts of expensive zinc from volatilization.[47] Goss centralized such plant services as stores, soldering, plating, and costing. He located his superintendent's office in the heart of the plant and worked to make the foremen more accountable to company management. In 1908 he met informally with them to discuss "means of developing a higher degree of good fellowship" and in 1913 created the foremen's association and clubhouse, complete with restaurant, billiard tables, and game rooms.[48] Foremen were now to think of themselves as a cohesive subgroup of management.

At the same time John Goss was intervening in both the time-keeping and hiring procedures of the mills to appropriate some of the foremen's authority. Even as assistant superintendent in 1905 he attempted to reverse old practices that had allowed many men in the plant to come and go at will without losing pay and ordered that "hereafter actual time in attendance during working hours must be reported by your time-keepers for everybody, including for men," implying that more rigorous timekeeping systems for women operatives had long been customary at Scovill.[49] A report Goss requested in 1905 recommended that a centralized timekeeping department be given authority to impose uniform standards throughout the plant. "The main trouble at present," the report argued, "is due to the fact that the force on the payroll in the main office have apparently no authority to stop a method that is wrong and that has crept into a department system, but seems as much controlled by the precedent in each department as the clerks in that department itself are. They at least consider that they have no authority to compel the superintendents of departments to stop such a practice."[50]

Hiring was largely in the hands of foremen, who naturally tended to hire friends, relatives, or members of their own ethnic groups; some took bribes in return for jobs.[51] People looking for work roamed the plant yards and added to the confusion. As soon as he became general superintendent Goss tried to halt this practice by requiring foremen to hire workers at the gatehouse rather than in the plant itself. In 1910 he complained that he was still "having considerable difficulty at the present time in keeping men, women and children who do not belong here out of the yard . . . . strangers or former employees go about the shop and ask the foremen for work, and are sometimes given jobs." He forbade family members to continue the custom of bringing dinner pails to the shops, and announced that anyone discovered seeking work in the yard should be brought to the gatehouse. No one who entered the factory in this way would be hired. Nonetheless, it would take another ten years to assume the kind of control over both timekeeping and hiring at Scovill that Goss desired. That control was heavily dependent upon the growing sophistication of cost accounting and record keeping.[52]

The key to more authority for the central timekeeping office was to require more thorough paperwork. By assigning each employee a labor rate card at the main office and not allowing foremen to assign overtime or changes in rates, no "special" arrangements could occur. Daily time cards made out by timekeeping clerks in duplicate were to strictly record the actual time worked, with any questionable hours, such as for power outages, to be computed by the main office. While these new methods "would entail more work in the main office on the books," they would also "make that force more responsible than now for errors, which is certainly better than the divided unchecked resonsibility now in force."[53]

The new costing and timekeeping methods began to pay off within a few years of their institution. By 1911 company accountants assured Goss that it would be possible by the end of the year to find "a tentative cost . . . for the output in all the producing departments of the Company. A method will thereupon be available as has already for some years been in successsful use in the more intricate and complex manufacturing departments for finding in advance specific costs." The company could finally establish a complete set of cost accounting rules for the entire plant. These rules and the records they would produce would give the company a week-to-week account of profit and loss, and as important, running accounts of inventory. "Bases will be established for present use and future comparison," one of Goss's managers reported. "The classified facts will compel attention to points of extravagance and weakness, if there are any such."[54]

New work order methods were instituted to make foremen and department heads more accountable for indirect labor costs. Estimates had to be checked by the cost department before work orders could be issued.[55] Goss reminded foremen that

> No charge or credit should be made by a department unless supported by a copy of the order . . . signed by the foreman . . . requesting the work, and giving the . . . Factory Account Number . . . . This responsibility rests with the foreman and . . . is of vital importance to him, because if he does not get the proper order or account number on daily time tickets and . . . requisitions, these charges will remain against the department . . . . In other words, a foreman should look on this as a means for getting credit for everything done in his department, the importance of which cannot be overestimated for correct accounting.[56]

In 1918 all factory timekeepers and clerks were placed under the supervision of the cost office.[57] Its manager prepared an elaborate set of directions for timekeepers to use in the shop and attempted to assume as much control as he could, not only over the work but also over the timekeepers, a move shop managers predicted would cause acrimony among the foremen. In fact, the directions for factory clerks were printed into shop manuals in 1919 but never distributed.[58] Goss was aware that such absolute appropriation of the foremen's authority was unrealistic. The new system of automatic time clocks, time cards, and use of clerks to extend time card totals on comptometers in the central office could all be instituted without formally "divorcing the timekeepers from the foremen . . . . I think one thing we ought to avoid now," said Goss, "is too many radical departures from our present practice." With tempers running high and the dramatic strike of 1919 just over the horizon, Goss had to draw back.[59]

More centralized timekeeping and factory clerking got women into some of the plant manufacturing departments where they had never been allowed as industrial workers, including the rolling and casting mills. By 1917 women were working as clerks in all but a handful of departments, and by 1921, thirty-six of the fifty-six timekeepers at Scovill were women.[60] Women continued to be least represented in the mills. As late as the eve of World War II foremen in casting departments "kept the time records themselves," ostensibly so that they could "deal with absenteeism directly," but also so that they could handle their men "without the intervention of 'some remote staff department.'"[61]

The fact that so many of the timekeepers were women was more important than it might first appear. If the managers at Scovill were interested in breaking the grip of the foremen and in instituting new standards of timekeeping controlled by the front office, placing women as timekeepers on the factory floor was a good strategy. Women clerks would have to be separated from the men on the floor in a special office enclosure. Using women timekeepers, along with the new mechanical clocking devices, may have eliminated ties that had bound male timekeepers, many of them foremen, to male factory workers, ties that had probably made them susceptible to peer pressure to doctor cards. With relatively little in the way of shared work culture, it would be difficult for male workers to pressure "women from the office," who also wore the clothes of the business class, into changing cards.[62]

Timekeepers represented company interests rather than shop-floor work arrangements, and had become central to the new accounting and management techniques. The director of the timekeeping department at Scovill reminded John Goss in 1919 that factory clerks were the linchpins of a good factory accounting organization, for "it is upon them that the central offices depend for most of the records used in making up reports, payroll and costs. Such reports and records are misleading if factory clerical work is inaccurate. Reliable information is absolutely necessary."[63]

In his search for reliable data and greater control, Goss was trying to change work patterns that had existed at Scovill for decades. E. H. Davis, a self-appointed Scovill historian and ex-manager, recalled that Goss had admitted

his chief difficulty was not in arriving at a conclusion but in finding a way to put that into effect. It called for the shaping up and dissemination of new instructions. It was easy, he said, to express clearly what he had in mind. The difficulty was in getting just that thought into the reader's mind . . . . Every foreman, he said, had his own ideas and methods, and was, however unconsciously, reluctant to change them. Thus he would tend to interpret the new instruction so as to make the least alteration in his existing pattern . . . . he had to take much time to read, re-read, alter and re-phrase his message before its issue. And it usually had to be followed up to check the result, so it might be depended on. "It is my hardest task."[64]

Despite ongoing difficulties, Goss and his co-managers continued their reforms, often using new paperwork systems to take more extensive control. Along with changes in accounting and timekeeping methods came changes in employment procedures. The sudden burst of employment created by war orders in 1917 led to the establishment of a formal industrial service department. The employment department oversaw the new welfare measures provided by the company, including some dormitories and housing for workers, a small hospital, and the hiring of Helen Duncan, a special director of welfare work for women. She helped form the Scovill Girls' Club and recruited women for bowling and basketball teams. But the heart of the new department was a central employment office that took control of hiring away from the foremen.[65] The first page of the 1918 foremen's manuals spelled out the procedures for hiring and made it clear that while foremen could recommend future employees, they were to do so by sending a slip of paper to the employment office. The office was also to be in charge of all transfers and terminations.[66] The execution of these employment policies required fifteen clerical workers. In 1919 Scovill instituted new record-keeping devices for employment designed to centralize employment management and facilitate cost accounting. By assigning a check number to each employee, all timekeeping, payroll, and employment records could be transferred to cards and tabulated for statistical summaries or census tables. The installation of mechanical time clocks made for easier computation of payroll and cut down on absenteeism and tardiness; they also tended to eliminate disputes between employees and timekeepers and reenforce the authority of the latter.[67]

In 1919 organizational and accounting changes at Scovill culminated in the creation of a central factory accounting office and a comptroller's office with L. P. Sperry in charge. The comptroller was to oversee and integrate factory accounting (including timekeeping, payroll, and costs) and the department of supply (including purchasing, storeskeeping, and inventory control) with the general accounting ledger, on the basis of which he would prepare newly required tax statements for the federal government.[68]

The number of Scovill workers in the main offices, including clerks, managers, and executives, increased dramatically over the years from 1911 to 1920, and coincided with the new accounting, timekeeping, and employment policies. There were 149 male and female main office workers in 1911 and 568 by 1920; despite the fact that the overall work force had barely doubled in these years, the number of main office workers nearly quadrupled (Table 1). Both women and men were hired to fill these new positions. Harriet Goodyear first worked for John Goss on the new cost and payroll systems in 1905 and eventually wound up in the chief accountant's office. Edna Holihan came to Scovill in 1905 to work in the button office posting time cards and then moved to the central time office; after World War I she became an accounting clerk in the billing department. Herman Rehm did both billing and payroll work when he first came to Scovill in 1906 and was the first clerk to use a comptometer. He eventually became the head of his department. In 1904 Homer Senior began as a timekeeper at American Pin, an acquisition of Scovill. He became assistant manager of the central time office in 1911 and head of the department in 1919. Mollie Collins came to work in 1912 as a timekeeper and eventually became head dispatcher in the trucking department.[69]

World War I and government red tape also created new clerical positions. Elizabeth Kelly went to work in 1915 loading pellets in the primer house but during the war joined the employment office to prepare questionnaires and deferment claims. She was to work in that office for twenty-five years.[70] The statistics division of the research department alone required forty workers, most of them women, to make daily charts of alloy constituents to comply with federal regulations.[71] With the wartime creation of labor shortages other women moved from the factory to the office. Mary LaFrance came to work at Scovill in 1895 in the packing room. She became an inspector and in 1917 was recruited for office work.[72]

The mechanization of Scovill's office work picked up in pace in the late teens. In 1919 Scovill installed two switchboards and four telephone operators to connect a nine-hundred-telephone system. Using the telephone did not always come naturally; Goss had to urge clerks to stop sending so many memos and start using the phone.[73] In 1918 the research department added a Powers accounting machine to the company's collection of Hollerith machines, and the timekeeping department announced that it would be using

Table 1.
Time Office Count of Employees
at Scovill Manufacturing, 1911-20

	1911	1913	1915	1917	1918	1919	1920
Supply (purchasing, stores inventory control)	67	74	56	100	121	99	102
Factory accounting (time, payroll, cost)	0	0	33	50	76	92	135
Research and metals co.	22	22	39	146	183	221	285
Industrial service	0	0	0	15	38	41	45
Manufacturing offices	60	74	49	81	88	84	94
Planning and production	0	0	0	0	3	11	38
Total, main offices	149	170	177	392	509	548	699
Hospital and hygiene	0	0	0	0	0	0	19
Tool and machine	353	378	509	669	697	626	764
Electricans, steam, piping and plumbing	51	62	103	480	500	380	510
Yard, transportation and plant protection	272	291	439	1,124	1,500	861	1,021
Total, service departments	676	731	1,051	2,273	2,697	1,867	2,314
Manufacturing workers	1,943	1,862	3,112	7,568	5,989	2,011	3,342
Mill, casting, wire	810	817	1,104	2,324	na	1,334	1,641
Total, mill and manufacturing	2,753	2,679	4,216	9,892	na	3,345	4,983
Total, all workers	3,578	3,580	5,444	12,557	na	5,760	7,996

Source: Employee Census Data, SM, case 36, Scovill Manufacturing Company Collection, Harvard Business School Library.

more calculators and comptometers: "Will we do our adding and multiplying by the slow and tedious hand method when the work can be done so much more easily and quickly by calculating machines?" asked the *Scovill Bulletin* rhetorically. "The answer, of course, is no—use calculating machines." The planners of the new timekeeping system were as eager to apply scientific management techniques to clerical work as to factory work; "besides raising the standard of timekeeping," its manager observed, "the Timekeeping

Division is striving to reduce factory clerical cost." The old struggle to wrest the control of timekeeping from the foremen had to be continued: "Clerks are used in inefficient timekeeping methods, some rooms keep one clerk ten hours where the work can be done in a few hours, other rooms keep a reserve clerk to take the place of a clerk who happens to be out, etc. By placing the control of time-keepers in the Timekeeping Division, this work can be standardized and centralized and carried on with a smaller number of clerks."[74]

The company began a "calculator school" for women already working as timekeepers and office clerks, and after three or four weeks of training put some of them into a central extending department to compute time tickets and requisitions.[75] When Millicent Pond arrived in 1923 to devise evaluative tests for machinists, she continued the comptometer training school and set up performance tests for factory women who aspired to office work. Any employee who had been studying typing, stenography, or comptometer operating might apply for testing through the employment office. If the employee received a passing grade and there was a job opening, the employee could be reclassified and moved to an office job.[76]

Scovill management remained happy with its testing system and believed that training and testing were a better combination for job placement than educational qualifications alone. Pond, who as part of her job edited the company magazine, urged women factory workers who had completed the eighth grade to take the compto-meter test: "Let's see whether there are any girls . . . who care enough for the chance of a change from bench or machine work to factory clerical or comptometer work to come over here to the testing room and take the test of their own accord." Pond was aware that some women might find the "testing room" intimidating and added in a postscript: "Let us whisper something to you. There is no need to fear these tests because every one begins easily, and the explanations are very clear."[77] Some factory workers were able to move into clerical positions at Scovill using this system, although exactly how many remains unclear. Comptometer work in the timekeeping department seemed to be the kind of clerical work most akin to factory operative work; that connection was reflected by the generally working-class status of the comptometer clerks. Pond's 1933 study of female clerical workers at Scovill showed that although 79 percent of the stenographers had a high school diploma, only 39 percent of the comptometer clerks did.[78]

While many women clerical workers at Scovill used machines to do office work, including typists, comptometer operators, punch card and sorting machine operators, and mimeograph operators, their work was not necessarily highly specialized, despite some of the managers' dreams of thorough rationalization. Computing machine operators were most likely to perform routine operations in scientific management-style systems. When a woman statistics professor at the Drexel Insitute inquired about opportunities for women statisticians at Scovill in 1920, the chief of the research department, E. H. Davis, replied that there really were none. The tabulating and sorting machines had reduced most statistical work to simple clerical chores and no longer required experts. The statistical staff, which he headed, had a staff of seven clerks and one stenographer, all female. Davis thought the most useful training for such work would be in typewriting, although he also recommended skills in simple arithematic. The major techniques used in cost accounting, industrial statistics, and quality control were sheer categorizing and counting; "special statistical questions such as interpolation, correlation, etc . . . arise only infrequently."[79]

By contrast, Scovill made little progress in systematizing its stenographic work. A study of stenographers' output at Scovill in 1932 revealed that Scovill had only a handful of dictaphones and a widely varying rate of stenographic performance by stenographers and secretaries. Although Scovill employed seventy clerks who took dictation, only about 14 percent of their time was spent doing stenography. Scovill had postponed centralizing both its typing and stenographic services, and most male executives continued to dictate to women, not into machines. As a result, women stenographers were scattered around various offices and performed a variety of different tasks each day.[80]

Despite the failure of system to reach typists and stenographers at Scovill, it was generally true that managerial changes had resulted in a clear shift in the kind of workers employed and of the work they did. Foremen no longer had the control they once exercised. Traditional casting and rolling techniques had been undermined by scientific management, and native-born artisanal work forces often replaced by more recent immigrants and blacks. New kinds of male skilled labor had assumed considerably more importance. The machine and tool department more than doubled between 1911 and 1920. There had been no electricians at the plant in 1911; by 1920 there were 257, another 131 men in the steam department, and the piping and plumbing department numbered 102.

The number of clerks and managers had grown despite the large layoffs of manufacturing workers following the completion of Scovill's lucrative war contracts. Although 77 percent of all workers at Scovill had been in manufacturing in 1911, about 62 percent were so designated by 1920. And of these manufacturing workers, roughly 5 percent were clerks and managers, or what Scovill categorized as "nonproductive" workers.[81]

The decade following 1910 had also dramatically changed the constituency of the female work force. In 1914 only 750 women worked at Scovill, most as operatives in light manufacturing. War enlistments and a tight labor market increased labor turnover at Scovill, and war contracts for fuses and other materials produced the need for more workers in both heavy and light manufacturing. Scovill recruited women workers in large numbers. The work force reached a peak of 13,225 workers in 1918, including 3,705 women. Two years later only 7,700 of these workers remained, only 1,640 of whom were women. Departments where most factory women had worked during the war were particularly hard-hit by the armistice; the fuse and munitions departments, mainly staffed by women, were simply disbanded. Women never penetrated the heavy industrial departments or the tool room in more than token numbers. But new clerical operations provided jobs for women that lasted beyond the war. The women workers who remained at Scovill after the war were likely to be either factory operatives or clerical workers, whereas the male labor force at Scovill was far more diversified.[82]

Scovill's history demonstrates how new accounting and organizational methods produced a new office labor force with a hierarchy of occupations ranked, in large part, by gender and class. College-educated male executives like the Goss and Sperry brothers now headed many corporations. College-trained women like Millicent Pond and Ella Patchen might find a place in this hierarchy as personnel workers or secretaries. A tier of mid-level managers, most former male clerks like Herman Rehm, managed the office labor force, most of whom were women like Edna Holihan and Elizabeth Kelley, who had grammar school and high school educations. Male clerks continued to dominate clerking in such factory offices as shipping and plant protection.

The development of new office and managerial jobs at Scovill was typical. Between 1900 and 1920, American men and women took nearly three million new jobs in clerical work; in most communities, office jobs increased more rapidly than any others. By

1920 clerks made up a higher proportion of the workers in manufacturing establishments than ever. Overall, the ratio of manual workers to white-collar workers in American manufacturing establishments fell from 11.4 in 1899 to 5.8 by 1921. Outside manufacturing, in the insurance, banking, retail, and civil service sectors, the number of clerical workers increased even more dramatically.[83] The growing number of office workers was the most central change in the American labor force in the first half of the twentieth century.

When office clerical jobs are broken down by sex it is apparent that by 1930 the feminization of office work was significant, but by no means complete; men still sought jobs in offices and were still in clerical jobs in large numbers (Table 2). Women were more heavily represented in some job title categories of clerical work and in some kinds of offices than others, a fact that has made the feminization of office work seem more extensive than it actually was. Altogether, many more male workers held office jobs in 1930 than in 1900.[84] Jobs with the titles of "stenographer" and "typist" may be said to have been feminized as early as 1910, but the absolute number of male stenographers and typists did not decline until 1930, and even as late as 1920 men constituted more than 10 percent of all workers in this group.[85] Men continued to increase dramatically in both the "bookkeeping" and the "general clerks not elsewhere classified" categories. The increasing complexity of clerical and managerial functions at the turn of the century also required a growing number of specialized white-collar workers who were not "executives," "professionals," or "clerks"; they were, rather, lower-level managers, salesmen, tellers, advertisers, and insurance, credit, and real estate agents, and closer to clerical workers in status and salary than to anyone else (Table 2).[86] These categories supplied extensive new office employment opportunities for men.

The growing number of office workers, male and female, was part of an emerging pattern which, as at Scovill, reflected the changing division of labor in the United States. The 1920s saw an acceleration of trends earlier begun: declining proportions of the population engaged in basic production (agriculture, manufacturing, and mining) and increasing proportions engaged in the distribution and service industries (professions, clerking, sales, nursing, laundry, and waitressing). Overall, this trend led to somewhat lower employment rates for men, and to rapidly increasing rates of employment for women,

Table 2.
Selected U.S. Clerical and Office Work Professions,
1900-1930 (in Thousands)

	1900	1910	1920	1930
Bookkeepers/cashiers	232.0	446.8	615.5	738.2
Male	159.2	263.3	269.8	272.5
Female	72.7	183.6	345.7	465.7
Stenographers/typists	134.0	387.0	786.0	1,097.0
Male	38.0	76.0	80.0	66.0
Female	96.0	311.0	706.0	1,031.0
Machine operators	na	na	na	38.1
Male	na	na	na	5.4
Female	na	na	na	32.7
Clerical and kindred jobs, not classified elsewhere*	234.7	654.3	1,323.3	1,680.5
Male	223.8	578.5	990.9	1,260.7
Female	10.9	75.8	332.3	419.9
Managers, officials, salesmen and agents in selected categories†	340.8	441.4	641.1	1,043.1
Male	333.0	426.1	607.3	971.9
Female	7.8	15.3	33.8	71.2

Source: David L. Kaplan and M. Claire Casey, "Occupational Trends in the United States, 1900-1950," Bureau of the Census Working Paper no. 5, Washington, D.C.: Department of Commerce, 1958.
*For 1900-1920 includes office machine operators, dispatchers, bank tellers, shipping and receiving clerks, and clerical and kindred workers. For 1930 includes all of the above except machine operators.
†Includes buyers and department store heads; store and credit workers; purchasing agents and buyers; banking and other finance, insurance, and real estate managers, officials and proprietors; agents and collectors, bill and account collectors (not classified elsewhere); advertising agents and salesmen; insurance agents and brokers; real estate agents and brokers.

who, nonetheless, still made up a minority of working people. But recruitment of women for clerical and service jobs accounted for most of this increase in women's labor force participation rates. By the 1920s female typists, telephone and telegraph operators, stenographers, bookkeepers, clerks, and saleswomen constituted a significant subsector of the American labor force. As the proportion of women in manufacturing and domestic service declined with re-

Table 3.
Women's Labor Force Participation, 1910-50

	Operatives	Clerical Workers
1910	1,701,925	687,811
1920	1,747,738	1,614,246
1930	1,869,636	2,245,824
1940	2,451,786	2,700,383
1950	3,286,683	4,502,009

Source: David L. Kaplan and M. Claire Casey, "Occupational Trends in the United States, 1900-1950," Bureau of the Census Working Paper no. 5, Washington, D.C.: Department of Commerce, 1958.

spect to the growth in population, the prototypical "working girl" was a white-collar worker (Table 3).[87]

Before I return in chapter 4 to the burgeoning female clerical labor force, in the next two chapters I will explore the world of upper-level management inhabited by men like John Goss and a few women like Millicent Pond. Their professions—business administration and personnel management—were constructed according to gender and represented two different approaches to the management of work and workers in the twentieth century.

NOTES

1. John H. Goss, "The Place of the White Collar and Professional Worker," speech delivered at Wesleyan College, Dec. 5, 1935, SM, Case 58. For a discussion of the importance for corporate management of penetrating the secret of "the art of cutting metals," see David Montgomery, *The Fall of the House of Labor: The Workplace, the State, and American Labor Activism, 1865-1925* (Cambridge: Cambridge University Press, 1987), 171-213.

2. The story of Goss's rise from tool room to the superintendency was widely repeated in stylized form by himself and others. For example, see L. M. Bingham, "Fifty Years an Asset to Connecticut," *Connecticut Industry* (Oct. 1944): 4-6, 30-32. Goss fits the profile of what David F. Noble calls the "corporate reformer" of the late nineteenth century: a white male, of Anglo-Saxon Protestant, native-born background, son of a prosperous businessman, born between 1860 and 1880, and enjoying a comfortable upbringing in a small town in New England. Goss, however, was a liberal arts graduate of Yale, not an engineer. *America by Design: Science, Technology, and the Rise of Corporate Capitalism* (New York: Oxford University Press, 1977), 50-51.

3. On Packard see *Scovill Bulletin [SB]* Jan. 22, 1945, 6; on Murray, April

1926, 5; and on Patchen, Sept. 8, 1941, 4. In November 1926 Patchen recalled (3) that when she arrived at Scovill in 1901 there were only two women stenographers in the main office and one in the purchasing office. "We have grown quite a bit, haven't we?" she commented.

4. Goss, "The Place of the White Collar and Professional Worker." On Pond's testing techniques see "The Testing Room," SB, Jan. 1927, 7-8, and Millicent Pond, "The Value of Mental Tests," SB, Jan.-Feb. 1932, 11, 16-17, 20-21. Her results were summarized in "Selective Placement of Metal Workers, I: Preliminary Studies," Journal of Personnel Research [JPR] 5 (Jan. 1927): 345-66. A synopsis of Pond's "Selective Placement of Metal Workers, II: Development of Scales for Placement," JPR (Feb. 1927): 405, described her work as "one of the most important and extensive studies ever attempted in the selection of metal workers." The Personnel Journal stressed Pond's progress in developing a group of qualified candidates for internal promotion to "salesman, estimator, production clerk, stenographer, assistant foreman, clerk, etc." "News Notes," Personnel Journal [PJ] 7 (July 1928): 143-45. Goss served as a vice president of the Personnel Research Federation in 1929, but sent Pond to the federation's annual meeting in May. See Walter A. Bingham to John H. Goss, April 9, 1929, and Goss's handwritten note on it to Pond, April 16, 1929, SM, case 58.

5. Alfred D. Chandler, Jr., Strategy and Structure: Chapters in the History of the Industrial Enterprise (Cambridge: MIT Press, 1962), 472; Barbara H. Brock, The Development of Public Utility Accounting in New York (East Lansing: Graduate School of Business, Michigan State University, 1981), 16; Thomas K. McCraw, Prophets of Regulation: Charles Francis Adams, Louis D. Brandeis, James J. Landis, Alfred E. Kahn (Cambridge: Harvard University Press, 1984), 98; Roger H. Grant, Insurance Reform: Consumer Action in the Progressive Era (Ames: Iowa State University Press, 1979), 5; Marquis James, The Metropolitan Life: A Study in Business Growth (New York: Viking, 1947), 168; Alfred D. Chandler, Jr., The Visible Hand: The Managerial Revolution in American Business (Cambridge: Harvard University Press, 1977), 231-32; Susan Porter Benson, Counter Cultures: Saleswomen, Managers, and Customers in American Department Stores, 1890-1940 (Urbana: University of Illinois Press, 1986), 34-37; Anita J. Rapone, "Clerical Labor Force Formation: The Office Woman in Albany, 1970-1930," Ph.D. diss., New York University, 1981, 79; Leonard D. White, Trends in Public Administration (New York: McGraw Hill, 1933), 243.

6. See Robert H. Wiebe, The Search for Order, 1877-1920 (New York: Hill and Wang, 1967), especially 111-33. Wiebe does not include either engineers or accountants in his "new middle class," but the observations he makes about the self-consciousness of doctors, lawyers, and social workers may be applied to them as well.

7. Daniel Nelson, Frederick W. Taylor and the Rise of Scientific Management (Madison: University of Wisconsin Press, 1980), 9-11.

8. Joseph A. Litterer, "Systematic Management: Design for Organizational Recoupling in American Manufacturing Firms," *Business History Review [BHR]* 37 (Winter 1963): 369-91.

9. Chandler, *Strategy and Structure*, 459; George Sweet Gibb and Evelyn Knowlton, *The History of the Standard Oil Company of New Jersey*, vol. 1: *The Resurgent Years, 1911-1927* (New York: Harper and Row, 1956), 139.

10. As quoted by Gary J. Previts and Barbara Dubis Merino, *A History of Accounting in America: An Historical Integration of the Cultural Significance of Accounting* (New York: John Wiley, 1979), 134.

11. Frank Mann Stewart, *A Half-Century of Municipal Reform: The History of the National Municipal League* (Berkeley: University of California Press, 1950), 10; Brock, *Development of Public Utility Accounting*, 20; Grant, *Insurance Reform*, 41.

12. "With the Vanguard," *American City [AC]* 5 (July 1911): 54; Martin J. Schiesl, *The Politics of Efficiency: Municipal Administration and Reform in America, 1800-1920* (Berkeley: University of California Press, 1977).

13. As quoted by A. E. Buck, *Public Budgeting: A Discussion of Budgetary Practice in the National, State and Local Governments of the United States* (New York: Harper and Brothers, 1929), 4.

14. James, *Metropolitan Life*, 174-77.

15. Alfred D. Chandler, Jr., *The Railroads: The Nation's First Big Business, Sources and Readings* (New York: Harcourt, Brace and World, 1965), 99; Chandler, *The Visible Hand*, 267-68. For a technical description of the development of cost accounting in these years see S. Paul Garner, *Evolution of Cost Accounting to 1925* (Montgomery: University of Alabama Graduate School of Business, 1954). Garner argues (346) that factory engineers rather than formal accountants were the most likely to introduce new systems of accounting before World War I. Of particular significance, says Chandler, *The Visible Hand*, 277, "were the methods developed to relate overhead costs or burden to the fluctuating flow of materials through a manufacturing establishment." These "manufacturing burden" costs were in many ways the most difficult and elusive of all but were often the key to a profitable business. Isolating them through better accounting methods might also mean controlling them.

16. These ideas are clearly presented in Frederick Winslow Taylor, *The Principles of Scientific Management* (1911, repr. New York: W. W. Norton, 1967). For scholarly interpretations of Taylorism see Nelson, *Frederick W. Taylor*, and Judith A. Merkle, *Management and Ideology: The Legacy of the International Scientific Management Movement* (Berkeley: University of California Press, 1980).

17. David Montgomery, *Workers' Control in America: Studies in the History of Work, Technology and Labor Struggles* (Cambridge: Cambridge University Press, 1979), 44-46; Litterer, "Systematic Management," 369-91; Dan Clawson, *Bureaucracy and the Labor Process: The Transformation*

of U.S. Industry, 1880-1920 (New York: Monthly Review Press, 1980), 167-201.

18. Garner, *Evolution of Cost Accounting to 1925,* 110; Daniel Nelson, *Managers and Workers: Origins of the New Factory System in the United States, 1880-1920* (Madison: University of Wisconsin Press, 1975), 48-51, and Nelson, *Frederick W. Taylor,* 13-14.

19. Chandler, *The Visible Hand,* 277.

20. Hugh G. J. Aitken, *Taylorism at Watertown Arsenal: Scientific Management in Action 1908-1915* (Cambridge: Harvard University Press, 1960), 129-33. Aitken stresses that this is a description of the plan as it worked in the ideal, not necessarily in reality. One issue that Taylor and other engineers postponed discussion of was the extent to which such new methods significantly increased the cost of "nonproductive" (managerial and clerical) labor and a subsequent rise in overhead. Efficiency experts generally tried to argue that savings due to more scientific production would more than cover these costs. See, for example, Walter N. Polakov, "Planning Power-Plant Work," *Bulletin of the Taylor Society [TSB]* 2 (Jan. 1917): 22-23. Certainly the enormous profits of most kinds of industries in the teens tended to obscure this potential problem of scientific management, and, perhaps, to postpone its further examination until the late 1920s. Melman found that although administrative overhead costs of large firms increased significantly from 1899 to 1947, the firms were able to keep their administrative expenditures per dollar of production expense lower than small businesses. Although mechanization increased, there was an overall increase in administrative personnel that could only be attributed to the addition of new functions. Nonetheless, the larger the firm, the lower the unit cost of completing those functions. Seymour Melman, "The Rise of Administrative Overhead in the Manufacturing Industries of the United States, 1899-1947," *Oxford Economic Papers* 3 (Feb. 1951): 62-112.

21. Merkle, *Management and Ideology,* 13; Murray C. Wells, *Accounting for Common Costs* (Urbana: Center for International Education and Research in Accounting, 1978), 97-102; Marc Jay Epstein, *The Effect of Scientific Management on the Development of the Standard Cost System* (New York: Arno Press, 1978), 155-57.

22. As quoted by Previts and Merino, *History of Accounting in America,* 135. On public accounting and the state see Paul J. Miranti, Jr., "Associationalism, Statism and Professional Regulation: Public Accountants and the Reform of the Financial Markets, 1896-1940," *BHR* 60 (Autumn 1986): 438-68. For summaries of changes in corporate reporting practices see John L. Carey, *The Rise of the Accounting Profession: From Technician to Professional, 1896-1936* (New York: Institute of Certified Public Accountants, 1969), 54-63, and David F. Hawkins, "The Development of Modern Financial Reporting Practices among Manufacturing Corporations," *BHR* 37 (Autumn 1963): 135-36.

23. R. Carlyle Buley, *The Equitable Life Assurance Society of the United States, 1859-1964*, vol. 2 (New York: Appleton Century Crofts, 1967), 701-8.

24. Brock, *Development of Public Utility Accounting in New York*, 20-30; Forrest McDonald, *Let There Be Light: The Electric Utility Industry in Wisconsin, 1881-1955* (Madison: American History Research Center, 1957), 115-22.

25. For more detailed analyses of business and progressive reform see Gabriel Kolko, *The Triumph of Conservatism: A Reinterpretation of American History, 1900-1916* (New York: Free Press of Glencoe, 1963); Robert H. Wiebe, *Businessmen and Reform: A Study of the Progressive Movement* (Cambridge: Harvard University Press, 1962); and James Weinstein, *The Corporate Ideal in the Liberal State: 1900-1918* (Boston: Beacon Press, 1968); also see Leonard D. White, *City Manager* (1927, repr. Westport: Greenwood Press, 1968), ix.

26. The New York Bureau of Municipal Research grew out of the Association for Improving the Condition of the Poor, which first sought to apply "objective efficiency tests" to determine where help was needed. James H. Potts, "The Evolution of Municipal Accounting in the United States, 1900-1935," *BHR* 52 (Winter 1978): 527; also see Schiesl, *The Politics of Efficiency*, 88-110.

27. White, *Trends in Public Administration*, 23, and Potts, "The Evolution of Municipal Accounting," 524-25. In a series of papers issued between 1901 and 1908, the Bureau of Municipal Research developed a widely respected system of uniform municipal accounting and auditing that was also used by the Bureau of the Census to develop statistics on American cities. The Census Bureau also issued a series of pamphlets explaining the new accounting to urban managers. For examples of the distribution of these guidelines see W. M. Williams, "Municipal Accounting and Auditing," *AC* 1 (Nov. 1909): 106-8; Logan McKee, "Civic Work of the Pittsburgh Chamber of Commerce," *AC* 5 (July 1911): 16-17; and "Books and Pamphlets," *AC* 5 (Oct. 1911): 227.

28. Buck, *Public Budgeting*, 3-4. Buck was a graduate of the Training School for Public Service, founded by the New York Bureau of Municipal Research and funded by Mrs. E. H. Harriman; he began his career as a budget specialist for the New Jersey State Chamber of Commerce. Buck was tutored by Frederick A. Cleveland, professor of accounting at New York University, president of the New York Bureau of Municipal Research, and friend of F. W. Taylor. Potts, "The Evolution of Municipal Accounting in the United States," 527; Merkle, *Management and Ideology*, 266. As Merkle observes (68), this conjunction of businessmen, Taylorites, and progressive reformers helped move Taylorism from "the purely economic and industrial realm to the political arena." Also see Dwight Waldo, *The Administrative State: A Study of the Political Theory of American Public Administration* (New York: Ronald Press, 1948), 34.

29. Frederick C. Mosher, *The GAO: The Quest for Accountability in American Government* (Boulder: Westview Press, 1979), 33-35. Mosher believes (44) that accounting reform spread from cities to states and the federal government rather than vice versa because aside from the post office and military defense in wartime, "the national government did little that cost very much—in relation to the economy as whole or to governmental costs generally." Between 1900 and 1910 federal expenditures were only about 2 or 3 percent of the GNP and less than one-third of all public expenditures. Local governments footed nearly 60 percent of the public expenditure bill, 44. According to Leonard White, it was not until the years between 1917 and 1923 that there was "intense activity in the reorganization of state government, the adoption of budget systems and the extension of the administrative power of chief executives." *Trends in Public Administration*, 6.

30. Buck, *Public Budgeting*, 13-14; Previts and Merino, *A History of Accounting*, 130-31.

31. Previts and Merino, *A History of Accounting*, 134-35; Eugene Nelson White, *The Regulation and Reform of the American Banking System, 1920-1929* (Princeton: Princeton University Press, 1983), 160; James Don Edwards, "Public Accounting in the United States from 1913 to 1928," *BHR* 32 (Spring 1958): 74-101.

32. Chandler, *Strategy and Structure*, 56-61.

33. Chandler claims that retail department stores did not undergo the kinds of managerial changes experienced by railroads and industrial corporations, *Visible Hand*, 238. However, Susan Porter Benson has found that although department stores were likely to "federate" rather than to merge, and to leave daily operations to local managers, some groups of stores did standardize both their organizational structure and their accounting systems. *Counter Cultures*, 55-58.

34. Wells, *Accounting for Common Costs*, 125; Nicholas B. Wainwright, *History of the Philadelphia Electric Company, 1881-1961* (Philadelphia: Philadelphia Electric Company, 1961), 148-49.

35. Gibb and Knowlton, *History of the Standard Oil Company of New Jersey*, 1: 615-16. In 1912 the accounting division of Standard Oil of New Jersey had fifty-one employees, but had doubled in size by the mid-1920s. While the auditing and comptroller's departments were merged in 1918 and resulted in some savings in labor costs, the treasurer's department of eighteen employees in 1918 had quadrupled by the mid-twenties.

Hermon Bell, an accountant, recalled that new taxes were "applicable in a mild sort of way to 1909," but that after 1913 "taxes assumed a much more important aspect. Taxes could become a most important item especially when we began to have not only taxes based upon income but also taxes dependent in amount upon invested capital . . . . There were no experts on the subject at that time . . . . It was so new as to produce much congestion in work. In some cases basic credits were dependent not on a single year but upon results over a period or cycle of years. The amount of work involved was considerable. And the degree of care in employing basic data had large effect on taxes of present and future years." Hermon F. Bell, *Reminiscences of a Certified Public Accountant* (New York: Ronald Press, 1959), 78, 133.

36. Chandler, *The Visible Hand*, 460-61, and Chandler, *Strategy and Structure*, 138-52.

37. For accounts of the Eastern Rates case see McCraw, *Prophets of Regulation*, 92-94; Merkle, *Management and Ideology*, 58-60; Nelson, *Frederick W. Taylor*, 174-75; L. Urwick, *The Golden Book of Management: A Historical Record of the Life and Work of Seventy Pioneers* (London: Newman Neame, 1956), 60; and Wells, *Accounting for Common Costs*, 114. Urwick claims that the term *scientific management* was coined by a group of engineers meeting with Brandeis at the home of H. L. Gantt in October 1910, but Nelson points out that Taylor had already submitted his manuscript "The Principles of Scientific Management" to the American Society of Mechanical Engineers earlier in the year. *Frederick W. Taylor*, 174.

38. As quoted by McCraw, *Prophets of Regulation*, 92.

39. Edwin T. Layton Jr., *The Revolt of the Engineers: Social Responsibility and the American Engineering Profession* (Cleveland: Press of Case Western Reserve University, 1971), 163-66.

40. Brandeis made these remarks in his essay "Organized Labor and Efficiency" in 1911. This essay and several others, including "Life Insurance: The Abuses and the Remedies," were printed in Louis D. Brandeis, *Business: A Profession* (Boston: Small, Maynard, 1914). The quote is on 41.

41. As quoted by Urwick, *Golden Book of Management*, 60. For an analysis of the connection between scientific management and the conservation movement see Samuel P. Hays, *Conservation and the Gospel of Efficiency: The Progressive Conservation Movement, 1890-1920* (Cambridge: Harvard University Press, 1959). Hays observes (123) that members of the Roosevelt administration maintained close ties with such groups as the American Society of Mechanical Engineers, and that, in turn, "professional engineers felt a close kinship with the scientific and technological spirit of the Roosevelt administration." One of the best accounts of the popularization and wide-ranging impact of Taylorism is Raymond E. Callahan, *Education and the Cult of Efficiency: A Study of the Social Forces That Have Shaped the Administration of the Public Schools* (Chicago: University of Chicago Press, 1962), 19-41. For an analysis of scientific management and intellectuals, see David B. Danbom, *"The World of Hope": Progressives and the Struggle for an Ethical Public Life* (Philadelphia: Temple University Press, 1987), 112-49.

42. William G. Lathrop, *The Brass Industry in the United States* (New Haven: Wilson H. Lee, 1926); Thomas R. Navin, "The 500 Largest American Industrials in 1917," *BHR* 44 (Autumn 1970): 360-85, 374.

43. For a good summary of both workers and management in the brass industry in this period see Jeremy Brecher, Jerry Lombardi, and Jan Stackhouse, *Brass Valley: The Story of Working People's Lives and Struggles in an American Industrial Region* (Philadelphia: Temple University Press, 1982), 5-90.

44. See, for example Aitken's discussion of the attempt to Taylorize molding at the Watertown Arsenal: *Taylorism at Watertown Arsenal*, 135-57. For analyses of the metal-making industries and scientific management, see Montgomery, *Fall of the House of Labor*, 171-213; Chandler, *The Visible Hand*, 356; and Nelson, *Frederick W. Taylor*, 149.

45. This is the central argument of Chandler, *The Visible Hand*, especially as elaborated on 146. Lathrop claims that of Scovill's seven presidents up to the 1920s "all but one had had from 27 to 57 years of previous training in the plant." *The Brass Industry in the United States*, 104.

46. This account of Goss and Sperry is based on P. W. Bishop's typewritten history of Scovill Manufacturing Company (circa 1952), 28-68, SM, case 59.

47. Brecher, Lombardi, and Stackhouse, *Brass Valley*, 68-69; Lathrop, *The Brass Industry in the United States*, 113-21.

48. Typewritten memo (undated), of meeting held on Dec. 12, 1908, SM, case 26.

49. "Copies of Instructions Issued by J.H. Goss," Jan. 20, 1905, SM, case 34.

50. "Report Made to the General Manager on Timekeeping in the Departments," Feb. 22, 1905, SM, case 34.

51. Brecher, Lombardi, and Stackhouse, *Brass Valley*, 71-72.

52. See John H. Goss, "Notices to Foremen," Dec. 8 and 9, 1910, SM, case 34. Three weeks later (Dec. 31) Goss complained that "Men are constantly going out early and hanging around the hallways and the yard. Some of this is due to the fact that the clocks in the rooms are wrong, and men do not regard the whistle as the index of quitting time, because some of them say the whistle is wrong." Nor were these offenses confined to workers alone: "the foremen who persist in going out early cannot expect to have as good control over their help on this point as those who themslves wait until the quitting hour."

53. These measures had been suggested in the "Report Made to the General Manager on Timekeeping in the Departments."

54. FBK to John H. Goss, Nov. 23, 1911, SM, case 58. Elaborate bookkeeping and record-keeping procedures developed to produce the data the new records required. By 1911 Goss required the day's time cards to be "handed in person to the foreman by the head timekeeper, and endorsed by the head timekeeper, as evidence that he, or she, has carefully examined them." After examining the cards for correctness, the foreman was to sign the voucher and personally deliver the cards to the timekeeping office. Memo to E. J. Davis, Feb. 1, 1911, SM, case 34. In 1916 a limited number of

"System of Accounts" books, printed on fine paper in sturdy bindings, enu-
merated cost categories and methods for assigning costs and computing
them. The most elaborate accounting methods were developed for "indirect costs," or overhead expense. They included maintenance and repairs,
supplies not used in production, utilities, wages for "non-productive workers" like inspectors, foremen, and factory clerks, and "contingent labor"
(including "extra, unforseen operations," extra wages paid where estimates
proved too low, lost time, and overtime). By 1918 the receiving of supplies
required forms to be completed in quintuplicate and routed to the purchasing office, the general stores division, the central stores records, and the
storeskeeper. See *System of Accounts Scovill Manufacturing Company*,
1916, SM, volume 236 and Instruction no. 77, "Receiving, Recording, and
Issuing Materials and Supplies," Dec. 27, 1918, SM, case 34. For a description of the evolution of cost accounting at Scovill and the importance of
the new system of accounts, see E. H. Davis, typewritten comments, "System of Accounts," Nov. 8, 1943, SM, volume 236.

Garner suggests that the kind of elaborate cost accounting system for
manufacturing burden developed by Scovill was typical of large industrial
firms between 1900 and 1920. These accounting systems were particularly
important in the metal-producing industries, where scrap, wasted material, and spoiled work were difficult to factor in as costs. *Evolution of Cost
Accounting to 1925*, 135-42, 200, 300-346.

55. Memo from Goss "To All Foremen," May 7, 1919, SM, case 34.

56. Notice from Goss "To All Department Heads," Dec. 12, 1919, SM,
case 34.

57. Notice from Goss "To All Factory Foremen," Sept. 24, 1918, SM,
case 34.

58. "Information and Instructions on Factory Forms for Factory Clerks,"
9-17. A handwritten note on this manual (probably added by E. H. Davis)
noted that the booklets for factory clerks were printed in 1919 but never
distributed, SM, case 40.

59. Memo from Goss to B. P. Hyde, March 31, 1919, SM, case 28.

60. These figures are drawn from data in "Enumeration and Classification of Employees," Sept. 1, 1917, "Census of Employees," Feb. 10, 1922,
and "Occupations, Feb. 10, 1921," all in SM, case 36.

61. Bishop, "History of Scovill Manufacturing," 261.

62. I have never seen the issue of gender and timekeeping discussed, but
the "feminization of timekeeping" along with management attempts to assume greater control over male workers hardly seems coincidental. We
might further conjecture that these developments drove wedges between
male and female solidarity in plants and lowered the possibilities of men
including female clerical workers in unions.

63. Memo from R. F. Humphreys to C. E. Woods and J. H. Goss, Feb. 17,
1919, SM, case 28.

64. E. H. Davis, "EHD Recollections of Scovill and Waterbury, 1918-1968," 11, SM, case 55.

65. For accounts of the establishment of the employment department see Davis, "EHD Recollections of Scovill and Waterbury," 8, and Bishop, "History of Scovill Manufacturing," 232-38. In early 1918 federal investigators compared Scovill's labor policies, which included piece-rates and a ten-hour day, with those of a Detroit plant with an eight-hour day. The eight-hour-day workers were found to be more efficient, but the report concluded that "in other essentials of management, such as centralization of authority, cost-accounting system, planning department, invention of labor-saving devices and setting of piece rates, the [Scovill] plant ranks high among efficient competitors . . . ." However, low wage rates in the East and "a lack of effort to select workers in any way other than by the guess of the foremen" did lead to a whopping 176 percent labor turnover rate for Scovill in 1916 and 1917, the report concluded. Bishop thinks (232) that concern over employment issues raised by this report was directly responsible for the new employment and welfare measures at Scovill.

66. Copies of the foremen's manuals can be found in SM, case 34.

67. Notice from John H. Goss, Jan. 8, 1919 and "Minute (sic) of Conference between Messrs. C. E. Woods and E. H. Davis," Jan. 8, 1916, SM, case 55; Notice from Goss "To the Heads of Departments," May 16, 1919, SM, case 34; John H. Goss to W. H. Monagan, March 28, 1919, SM, case 26. E. H. Davis noted later that six lectures were given to foremen in 1919 by the assistant comptroller, C. E. Woods, to explain the new system. Notes on System of Accounts, SM, volume 236.

68. Notice by E. O. Goss, July 24, 1919, SM, case 34. See Garner, Evolution of Cost Accounting to 1925, 271, on the importance of integrating cost accounts with the general ledger.

69. These biographies have been taken from SB, Oct. 1930, 9, Jan. 7, 1946, Jan. 22, 1945, 6, and Dec. 11, 1944, 9.

70. Ibid., Sept. 8, 1941, 4.

71. Scovill had been actively pursing new production methods since the turn of the century, but during World War I the company formally created a research department under the supervision of another of Sperry's sons, Roger, an engineering graduate. He hired several engineers, statisticians, and chemists to design better machinery, analyze casting, the reclamation of scrap, and provide more elaborate daily tests of the quality of alloys. These were partly necessary because of new government specifications for war contracts that required that chemical constituents of alloys be listed and that lead and other chemical impurities be kept to a certain minimum. See E. H. Davis, "Research Dept. in World War One," Jan. 1967, SM, case 55.

72. SB, Nov. 1925, 7.

73. Ibid., Jan. 1919, 8-9; J. H. Goss to Department Heads, Nov. 17, 1922, SM, case 34.

74. E. H. Davis to R. S. Sperry, Oct. 10, 1918; E. H. Davis, "Statistics Work to be Transferred to Research Dept. from Cost Office," Dec. 12, 1918, SM, case 55; Memo from R. F. Humphreys to C. E. Woods and J. H. Goss, Feb. 17, 1919, SM, case 28; SB, Jan. 1919, 8-9.

75. The calculator school is discussed in ibid., Jan. 1919, 8-9, and Feb. 1919, 8-9. See the Scovill Foremen's Manual, Oct. 15, 1930, SM, case 34, for directions on taking the tests.

76. Millicent Pond, "The Value of Mental Tests," SB, Jan.-Feb. 1932, 11, 16-17, 20-21.

77. "Employment Tests", SB, Dec. 1926, 16.

78. Typescript, "Job Evaluation of Clerical Employees" (1939), 5, SM, case 33.

79. Leda F. White to R. E. Platt, May 1, 1920; copy of E. H. Davis to White, May 5, 1920, SM, case 55.

80. Report submitted to Allen Curtiss by H. B. Berngston, Dictaphone Corporation, April 6, 1932, SM, volume 345.

81. SB, May 1919, 5; "Labor Statistics as Reported to the U.S. Department of Labor," SB, Nov. 1918, 8; "Scovill Nationalities in the Strike," SB, May 1920, 4; Memo from H. R. McCory and H. T. Wayne to R. E. Platt, May 1, 1919, SM, case 33C. Also see Scovill Manufacturing Company Employment Office, basic census figures to July, 1934, SM, case 36. E. H. Davis thought Scovill had employed as many as fifteen thousand workers at the peak of wartime production and warned that the plant employee census records accumulated before 1922 were somewhat inaccurate. Davis, "Recollections," 5, 17. After Millicent Pond arrived in 1923 she compiled a census tally that reconstructed the earlier years.

82. I arrived at figures for male and female office workers by tallying the numbers and proportions of female and male clerks listed in "Enumeration and Classification of Employees," Sept. 1, 1917, and "Census of Employees," Feb. 10, 1921, SM, case 36. A tally of employees on September 1, 1917 showed 11,292 at work. Of these only 487 were clerks, 249 of them men, and 238 of them women. In 1917, then, male clerks were only about 3 percent of all male workers at the plant, and women clerks about 7 percent of all women workers. By February 10, 1921, the Scovill workforce had declined to 4,704 employees. But while the number of male office workers declined to 221, the number of female office workers rose to 312. Both male and female clerks were now a larger proportion of the workforce at Scovill than they had been in 1917, but although only 6 percent of all male employees were office workers, female clerks were more than 27 percent of all the women who worked at Scovill.

The unique census tally of Scovill employees for 1917 listed "clerical, administrative and technical" personnel separately from artisans and laborers. Administrative and technical personnel in the main office may be assumed to be executives and office managers, while most of those in mill and manufacturing were probably largely foremen and women.

Scovill Employees, 1917

	Main Offices			Mill and Manufacturing		
	Male	Female	Total	Male	Female	Total
Administrative/ technical	89	0	89	162	3	165
Clerical	137	171	308	112	67	179

The 1921 census of administrative and clerical employees did not differentiate between main office and factory clerks, but the growing centralization of factory accounting probably meant that more of the clerks were in the main office than had been in 1917.

Administrative and Clerical Employees, 1921

	Male	Female	Total
Executives	33	1	34
Foremen	164	0	164
Clerks	221	313	534

83. For changes in male and female occupations between 1870 and 1930 and the new importance of office work, see Alba M. Edwards, *Comparative Occupation Statistics for the United States, 1870-1940* (Washington, D.C.: GPO, 1943), 100-103, and H. Dewey Anderson and Percy E. Davidson, *Occupational Trends in the United States* (Stanford: Stanford University Press, 1940), 584-99. On the ratio of clerical to manufacturing employees, see Jurgen Kocka, *White Collar Workers in America, 1890-1940: A Socio-Political History in International Perspective* (London: Sage Publishers, 1980), 94.

84. Adding the categories of bookkeeper-cashier, stenographer-typist, machine operator and clerical and kindred from Table 2 gives a total of 421,000 men in clerical work in 1900 and 1,604,600 in 1930. All census figures for clerical categories should be used as rough guides and with considerable caution. The category "clerks not classified elsewhere" contained both machine clerks and those with general skills or job titles until 1930. Only stenography, typing, and bookkeeping were listed as separate categories, and "machine operators" (and who these were is not entirely clear) were not separated until 1930. See David L. Kaplan and M. Claire Casey, "Occupational Trends in the United States, 1900-1950," Bureau of the Census Working Paper no. 5 (Washington D.C.: Department of Commerce, 1958). For further elaboration on the census and clerical work, see Margo Anderson Conk, *The United States Census and Labor Force Change, 1870-1940* (Ann Arbor: UMI Research Press, 1978), 68, and Sharon Hartman Strom, "'Machines instead of Clerks': Technology and the Feminization of Bookkeeping, 1910-1950," in *Computer Chips and Paper*

Clips: Technology and Women's Employment, ed. Heidi Hartmann (Washington, D.C.: National Academy Press), 2:78-83.

85. The census figures for male stenographers and typists in 1930 may reflect changed categories used by census takers more than an actual decline in male members of this group; in 1940 the number of male stenographers and typists had surpassed its 1920 total to reach more than eighty-one thousand. Margery W. Davies found that men were still a substantial majority of all private secretaries in Massachusetts in 1902 and that most advice books to private secretaries were intended for men as late as World War I. These materials were directed to both men and women in the 1920s and did not become "women's material" until after 1930. Margery W. Davies, *Woman's Place Is at the Typewriter: Office Work and Office Workers, 1870-1930* (Philadelphia: Temple University Press, 1982), 158-61.

86. Although it is not possible to sort out these specialized white-collar workers from upper-level managers and proprietors in the census, a sampling of some of the major categories indicates how rapidly they were growing and that men outnumbered women in them substantially. There were, for example, about 77,000 male insurance agents and brokers in 1900 and nearly 244,000 by 1930. Women made substantial progress in this field, where their numbers rose from about a thousand in 1900 to nearly thirteen thousand in 1930, but they were still only 5 percent of the total.

87. In 1880, about 79 percent of all men of working age were employed and 15 percent of all working-age women; by 1930, 76 percent of the men and 22 percent of the women worked. An especially useful summary of these trends is National Industrial Conference Board, *Women Workers and Labor Supply* (New York: NICB, 1935). By the NICB's accounting (18), by 1930, 1.886 million women were in manufacturing, 2.379 million were in clerical occupations (including telephone and telegraph operators), and another half million were in sales.

2

Gender and the Masculine Business Professions

THE TRANSFORMATION of office work took place during the last, most vigorous stage of the suffrage movement. By 1920 two million women belonged to the National American Woman Suffrage Association, and thousands had participated in demonstrations, political campaigns, and lobbying efforts. During World War I women were hired for jobs previously thought suitable only for men: railroad yard work, streetcar conducting, lower-level managerial jobs in business, and administrative jobs in government. The coincidence of these economic and political opportunities and the optimism of the Progressive years created an atmosphere of confidence and continuing expectation. Many middle-class women, especially those with college degrees, thought themselves in a halcyon day. Almost anything seemed possible, including successful attacks on the exclusion of women from the male-dominated professions. Marjorie Nicolson, a 1914 graduate of the University of Wisconsin, later recalled the euphoria of her generation. Nicholson claimed she and her peers "came late enough to escape the self-consciousness and belligerance of the early pioneers," and "to take education and training for granted . . . . This was our double glory. Positions were everywhere open to us; it never occured to us at that time that we were taken only because men were not available . . . . The millenium had come; it did not occur to us that life could be different."[1]

Advice books and vocational guidance experts predicted that new openings in business administration, accounting, statistics, and personnel management would create unprecedented opportunities for middle-class women with college educations, expanding occupational choices beyond teaching and the other "women's professions." There seemed to be no good reason why women could not enter the ranks of the managerial experts required for the growing specialization of office work. It seemed particularly portentous that the granddaughter of Elizabeth Cady Stanton, Nora Blatch, was one of a handful of courageous young college women who entered the engineering profession. Blatch was a "Sibley Sue," a graduate of the Sibley College of Engineering at Cornell in the top five of her class. She was also, in the tradition of her grandmother and her mother, Harriet Stanton Blatch, an ardent suffragist and rode across New York state on a horse in 1913 to promote the idea of votes for women.

Many college women thought, like Marjorie Nicholson, that if women wanted managerial and professional jobs, they could have them. Jeanette Eaton and Bertha M. Stevens, who investigated opportunities in Cleveland before the war began, declared in 1915 that while at the moment women in offices did "most of the subordinate and mechanical work" and men held "the majority of responsible, executive and highly paid positions," the future might be quite different. Making it so depended largely on women's determination and growing professionalism: "Prejudice against women *per se* is giving way before the advance of efficient professional women," continued Eaton and Stevens. "A few women who climb to responsible positions win the confidence of men for the whole sex and point the way to their younger sisters at the foot of the ladder." A popular magazine writer, Katherine L. Chamberlin, echoed these sentiments when she announced that there was "no limit to women's future business possibilities. Their success or failure rests with themselves." Even more cautious predictors of the future like Elizabeth Kemper Adams, author of the carefully researched *Women Professional Workers* in 1921 for the Women's Educational and Industrial Union, thought the war represented a turning point in both women's self-perceptions and the gendered identity of the professions: "Women are thinking of themselves as professional workers, and men are thinking about them, with a new seriousness and a new vividness . . . . This new professional awareness of women comes fortunately at a time when . . . . the professions themselves are acquiring an unprecedented public importance and new flexibility of mind."[2]

These writers were all more optimistic than they should have been about the possibility of women entering the business professions. Competence, intelligence, and dedication could get women only so far, because it was partly the exclusion of women and other "undesirables" that made the new business professions attractive to men. Traditional male jobs in both clerking and the professions were undergoing profound changes. The growing rationalization, mechanization, and feminization of office work was beginning to limit middle-class men's opportunities in traditional clerking. The expansion of academic training in the business professions and the growing importance of the professions in general gave middle-class men, along with upwardly mobile men from the working class, a new set of occupational alternatives. Men from older elites also had a vested interest in the new business expertise. They were seeing the traditional influence of medicine, law, and the ministry threatened by the rise of corporate business and were under pressure to find more modern ways of exercising power. This chapter and the next will discuss how these forces interacted to produce a particularly virile (the word is used intentionally) professional identity in business administration and engineering, and a somewhat more ambivalent sexual identity in accounting, statistics, and personnel management. It was no accident that these identities emerged just as white, upper-middle-class, college-educated women were able to launch a real assault on the bastion of male professional privilege. As male professionals oversaw the feminization of the lower levels of office work, they were determined to keep their own world as free of women as possible.[3]

The exclusion of women from the business professions was not completely successful. Although the opportunities were not as numerous as enthusiasts such as Eaton, Stevens, and Adams claimed, women certainly had more chances to wield influence in business by 1930 than had been the case in 1900. Few women became engineers or business executives, but some managed to be accountants, statisticians, and personnel workers. The overall picture of women in business remained bleak, despite the surge in numbers of women professionals.

Between 1900 and 1930 the census showed that numbers of professional, technical, and kindred workers grew by more than two million. Altogether there were 2.68 times as many of these workers in 1930 as there had been in 1910. Women seemed to maintain their share of the professional pie; they constituted about 35 percent of all professional workers in 1900 and 45 percent of them in

1930. However, they were overwhelmingly concentrated in professional occupations which were considered appropriate for women, even though most of the professions required equivalent levels of undergraduate training (Table 4). In fact, the decades in which the business professions emerged saw a greater polarization than ever of the professions along lines of gender. Men sought to fend off the challenge that the women's rights movement was raising to their dominance of public and professional life by restricting access to professional education and training; they claimed the more prestigious professions were inappropriate for women. As the professions became more important in American life, their gendered identities seemed to take on even more significance. As historian Nancy Cott has argued, "Male professions fending off female interlopers suggested that they considered the presence of women colleagues above a certain point incompatible with their own vision of professional excellence, a threat to professional esteem. Unambiguous male predominance became an implicit and essential condition of continued professional identity and distinction."[4] Both women and men found it difficult to avoid signifying the gender of the business professions. Sexual difference became an important typology for evaluating and encoding them.

Table 4.
Selected Professional Occupations in the United States in
Order of Numerical Importance, 1900 and 1930

	1900	Percent Female	1930	Percent Female
Teachers	435,642	75	1,044,016	82
Nurses	11,804	94	294,189	98
Engineers	37,467	—	217,246	—
Accountants and Auditors	22,916	6	191,571	9
Lawyers	107,620	—	160,605	2
Physicians and Surgeons	131,477	5	156,603	4
Social and Welfare	—	—	70,801	70
Librarians	2,915	72	29,613	91
Architects	10,581	1	22,850	2

Source: David L. Kaplan and M. Claire Casey, "Occupational Trends in the United States, 1900-1950," Bureau of the Census Working Paper no. 5, Washington, D.C.: Department of Commerce, 1958, 6.

"We Have No Other Merchandise than Ourselves": The Professions and Professionalization in American Life

As their numbers and importance grew after 1900, professionals became more self-conscious as a class and more aggressive in promoting their own interests. They faced an occupational contradiction; although the professions were more central than ever to American life, many professionals were losing their traditional independence. The professional was increasingly likely to be a salaried employee hired to provide specialized expertise in the production of human resources, technology, science, and knowledge. One contemporary observer described the professional worker of the teens as a person who sells "experience, judgment, advice. We have no other merchandise than ourselves."[5] In Barbara Ehrenreich and John Ehrenreich's definition, the professional-managerial class is a group of "salaried mental workers," that does not own the means of production or produce goods; it manages, teaches, and pacifies those who do. The professional managerial class, in other words, becomes a buffer between those who own or control the means of production and those who sell their labor for wages.[6]

The professions of engineering, accounting, business administration, and personnel management were especially likely to be cast in the role of "producing capitalist class relations." These professions gained new importance just as the more traditional professions were undergoing dramatic change. At the turn of the century, most professional groups replaced a haphazard system of education, training, and apprenticeship with more stringent and formalized requirements. It took several decades to accomplish the upgrading of the professions, but the growing trend was toward requiring new combinations of standards for professional status, including college degrees, certifying examinations, licensing regulated by the states, and, frequently, postgraduate training as well. While some of these changes were aimed at improving training, they were also designed to limit access. In an increasingly democratic and widely educated society, women, people of color, and the working class posed more of a threat to the dominance of white, upper-class men than they had in earlier decades.[7]

Ironically, the ideology of professionalism at the turn of the century seemed to present an opening for womanly influence. Elizabeth Kemper Adams observed that professionals might be viewed as "workers in the public interest and officially or unofficially in the public service . . . . In many ways they seem to stand at present as the ideal mediators between capital and labor."[8] The supposed detachment of professionals from the interests of both the ruling and working classes appeared to put them in a position to defuse the conflict between haves and have-nots that was so frightening to middle-class Progressives in the teens. As purveyors of middle-class culture in the nineteenth century, women volunteers had seemed ideal intermediaries. Some of the women's professions that appeared at the end of the nineteenth century, like social and library work, were to some degree extensions of this idea.

Middle-class benevolence, however, was different from the commanding expertise that the redesigned professions hoped to offer. Business professionals in particular did not see womanly benevolence (or womanliness in general) as positive qualities. Promoters of the new professionalism like Frederick W. Taylor and Louis D. Brandeis, emphasized its inherent manliness. They wanted to dissociate their practical, tough-minded solutions to society's problems from what they viewed as the "effeminate" tendencies of old-fashioned social reform or the utopian thinking of turn-of-the-century visionaries like Edward Bellamy. In their handbook on personnel management in 1921, for instance, two psychologists promised to forego the "kind of pablum" administered by the "old women of both sexes" who had run old-fashioned welfare programs in industry.[9]

Engineers, according to one historian, saw "their proposals as substitutes for progressive reforms, not as supplements to them." Their epithets for Progressive reformers included "utopist" and "dilletante," terminology frequently used in the past to question the sexual identity of male reformers.[10] The business professions were not only careers, they were also masculine callings central to the maintenance of an orderly society. They would impose disciplined system on the chaos of capitalism so that the social and sexual order would be preserved. Even though women had helped to mediate social problems in earlier decades, they now needed to step aside or to confine themselves to assisting roles.

Harrington Emerson, an early scientific management engineer, evoked a clear sexual division of labor in explaining why the primary goal of his generation (of men) was to eliminate waste and make efficiency a political ideal. Society was moving to a new level of organization that required group planning and enterprise. Women, Emerson claimed, could be credited with "the germs of civilization" because of their endurance and intuition. But manly ways of thinking, or what Emerson termed "principles of efficiency," were required to "take over and develop on a gigantic scale" what women had begun: "woman makes tepees, but men build . . . sky-scrapers; . . . . [and] organization must replace intuitions." As Samuel Haber has observed, the gendered outlook required for the new professions was indisputably masculine: "An efficient person was an effective person, and that characterization brought with it a long shadow of latent associations and predispositions; a turning toward hard work and away from feeling, toward discipline and away from sympathy, toward masculinity and away from femininity."[11]

Many intellectuals of the Progressive period, including the founders of the business professions, sought to link their academic training and intellectual values to a masculine American tradition of heroism rooted in pragmatism, experimentation, and exploration, while rejecting pure idealism as inherently feminine and merely sentimental.[12] Casting activities of the new professions in the heroic mold was critical to making them manly. What might be viewed by others as technical labor, paper-pushing, delegation of important tasks to others, and mere money-making had to be portrayed as adventurous, noble, and indispensable to the national purpose. Engineers and businessmen emphasized the ways in which they were pioneers conquering "new frontiers," subduing industrial disorder in much the same way their ancestors had "tamed" the wilderness. According to Arch W. Shaw, business publisher and early instructor at the Harvard Business School, "the manufacturer-merchant" had "become a pioneer on the frontier of human desires and needs." Louis Brandeis thought the best businessmen were pioneers breaking new paths that "will become the peopled highways."[13] This posturing as pioneers, perhaps, reflected the same kind of crisis of masculinity and search for heroism found in the life of Theodore Roosevelt, whose affinity for both western-style adventure and engineers was well known.

Sometimes business professionals made their fantasies of classic male adventurism explicit. At the General Electric Company, for example, male managers and executives were sent to summer camp, beginning in 1922, to encourage company loyalty and solidarity. They performed forest rituals and dressed up like Indians, lumberjacks, and Roman soldiers. No women were ever invited, and the camps became, according to historian David Nye, "a sanctuary where regression to premarital bonding was actively encouraged."[14]

The new professionals often made claims for masculine identities that bordered on the grandiose. One engineer thought the engineering "way of thinking . . . enables us successfully to think of any kind of thing," and another asserted that "it matters not whether the problems before him are political, sociological, industrial or technical, I believe that the engineering type of mind . . . is best fitted to undertake them." George S. Morison, who spoke to fellow engineers at the American Society of Chemical Engineers in 1895, claimed that engineers "are the priests of material development, of the work which enables other men to enjoy the fruits of the great sources of power in Nature, and of the power of mind over matter. We are priests of the new epoch, without superstitions."[15] E. E. Hunt, a self-proclaimed Taylor disciple and assistant to U.S. Secretary of Commerce (and engineer) Herbert Hoover, claimed in 1924 that "scientific management is becoming a part of our moral inheritance. Taylor has won a victory for the science of management which is no less overwhelming than Pasteur's victory for bacteriology." Taylor himself claimed that engineers could educate "not only the workmen but the whole of the country as to the true facts." H. L. Gantt described the engineer as "a man of few opinions and many facts, few words and many deeds," who "should be accorded the leadership which is his proper place in our economic system."[16] The necessity of maintaining the sexual purity of a profession that thought of itself as a priesthood was self-evident.

These kinds of claims often gained support from many social critics and Progressive reformers who, like Thorstein Veblen and Theodore Roosevelt, found the alleged objectivity and practical know-how of the engineer appealing.[17] As the earliest proponents of scientific management, engineers were often as critical of big business and political corruption as Progressive reformers. Taylor repeatedly argued, as did his disciples, that reform in industry must come largely within management itself. The engineer Morris Cooke was an outspoken critic of urban utilities, an advocate of municipal reform, and a hero of Progressivism. But the average engineer's tendency to ally with the business class ultimately made him more a servant of the corporation than its effective critic, more an advocate of social control than of social change.[18] Real power was likely to be exercised by those who owned or directed the means of production: businessmen and chief executives. Business or public administration—the science of managing large organizations—came to have more esteem than the technical knowledge of engineering.

The engineer never quite achieved the powerful status Gantt and others claimed for him, partly because the professional business administrator began to push him out of the limelight. By World War I the corporate executive was becoming an icon of the American character. Louis Brandeis, who had been so attracted to scientific management in the Eastern Rates case, proclaimed the virtues of big businessmen in his essay "Business: A Profession." He asserted that the successful corporate businessman performed "achievements comparable . . . with those of the artist or the scientist, of the inventor or of the statesman." As businessmen became more professional and therefore more socially responsible, Brandeis argued, the term *big business* would lose its "sinister meaning," and would take on a new definition: "'Big Business' will then mean business big not in bulk or power, but great in service and grand in manner. 'Big business' will mean professionalized business, as distinguished from the occupation of petty trafficking or mere money-making. And as the profession of business develops, the great industrial and social problems expressed in the present social unrest will one by one find solution."[19]

Leon C. Marshall, author of a rigorous textbook on business administration and a professor at the University of Chicago Business School, also claimed broad influence for the professionally trained businessman: "Business is, after all, a pecuniarily organized scheme of gratifying human wants, and, properly understood, falls little short of being as broad, as inclusive, as life itself in its motives, aspirations, and social obligations[,] . . . as broad as all science in its technique."[20] The business professional, in the words of another promoter, was unquestionably male, upper-class, and deserving of wide-ranging influence: "A successful banker is composed of about one-fifth accountant, two-fifths lawyer, three-fifths political economist, and four-fifths gentleman and scholar—total ten-fifths—double-size. Any smaller person may be a pawnbroker or a promoter, but not a banker."[21]

Nonetheless, promoters of the profession of business administration faced a number of problems in establishing its legitimacy. Classical academia had always scorned anything connected to money-making as beneath the lofty activity of pure thought or professional service. Yet most men who graduated from college at the turn of the century went into business, a fact traditional educators began to feel they had to acknowledge more formally. The growing need for college-trained executives and administrators was also apparent. Male college graduates needed professional degrees to assume executive positions. Such credentials would legitimize their power and set them apart from both commercial college graduates and technicians (including engineers), who were increasingly from middle- and working-class backgrounds. While president Charles Eliot was initially reluctant to bring the study of business to Harvard, he noted that more than half of the class of 1907 had gone into business as he sanctioned the establishment of the Harvard School of Business Administration in 1908. A flurry of speeches and articles surrounded these attempts to put the professional in business on a par with his colleagues in law and medicine.[22]

By the 1920s there were enough business degree holders to compete with the engineers, who had laid initial claim to many upper-level managerial positions.[23] Although there would continue to be a vocal group in big business which argued the "college man" was of no use to business because he had not been brought up through the ranks, most of the industries in the forefront of scientific management techniques thought highly of placing college graduates in administrative positions. They held men with advanced degrees from institutions like Harvard, the University of Pennsylvania, and the University of Chicago in particular regard. A Westinghouse Electric executive complained that although "there are not enough of the best men, men who become recognized leaders," and far too many of "the lower grades of college men . . . there are of course the cases of men who have done advanced work in certain lines and are worth much more than the ordinary 'run of class' graduates."[24]

Initially, there was a great deal of confusion over what should constitute a business curriculum in a university setting. One thing was definite: university business training should not replicate what the commercial colleges did by teaching specific skills in bookkeeping, typing, and stenography. Accounting was obviously integral to the study of business on the university level, but it was also very popular in correspondence schools, night courses, and business colleges. Economics was a discipline that seemed to belong in the academic study of business, but it had already found a home in the social sciences and usually remained in colleges of arts and sciences. Educators at the elite institutions of business administration thought scientific management might integrate all of these fields and give them a discrete academic identity. Frederick W. Taylor regularly talked to deans of business and engineering schools and was approached by Dean Edwin Gay of the Harvard Business School to teach courses in scientific management. Indeed, the first curriculum at Harvard was designed around Taylorism at its core.[25]

A final problem remained, however: to establish just what it was that distinguished business administrators from engineers and accountants. In the grander conceptions of business administration, graduates of the prestigious professional schools portrayed themselves as conceptualizers of scientific management, and engineers as its technicians. In this scheme of things, it was the professional administrator, not the engineer, who would actually chart the course of the ship of business: engineers, accountants, managers, and salesmen would simply execute his orders.

The purported ability of the male business professional to employ the scientific method was a critical aspect of his power. The way in which the Taylorites acquired the mantle of science for the new business professions—partly by the simple fact of changing the term *systematic management* to *scientific management*—was a stroke of genius, even if an obvious one. The growing prestige of professionals at the turn of the century was in large measure based on the idea that advanced education, particularly in the scientific method, would bring both objectivity and modern methods to old ways of doing things.[26]

Employing subjective ideas about women's biology, early commentators tried to argue that women were simply unsuited to the rigors of scientific thought.[27] But the widespread movement of women into higher education quickly dispelled the possibility that women and their male allies would accept such rhetoric at face value. More overt methods of excluding women would have to be found if they were to be kept out of the male-dominated professions.

Maintaining Sexual Purity: Engineering and Business Administration

By 1910 nearly 40 percent of all college students were women, as were 47 percent of all students in four-year colleges by 1920. Although most elite institutions in the country were closed to women, fine women's schools and coeducational universities offered women first-rate educations. By 1915-16, in fact, 75 percent of all women college students attended coeducational institutions. They were determined not only to obtain college degrees, but also to study science and to enter the professions.

Women college and university students faced stiff opposition in some quarters. Leaders of many coeducational institutions had become alarmed over the growing "feminization" of college life. The presence of so many women reenforced an already keen sense of inferiority to eastern Ivy League schools. At Chicago, where between 1892 and 1902 women received 56.3 percent of all the Phi Beta Kappa awards and by 1912 were 52 percent of the student body, sex-segregated classes were instituted in large courses. At the University of California, President Benjamin Wheeler advocated a new junior college system partly on the grounds that women would be more likely to attend college in their local communities and thus leave the university to qualified men. At Stanford, where women were winning many academic awards and nearly equaled men in the graduating class of 1901, administrators turned to a quota system that admitted three men for every woman; the policy was not overturned until 1933. Wesleyan abandoned coeducation altogether in 1912 and did not resume it until 1970.[28]

Those women who were admitted to coeducational schools often faced hostility from male faculty and students. They were often discouraged from entering professional schools or faced outright discrimination if they applied. In fact, the emergence of the new professional curricula at many large state institutions was partly seen as a way around the "problem" of coeducation, or, in other words, as a way for male students to avoid taking classes with women. Charles R. Van Hise of Wisconsin was particularly interested in the possibility of using specialized programs in business and engineering to create academic spheres for men that would be uncontaminated by women. "Segregation by choice of vocational or technical school is good," he claimed, "and will go farther . . . . At the present time, provision has been made for nearly complete segregation on a large scale by the establishment of courses and colleges which are practically for one sex or the other. The colleges of engineering, law, commerce and medicine are essentially men's colleges." Although Van Hise claimed these schools were open to women, he assured educators "their opportunities have been taken advantage of only to a limited extent" by female students. The result was that at an institution like the University of California, where women comprised about 40 percent of the student body between 1898 and 1913, most of the professional schools and vocational departments were 90 to 100 percent male. The low proportions of women in professional schools had little to do with lack of interest in studying science; at California more than half of all the students in the natural sciences were women.[29]

The professions used several methods to exclude women. These began at the college level and continued on to professional training.

Medical schools were the first to be besieged by significant numbers of women applicants, which came just as medicine was trying to upgrade training and professionalize in the late nineteenth century. Medical schools hit upon quota techniques for limiting the number of women (and some categories of men, particularly Jews and African Americans). While giving the appearance of fairness by not excluding the undesirables altogether, quotas made it extremely difficult for more than a selected few of the outside groups to achieve professional status. The effect of quotas was amplified by strictly limiting opportunities for apprenticeship training (such as hospital internships) and through a tacit understanding among members of the medical profession that undesirables should not be allowed to practice at the better hospitals. Medicine and other professions managed to severely limit the number of "undesirables" who could practice. The effect on women in medicine was clear. The proportion of physicians who were female reached a peak in 1910, and by 1930 there were fewer women physicians than there had been twenty years earlier.[30]

Engineers faced an easier task than doctors in excluding women. Women did not seem to be as attracted to engineering as they were to medicine, and those who were found nearly insurmountable obstacles to training for employment. Engineering became a profession literally overnight; between 1890 and 1900 alone the number of students studying engineering in college grew from about a thousand to about ten thousand just as increasing numbers of women were entering colleges and universities. Most engineering schools were established for male students between 1870 and 1890 as technical institutes, and most continued to deny admission to women. But universities and coeducational colleges developed engineering curricula as well, and many of these were theoretically open to women. The dean of the College of Engineering at the University of Colorado reported that in 1923 three women were enrolled at the school and that a few former women students had been successful in finding employment. Alice C. Goff, a 1915 graduate of the University of Michigan, managed to find work with a Youngstown steel company and by 1924 was a squad boss in charge of eight to twelve men, although she found "that many firms were prejudiced against employing young women."[31]

Educators at Michigan and Colorado seemed to be exceptions to the rule against encouraging women students in engineering. Coeducational schools with engineering departments were often actively hostile when women tried to enroll. At Cornell's highly regarded engineering school the hostility of male students was legendary, and the administration remained ambivalent about women's presence well into the twentieth century. By failing to provide adequate on-campus housing for women students, both Cornell and MIT effectively used bed space to prevent significant numbers of women from entering prestigious professional programs. Florence Luscomb, who lived in Boston and thus could attend MIT as a nonresidential student, graduated in architecture in 1909. She recalled that there was a record number of twelve women in her class, in either chemistry or architecture. Most of the student societies, such as the Engineering Club, did not accept women members, and it was the tradition at MIT for men not to associate with women students. One of Luscomb's classmates had originally enrolled in engineering "but shortly . . . became convinced that she could never get a job with any engineering firm, and as she had to earn a living she switched to architecture."[32]

The professional engineering societies were also often unwilling to encourage women engineers. Nora Stanton Blatch became a junior member of the American Society of Civil Engineers when she graduated from Cornell but was refused full status in 1916, when the Society of Civil Engineers voted 1,746 to 1,352 to exclude women. She was dropped from the list of members despite her protestation that she met all the listed requirements. She sued the ASCE in court for excluding her but lost her case. By 1922 the American Institutes of Civil, Mechanical, Electrical, and Mining Engineers had a combined total of sixteen women members. Alfred D. Flinn, director of the United Engineering Society, reported to Emma P. Hirth of the Bureau of Vocational Information in 1922 that "in 30 years' experience as a civil engineer" he had encountered very few women in engineering. Although most of the schools and engineering societies did not actively bar women, Flinn thought that unnecessary; the loneliness of women's lives as engineering students and society members was all too obvious.[33]

Most male engineers treated the subject of women in engineering with disdain. James F. Kemp, an instructor of geology at Columbia, stated flatly that women would be as welcome in mining engineering as "snakes in Ireland." A Pittsburgh engineer, John Needles Chester, noted that although engineering was theoretically "open to all who aspire to succeed," he did not "approve of women entering any field" that would "subtract from their womanliness . . . . Next to military leadership," he asserted, "the profession of engineering is the most masculine . . . . [E]ngineering incorporates everything from the kid glove position to the roughest and most hazardous field work .... I believe ... it will be years before women could place themselves at parity with men in this field, either as to responsibility that would be entrusted to them, or compensation meted out."[34]

Engineering remained the most difficult of all the professions for women to enter throughout the twentieth century, and without access to engineering women were essentially excluded from the material development and managerial structuring of the corporate process. The recruitment of large numbers of engineers began with the growth of corporations and other kinds of bureaucratic institutions in need of designers, planners, and managers. By the turn of the century new specialities in mechanical, electrical, and mining engineering were beginning to overshadow civil engineering, but all of the varieties still involved hands-on work in the industrial process itself, which was inherently viewed as "men's work": the building of bridges, the design of factories, the invention of new mechanical processes for industry, and the efficient use of human labor. Engineers were, at least early on, asked to perform administrative and personnel functions, and many of them rose to positions of executive responsibility in the teens and twenties. The engineering profession seemed especially unsuitable to women.

With few chances for engineering education and even fewer chances of employment, women could not afford to challenge male dominance in engineering. The number of engineers climbed to about 130,000 in the census of 1920, but only forty-one were women. Helen A. Smith had a degree in electrical engineering and worked for the Rochester Gas and Electric Corporation, but she spent her days promoting the consumption of home lighting and designing store windows. Helen Klein, a radio engineer for the Crosley Radio Corporation, dejectedly admitted in 1930 that there were few opportunities for the handful of women trained in engineering, partly because engineers were assumed to be potential managers. Even if the woman engineer could obtain an engineering job, she could not expect to be promoted to a managerial position because "a woman controlling a department of men is often unsuccessful. They resent her position and co-operation is never obtained." Some male engineers thought women might be suitable in engineering if they confined themselves to stenography and drafting. Women engineers corroborated this point. "There is a strong tendency on the part of employers to keep women at drafting and computing," said Nora Stanton Blatch. The former wife of Lee De

Forest, inventor of the vacuum tube, Blatch finally established her own business in order to do "real engineering." Kate Gleason of Rochester, who had learned the art of machine design in her father's workshop, graduated from Cornell and then took charge of his car works factory. But Gleason and Blatch had connections and capital that were clearly beyond the reach of most women in engineering.[35]

Women were studying mathematics and the sciences successfully by 1900 and entering most other professions in significant numbers if not large percentages. There is no reason to believe that engineering required some special intellectual ability that put it on a different plane from the other scientific disciplines; outright discrimination seems the most likely explanation for the almost total paucity of women. When the degree of discrimination and exclusion was added to the condemnation women faced for taking up a "masculine pursuit" like engineering, the obstacles may very well have been so overwhelming as to convince them there was really no point in even considering engineering throughout most of the twentieth century. Hence Alice Rossi's finding in 1970, when women were still only 2 percent of all students in engineering colleges, that most young women "could not assimilate the notion of becoming engineers," and "there was no single occupation that they thought their male contemporaries and their parents would be less pleased to have them pursue."[36]

Male business administrators faced greater obstacles to discouraging women than did engineers. Business administration did not require hazardous field work and was fundamentally a "desk job." Women had access to the general kind of training required for the field. Vocational business colleges had always been open to women, and many coeducational schools also offered business courses, although business curricula at collegiate schools were widely diverse in character. Some were two-year programs in the junior and senior years, as at Wisconsin and Minnesota, others were four-year, degree-granting programs as at the Wharton School and the University of Chicago, and beginning with the Harvard Business School in 1908, a few offered postgraduate degrees in business administration. While the elite graduate institutions forged ahead in developing a curriculum around the principles of scientific management, what should constitute a course of business study at more inclusive schools remained murky. Whatever their design, business curricula were immediately popular. By 1926, the Federal Bureau of Education estimated that more than fifty-seven thousand undergraduate students were majoring in business programs at the college or university level.[37]

Columbia University developed its business program out of a set of adult extension classes offered through the Teachers' College, and the program had initially attracted many women students. Some of the women who studied business at Columbia were former college students seeking training so they could get jobs other than teaching; others worked in offices in New York City and took business courses at night in the hopes of obtaining better jobs. Although male undergraduate students and evening students originally took the same courses, there was growing concern at Columbia to develop a professional business school that would be on a par with prestigious business schools at other universities. In 1913 students seeking secretarial training were separated from business students, who were put into a professional degree curriculum. The secretarial students were offered a one-year certificate. The result was a clearer separation of female and male students into "appropriate" areas of business, with added benefits for Columbia as an employer as well. Although some women continued to take academic courses in business, the Columbia Business School's historian, Thurman Van Metre, noted that its secretarial certificate program "developed a supply of efficient, intelligent secretaries," some of whom were employed in the offices of the university. In 1916 Columbia went further by requiring that business degree candidates have two prior years of liberal arts training, at either Columbia or Barnard, and in 1931 the business school faculty was formally separated from the extension staff of the Teachers' College and moved to the Columbia faculty.[38]

Schools of business at other men's schools sought to hold the line against admitting women students. The Wharton School did not admit women students until 1938, and then on a limited basis in especially designed courses such as "Consumers' Problems in Marketing." The Harvard Graduate School of Business Administration kept its doors barred to women until 1963. Henry T. Copeland, an early faculty member and assistant to the first dean, admitted that "within a few years after the Business School was opened, inquiries and even strong demands had come from several women who wished to be admitted to the School."[39] Beatrice Doerschuk, assistant director of the Bureau of Vocational Information, was researching women's access to business education in 1920. She wrote to Copeland asking whether the Harvard Business School had any plans to open its doors to women. Copeland responded that although "the question of admitting women . . . has arisen on two or three occasions in the past . . . . the school has not considered it expedient to modify the restrictions on admission."[40]

One alternative to the exclusion of women at the elite business administration schools would have been the establishment of collegiate programs of business at the more exclusive women's colleges. But women's private colleges in the East continued to focus on liberal arts training and to view vocational curricula with suspicion. Like their counterpart Harvard, they saw undergraduate study in the liberal arts as crucial preparation for professional training in the sciences, education, medicine, and law. The "Seven Sisters" (Mount Holyoke, Vassar, Smith, Bryn Mawr, Barnard, Wellesley, and Radcliffe) did send a larger proportion of their students on to professional careers than other schools. But women educators at the elite schools remained ambivalent about the new emphasis on business and vocationalism in education because it was precisely the absence of these that made their institutions parallel to the highly thought of schools for men.[41]

Early generations of faculty and administrators at the Seven Sisters also had doubts about encouraging women to work in heterosocial but male-dominated environments like corporations. They were committed to building female institutions, where women could perpetuate feminine morality and friendship. They wanted to expand the number of occupations open to women, but their thinking about sexual differences remained ambiguous. Although they wanted to show that women were the intellectual equals of men, they also tended to think that women were more sensitive, more caring, and generally morally superior. Women educators were all in favor of producing more women doctors and lawyers, partly because the discrimination against women in these professions, suddenly worse than ever, was a long-standing bone of contention in the women's rights movement, but also because these seemed to be the "nobler" professions, not connected, at least in their minds, with baser motives of profit-making and materialism.[42]

After 1910 this ideology began to break down somewhat, although it remained a potent force at most elite women's schools. Many of those who attended college in the teens and twenties were impatient with the homosocial environment of women's colleges. Younger college women were also clamoring for occupations other than teaching. Home economics, nursing, psychology, and social work were all fields that welcomed women and provided real alternatives to the classroom, and many women's schools began to offer at least some of these courses of study as alternatives. Most women's schools offered courses in economics and statistics, and nearly all schools offered limited credit or noncredit courses in typing and stenography, well aware that many of their graduates would have to fall back on office work for earning a living. The Katharine Gibbs secretarial schools specialized in the training of college women for office work, but women students had to turn elsewhere for teaching in business administration, accounting, and engineering.[43]

There were very real practical obstacles to establishing business curricula at the elite women's schools. No doubt the danger of turning into a glorified "secretarial science" school loomed large in the minds of educators at places like Radcliffe, Barnard, or Bryn Mawr.[44] Many potential donors and alumni probably disapproved of women's study of "masculine" pursuits; most jobs in the business professions were closed to women anyway. The cost of adding new schools or courses was substantial and remained formidable. Most prestigious women's schools ran their operations on a relative shoe-string, especially in comparison to their better-heeled male counterparts. In 1925 and 1926, for instance, Harvard received more than $9 million in gifts, and Wellesley, which of all the Seven Sisters raised the most that year, received only three-quarters of a million.[45]

A rare but important exception to the general exclusion of business curricula at women's schools was Bryn Mawr's Carola Woerishoffer Graduate Department of Social Economy and Social Research, which offered study in industrial relations and personnel administration. The Woerishoffer Department, established in 1915, was originally intended to train students for "organized activities for social welfare," and encouraged strong training in the social sciences. In 1918 it became one of the most important locations of the new training programs for women employment managers, under the direction of the economist and statistician Anne Bezanson.[46] Radcliffe College, by contrast, did not develop a program in personnel and business management until 1937. In a sense, however, both the Bryn Mawr and Radcliffe programs remained within acceptable gender boundaries because they steered women toward the most "feminine" of the business professions, personnel management, and were seen by some male educators as a way of staving off women's demands for admission to graduate schools of business administration.[47]

Despite all of these obstacles to studying business administration, women were taking business curricula in large numbers at

other kinds of institutions by the 1920s. A survey of four-year programs at colleges and universities by the Federal Bureau of Education showed that 2,534 women obtained degrees in business
between 1914 and 1928, with significant increases toward the end
of the twenties; by 1928 women received slightly more than 17 percent of all the degrees granted.[48] Many others took some business
courses while they majored in another discipline.[49]

Whether these business courses counted as the real thing was a
different matter. At coeducational institutions such as Stanford,
the University of Chicago, New York University, and the large midwestern state universities, women took legitimate courses in accounting, statistics, and employment management. But approximately one-third of the coeducational collegiate schools of
business offered a curriculum in secretarial science, and many
women who took business courses were acquiring typing and stenography skills to qualify themselves for work in the "real world"
after they graduated.[50] Student demand and administrators' ideas
about women's roles in business both influenced these choices. "It
is probably true that a school of business associated with a state
university will feel the urge to establish secretarial work more
keenly than some others schools do," said one college administrator. "Schools located in large cities might feel this urge because
there is a strong demand for college-trained secretaries and because
the institution owes it to its student body to provide the training."
Because women were "not wanted in public accounting" and were
"barred from most other first-class positions that commerce boys
usually enter," he went on to say, the business school was obligated
to offer them commercial courses.[51] Business curricula, then, frequently steered women into clerical work and diffused any aspirations they might have had to enter business adminstration or
accounting.

More Ambiguous Ground: Accounting,
Statistics, and Bookkeeping

Business administration seemed to emerge out of whole cloth in a
single decade, but bookkeeping and accounting had a long history
and an enormous constituency. Although some firms had to be sold
on the importance of executives trained in business administration,
accounting's importance to the new methods of doing business and
to government was undeniable. The expansion of accounting and
the collection of statistics lay at the heart of changes in office work

after 1900. As accounting procedures surged during World War I, demand for statisticians, accountants, and bookkeepers was intense. The growing number of human computers reflected these trends. In 1900 there were nearly 23,000 accountants and 232,000 bookkeepers; by 1930 there were 191,600 accountants and more than 738,000 bookkeepers. The sexual division of labor in bookkeeping and accounting was pronounced but not as absolute as in most other office occupations. Bookkeeping was not as feminized as stenography and typing, and accounting and auditing were not as exclusively male as engineering. By 1930 about 63 percent of bookkeepers were women, as were nearly 9 percent of accountants (Table 5).

The goal of those committed to the professionalization of accounting was to develop and maintain distinctions between bookkeeping and accounting. Because computing clerks and bookkeepers could claim a role in doing accounts, the professionalization of accounting required the separation of theories of accounting from the mere techniques of bookkeeping. But accountants were not as successful as other professionals in separating "technique" from "theory."[52]

Part of the difficulty in determining who might designate themselves as a professional accountant was in defining exactly what accountants did. There were two main categories of accounting.

Table 5.
Accountants and Bookkeepers in the United States,
1900-1940 (in Thousands)

	1900	1910	1920	1930	1940
Accountants/ auditors	22.9	39.2	118.5	191.6	238.0
Male	21.5	35.6	105.1	174.6	218.3
Female	1.4	3.6	13.4	17.0	19.7
Bookkeepers/ cashiers	232.0	446.8	615.5	738.2	721.1
Male	159.2	263.3	269.8	272.5	248.4
Female	72.7	183.6	345.7	465.7	472.8

Source: David L. Kaplan and M. Claire Casey, "Occupational Trends in the United States, 1900-1950," Bureau of the Census Working Paper no. 5, Washington, D.C.: Department of Commerce, 1958, 6.

Public accounting (initially a form of auditing, or checking account books for errors or fraud) became important at the turn of the century as the financial records of large institutions were subjected to more extensive scrutiny by management, stockholders, and government. The public accountant's job was to vouch for the accuracy and integrity of books, to advise on taxes, and to offer independent consultations. The states began to certify some public accountants, and public accounting firms in large cities offered the services of these licensed experts.

By 1910 a second kind of accounting emerged: managing the finances and cost accounting systems of corporations. The National Association of Cost Accounting was formed in 1919 to link managerial and system designing accounting with the scientific management movement. Comptrollers and treasurers were now more likely to be college-educated accountants who assembled staffs to provide and interpret reams of bookkeeping detail for future planning.[53] Joseph Sterrett of the prestigious public accounting firm Price, Waterhouse told a New York reporter in 1921 that he thought it was still possible for ambitious young men to take up accounting with a high school diploma, but would prefer to see those who wished to enter the profession take a "full college course in general subjects, followed by post-graduate work in accountancy."[54]

Those who claimed an administrative role for accountants staked out a claim that went beyond what some perceived as the "glorified bookkeeping" of public accountants. The executive accountant, they insisted, was an essential complement to engineers and business administrators in the proper execution of scientific management. Sterrett, a promoter of this view, sought to explicate the differences between public and managerial accounting: "One is analytic as typified by the audit and the examination. The other is synthetic or constructive, instances of which are found in the construction and installation of cost and other systems of accounts . . . . Accountancy . . . will, if those in whose hands its fortunes are entrusted fulfill their part, expand . . . until it will stand shoulder to shoulder in the estimation of the public with those older professions whose courses have been a laborious evolution of years and centuries."[55]

Whether managers or CPAs, accountants continued to articulate what they thought made them different from bookkeepers. Bookkeepers were often described by accountants and managers in the same way that doctors described nurses. Like nurses, bookkeepers were to stay in their place and not entertain ideas of self-importance. The office management expert William Henry Leffingwell thought that the importance of bookkeeping, which was really just "a series of checks and counter-checks on accuracy," was often "overexaggerated." Bookkeepers should realize their mission was to assist professionals who had an overall sense of how things actually worked. Bookkeepers had to keep accurate records but should never aspire to interpret them. The accountant must be the one to confer with the business executive when plans and decisions were to be made. Knowing this fact, Leffingwell claimed in 1917, might enable the bookkeeper to "read into the dull, uninteresting rows of figures real romance and exciting narratives," because "in their books lie valuable data on the solution of almost every business problem."[56] But whereas nurses were clearly female and doctors male, bookkeepers and accountants could be either.

Nor could accountants always define the boundaries between bookkeeping and accounting. George E. Bennett, an advisor on the installation of accounting systems, admitted that the difference between bookkeeping and accounting was often a matter of size and complexity, not a distinct difference in technique: "Bookkeeping records business transactions in Journals and Ledgers. Accounting analyzes and interprets these records. Hence, it is the bookkeeper who compiles data for the accountant. The terms 'bookkeeping' and 'accounting,' therefore, are not synonymous. But as a practical proposition, it is not always possible to make the above sharp theoretical distinction or separation, since frequently the bookeeper acts as an accountant; in general, it is only in a business that is at least of fair proportions that the fields of bookeeping and accounting are rather sharply divided."[57]

Accountants turned to the states for licensing legislation in their ongoing effort to separate themselves from bookkeeping technicians, to "raise standards," and to exclude undesirables. Because most early public accounting firms were in New York City, New York was the first state to institute examinations for the licensing of "certified public accountants" in 1896. But in response to intense lobbying from those already calling themselves accountants, the examination was waived for those who had practical experience. By 1914 thirty-three states had CPA licensing laws, but most allowed "grandfathering," or the substitution of a sufficient number of years of experience for the test. A new professional organization, the American Association of Public Accountants, later the Institute of Certified Public Accountants (AICPA), was formed in 1916 to advocate examination, college training, and experience as requirements for certification in all of the states. By 1921 examinations prepared by the AICPA were used in thiry-six states, but resistance to the examination continued. Only 13 percent of all those who took the examinations in 1921 passed. While the low passing rate might have been an indication that many would-be CPAs had inadequate training and were probably better trained in bookkeeping than in auditing, it also lent credence to the "undesirables'" claims that high-placed public accountants were using the examination's difficulty and arbitrary grading to maintain a monopoly on business for themselves.[58]

The way in which the new professional standards might elevate an accountant into an illustrious career appeared in Hermon F. Bell's progression from lowly bookkeeper to prestigious cost accountant. Bell grew up in New England, where his father owned a retail furniture store. The younger Bell graduated from Amherst in 1901 with a liberal arts degree and took postgraduate courses at Yale in philosophy and religion. In an abrupt departure from his college work, he entered business in 1905 as a sales clerk in a New York department store and then drifted into bookkeeping. In 1908 his employer's books were audited by a small accounting firm, and he recalled that "one of the staff told me that I was wasting my time in bookkeeping and that better jobs would be available in public accounting." He took some accounting courses at a business college and lessons from a downtown accountant to prepare for the CPA examination, which he repeated three times before passing. Meanwhile, he had also gained the practical experience required for certification. After taking some additional courses at the recently established Pace Institute, Bell took a new job at a better firm on Wall Street in 1911 but was still forced to spend most of his time on the road, auditing. In 1913 he moved to the prestigious firm of Lybrand, Ross Brothers and Montgomery, whose owners were actively involved in the formation of the National Association of Cost Accounting. Bell's firm developed uniform cost accounting for department stores, created a specialty in income tax consultation, and, during the war, worked out cost accounting methods for war contracts.[59]

Bell's trajectory to the top of his profession remained exceptional. Most accountants continued to ignore Sterrett's advice to gain a college degree. Application to take state-certified public accountant examinations did not indicate any standard form of education or training. The AICPA found that of its members admitted between 1917 and 1926, only 22 percent were college graduates, and as many as 40 percent did not even have high school diplomas. New York State, which continued to be among the most rigorous CPA licensors, passed legislation requiring college degrees in 1926, but allowed for a twelve-year phasing-in of the new requirement.[60]

Accountants were unable to develop the distinctions that would clearly set accounting off as an elite profession. Accounting continued to be taught in correspondence courses, night schools, private business colleges, and universities.[61] The failure of the elite accountants to exclude the irregulars, some thought, led to lower salaries than in the other professions. "In view of the fact that for many years past such large numbers of college men have been entering the rather limited field of accountancy *per se*," said one observer, "there is some question as to whether there has not been some overcrowding in this occupation." Even accountants trained at the more prestigious business schools felt the effect of an open-door policy. Graduates of the Wharton School of Business, for instance, reported "substantially lower" incomes than their peers in other lines of business.[62] Accounting remained one way for individuals from nonelite groups to enter the business professions just as other doors were closing. Given the rapid growth of the profession, the need for expert accountants, the insatiable demand for computing clerks, and the blurring between bookkeepers' and accountants' tasks, the outright exclusion of women from accounting education and accounting jobs was impossible to maintain. Because increasing numbers of bookkeepers were women and accounting frequently descended into mere bookkeeping—or bookkeeping often turned into sophisticated accounting—the division of labor in business computing was not as clearly delineated as it was in either engineering or medicine. As a result the sexual division of labor in computing remained imprecise, never a good sign for the establishment of an elite profession.

Women seized on the ambivalence in accounting with enthusiasm, partly because occupational advisors urged them to do so. As early as 1914 advisors argued that a woman stenographer or bookkeeper in a public accounting office might "gain sufficient experience in accounting methods to become an assistant accountant," and that "if she were sufficiently interested and able in accountancy and possessed those inborn qualities which inspire confidence, a new field might be hers to develop." The Intercollegiate Bureau of Occupations agreed that "bookkeepers who possess initiative are sure to press on into the more highly specialized fields of expert accounting and cost statistics."[63]

Business college entrepreneurs immediately grasped the extent of the potential market for teaching accounting to women as well as to men. Pace Institute added women accountants to its teaching staff and advisory board, and openly encouraged women to enter the field. Mrs. Florentine D. Goodrich, a Pace graduate and an accountant with the Reo Sales Motor Company of New York, was quoted in Pace advertising brochures specifically aimed at women: "My own commercial experience has shown me that there is a growing demand for Accountancy . . . . I constantly recommend Pace Institute's course of training to women, who, in my opinion, have natural accounting and executive ability."[64]

Despite these opportunities for education in accounting, no woman could expect to follow Hermon Bell's starlike trajectory in the profession. Public accounting had first emerged in England, with a distinct antifemale bias. Most of the English professional societies excluded women, a matter that became a controversy in the British suffrage campaign and was resolved in 1918 when the Incorporated Society of Accountants and Auditors reluctantly amended its charter to admit women. Although "women might make excellent bookkeepers," contended one English accounting expert, "there is much in accountancy proper that is, we think, altogether unsuitable for them."[65] American firms, many of which began as British transplants, continued these prejudices. Hermon Bell recalled that his first employer, a crusty Scotsman, would not even employ women as typists, let alone as accounting clerks. The more prestigious public accounting firms in the United States refused to hire women as junior accountants. Women's exclusion from public accounting firms was critical because practical experience as well as passage of the CPA examination was required for state licensing. In New York, for example, public accountant candidates had to practice accounting for five years, at least two in the employ of a practicing CPA with the rank of at least "junior accountant."

The life of an accountant was initially considered unsuitable for women. In the early years of the century, public accounting was mainly auditing. Accountants spent days or even weeks away from home in boardinghouses and hotels, where they could conceivably gamble, drink, and seek out prostitutes. But by World War I it was possible for professionals to work all year in their home offices. Women accountants, like women architects, could establish their own businesses and compete for clients.[66] Some women did manage to take and pass the CPA test and find jobs with public accounting firms or establish their own; by 1920 there were a handful of women certified public accountants. Alice M. Hill, once a clerical assistant, was a Massachusetts CPA and a supervising accountant with Jordan, Marsh and Company.[67] A woman named Lowenstein who had passed the New York State bar examination had also recently taken the CPA test and decided to go into accounting because she thought the profession offered fewer obstacles to women than did the law. Her Manhattan office suite was said to be located "in one of the finest buildings in lower Manhattan," and she was said to have "so many clients that a half a dozen busy assistants are necessary to do the work." The appeal of accounting as a more open profession than many others had clearly played a role in Lowenstein's choice:

> She said that it is one of the new professions in which women are absolutely unhandicapped by their sex. "For one thing, they can receive the same preparation as men, and that is not true in many other connections. When, for instance, three of five law schools in New York are closed to women and most of the foremost medical schools still reject women students, a woman desiring to enter either profession finds herself handicapped at the very outset. Many women have made conspicuous successes in both fields, but this discrimination against them by schools and colleges is an obstacle that turns many bright women to other fields of endeavor. Accountancy is also one of the few professions in which a woman can reach the topmost pinnacle."[68]

These claims for accounting's acceptance of women were far too sweeping. Only a handful of women took and passed the CPA examination before World War II. But because many men passed themselves off as professional accountants without taking the test, some women did too. Extraordinary success stories surfaced from time to time. Mrs. Caroline Wylie of Sioux City, Iowa, spurned her family's advice to take up teaching and became an office worker in the stockyards instead. The *New York Evening Post* reported in 1921 that her employer insisted she keep a loaded pistol on her desk in case she faced trouble from "the rougher elements." Although she never had to use her gun, she did learn to handle cash inflows of $100,000 a day. Later, when she lived in New York and her husband became ill, she went to work for a lawyer and "gradually became recognized as an expert accountant, and her responsibilities have increased until now she is a recognized public accountant in downtown New York and regularly handles the books of several large corporations."[69]

Most women who studied accounting became accounting or statistical clerks in the employ of business or government and never attempted to become CPAs or to set up their own firms. Business schools cleverly incorporated this reality into their advertising. While an advertisement for the Walton School of Commerce in Chicago in 1918 was clearly aimed at men—"Be a Walton-Trained man"—an advertisement from Pace was aimed at both sexes: "The demand for trained accountants, both men and women, is increasing daily, hourly."[70] The Walton School boasted that many of its students had successfully passed the CPA examination in Illinois and received top-level jobs with corporations and public agencies. Pace did not even mention training for the New York CPA examination and described its graduates as "business technicians," not as professionals. Women who inquired about Pace's courses might also not be directed into accounting but to a "shorter course in accounting for women," which was in reality a glorified bookkeeping course. Nonetheless the advertisement for this course vaguely implied it might lead to something big: "Mastery . . . prepares women for successful entrance into Business through the avenue of accounting records . . . . Women who have this kind of knowledge are in growing demand and are rapidly winning promotion. Beginning as bookkeepers and clerical employees, they can soon aspire to positions of executive consequence."[71]

Accounting remained a profession to which office clerks and bookkeepers, including those who were women, could aspire. The explosion of new accounting systems by 1910 required the hiring of vast numbers of "computers" at every level of the office hierarchy. The widespread availability of accounting instruction combined with the sudden surge in demand for accountants and computing clerks during World War I to open the profession to women in ways that were unheard of in engineering or business administration. While corporate managers did not view women as potential executives, they did hire them as assistants to accountants and statisticians. Smaller businesses might find it to their advantage to hire women as bookkeepers or accounting clerks; discrimination had created a large pool of college-educated women who were qualified for much higher-level work.

Some women bookkeepers did make their way into interesting jobs that bordered on accounting. A survey of "Opportunities for Trained Women in Cleveland Factories" in 1919 found that women headed four of the cost accounting departments of the 125 factories surveyed, and in several were the heads of payroll departments.[72] A middle-aged bookkeeper who lived in Los Angeles worked in a small factory in 1925 and had duties that made her the president's chief assistant. She supervised the plant when the president was away, prepared income tax reports, and handled all financial matters.[73] An unidentified investigator sent out by the Bureau of Vocational Information to observe women working in accounting, auditing, and statistical offices in New York and Pittsburgh in 1919 was disappointed to find only four who could be classified as professional statisticians or accountants. "Financial men," she concluded, "do not seem inclined to give to women the responsibility of final figures." But she uncovered hundreds of women clerks compiling, computing, graphing, and summarizing data.[74]

The federal government hired several thousand women statisticians during World War I. Elizabeth Kemper Adams observed that women graduates of coeducational business programs came to Washington with their professors, "who were acting as experts in various capacities for the government. They collected and organized information . . . . They constructed price tables; they made shipping and tonnage charts . . . . They grew to be authorities on wool and leather and sugar and wheat."[75] It was claimed that these positions were largely beneath the dignity of male business graduates, who could expect to find much better-paying jobs in the private sector.[76]

Wartime shortages of labor and the new importance of figures landed women in statistical and accounting jobs, both in industry and government. A 1909 graduate of Cornell with a degree in history worked as a teacher for a year. She spent the next eight years as a statistical clerk and examiner for the Board of Education of New York City. After taking a year of accounting at Pace she became a statistician for the U.S. Shipping Board in 1919 and then when the war ended moved to a private firm, Arthur and Walter Price Inc. of Paterson, New Jersey. A geology major from the University of Iowa prepared and analyzed cost data at Consolidated Steel Corporation in 1919. A woman who had attended Wellesley College for two years began working in the collection department of Lee Higginson and Company in Boston in 1917. After taking night courses in income tax and corporation finance at Boston University, she was promoted to statistical and income tax clerk.[77]

The most prominent woman to be found doing accounting work in the federal government was a career civil servant who received an appointment to head a division of the Internal Revenue Service. She had been educated at Indiana State Normal but had never worked as a teacher; she came to Washington in 1900 instead to work in the census office. She obtained a B.S. degree from George Washington University in 1910 and a law degree from the Washington College of Law in 1912. After a five-year stint in the Children's Bureau between 1914 and 1919, she was promoted to a $5,000 a year position with the Internal Revenue. But this case was exceptional. A woman supervisor in the U.S. Office of Agricultural Insurance knew of many women employed as statistical clerks by the federal government, but was "convinced that not more than one percent of these women get beyond the drudgery stage in statistical work."[78] Most of the employees at the U.S. Bureau of the Census in 1921 were women, but of the 2,024 women employed, only ten percent were "expert chiefs" or "statistical experts" earning $2,000 or more a year; the rest were stenographers, clerks, and operatives earning $1,800 or less.[79]

Once in jobs and performing them well, these women resented their inability to go further. A woman with a Ph.D. from Cornell had worked at the New York City Department of Finance since 1913. Although she had taken the civil service examination with almost two hundred men and placed at the top of the list, she was categorized as a "statistician" instead of as "examiner" or "investigator." The result was her appointment "at the minimum salary of the next lower civil service salary grade," although she claimed she did work "similar to men who have titles of examiner and investigator." Other women interviewed by the BVI in 1919 believed that they earned less than men doing similar work and that they were passed over for advancement to higher positions despite their qualifications. An actuarial clerk at the New York State Insurance Department reported in 1919 that the chances of "using initiative or taking responsibility . . . are very little for a woman . . . . Men are given opportunity for advancement but women are kept to details and are given poor salaries." "There is no particular method in assigning work here," said one of her co-workers, "nor any particular method of advancement nor of paying salaries . . . . Men are usually paid from one and one half to twice what women are for the same work." A statistician at the Port and Zone Transportation Office said "men make *at least 50% more.*" A woman who worked at the National Industrial Conference Board in Boston complained that "men are put ahead of women, even knowing less and of much less ability."[80]

The complaints, however, need to be put into context. These largely college-educated women felt entitled to complain because their expectations had been heightened. Many preferred their accounting and statistical jobs to their old occupations, because their new ones were better paying and more interesting. The psychological climate induced by the suffrage movement and changes that made the Civil Service more open to women reinforced a sense that things had to improve eventually. A statistical clerk with the Children's Bureau agreed that men were paid more than women, but emphasized, "this is better than social work!" A statistical clerk in the Department of Commerce thought things were "becoming more favorable in government positions since the federal clerks formed their union and demanded equal pay for equal service regardless of sex." Many hoped that widening opportunities for women might some day include positions of real importance. The IRS department head who earned $5,000 year was predictably optimistic: "perhaps *highest* places not open to women yet, but that is more a question of time."[81] Such optimism was understandable, given the progress women had already made. But the 1920s would not see any significant gains for women at the upper levels of management.

Women and the Executive Taboo

There was one limited exception to the general rule that women could not be appointed upper-level managers. A few women were made heads of "women's departments" in banks, insurance firms, and investment houses in the years surrounding World War I and received considerable attention in the press. Financial firms hoped to capitalize on the investment needs of women, some of whom were both independent and well-heeled. The success of the feminist movement suggested to financiers that some women would be investing money on their own, but the same financiers also assumed that women needed special assistance because of limited financial experience.[82] The first women's department at a New York bank appeared in 1907 at Columbia Trust and was headed by Virginia D. H. Farnum. Farnum was greeted by the New York State Suffrage party and the Women's City Club as a harbinger of things to come. Mrs. Natalie Laimbeer, a widow with three children, was put in charge of a similar department at National City Bank in 1919.[83] S. W. Straus and Company, an investment house in Chicago, hired Eleanor L. Hall to head its women's department in 1925.[84]

These women, however, were not part of a new vanguard of women executives. As one observer made clear, they were "chance appointments . . . who happened into places through luck or friendship."[85] In a BVI interview in 1925 a secretary to an officer at a large New York bank said these kinds of positions were "given to society women—who add prestige to the bank."[86] Farnum's father was president of a large New York bank, and Natalie Laimbeer was described as "an experienced and able hostess, [who] had travelled widely, was gifted with exceptional good looks and . . . a magnetic personality . . . and had a wide acquaintance among well-to-do families in New York and Paris." Eleanor Hall, who was also acting director of the Woman's City Club, was said to be from one of Chicago's oldest families. The appointments were obviously designed to lure well-to-do women customers to particular banks, insurance firms, and securities firms, not to grant women any systematic employment or authority. Most of the women's departments disappeared during the early years of the Great Depression.[87]

Banks in particular remained bastions of male privilege. At most, women could aspire to be private secretaries or assistants to powerful men, a reality that caused smoldering resentment in women with professional training and aspirations like a California woman interviewed in 1925. She received a B.S. degree from Stanford in 1915, taught high school in Santa Barbara for three years, and then served in Paris during the war doing emergency relief work as a YMCA officer. After the war she trained in office work at a business college and secured a position as a secretary to a vice president at a large San Francisco bank. After a year of evening courses at the American Institute of Banking, she and her immediate boss had hoped she might become a bank officer. "But the policies of the bank were against women," she reported. Although she thought the banking industry provided "an almost unlimited chance to study and grow in usefulness, . . . in most secretarial positions the limit is reached all too soon. The time comes where there's nothing to improve, nothing new to learn . . . . The salaries are shockingly inadequate." Instead of taking center stage, the private secretary was forced to orchestrate a puppet show, pulling strings while the boss received the applause. When asked to list the qualities required for secretarial work, she responded that the secretary must have "*the mind to conceive and do*, but the wit to make your superior believe he is doing it all. Many men in executive positions (especially in banks) are of mediocre intelligence: they like to have a secretary who will do all their work, but not 'rub it in,' as it were." She left her job in late 1924, listing "poor salary, no future," as her reason for quitting, and took a job with a community arts association.[88]

High-level male managers and executives were not unaware of the psychological effect of the clear convention that women could not be "in charge." In 1933 F. W. Rowland, a management specialist, worried over the problems this stricture was producing in large banks and corporations:

> Some of my studies have revealed the extent to which firms employ-ing women . . . have used and promoted women so extensively that there is an absolute absence of men in the upper levels from which promotions to junior executives can be made. We checked the private secretaries and assistants to executives in one company, and found that in eighteen cases, fourteen assistants to executives were women who, if the executive went out of the organization could not be pro-moted. Indeed at the time of our study some of these women were al-ready falling down on the job because they were sure that they would not be promoted and could not see why they should work very hard any longer. In this firm some of these secretaries and assistants were college-trained women, high-grade women.[89]

Men who dominated elite business professions were happy to re-cruit women as assistants as long as they respected the central rule: men were in charge and would remain in charge. Women could not be in charge, not because they lacked qualifications or proper edu-cational training, but because they were women. The very identity of the masculine business professions depended on the exclusion of women.

As time went on, however, the internal contradictions of such policies, particularly in an era of growing opportunities and politi-cal participation for women, were bound to become more apparent. Discrimination against women meant that many women would be-come disaffected and resentful because of their inability to be pro-moted. The talents of college-trained women as managers and experts were largely lost, and male executives had to be imported, frequently from outside the corporate ranks. But the gains, for the moment, outweighed the costs. Discrimination guaranteed a large pool of capable women who could be hired as secretaries and assis-tants. Male college graduates and executives could be guaranteed a separate career ladder and an assurance that the virility of the masculine business professions had not been diluted. In personnel management, however, a touch of feminine influence was not only desirable but also necessary to survival.

NOTES

1. As quoted by Patricia Albjerg Graham, "Expansion and Exclusion: A History of Women in Higher Education," *Signs* 3 (Summer 1978): 765. A survey of data collected by the United States Office of Education on 6,665 women matriculants of land grant colleges and universities showed that the generation that graduated between 1919 and 1922, compared with three earlier groups of classes (1889-92, 1899-1902, and 1909-12) had been the most successful: "It was the woman who left college during and just after the Great War who seemed to have had the greatest success in non-teaching fields." Chase Going Woodhouse and Ruth Yeomans Schiffman, "Occupations, Earnings, Families and Some Undergraduate Problems," *Institute of Women's Professional Relations Bulletin* 4 (May 1932): pt. 1, 34.

2. Jeanette Eaton and Bertha M. Stevens, *Commercial Work and Training for Girls* (New York: Macmillan, 1915), 198-99; Katharine L. Chamberlin, "Women in Business," *Office Economist* [OE] 2 (April 1920): 55, 62; Elizabeth Kemper Adams, *Women Professional Workers: A Study Made for the Women's Educational and Industrial Union* (Chautauqua: Chautauqua Press, 1921), 20.

3. For discussions of women in the professions in these years see Joan Jacobs Brumberg and Nancy Tomes, "Women in the Professions," *Reviews in American History* 5 (June 1982): 275-96; Frank Stricker, "Cookbooks and Lawbooks: The Hidden History of Career Women in Twentieth Century America," *Journal of Social History* 10 (Fall 1976): 1-19; and Nancy F. Cott, *The Grounding of Modern Feminism* (New Haven: Yale University Press, 1987), 216-25.

4. Cott, *Gounding of Modern Feminism*, 223. Gerda Lerner was one of the first scholars to suggest a link between more rigorous professionalization standards, democratization, and the exclusion of women. See "The Lady and the Mill Girl," *American Studies* 10 (Spring 1969): 5-15; also see Graham, "Expansion and Exclusion," 759-60. For a discussion of the role such ideological forces can have on the exclusion of women from professional and managerial jobs and their underlying economic rationality, see Samuel Cohn, *The Process of Occupational Sex-Typing: The Feminization of Clerical Labor in Great Britain* (Philadelphia: Temple University Press: 1985), 232-36.

5. As quoted by Adams, *Women Professional Workers*, 20.

6. Barbara Ehrenreich and John Ehrenreich, "The Professional-Man agerial Class," *Radical America* 11 (March-April 1977): 12.

7. For two helpful discussions of the concept of professionalism see Burton J. Bledstein, *The Culture of Professionalism: The Middle Class and*

the *Development of Higher Education in America* (New York: W.W. Norton, 1978), 80-128, and Barbara Melosh, *"The Physician's Hand": Work Culture and Conflict in American Nursing* (Philadelphia: Temple University Press, 1982), 15-36. On the professionalization of medicine, see Mary Roth Walsh, *"Doctors Wanted: No Women Need Apply": Sexual Barriers in the Medical Profession, 1835-1975* (New Haven: Yale University Press, 1979), and Barbara Solomon, *In the Company of Educated Women: A History of Women and Higher Education in America* (New Haven: Yale University Press, 1985), 130-33. On engineering and business, see Margaret W. Rossiter, *Women Scientists in America: Struggles and Strategies to 1940* (Baltimore: Johns Hopkins University Press, 1982), 90-91; Edwin T. Layton, Jr., *The Revolt of the Engineers: Social Responsibility and the American Engineering Profession* (Cleveland: Press of Case Western Reserve University, 1971), 30-31; and Alfred D. Chandler, Jr., *The Visible Hand: The Managerial Revolution in American Business* (Cambridge: Harvard University Press, 1977), 464-67.

8. Adams, *Women Professional Workers*, 10; also see Louis D. Brandeis, *Business: A Profession* (Boston: Small, Maynard, 1914), 2-3.

9. Walter Dill Scott and M. H. S. Hayes, *Science in Working with Men* (New York: Ronald Press, 1921), 8.

10. Layton, *Revolt of the Engineers*, 65.

11. Harrington Emerson, "The Twelve Principles of Efficiency," *Engineering Magazine* 41 (Aug. 1911): 811-12; Samuel Haber, *Efficiency and Uplift: Scientific Management in the Progressive Era, 1880-1920* (Chicago: University of Chicago Press, 1964), ix. Haber's lively and insightful book frequently captures the psychological characteristics of the efficiency movement. Also see David B. Danbom, *"The World of Hope": Progressives and the Struggle for an Ethical Public Life* (Philadelphia: Temple University Press, 1987), 112-49.

12. For an interesting discussion of this typology see Ruth Schwartz Cowan, "Women and Technology in American Life," in *Dynamos and Virgins Revisited: Women and Technological Change in History, an Anthology,* ed. Martha Moore Trescott (Metuchen: Scarecrow Press, 1979), 30-42.

13. A. W. Shaw, *An Approach to Businesss Problems* (Cambridge: Harvard University Press, 1916), 104; Brandeis, *Business*, 12.

14. On Roosevelt's connections to engineering and scientific management, see Samuel P. Hays, *Conservation and the Gospel of Efficiency: The Progressive Conservation Movement, 1890-1920* (Cambridge: Harvard University Press, 1959), 122-27. For an interesting parallel to Roosevelt, see the biographical profile of Taylor in Haber, *Efficiency and Uplift,* 3-4. The obvious delight Taylor took in the link progressives made between scientific management and the conservation movement (thus pairing him with Roosevelt) is another example of the pscyhological affinities among scientific management, Progressivism, and American notions of masculinity in the teens. One needs only to turn to Frederick Jackson Turner's

essays on the significance of the frontier in American history to sense how anxiety-ridden this generation of male intellectuals was about fitting themselves into a historical narrative in which conquering "a frontier" was essential to masculine identity.

Feminist textual criticism has emphasized the extent to which narratives that emphasize a flight from domesticated civilization across boundaries and the conquest of the physical world, space, or the "wilderness" are, symbolically, attempts to tame the disorder linked with animality (in turn associated with women's nature). By definition, of course, women cannnot be members of the heroic group, or it will be contaminated by the feminine and the desire "to know" cannot be achieved. The narratives of both male engineers and business administrators seem to fit this mold. For a helpful theoretical exposition of this idea, see Theresa deLauretis, *Alice Doesn't: Feminism, Semiotics, Cinema* (Bloomington: Indiana University Press, 1984), 103-24. On the General Electric summer camps, see David E. Nye, *Image Worlds: Corporate Identities at General Electric, 1890-1930* (Cambridge: MIT Press, 1985), 96-100.

15. As quoted by Layton, *Revolt of the Engineers*, 66, 58-59. Layton observes that Morison's speech set the tone for similar addresses at ASCE for years to come.

16. Edward Eyre Hunt, ed., *Scientific Management since Taylor: A Collection of Authoritative Papers* (New York: McGraw-Hill, 1924), xiv; Frederick Winslow Taylor, *The Principles of Scientific Management* (1911, repr. New York: W. W. Norton, 1967), 18; Henry L. Gantt, *Organizing for Work* (New York: Harcourt, Brace and Howe, 1919), 19-20.

17. Thorstein Veblen, *The Engineers and the Price System* (New York: B. W. Huebsch, 1921).

18. Layton makes this argument quite convincingly in his discussion of "the ideology of engineering," *Revolt of the Engineers*, 53-78; also see David F. Noble, *America by Design: Science, Technology, and the Rise of Corporate Capitalism* (New York: Oxford University Press, 1977), 50-65. Engineers were more likely to come from elements of the middle class that might, in an earlier day, have been drawn to clerking; a questionnaire distributed in 1924 showed that the most dominant occupation of fathers of engineering freshmen at a number of institutions was that of small businessman, Layton, *Revolt of the Engineers*, 9-10. Engineers were, along with teachers and nurses, the most likely of professionals to be salaried employees. Their recruitment in large numbers really began with the growth of corporations in need of designers, planners, and managers and their jobs depended on the perpetuation of the business class.

19. Brandeis, *Business*, 12; also see Haber, *Efficiency and Uplift*, 75-82, Wallace B. Donham, "The Social Significance of Business," *Harvard Business Review [HBR]* 5 (July 1927): 406-19; and A. Hamilton Church, *The Making of an Executive* (New York: D. Appleton, 1923), 1.

20. Leon Carroll Marshall, *Business Administration* (Chicago: Univer-

sity of Chicago Press, 1921), vii. The Marshall textbook is a remarkable collection of original writing and reprinted articles from scholarly journals, trade magazines, and government publications. It includes pieces on psychology, labor unions, fatigue theory, factory site selection, accounting methods, principles of scientific management, personnel management, finance, and relevant historical and social science selections. Marshall's aims seem to be extraordinary: integrating all of these into a kind of "universal" thinking businessman who can at the same time use the case method of solving particular problems.

21. C. H. Wolfe as quoted by Adams, *Women Professional Workers*, 256.

22. Eliot as quoted by Melvin T. Copeland, *And Mark an Era: The Story of the Harvard Business School* (Boston: Little Brown, 1958), 16-17; also see "College Graduates in Business," *Journal of Personnel Research [JPR]* 1 (1922-33): 452; A. Lawrence Lowell, "The Profession of Business," *HBR* 1 (Jan. 1923): 129-31; and Wallace B. Donham, "The Emerging Profession of Business," *HBR* 5 (July 1927): 401-5.

23. Church, *Making of an Executive*, 2; James H. S. Brossard and J. Frederic Dewhurst, *University Education for Business: A Study of Existing Needs and Practices* (Philadelphia: University of Pennsylvania Press, 1931), 39-41. Engineers still did plenty of administrating. Leonard D. White, for instance, found that nearly half of all the city managers in the country in 1927 were former engineers. *City Manager* (1927, repr. Westport: Greenwood Press, 1968), 335. On engineers as managers, see Noble, *America by Design*, 310-15. As Noble points out, there was nothing to prevent engineers from outfitting themselves with degress in business administration, and they were actively recruited by the professional business schools.

24. Brossard and Dewhurst, *University Education for Business*, 44; C. S. Coler, "The College Man in Industry," *Personnel* 6 (May 1929): 29-32. For examples of the debate on using college graduates in business see Charles F. Thwing, *College Training and the Business Man* (New York: D. Appleton, 1904); Lyon, *Education for Business*, 83-84; and Brossard and Dewhurst, *University Education for Business*, 34-35. More businessmen at the executive level were likely to be college graduates as the century progressed. A study of 190 business career men "who were at the apex of some of the mightiest organizations the world up to then had seen" (circa 1910) showed that they were almost entirely drawn from traditional ruling elites in America: white, nativeborn of native-born parents, Protestant, northeastern, with fathers who had been prosperous businessmen or professionals. Even at this early date, 41 percent of these career men had attended some college or were college graduates. An American Management Association survey showed that in the 1920s nearly 40 percent of all new supervisory, staff, and professional positions in business paying at least $4,000 a year were college graduates. William Miller, "American Historians and the

Business Elite," *Journal of Economic History* 9 (Nov. 1949): 184-208; R. I. Rees et. al., "The Supply of and Demand for College Graduates," *Personnel* 8(Feb.-May 1932): 67-84.

25. "To the teachers who were called upon to find the answer to the demand of business, to give classroom expression to vague aspirations, the first and, indeed, the abiding question was, *what* is essential to be taught, and *how* can it be taught?" Edwin F. Gay, "The Founding of the Harvard Business School," *HBR* 5(July 1927): 398; also see Leon C. Marshall, "A Balanced Curriculum in Business Education," *Journal of Political Economy* 25 (Jan. 1917), 84-105; Wallace B. Donham, "Essential Groundwork for a Broad Executive Theory," *HBR* 1 (Oct. 1924): 1-10; and Frances Ruml, "The Formative Period of Higher Commercial Education in American Universities," *Chicago Journal of Business* 1 (April 1928): 238-55. On Gay's interest in Taylor see Herbert Heaton, *A Scholar in Action: Edwin F. Gay* (Cambridge: Harvard University Press, 1954), 73; Copeland, *And Mark an Era*, 26; Judith A. Merkle, *Management and Ideology: The Legacy of the International Scientific Management Movement* (Berkeley: University of California Press, 1980), 74-75; and Daniel Nelson, *Frederick W. Taylor and the Rise of Scientific Management* (Madison: University of Wisconsin Press, 1980), 186-87. Nelson observes that Taylor was not at all happy with the liberal arts education that usually preceded study at the Harvard Business School and remained generally distrustful of "college men." But in 1919, after Taylor's death, the Taylor Society held its meeting at the Harvard Union under the sponsorship of the School of Business Administration. "Comment," *Bulletin of the Taylor Society [TSB]* 4 (Dec. 1919): 1.

26. Janice Law Trecker has perceptively observed that the rise of more rigorous science in America in the late nineteenth century was viewed as "a liberating intellectual force." As such, it was "not seen simply as a means of exploring nature and matter, but as tools for approaching moral and social problems as well." "Sex, Science and Education," *American Quarterly* 26 (1974): 352-57.

27. Solomon, *In the Company of Educated Women*, 60.

28. President Charles Eliot of Harvard had haughtily commented in 1883 that coeducation "may . . . be justifiable in a community which cannot afford anything better." As quoted by Thomas Woody, *A History of Women's Education in the United States* (New York: Octagon Books, 1966), 2: 257. While many of the male leaders in the coeducation movement were inspired by equal rights for women, Woody notes that economy was also frequently given as a reason for establishing coeducational state universities. Thus by implication an education at an institution for both sexes was cut-rate and not comparable with either the male or female elite schools in the East. For discussion of the retreat from coeducation see Woody, 280-95, and Solomon, *In the Company of Educated Women*, 58-59.

29. Woody, *History of Women's Education*, 2: 291; Solomon, *In the Company of Educated Women*, 230, fn. 9.

30. Rosalind Rosenberg, *Beyond Separate Spheres: Intellectual Roots of Modern Feminism* (New Haven: Yale University Press, 1982), 107-10; Solomon, *In the Company of Educated Women*, 131-33; and Walsh, "Doctors Wanted"; Graham, "Expansion and Exclusion," 759-60.

31. For a history of engineering education, see Charles R. Mann, "A Study of Engineering Education," *Carnegie Foundation for the Advancement of Teaching Bulletin* 11 (1918): 1-20; Esther Lucile Brown, *The Professional Engineer* (New York: Russell Sage Foundation, 1936), 10-39; and Noble, *America by Design*, 20-49, 167-223. Beatrice Doerschuk of the BVI assembled a list engineering schools that admitted women in 1922, and received letters from H. S. Evans, dean of the College of Engineering at Colorado, Oct. 31, 1923, and from Alice C. Goff, March 10, 1924, all in BVI, folder 117.

As late as 1954, the following engineering schools did not admit women: California Institute of Technology, Colorado School of Mines, Worcester Polytechnic Institute, Polytechnic Insitute of Brooklyn, Case Institute of Technology, Texas A and M College, and the Stevens Institute of Technology. Undergraduate programs at Notre Dame, Johns Hopkins, Harvard, Princeton, Yale, Villanova, and the University of Pennsylvania were also closed to women. "Employment Opportunities for Women in Professional Engineering," *Women's Bureau Bulletin* [WBB] 254 (1954): 32-36.

32. A survey of 6,665 women graduates (about 55 percent of whom were gainfully employed) from land grant institutions between 1889 and 1922 revealed four women working as engineers. Woodhouse and Schiffman, "Occupations, Earnings, Families and Some Undergraduate Problems," 36. By 1970, Cornell, supposedly a coeducational state university, had the following female percentages in its professional schools: Industrial and Labor Relations, 10 percent; Law, 7 percent; Business and Public Administration, 3 percent; and Engineering, 2 percent. Charlotte Williams Conable, *Women at Cornell: The Myth of Equal Education* (Ithaca: Cornell University Press, 1977), 153.

On MIT, see interview with Florence Luscomb by Steven Halpern and Sharon Hartman Strom, Tamworth, N. H., July, 1972. Why did women take architecture and chemistry and not other disciplines at MIT? Some of the tradition of women in chemistry had been established by Ellen Swallow Richards, MIT's first woman enrollee, one of the founders of home economics and still at MIT in 1909, where she was an informal advisor to women students. Architecture could be practiced in small-scale firms that women might have some expectation of founding for themselves. Luscomb first worked in the Waltham firm of Ida Annah Ryan, an earlier graduate of MIT. On women in architecture before 1910, see Elizabeth G. Grossman and Lisa B. Reitzes, "Caught in the Crossfire: Women and Architectural

Education, 1880-1910," in *Architecture: A Place for Women*, ed. Ellen Perry Berkeley and Matilda McQuaid (Washington: Smithsonian Institution Press, 1989), 17-40.

33. On Blatch's experience with the ASCE and the formidable requirements for membership in professional engineering societies, see Rossiter, *Women Scientists in America*, 91 and 389, fn. 15. A BVI memorandum of Sept. 22, 1922 gives these figures for women members of the engineering societies, and Flinn's comments are in his letter to Emma P. Hirth, Nov. 27, 1922, both in BVI, folder 117.

34. Quoted in "A Symposium of Views of Leading Engineers on the Opportunities in the Engineering Profession for Women," *The Business Woman* (July 1923): 12-13.

35. Letter from Helen A. Smith to Beatrice Doerschuk, Jan. 17, 1924, BVI, folder 117; Helen Klein, "The Radio Engineer," in *Careers for Women: New Ideas New Methods, New Opportunities—to Fit a New World*, ed. Catharine Filene (Boston: Houghton Mifflin, 1934), 251; typewritten copy of letter from Nora Stanton Blatch to Emma P. Hirth, Jan. 26, 1921, BVI, folder 117; Ada Patterson, "A Woman Engineer" (Kate Gleason), circa 1919, BVI, folder 118; comments by Olive W. Dennis, circa 1921, BVI, folder 117.

In 1940, on the eve of World War II, a total of 730 women were employed as engineers. The first real growth of women in engineering came during the 1940s as a result of labor shortages during the war and the expansion of engineering during the cold war. The continued small number of women in engineering has been explained in a number of ways, most of which involve the alleged pyschological makeup of women; it has never, as far as I know, been suggested that engineering might incorporate certain psychological stances of men that preclude women. I would not disagree that female socialization has played some role in discouraging women from taking up engineering. I am, however, also arguing that there was a concerted effort to bar women from engineering, a factor rarely discussed at any length in the professional literature. As late as 1969 one author in a collection of scholarly articles on the engineering profession sought to explain "why engineering is so little manned [*sic*] by females" by arguing that because engineers in general were low in "emotionality, sophistication, extroversion and intellectual urbanism," and these traits were more characteristic of women students, women were likely to avoid engineering. Somehow what appear to be the superior qualities of women students were interpreted to mean that "the dysfunction of the female student role helps explain the paucity of female engineers." This article contains no mention of the long history of discrimination in engineering schools, the anti- female bias of most engineering students and instructors, and, on the eve of affirmative action programs, made no positive suggestions for increasing the number of women engineers beyond the vagaries of changing social norms. Stanley S. Robin, "The Female in Engineering," in *The Engineers and the Social System,* ed. Robert Perrucci and Joel E. Gerstl (New York: Wiley and Sons, 1969), 203-18.

36. As quoted in Cowan, "Women and Technology in American Life," 41.

37. Brossard and Dewhurst, *University Education for Business,* 254. On the history of collegiate business education see Lyon, *Education for Business,* 371-73; Willis J. Winn, *Business Education in the United States: A Historical Perspective* (Princeton: Princeton University Press, 1964); and Brossard and Dewhurst, *University Education for Business,* 251-53.

38. Thurman W. Van Metre, *A History of the Graduate School of Business Columbia University* (New York: Columbia University Press, 1954), 1-69. Solomon notes that most women from Barnard interested in the professions went into the Teachers' College or the School of Journalism, so removing the business curriculum from the Teachers' College was a critical step for the exclusionists, *In the Company of Educated Women,* 84.

39. Saul Sack, *History of Higher Education in Pennsylvania* (Harrisburg: Pennsylvania Historical and Museum Commission, 1963), 2: 565; Copeland, *And Mark an Era,* 132.

40. Doerschuk asked "Has the question ever arisen of admitting women to the Graduate School of Business Administration, or is the fact that there are no women students due simply to the lack of organization on their part?" Carbon of letter from Beatrice Doerschuk to Melvin T. Copeland, Jan. 26, 1921, and reply from Copeland, Jan. 26, 1921, BVI, folder 347. In 1937 the Harvard Business School fended off another attack from women by establishing a one-year management training program at Radcliffe for Radcliffe graduates instead of allowing them to apply to the business school. After World War II, when a handful of women were being admitted to both Harvard Medical and Law, pressures on the Harvard Business School became more intense. The Business School conducted a survey of women in managerial positions in business and industry and concluded that "only a few were occupying top executive jobs." While it might have been possible to conclude from such findings that if there were more women graduates of the top business schools there might be more women executives, the business school instead interpreted the results to mean women should continue in a segregated but obviously inferior program. See Copeland, *And Mark an Era,* 132-33, and Jane Knowles, "Harvard-Racliffe Program in Business Administration," *Radcliffe Quarterly* 73 (Dec. 1987): 27-29.

41. Solomon, *In the Company of Educated Women,* 80-85; Joy K. Rice and Annette Hemmings, "Women's Colleges and Women Achievers: An Update," *Signs* 13, no. 3(1988): 546-59.

42. Estelle Freedman, "Separatism as Strategy: Female Institution-Building and American Feminism," *Feminist Studies* 5 (Fall 1979): 512-29. For a similar argument about women's colleges in England, see Martha

Vicinus, *Independent Women: Work and Community for Single Women, 1850-1920* (Chicago: University of Chicago Press, 1985).

43. On college women between 1890 and 1920, see Lynn D. Gordon, *Gender and Higher Education in the Progressive Era* (New Haven: Yale University Press, 1990). On college women in the 1920s, see Elaine Kendell, *"Peculiar Institutions": An Informal History of the Seven Sister Colleges* (New York: G.P. Putnam's Sons, 1975), 167-84; Brown, *Setting a Course,* 127-64; and Cott, *Grounding of Modern Feminism,* 148-49.

44. In 1917 M. Carey Thomas complained that "Japanese Geisha schools are springing up on all sides. Practical vocational courses are to be given . . . . Now is the time for us to fight for our lives, for our educational convictions, and save, if we can, at least the girls of the East by refusing to give up our present college curriculum. It is our highest duty as educated women to pass on unimpaired . . . this precious intellectual heritage." As quoted by Dorothy M. Brown, *Setting a Course: American Women in the 1920s* (Boston: Twayne Publishers, 1987), 136.

45. Willystine Goodsell, "The Educational Opportunities of American Women: Theoretical and Actual," *Annals* 143 (May 1929): 4.

46. See the description of the Woerishoffer Department in the Bryn Mawr calendar, 1916, and in Bryn Mawr *College News*: "Bryn Mawr Asked to Train Women to Be Supervisors," May 30, 1918; "Aims of Bryn Mawr Industrial Course," Dec. 12, 1918; "Many Firms Cooperate to Make Industrial Course Successful," Dec. 19, 1918. All in Bryn Mawr College Archives, Bryn Mawr, Pennsylvania.

47. Knowles, "Harvard-Radcliffe Program in Business Administration."

48. Brossard and Dewhurst, *University Education for Business,* 254-55.

49. In 1922, for instance, the Bureau of Education said that 44,768 men and 7,890 women were enrolled in collegiate schools and departments of business. As reported by the BVI, *Training for the Professions and Allied Occupations* (New York: BVI, 1924), 130.

50. In 1931 there were forty-two accredited member schools of the American Association of Collegiate Schools of Business. In 1924 the Bureau of Vocational Information listed thirty-two accredited collegiate schools of business that were open to women, eleven of which offered secretarial sciences courses. Brossard and Dewhurst, *University Education for Business,* 263; BVI, *Training for the Professions,* 132-43, 229.

51. Edward Wiest, "Secretarial Training in Schools of Business," *Journal of Business of the University of Chicago* 3 (Oct. 1930): 59-60. In the discussion that followed Wiest's remarks, the dean of the business school of Syracuse University reported (65) that of 250 women enrolled as business students (presumably for 1929-30), 195 were in secretarial science and business education.

52. Physicians and surgeons had slowed their rates of growth considerably: there were only twenty-five thousand more of them in 1930 in 1900, and an absolutely clear-cut division between themselves and nurses. No

such division could be implemented, at least at this time, between accountants and bookkeepers.

53. Henry P. Kendall, "Types of Management," in *Scientific Management since Taylor*, ed. Hunt, 15.

54. Max Watson, "An Interview with J. E. Sterrett," *New York Evening
Post*, Jan. 18, 1921.

55. J. E. Sterrett of Price, Waterhouse and Co. in 1909, as quoted by
Gary John Previts, *The Scope of CPA Services: A Study of the Development
of the Concept of Independence and the Profession's Role in Society* (New
York: John H. Wiley and Sons, 1985), 37-38; also see "The Management
Aspect of the Comptroller's Work," *HBR* 5 (Oct. 1926): 21-26.

56. William Henry Leffingwell, *Scientific Office Management* (Chicago: A. W. Shaw, 1917), 116-17. For a later explicit comparison between
doctors and nurses and accountants and bookkeepers, see Stewart
Schackne, *Designers of Order: The Story of Accountancy Briefly Told*
(New York: American Institute of Certified Public Accountants, 1970), 5.

57. George E. Bennett, *Accounting Systems: Principles and Problems of
Installation* (Chicago: A. W. Shaw, 1926), 3. Lee Galloway, a professor of
business at New York University and author of a well-known book on office management, acknowledged that the accounts of small firms might
"easily be handled by three or four clerks with a head bookkeeper in
charge; its cost accounts and records could be compiled by a cost clerk who
is thoroughly conversant with this branch of accounting, and who, if necessary, would be assisted by two or three girls." *Office Management: Its
Principles and Practice* (New York: Ronald Press, 1921), 421.

58. On CPA examination and licensing, see Gary J. Previts and Barbara
Dubis Merino, *A History of Accounting in America: An Historical Integration of the Cultural Significance of Accounting* (New York: John Wiley,
1979), 96-100, 205-9, and John L. Carey, *The Rise of the Accounting Profession: from Technician to Professional, 1896-1936* (New York: American
Institute of Certified Public Accountants, 1969), 1: 271-75, 279-86.
Previts and Merino note (148-49) that there were many complaints that
exaaminations in states like New York, Pennsylvania, and Illinois were "ar-
bitrarily graded" and designed to maintain a monopoly of CPAs.

59. Hermon F. Bell, *Reminscences of a Certified Public Accountant*
(New York: Ronald Press, 1959). Bell became an expert in department store
accounting and published two editions of *Retail Merchandise Accounting*.

60. Carey, *Rise of the Accounting Profession*, 1: 270. In 1950 only 36
percent of all male and only 14 percent of all female accountants and auditors were college graduates, and by 1968 only twenty-seven of the fifty-
four jurisdictions recognized by the AICPA required accountants to have
four-year college degrees. "Employment Opportunities for Women in Professional Accounting," *Women's Bureau Bulletin* [WBB] 258 (1955): 7;
Carey, *Rise of the Accounting Profession*, 2: 312.

61. On correspondence school courses, see Benjamin R. Haynes and

Harry P. Jackson, *A History of Business Education in the United States* (Cincinnati: South-Western Publishing, 1935), 97-102. Previts and Merino note that although there were no B.S. degrees in accounting offered by colleges in 1900, three hundred institutions offered the degree by 1930, *History of Accounting*, 213.

62. Brossard and Dewhurst, *University Education for Business*, 43-44. Several studies showed that although accounting was one of the most widely studied of curricula in business schools, salaries for accountants were generally lower than those for other business professions. According to Carey, "CPAs began to complain about work solicited by management consultants in the areas of systems and procedures, which the accountants claimed could have been done better by themselves, and for which the consultants received fees greatly in excess of those ordinarily obtained by accountants." *Rise of the Accounting Profession*, 1: 148.

63. Eleanor Martin and Margaret Post, *Vocations for the Trained Woman* (London: Longmans, Green, 1914), 120-21; Intercollegiate Bureau of Occupations, "Opportunities in Occupations Other Than Teaching," pamphlet no. 8627, Schlesinger Library, Radcliffe College. Also see Eleanor Gilbert [Anne Rosenblatt], *The Ambitious Woman in Business* (New York: Funk and Wagnalls, 1916), 241-43.

64. Printed page from Pace and Pace publication, circa 1921, BVI, folder 511. Alice Hill and several other accountants are described in another Pace and Pace pamphlet, "Making Good" (1920), BVI, folder 73. A BVI lecturer in 1915-16 listed a variety of daytime and evening courses in the New York City region for studying accounting. These included a $270 course at Pace and Pace, a $150 course at the New York School of Accountants, a $190 course at the Plymouth Church in Brooklyn, and other courses at the National Business Institute and "a number of correspondence schools." Elizabeth E. Cook, "Women on Wall Street and in Banking," April 11, 1916, 40-41, BVI, folder 23.

65. As quoted by Nicholas A. H. Stacey, *English Accountancy: A Study in Social and Economic History, 1800-1954* (London: Gee, 1954), 84-85, 95. Stacey notes (99) that cost accounting in England was at first dismissed by public accountants and older professional societies as "unprofessional work . . . employed in the service of traders."

66. Cook, "Women on Wall Street and in Banking," 46-47.

67. Eaton and Stevens noted in 1915 that women in Ohio could not be legally certified as public accountants, *Commercial Work and Training for Girls*, 189. I have been unable to find any systematic description of women's access to the state CPA examinations. In 1924 the American Institute of Accountants, whose membership was limited to practicing public accountants who had also passed the CPA test, listed seven women members, BVI, *Training for the Professions*, 162. The Women's Bureau stated that by 1933 "only a few more than 100 accounting certificates were issued to women by all States conducting examinations." "Employment Oppor-

tunitites for Women in Professional Accounting," 3. After World War II these figures began to change dramatically.

68. Cook, "Women on Wall Street," 46-47.

69. Adelaide A. Lyons, "Caroline D. Wylie, Expert Accountant," *New York Evening Post*, 1921, exact date unclear, BVI, folder 511.

70. *System* 34 (Aug. 1918): 259, (Nov. 1918): 767.

71. The "Shorter Course in Accounting for Women," is described in a 1917 Pace Institute pamphlet, BVI, folder 73.

72. Florence L. Sullivan, "Opportunities for Trained Women in Cleveland Factories," 1919, pamphlet no. 8646, Schlesinger Library, Radcliffe College.

73. Bureau of Vocational Information Woman Secretary Survey [BVIWS], 327 (88), California.

74. "Survey as to Statisticians," typewritten report, Sept., 1919. BVI, folder 334.

75. Adams, *Women Professional Workers*, 242.

76. Brossard and Dewhurst note that "only an inconsiderable number of students enroll in business schools for the purpose of preparing themselves for government positions," which were not comparable to "most of the higher positions available in industry, transportation, banking, and distribution . . . which involve in some degree the common function of operating management, i.e., the control and direction of human effort in the operation of business enterprise." *University Education for Business*, 47.

77. These profiles are drawn from questionnaires filled out by "women statisticians" (a category that included accounting clerks) for the BVI from 1919 to 1921, BVI, folders 337-50. Although only impressionistic conclusions can be drawn from such a widely varied and small sample, the BVI survey of statisticians reveals some interesting general information. Of the thirty-nine women I categorized as working in 1921, about 75 percent had attended college, and another 25 percent had postgraduate training or degrees as well. The importance of the new university-level business courses or accounting programs was clear for this group; Pace and Pace, Columbia School of Business, New York University, and Boston University were all on the list of postgraduate schools offering the courses in business, accounting, and economics they had attended. A third of those interviewed were former teachers, and most of them abandoned either clerical work or teaching to take better-paying and more interesting jobs in 1918 and 1919, indicating that the war had played an important role in their initial hiring and subsequent advancement. The sample worked in a wide variety of settings, including private industry, state and municipal departments and agencies, and executive departments of the federal government. The majority of the women statisticians in the BVI study earned between $1,200 and $2,000 per year.

78. BVI, folders 341-42.

79. Letter from Wm. M Stewart to Beatrice Doerschuk, April 22, 1921,

BVI, folder 341. The Women's Bureau found four women accountants and auditors and 181 accounting and auditing assistants working in executive departments of the federal government in 1925. Bertha M. Nienburg, "The Status of Women in the Government Service in 1925," *WBB* 53 (1926): 47; also see Bertha M. Nienburg, "Women in the Government Service," *WBB* 8 (1920), and Susan Ware, *Beyond Suffrage* (Cambridge: Harvard University Press, 1981), 60-64. At the peak of government employment during World War I, women constituted 75 percent of appointments to government positions. After a sharp drop following 1919, appointments of women rose steadily until the onset of the depression.

80. BVI, folders 341-45.

81. BVI, folders 341-42.

82. See, for example, "Life Insurance for Women," *BVI News Bulletin* [*BVINB*], 1, Dec. 1, 1923, 1-2 and 6, and Adele H. Kirby, "Banking for Women," *BVINB*, Nov. 1, 1922, 1-2, 6. Kirby was assistant secretary and treasurer at the Plainfield, New Jersey, Trust Company. Some women did serve as board members and bank officers at small banks, probably because of their position as stockholders. In 1929, Gildersleeve counted six chairs of boards, seventy-four presidents, and 197 vice presidents who were women. Whether many of these actually worked in managerial capacities in banks, however, is questionable. Genieve N. Gildersleeve, *Women in Banking: A History of the National Association of Bank Women* (Washington, D.C.: Public Affairs Press, 1929), 49.

83. On women's departments in banks, see Anne Seward, *The Women's Department* (New York: Bankers Publishing, 1924), 9-13, 36-38, 76-77.

84. "Womens Service Department Organized at Chicago Office," unidentified newspaper clipping, April 11, 1925, BVI, folder 511. Several examples of women's departments at investment houses are described by Cook, "Women on Wall Street," 16.

85. Seward, *The Women's Department*, 109.

86. BVIWS 109 (1850) and 146 (1858), both from New York.

87. One observer described Laimbeer as "rather in the capacity of an interested friend than that of a bank official. Mrs. Laimbeer gives advice on family as well as business finances, monthly housekeeping budgets or other personal matters which can be discussed more freely with one of their own sex by the women clients." Typewritten notes, June 11, 1921, BVI, folder 76.

88. BVIWS 217 (339), Washington, D.C. As late as 1944, even after the effects of labor shortages caused by World War II, estimates were that fewer than 1 percent of all executive and managerial posts in banks were held by women. Dorcas Campbell, *Careers for Women in Banking and Finance* (New York: E. P. Dutton, 1944), 21.

89. F. L. Rowland, "Present Status and Probable Trends in Office Management," American Management Association *Office Executive Series* 61(1933): 18-19.

3

"The Human Factor": Gender and Personnel Management

IN 1918 A WOMEN'S EMPLOYMENT bureau conducted a survey of women employment managers in factories, banks, department stores, and telephone companies. The surveyers wanted to know whether this relatively new profession had opened its doors to women. The responses were detailed and generally enthusiastic. Jane Mundy Kinsley of the Broadway Department Store thought opportunities for women were increasing, and that salaries for men and women compared "favorably." Sallie Eugenia Wallace at Guarantee Trust Bank of New York agreed that "in salary women do fairly well," but felt that promotion possibilities for women could not "compare with the opportunities for men, as a general thing." But, she thought executive positions would someday "be opened to women who have natural gifts for organization." Heloise Arnold, formerly of Sears and Roebuck, was also upbeat: "The opportunity for progress and service in employment work," she thought, was "the biggest opportunity for business women today. The growing desire of business firms for the right placement of their employees, and their growing recognition of the disastrous results of misplacement, has opened a field to the woman of vision and insight."[1]

Employment management, increasingly known as "personnel management" after World War I, appeared to be both more receptive to women and to catch their imaginations in ways which engineering and business administration had not. Athough only a handful of women attended the national conference of the Employment Managers Association in 1917, more than a hundred did so in 1919, and by 1922 the Bureau of Vocational Information reported that employment management ranked sixth in frequency of requests for information from women on specific occupations.[2] Advice books unequivocally endorsed personnel management as a suitable and stimulating career for ambitious women.[3] It appeared true that at least one of the new business professions appealed to women, was suited to their supposed gender characteristics, and offered them real chances of employment.

The alleged gender characteristics of personnel management were wide-ranging. They reflected long-standing assumptions about women's "natural" propensity for such maternal tasks as domestic management and social work, and also emphasized modern professional women's interest in efficiency, the scientific method, and the ability to move comfortably among both sexes. The journalist Ida Tarbell focused on the traditional when she commented on women employment managers in 1920: "All the best practice proves the wisdom of bringing in women to deal with women. They know what to do in the case of headaches and crying spells. They know the springs to touch in order to turn a sulky and indifferent worker into a cheerful and interested one." But Mary G. Kiepe, employment manager at a meat-packing firm in Buffalo, omitted any reference to sentimentality and defined personnel management in modernist terms: "the necessity of conserving human beings and making them efficient; of applying to men what we are beginning to apply to things—principles of efficiency."[4]

Elizabeth Kemper Adams, a professional researcher and writer for the Women's Educational and Industrial Union, also took the more modern view. While granting that employment management was being "widely heralded as a 'new profession for women,'" she also insisted "that it requires far more of its practitioners than a 'natural liking for people and a few undergraduate courses in labor problems' and psychology . . . . They must be supplemented by rigorous special training and practical experience of a kind new to most women." She thought employment management was one field where women might have the opportunity to prove their worth to organizations as people, not as women, if they sought the proper training and took it up as a serious profession: "Women must realize that both for the sake of the profession and for the sake of the permanent position of women within it, those who enter it to-day [sic] should do so with a . . . strong sense of their professional responsibilities and obligations." At the heart of the successful personnel manager, Adams contended, was a no nonsense persona, one that might be cultivated by "young women of vigorous and unsentimental personality, resourcefulness, and determination."[5]

Women left a greater imprint on personnel management than any of the other new business professions. Their ambivalence toward its gender identity, articulated by Tarbell and Adams, runs through its early history. One of the reasons there was room for women in personnel management was that the profession itself contained the same ambivalence. Personnel management had a distinctly feminine aspect, whether its practitioners were male or female. It was always the soft or more womanly side of business administration, a hybrid of dispassionate system and liberal feeling.

The feminine and masculine sides of personnel management could be espoused by either sex; these were gendered traits of ideas and philosophies, not necessarily of individual sexes. Men and women contributed to the feminine aspect of personnel management, and both women and men sought to toughen the profession. In contrast to the more "masculine" business professions like business administration and engineering, personnel management purposely sought to incorporate an understanding of human behavior into the administration of capitalist enterprises. But most personnel managers emphasized that their methods were both systematic and profit-producing. Their expertise, they claimed, was just as integral to the proper functioning of scientific management as the other business disciplines.

In order to be heard by those who counted, personnel managers aligned themselves with the ideas of scientific management, the most powerful business and reform ethos of the period. Their simultaneous attempts to add "the human factor" to scientific management produced an intriguing mixture of both challenge and accommodation to capitalist and gender-based hierarchies. It also provoked some serious thinking about women's roles in the modern economic order. Were women to bring a feminine touch to the corporate enterprise, or should they present themselves as sex neutral professionals? How did feminist politics fit into humanized scientific management? The answers to these questions were not always so obvious.

The implications of personnel management for women should not be considered strictly by individual women's successes in rising to executive status. Many women came to personnel management with a reformist agenda. They were attracted to the discipline precisely because of its potential for reforming the traditional sexual division of labor. Changes in civil service work are a case in point: the expansion of federal employment, the hiring of more women civil service employees, and the labor shortages of World War I created a successful climate for a less sex biased civil service system. Modern personnel practice provided the techniques for establishing that system. The creation of federal personnel commissions and more systematic policies of employee selection, job classification, wage rates, and promotion procedures linked personnel management reform with sexual equality. Perhaps for precisely that reason, the reformist and often feminist roots of personnel management continued to make it suspect to the masculine business professions, even as the more tough-minded techniques of scientific management failed because they did not take in the "human factor." Personnel management threatened not only to introduce women but also "the feminine" into the inner sanctums of masculine management circles.

Personnel management emerged in the late teens from three occupations, all of which had reformist tendencies: psychology, vocational guidance, and welfare work. All three drew women into personnel management and allowed them to influence its development. The vocational guidance movement, which came out of social settlement work, college placement bureaus, and attempts to keep youngsters in high school, attracted women and gave them expertise in one aspect of early personnel work. College women's access to undergraduate and graduate training in psychology, particularly applied psychology, created a contingent of female psychological experts available to work as managers and researchers. As employers turned toward welfare departments to reduce labor turnover and to foster company loyalty, new managerial positions were created. Women often managed early welfare and employment departments in insurance companies, department stores, and factories where large numbers of women were employed. As these businesses expanded their functions to include personnel work, women welfare workers were in a position to move into personnel management.

The academic discipline of psychology, and its applied offshoots, particularly industrial psychology, provided personnel management with a theoretical framework. Vocational guidance added a progressive reform consciousness; welfare work supplied jobs in industry for both the ambitious and the reform-minded. Many of those who gravitated toward these three fields of work hoped to find ways of easing conflict between capitalists and workers, government and citizens, the haves and the have-nots, and later turned toward personnel management. But to be accepted by managers and business executives, these more sentimental (and effeminate) approaches had to be tempered by the necessities of profit and loss, by a tougher-minded pragmatism, and in general made more masculine.

The explosion of labor management problems created by the working conditions of World War I, including the rapid recruiting of women for industrial jobs, the mushrooming of clerical staffs, high labor turnover, and a general shortage of trained managers, all made it possible for women to seize new opportunities in personnel management. As the war ended, however, women found themselves closed out of the highest levels of this new business profession, where animosity to both women and the feminine continued to persist.

Psychology, The Scientific Method, and Feminism

Early American psychologists had not been very sympathetic to changes in women's roles. Largely armchair philosophy, the discipline of psychology was given new direction in the late nineteenth century with the incorporation of experimental psychology, a combination of German research methods and the American philosophy of pragmatism.[6] Experimental psychologists said they wanted to see what people did rather than prescribe how they should behave. Their point of view could be sympathetic to women and inviting to those interested in demonstrating women's mental capacities for better jobs and political equality. Many experimental psychologists were willing to teach women graduate students as well as take their work seriously.[7]

Psychology immediately appealed to women as an academic discipline, and it was readily available to them by the turn of the century at co-educational institutions and women's colleges.[8] Students preparing for "women's occupations" like education and social work often sought undergraduate training in psychology. The opening of more graduate programs at universities allowed women to seek advanced degrees in the field. By 1910 women could take graduate work in psychology at a wide variety of institutions, including Pennsylvania, Columbia, Yale, Clark, Cornell, Radcliffe, Bryn Mawr, and the universities of Chicago, California, and Wisconsin.[9]

Feminist graduate students in psychology soon saw the possibility of using psychological research to challenge traditional ideas about women. The "greater variability" theory was especially detrimental to women's equal participation in politics, the academy, and nontraditional occupations; it argued that men's intelligence was more varied than that of women and therefore justified men's monopoly of important positions and occupations. Women's less varied intelligence suited them, not surprisingly, to domestic life, child-rearing, and the women's professions. John Dewey's student at the University of Chicago, Helen Bradford Thompson, conducted meticulous experiments to determine whether significant sex differences existed in men's and women's motor and mental performances. She found that there was a wide variation between the performance of individuals but hardly any important differences between those of women and men; sex was not a significant variable in performance.

Leta Stetter Hollingworth, who could not obtain a teaching position in the New York City school system because she was married, entered the graduate program in psychology at Columbia in 1911, where her husband was a young instructor, and earned a Ph.D. She demonstrated that women's mental and motor performance was not affected negatively by menstruation; the claim that women could not perform men's jobs because they were incapacitated by menstruation had long been used by traditionalists to bar women's employment in responsible positions.[10] In 1916 Leta Hollingworth contributed a chapter to her husband's widely respected book on vocational aptitude and guidance and argued that scientific evidence accumulated thus far revealed no significant sexual differences in mental traits. These findings had immediate relevance for women in the world of work: "The social gain would be very great," she concluded, "if the public could be brought to recognize intelligently that to many of the questions regarding the vocational aptitudes of women no definite answers can at present be given . . . . So far as is at present known, women are as competent intellectually as men are, to undertake any and all human vocations."[11] Psychology gave women an opportunity to practice the scientific method and could accommodate a feminist consciousness as well.

Whatever the attractions of the discipline, women took up psychology in ever greater numbers after 1910. By 1921, 20.4 percent of all the psychologists were women, a far higher proportion than in any other scientific field except nutrition. Of all doctorates awarded in psychology between 1920 and 1923 more than one-third went to women, and roughly 20 percent of the members of the American Psychological Association before World War II were women. But difficulty in obtaining academic positions continued, and many female psychologists gravitated toward applied psychology in business, government, and education.[12]

Applied psychology, like engineering, was an amalgam of academic theory and hands-on experiments in the real world. The industrial psychologist Hugo Munsterberg, a dynamic German instructor whom William James had brought to Harvard, encouraged students to find applications for pyschology outside academia and wrote one of the earliest texts on industrial psychology. By 1910 business was approaching psychologists for help in developing employee selection tests, particularly for skilled machine clerks, telephone operators, and salespersons. In 1915 Walter V. Bingham was invited to direct a division of applied psychology, later dubbed the Bureau of Personnel Research, at the Carnegie Institute of Technology. The bureau actively sought to develop links between university research and industry. Pools of corporations, insurance companies, and department stores provided Carnegie with funds for research in salesman selection tests and retail training. By 1922 the institution was receiving $237,000 a year from corporations for its research.[13]

The search for practical uses of psychology attracted women from the beginning. So many women students attended Hugo Munsterberg's classes that a separate laboratory was established for them at Radcliffe. Women psychologists were published in the professional literature and had a significant impact on the field's developing theory. Some did industrial psychological research at institutes like Bingham's at Carnegie Tech; others were hired directly by corporations to engage in research that could be applied to hiring and employment policies. Elsie O. Bregman, a graduate student at Columbia University from 1919 to 1921, developed employment tests for R. H. Macy. Anne Bezanson, originally director of industrial courses at Bryn Mawr, later did work on labor turnover in the coal mining industry at the Industrial Research Department of the Wharton School. Grace E. Manson, a Ph.D. at the University of Michigan, did research on salespersons' application blanks and the abilities required for successful retail selling. Marion A. Bills attended the University of Michigan, received a Ph.D. in psychology at Bryn Mawr, taught at the University of Kansas, and then went to Bingham's Bureau of Personnel Research in 1922 to develop clerical tests for the insurance industry. She became one of the most respected office management consultants in the country. Millicent Pond did graduate work at Bryn Mawr and

Yale. As supervisor of employment testing at Scovill Manufacturing she developed aptitude tests and training programs for machinists and other skilled workers.[14]

Standardized testing was the most eagerly sought-after application of psychology in the early twentieth century. Unlike the work of Leta Stetter Hollingworth and Helen Bradford Thompson Woolley, most of this testing, intentionally or not, was used to justify the status quo. Many psychologists turned to the testing of immigrants and blacks and, not surprisingly, produced results that bolstered middle-class, native-born white beliefs in the superiority of their own groups. Psychologists "found" that low intelligence, as measured by tests, could be correlated with darker skin, southern European backgrounds, or the "antisocial" behavior of the poor.[15]

There is no evidence to suggest that women psychologists as a group were particularly immune to the elitist and racist biases of early testers.[16] Liberal feminists were often committed to the notion that class hierarchies were both natural and desirable; what they wanted was a chance to prove the competence of women so that they could take their proper place in those hierarchies alongside the professional men who were already in control. When combined with the new field of vocational guidance, testing could validate channeling some boys and girls to vocational programs in high school and the sending of others, usually white and native-born, to college. Testing could make American society more efficient and productive by sorting people according to their intelligence and talents into the occupations for which they were best suited. Vocational guidance and testing were pursued by many feminists and educators as at least partial solutions to American problems of inequality and class confrontation.[17] Hierarchies based on "scientific placement" could be defended as reasonable forms of social organization.

Vocational Guidance and Personnel Work

The founders of the vocational guidance movement came from several factions of reformers. The first faction wanted to do something about unemployment and the pinched lives of the working poor by providing vocational training and employment guidance to young unskilled workers. These men and women often came to vocational guidance from settlement house and community center work and were advocates of trade unions and municipal reform as well. Educators who wanted to expand the offerings of American high schools in order to keep children in school longer were a second contingent. A third group, including college-educated feminists, wanted to use vocational guidance to expand suitable occupations for women and, sometimes, other groups of individuals who faced stereotyping and discrimination in the work force. All these factions shared the theoretical conviction that workers should seek "vocations," occupational callings to which they were suited by temperament and aptitude, not just "jobs" that put bread on the table or fulfilled stereotyped destinies. If individuals could be directed to suitable occupations, both schools and the industrial order might prove to be compatible with American ideals of equal opportunity.[18]

The emergence of vocational guidance in Boston demonstrates the complicated ties between early-twentieth-century reform, feminism, and personnel managment. Although Frank Parsons and Meyer Bloomfield are the best known public figures of the Boston movement, Mary Parker Follett was arguably more important as a main mover and theoretician behind the scenes. After a summa cum laude graduation from Radcliffe in 1898, Follett did temperance and suffrage work and participated in school committee politics. She pioneered in creating evening classes and social activities in so-called "social centres" for young men and women in East Boston in 1910, a program sponsored by the Women's Municipal League. With the funding help of the philanthropist Pauline Agassiz Shaw, Follett began promoting the work of Boston's Vocation Bureau to round out her social center services. The hope was to provide better employment opportunities for those who had to leave school early or were stuck in dead-end jobs. The bureau's board, upon which Follett served and had a major influence, convinced a municipal reform colleague of hers, Meyer A. Bloomfield, to act as executive director.[19]

In 1909 the superintendent of Boston's public schools invited the Vocation Bureau to propose a plan for vocational counseling in the city school system. The bureau set up a training plan for school counselors. Vocational guidance reformers believed that one solution to poor school attendance, unemployment, and poor wages might be a combination of specialized vocational education, vocational guidance, and individual placement in suitable jobs. The first citywide vocational information department and placement bureau in a public school system in the country emerged in Boston in 1912, and in 1917 the School Committee of Boston agreed to finance all its activities with public funds. Follett worked effectively behind the scenes to bring the school guidance program to fruition, although her chief concern remained the development of "initiative and will-power" and the provision of "self-expression, that most fundamental need of man" in her social center work.[20]

Follett remains difficult to pigeonhole in any one social reform category or intellectual group. She was primarily interested in reconciling the potential of individual citizens with the ongoing functioning of the state and industrial capitalism. Not a radical or a socialist, she was committed to community and workplace organizational structures that would "give people training for that larger democracy which we see coming, to help them to learn how to work and play together, how to live together, not only harmoniously, but also effectively."[21] These ideas would prove to be very attractive to the liberal (and feminine) wing of personnel management.

In the late teens and 1920s Follett presented her ideas about organizations in essays, speeches, and two books, the most famous of which was *The New State*, published in 1918. She argued that the successful administration of organizations required both citizens and workers to be managed in ways that would elicit cooperation but also release the potential for self-expression. Her ideas seemed to reassure a liberal constituency of the business class in both England and the United States that workplace democracy could be expanded without fundamentally rearranging the class hierarchy or its wage system, while, at the same time, creating a happier work force. Through the study of human psychology and more systematic management methods, Follett held that individual creativity might be mobilized more effectively for the common good. Her work in Boston reform brought her into contact with Edward A. Filene, the department store magnate, and she also had a longstanding friendship with Henry A. Dennison, the manufacturer. Both men were known for their progressive sympathies and modern management techniques. Follett became a kind of consultant on the solving of "human" problems in business through "industrial democracy" and an advisor to progressive businessmen in Boston. After Henry Metcalf, an early expert on personnel administration, helped to set up training programs for employment managers in federal munitions and shipyard installations during World War I and moved into a national circle of policymakers, he helped to widen Follett's influence considerably. She was invited to lecture at annual conferences sponsored by the Bureau of Personnel Administration. Her speeches emphasized the art of discussion rather than dictation, of "constructive conflict," and of using differences to achieve a newly integrated whole. When Henry Dennison spoke before the Bureau of Personnel Administration in 1929, he referred explicitly to Follett's influence. "In this talk," he began, "I am going to use Control in the dynamic sense, as an influence or force. Among many men who have been interested in Scientific Management . . . the word is coming to mean a very different thing,—to mean records of performance . . . . Miss Follett . . . has discussed what Control in this sense actually means and hence what considerations limit its proper exercise. She has brilliantly contrasted power-over against power-with and has given to the word 'integration' a new and wide currency. At its roots my talk must be her talk, only above ground will it vary." Follett's ideas would eventually contribute to modern personnel practice in both England and America.[22]

Attempts to find meaningful work for both men and women had been one of Follett's early concerns. Middle-class feminists also turned to vocational guidance as a way of opening more occupations to women, especially college-educated women. Employment bureaus for college women appeared in most major cities after 1910, with many of them attempting to place graduates in positions other than teaching. The most influential of these was the Intercollegiate Bureau of Occupations, formed in 1911 in New York and directed by Emma Hirth. Reorganized in 1919 as the Bureau of Vocational Information (BVI), the agency abandoned placement and conducted path-breaking studies of women in various occupations, including chemistry, employment management, department store managing, and statistical and secretarial work. The BVI also provided up-to-date information on how women could obtain training for a wide variety of occupations, insisting upon "the power of facts as the best guide into occupational life" and "the ability of mature women to choose their proper work when once given such fundamental facts."[23]

Vocational guidance was to become an important and influential strand of the expanding field of personnel management directly following the war. Hirth and other feminist educators were attracted to vocational guidance because it held out the possibility of putting people into positions on the basis of their training and merits rather than their family connections, race, sex, or appearance. It seemed a logical extension of the suffrage movement's attempts to promote equality in the public sphere. Vocational guidance remained one of the more marginal aspects of personnel management in business, but even on the periphery it could legitimize efforts to suit jobs to people and to develop internal promotion systems based on fair and reasonable critera.

Welfare Work and the Origins of Personnel Management

Another strain of personnel management came from early welfare work in business.[24] Paternalistic factory owners first provided welfare services for employees in the nineteenth century. Welfare programs might have included one or more of a variety of services: bathhouses, company housing and stores, libraries, and lunchrooms. More systematic welfare programs appeared at the turn of the century. Edward A. Filene and his brother, German Jews with Old World socialist and New World progressive sympathies, developed welfare programs in their huge Boston department store in the 1890s. They installed savings, loan, and insurance plans, a medical department, and arranged for recreational activities. Similar programs emerged at National Cash Register and Dennison Manufacturing, where owners John Patterson and Henry Dennison were more interested in preventing high turnover and labor conflict than in sentimental reform. They insisted that welfare work could be made to pay.[25]

Firms that were installing highly rationalized assembly-line labor processes may also have been motivated by the realization that better-rested, fed, entertained, and exercised operatives would be more productive and efficient. H. J. Heinz, AT&T, General Electric, and Sears and Roebuck, all employers of large numbers of young women who performed repetitive tasks at a fast pace, systematically introduced welfare programs.[26] Manager Elmer Scott of Sears and Roebuck eliminated night work in 1902. He claimed that "the morale and effectiveness of the employees was improved noticeably by the reform," and that "the immense increase of business in December, 1903, was carried on with greater speed, greater accuracy, and with infinitely better results." He went on to establish an elaborate "Seroco" welfare program.[27] There were no reasons why such measures had to be incompatible with ruthless managerial methods; both National Cash Register and AT&T were so committed to the drive system that they eventually evoked employee resistance and strikes. Although Scott abolished night work, he instituted piecework and bonus plans. Firms in which women interacted with the public, for example, department stores and telephone companies, hoped to inculcate appropriate workplace behavior by molding employees through welfare programs.[28]

Firms with large numbers of female employees were especially likely to consider the installation of welfare programs. When early textile mills in New England tried to attract native-born farm women as workers they assumed it would be necessary to "stand in" for parents as guardians of the young women's welfares, and also that provision of housing and other amenities might substitute for higher wages.[29] Sixty years later many employers still took seriously the notion that they stood in loco parentis to young women workers, many of whom were still in their teens, and they saw both the psychological and material advantages of continuing a relationship of dependency through welfare programs. Some welfare work programs included home visits and employment interviews with mothers. Others gave their managers authority to contact parents if employees were repeatedly tardy, badly dressed, or unhappy at work. Some assumed a didactic responsibility for instilling proper domestic virtues in their female charges. The Ballard and Ballard Flour Company of Louisville reported in 1913 that it provided a separate lunchroom for its thirty women clerical workers, where "each day a certain number of the girls are detailed to do the cooking, others set the table and still others to clear the table." The company proudly boasted that every one of its female employees would "learn to make bread and biscuit—a measure for which the coming generation of Louisville husbands and children of these girls will certainly have cause to thank Ballard and Ballard."[30]

Other factors spurred welfare programs as well. Interest in working conditions in reform circles and the public press during the Progressive period made employers anxious to prove to the general public that they could provide safe and pleasant jobs without government and union interference. Unions had made employers' dealings with male workers far more problematic. The growing numbers of clerical workers, managers, and salespersons in corporations created special work forces that, theoretically, needed to be treated differently from factory workers and from each other. In a period that still stressed the social propriety of separating the sexes, women clerks and factory workers needed spaces within plants and large office buildings where they could eat their meals, rest, and socialize away from men. Employers were also anxious to make certain that the lunch hour was taken with dispatch. The temptations to wander leisurely around town in search of food and to shop during the lunch hour often resulted in late employees, so providing lunch services on the premises gave employers more control.

It seemed logical to employers to put most of these burgeoning welfare programs in the hands of new kinds of managers.[31] The YWCA offered instruction for "welfare secretaries" as early as 1904, and in 1905 Gertrude Beeks, in charge of a special welfare secretary consultation service for the National Civic Federation, claimed the status of "a new profession" for the welfare secretary.[32]

Women welfare secretaries, although usually middle class, had varied educational preparation. The 1918 Intercollegiate Bureau of Occupations located nineteen women welfare workers. These included ten former teachers, seven former social workers, three librarians, three clerical workers, two nurses, two forewomen, and one pharmacist (some had held more than one occupation). Of the fifteen who reported on the sizes of their firms, ten worked at establishments hiring a thousand or more, including Electric Auto-Lite Corporation, Westinghouse Air Brake, the Ohio State Telephone Company, and Guarantee Trust Bank of New York. Most had been hired since 1915, and about two-thirds were in charge of both male and female employees.[33]

The hiring of women welfare secretaries to supervise both men and women required some new thinking, but traditional ideas about gender were often helpful in making the transition. One advocate of women employment and welfare managers recounted the story of a woman who had expanded her jurisdiction in a factory by combining professionalism with a mother's concern:

> much . . . opposition was felt even to turning over the employment of women to a woman employment manager. While this was being carefully worked out, the men . . . began to feel slighted and seemed to welcome any meager attention the woman employment manager had time to give them in her trips through the plant. So many evidences of improvement were noticed in regard to the women that it was decided to also centralize the employment for the men. But how could the woman who was already in the plant employ foreigners, rough laborers of all kinds—they might come into her office under the influence of liquor . . . . And oh, the mechanics and skilled workers, what about them! After much discussion, it was decided to let her try anyway, and at the end of her first year in the plant, all the employment problems . . . were being taken care of by her . . . . At the end of her first year's vacation, the fine Scotch foreman who had at first been so hard to win, was waiting anxiously for her to help him save one of his best workmen from the wrath of the Superintendent . . . . Since all

discharges were made by her, she was able to support a good foreman, and save a valuable workman.[34]

The welfare secretary struggled to define a new profession and its identity. The teacher, the social worker, the nurse, the missionary, and the mother were analogous roles upon which early welfare workers drew for inspiration. Many saw themselves as middle-class custodians of working-class virtue. The welfare secretary at Ballard and Ballard Flour Company, Urith Pope Galt, found her job to be essentially a maternal one: "I describe my part as being only 'old-fashioned housekeeping,' and the care that any Mother would give to her household." She had received her most valuable training for her job, she reported, "in my Father's household and as a member of the Protestant Episcopal Church."[35] Other secretaries were equally directive and controlling, seeing themselves as molders of characters, upholders of proper moral values, and instructors in citizenship. Others held ideological positions that connected them to middle-class reform movements of the day. Mary Belle Brown of the Walter M. Lowney Company in Boston thought "Girls of this type of factory worker are hard to interest in higher things," but "one feels that the work is much needed especially among the foreign people as they need to be Americanized." Miriam Spencer, welfare director of a small factory in upstate New York, sought to provide wholesome recreation to keep her working girls out of public dance halls and back rooms in saloons. Jeanne Reeves of the I. Magnin Department Store thought she should teach her saleswomen "the value of their American citizenship, what it means and how they can best help."[36]

Others emphasized their commitment to improving both working conditions and group morale. Ada Trevor Fox of the Electric Auto-Lite Corporation, in charge of welfare work for 2,900 workers, most of whom were men, thought her achievements included "getting all labor laws complied with, bringing about a more contented feeling, doing away with the fear of superiors, . . . bringing about confidence in officials and foremen; giving pleasures they have not had before; providing more conveniences in workrooms and dressing rooms—someone 'interested' in them." Mary G. Kiepe's Buffalo packing company employed about 1,600 men and 400 women. She had been able to establish a welfare department that provided, among other things, showers, a library, a gymnasium, and a roof garden. But Jeanne Reeves of I. Magnin wistfully admitted that keeping a balance between proper welfare work and employer interests was sometimes difficult: "It is hard to coordinate one's social service viewpoint with some of the . . . commercial aspects of business. One has constantly to remember that primarily a business is to make money. The effort has to be the greatest good for your people with the least friction over existing conditions."[37]

Outside observers also commented on the contradictions faced by caring welfare workers. Eleanor Gilbert noted in her advice book in 1916: "Sometimes [the welfare secretary] acts as a sort of buffer between the management and the workers, for it is inevitable that even in the best managed organizations there are employees with the ineradicable class-consciousness that makes them suspicious . . . . The task of the welfare secretary is to sift the real from the fancied complaint and to see that justice is recognized."[38]

These sentimental ideas about welfare secretaries were carried over by some to personnel work. The casting of woman personnel workers as feminine peacemakers between capital and labor was sometimes carried to extremes. In the vision of Miriam Leuck, author of an advice book on occupations for women in 1929, the woman personnel worker became the mother of the workplace family, charged with explaining the arbitrary decisions of the boss, or father, to her children, the workers. Sometimes she might, through delicacy and tact, be able to negotiate rewards and privileges for them by appealing to the better instincts of the patriarch: "As the fairy godmother of the plant . . . . she is omnipresent, ever useful . . . . she interprets both sides in the war between labor and capital, to the benefit of production and good feeling." While the engineer "assures that the machinery moves smoothly" and "the treasurer places funds wisely, she adjusts and places the human factors of her establishment."[39]

But Leuck's characterization of the personnel worker as a "fairy godmother" and his or her earlier manifestation as a welfare worker were images most professional personnel people, male and female, were anxious to discard. Such stereotypes cast aspersions on the gender identity and effectiveness of the personnel department and needed to be tempered by heavy doses of masculine scientific management. Women were involved in the evolution of both welfare and personnel work, but by sanitizing themselves in the atmosphere of "objectivity" and pragmatism surrounding scientific management, they were able to lose some of their reputation for tender-heartedness and appear to be strong-minded enough to participate in the world of managerial work.

Scientific Management and the Human Factor

Although psychology, vocational guidance, and welfare work were all on the upswing in the teens, they remained suspect in business and engineering circles because of their "soft-hearted," effeminate overtones. On the other hand, those who were endeavoring to modernize managerial practice under the guise of Taylorism were finding that pure scientific management was almost too "hard-hearted" and required a human touch. Scientific managers began to argue after 1910 that their strategies should pay as much attention to "the human factor" as to rationalization, technology, and the techniques of cost accounting. The ruthlessness of earlier Taylorist methods, immediately understood by workers, had to be disguised by a smokescreen of incentives and manipulative management policies in order to gain employee consent.[40]

Taylor had not foreseen this problem. He had assumed the implementation of "a fair wage for a fair day's work" would ensure cooperation from workers and be all that their employers need provide. Taylor and other scientific management engineers tended to view welfare workers as interfering busybodies. The early years of the century saw something of a standoff emerge between welfare managers and the Taylorites, with the scientific managers opposing welfare work as antiquated sentimentalism, and welfare managers perceiving the Taylorites as ruthless implementers of the drive system.[41] But aspects of Taylorism anticipated both welfare work and personnel management: wresting employment and promotion powers from the foreman and placing them in the hands of management; studying in as detailed a way as possible the actual procedures of individual jobs with an eye to standardizing them; fixing wages according to a rational formula; and providing rest periods, decent working hours, proper tools, and good safety conditions to achieve maximum efficiency. But Taylor did not see any new discipline emerging to handle these functions. He thought most of them could be handled by engineers in a planning room close to the shopfloor and appears not to have envisioned the massive administrative and clerical "nonproductive" apparatus the new functions would require.[42] His death in 1915 opened the door to wide-ranging modification of his ideas and conveniently allowed his disciples to search his minimal body of written texts for endorsements of a wide array of schemes and positions he had probably never envisioned. Whether or not Taylor's plans were followed precisely, the enthusiasm for what was perceived to be his philosophy remained unbounded. After 1915, managers often sought credibility by claiming they were using "scientific management." Taylorite disciples helped to create the impression that Taylor had provided the intellectual basis for personnel management and given it his blessing.[43]

The new approach to scientific management showed up in the first issue of the Taylor Society's bulletin in 1915. It included an essay by Ernest M. Hopkins, manager of the employment department at Curtis Publishing, on "The Supervisor of Personnel." Hopkins thought that the attention of most industrialists had originally been drawn, of necessity, to "the machines . . . [of] the plant . . . and its arrangement within." Not only had the laborer been "taken for granted," but it had also been assumed that "industry was getting to the point where it would be less dependent upon the human factor." Nothing, however, could have been further from the truth. In an age of shrinking profits, increased competition, and the impossibility of gaining a significant edge in machine methods, "varying grades of success will be determined by the intelligence of selection of the personnel and the reasonableness of the adjustments with it."[44]

Eugene Benge, who trained at the Personnel Research Bureau at Carnegie and then went on to personnel management positions with several major corporations including the Atlantic Refining Company, observed in his textbook of 1920 that "unfortunately the Taylor and similar systems too often regarded men as seekers of pay *only*, and the industrial enterprise as existing for the stockholders only." Personnel management had changed all of that forever: "A new profession has arisen. Out of the nebula of efficiency, paternalism, exploitation and strikes which have hitherto floated like a wreath of good and evil over an enterprise, there has formed the new profession of industrial relations, whose aim it is to educate management and men alike to understand and help each other."[45]

Taylor disciple Henry P. Kendall was certain that Taylor would have approved. He recalled in 1924 that Taylor had once been asked "why he had not turned his attention to personnel, sales and other aspects of business." Taylor, Kendall reported, "said he felt his life would be too short to attempt . . . the application of his point of view to those fields; that the most and best he could do was to make a thorough demonstration in the field of production management; that others on the basis of that demonstration could carry [it] . . . into other fields of management."[46] As long as it could be claimed that the methods in "other fields" paid off, that they increased efficiency, that they had been arrived at through a procedure vaguely resembling the scientific method, they could be stitched to the ever-growing patchwork quilt of scientific management.

More than a few women, some of them critics of the excesses of industrialism, others feminists or early personnel managers, were instrumental in assembling this quilt. Their interest in the faith of scientific management grew from several perceived affinities. Many women welfare workers and employment directors welcomed Taylorism because of the opportunity it gave them to appear to be tough-minded and efficient in their techniques and attitudes. Those who were feminists saw in Taylorism a chance to judge workers on the basis of aptitudes and productivity, and therefore saw an opening for more equal consideration of women. The ideology of scientific management, if applied justly, seemed to fit in well with the principles of vocational guidance; the worker should be suited to the job. Progressive reformers saw no necessary contradiction between protective legislation for women workers, trade union organization, less stressful working conditions, and the introduction of scientific management techniques. They believed that the "scientific" organization of production and machinery might eliminate seasonal work and overtime, reduce fatigue, provide higher wages, end conflict between managers and workers, and open opportunities to the talented. Taylor had eloquently promised as much.

Ida Tarbell, who was writing for *American Magazine* when Taylor submitted his first popular article on scientific management to it in 1910, thought his ideas would solve the strife and dreadful working conditions she later saw in her visits to American factories between 1912 and 1916. She insisted that scientific management was nothing more than "the practical application of the golden rule" and was an early and enthusiastic popularizer. In 1924 she declared that "no man in the history of American industry has made a larger contribution to genuine cooperation and juster human relations than did Frederick Winslow Taylor .... He is one of the few—very few—creative geniuses of our time."[47]

Sue Ainslie Clark and Edith Wyatt studied women factory workers for a Consumers' League project that became widely known among advocates of wage-earning women. At plants where scientific management had been applied, Clark and Wyatt concluded, women received higher wages and worked shorter hours than the norm. Although they were not so convinced that Taylorism had always been beneficial to women's health, they thought its "whole tendency" was "toward truth about industry, toward justice, toward a clear personal record of work, established without fear or favor." It "had inspired something really new and revolutionary in the minds of both the managers and the women workers where the system had been inaugurated." On balance, thought Clark and Wyatt, "this sense of cooperation on both sides" was the most "stirring and vital" aspect of scientific management and worth "the occasional strain on health" when it was imperfectly applied.[48]

Josephine Goldmark was more critical of the effects of scientific management on women operatives in her classic work on fatigue in industry. She argued that the gains in efficiency secured by the new methods had not always been repaid by capitalists to workers, particularly in shorter hours. But like Tarbell, Wyatt, and Clark, she was struck by the utopian possibilities of scientific management, which she described as "a new system . . . slowly spreading through the world" and whose "results have intoxicated the imagination." She warned that "unscrupulous men can easily pervert it to their own uses. Its mechanical features . . . are easily copied, and unless they are correctly applied the workers can thereby be exploited more relentlessly than ever before. But such perversions cannot fairly be charged against the system itself."[49]

The Taylor Society attracted women reformers and personnel managers, heard their speeches, and remained receptive to the idea of protective legislation for women. In 1926 the group sent Lillian M. Gilbreth, the efficiency expert, Pauline Goldmark, Josephine's sister, and Mary van Kleeck, the industrial sociologist, as its delegates to a Women's Industrial Conference sponsored by the Women's Bureau.[50] The three women reported negatively on the Woman's party's attempts to eradicate protective legislation. During the 1920s, an Industrial Code Committee of the Taylor Society met to discuss the drafting of an industrial relations platform that might be used by employers who wanted to institute above-average employment standards in the United States. Van Kleeck, Gilbreth, and Florence Kelley served on the committee and helped in the drafting of the document. Among other reforms, the code endorsed a work day of eight hours as standard and urged the avoidance of night work, especially for women.[51] Rose Schneiderman, then president of the Women's Trade Union League, admitted that while "labor folks have looked upon scientific management with a great deal of misgiving," she had read the code and was pleasantly surprised to find "that management is going in the direction which will make for happier civilization."[52] Although the code was never more than a series of suggestions to industry, it reaffirmed the links between scientific management, social reform, and a feminist influence in personnel management.

Mary Barnett Gilson: Feminism and Personnel Management

Mary Barnett Gilson was the most influential and articulate woman advocate of Taylorism. She laid out a coherent plan of scientific personnel management for a well-known business firm, argued that the new management techniques could further feminist goals, and tried to guarantee a place for women employment managers in the new system.

Gilson grew up in Pittsburgh, where her father was the editor of a religious newspaper, and she witnessed first-hand the effects of horrible working conditions in the Carnegie steel works. She remembered her college years at Wellesley as a time when she "floundered around," with the memorable exception of attending a stirring campus speech by social reformer Florence Kelley of the Consumers' League. Although Gilson thought that "most women who went to college in the nineties were serious in their vague hope to be of some use, not mere parasites," few options existed for executing this hope. She had no real interest in marrying and seemed to take pride in the fact that her red hair reminded her relatives of her "spinster great-aunt Jane." Teaching seemed the only possible career, and although one bold instructor suggested journalism, Gilson settled on library work in Pittsburgh, where she attempted to introduce books to slum children.[53]

Having moved to Boston with a woman friend, Gilson took up training for department store girls at the Women's Educational and Industrial Union in 1910. Boston was the center of the developing vocational guidance movement, and Gilson arrived just as it was coming into its own. While working in department stores to research saleswomen's jobs, Gilson met Mary LaDame, who was in charge of training junior women workers at Filene's, and through her met Meyer Bloomfield, head of the Boston Vocation Bureau and colleague of Mary Parker Follett. Gilson decided to train with the bureau as one of the new vocational counselors at the Boston Trade School for Girls. "It was all new and exciting," she recalled. "We lived in hope that we could ultimately place all the round pegs in round holes and all the square pegs in square ones." But her work at the Trade School for Girls ultimately proved to be frustrating:

"there was no really scientific method of detecting the motor-minded, so incomes, grades, the advice of teachers, and the will of parents were in essence the divining rods." After the schools provided guidance and training, the jobs offered to students were still low-paying and working conditions unpleasant; most girls found positions in garment-making sweatshops.[54] Vocational guidance alone was not enough.

Gilson was finally infused with a militant new sense of direction when Taylor came to Boston to give a series of lectures. "Those," she fervently recalled, "left me in the state of a person who has suddenly 'got religion.'" Here was the key to ameliorating the deplorable conditions of the working-class women she encountered and a way to carve out a niche beyond that of sentimental reformer for herself. Creative and responsible management might restructure the nature of work so that it would benefit workers and business alike. "To one who has not seen so many examples of mismanagement as I had at that time, I always found it hard to explain the inspiration he [Taylor] furnished . . . . more than anything else his stress on the responsibility of management impressed me. The time had come, he said, when we should stop lecturing workers about their failures and duties *until* we had awakened management to its own responsiblity for good workmanship."[55]

Gilson was given an opportunity to do something with her new-found religion. In 1913 she was invited to become the service and employment director at Clothcraft Shops in Cleveland, a large garment factory that produced men's clothing and employed several thousand workers, nearly three-quarters of whom were women. Richard A. Feiss, the young works manager in an old family business, Joseph and Feiss Company, producer of the Clothcraft label for men's garments, had also been bitten by the bug of Taylorism. Feiss had a number of Boston connections who put him in touch with the vocational guidance and enlightened welfare work proponents there. He graduated from Harvard Law School in 1903, and found Gilson through Meyer Bloomfield.[56]

Feiss was, like Gilson, in need of an overarching theory for his modernist sympathies. Having joined the family business in 1904, he had overseen the construction of a new factory. He also committed the firm to an abandonment of "outside work," the practice of consigning batches of garment-sewing tasks to homeworkers. But the factory could only compete with homework and sweatshops if it adopted more efficient systems and became productive enough to pay for overhead. Feiss instituted the most modern sewing equipment, good lighting, and fatigue-saving seats and table heights. He developed a special routing and scheduling system to approximate a garment-producing assembly line. He did time and motion studies, modified piece rates according to new engineering principles, and paid workers bonuses for goods produced over the daily limit. Like Dennison he saw the ending of seasonal unemployment as a crucial factor in worker morale and productivity. New paperwork systems kept track of goods produced by individual workers and those of the company as a whole. By the time Gilson arrived in Cleveland in 1913, Clothcraft was already known for its good working conditions, its higher-than-average wages, its rest periods, and its relatively short work week.[57]

Feiss had done most of the things Taylor and other scientific manager engineers suggested. He had also established up-to-date welfare measures. But the "human factor" remained problematic. His firm was still plagued by typical employment woes of the garment industry: high labor turnover, tardiness and absenteeism, and seemingly untrainable workers, many of them non-English-speaking immigrants. Gilson was charged with systematizing employment and using welfare programs to create a more efficient and loyal labor force. Feiss gave her, evidently, a free hand in devising her system of management and made room for her feminist commitments too.[58]

Feiss described the work of Clothcraft's personnel department in a lengthy address to the Taylor Society in 1915, and in her autobiography Gilson recounted many of the changes she helped to implement. Her title was changed from welfare secretary to service and employment manager soon after she arrived. She immediately attacked the problem of hiring, which had formerly been left to foremen, who picked out prospective employees from hopefuls milling around the front vestibule. All hiring was transferred to Gilson's jurisdiction. Feiss's address was clear on the point that proper scientific management required a managerial-level personnel director, and Gilson remained, throughout her life, a militant advocate of the idea that foremen should not do hiring. Although the psychological specialist Walter Dill Scott was consulted to devise intelligence and dexterity tests, Gilson felt more comfortable in using lengthy application blanks and better interviewing techniques to place employees. The tests remained somewhat useful in sorting out "cases of exceptionally low-grade intelligence."[59]

For Gilson and Feiss, the most important key to happy workers and an efficient plant was proper placement; vocational guidance had moved from the school to the workplace. It was the special role of the employment manager to find the job best suited to the applicant and to draw on existing personnel as much as possible for positions beyond those of operatives. Feiss and Gilson both thought that effective placement, higher wages, internal promotion, and good welfare programs would undercut labor turnover, and did demonstrate turnover rates much lower than average for the garment industry.[60]

The management innovations at Clothcraft did not alienate the efficiency experts, at least initially. Although Feiss and Gilson implemented scientific management techniques without the help of any of the Taylorite consultants and considerably cushioned some of their impact, Taylor privately described the Clothcraft shop as "the best plant anywhere." Frank Gilbreth, the time-and-motion study expert, also extolled Clothcraft's virtues, claiming "what Mr. Feiss has done in the clothing trade is a mark to come to. I have been through that factory and I believe (and I have exceptional opportunity to judge) that Mr. Feiss has absolutely reached the top niche of the clothing industry of the world."[61] And to Clothcraft came a steady stream of observers, reporters, employment experts, and reformers who wanted to see humanized scientific management in action.[62]

Gilson surely had an agenda that went beyond adding the human factor to Taylorism. For Gilson, good personnel work was also the key to issues of sexual equity in employment. She was offended by the discovery that recommendations for promotion from foremen were often the result of bribery or gifts. These had ominous implications in an establishment with male foremen and female operatives. She saw both the original application form and employee records, which were extraordinarily elaborate at Clothcraft, as a way of developing a pool of female labor from which promotions based on merit and aptitude could be made. The plant provided English classes and training programs for new positions. Factory operatives became forewomen, operatives moved into the office, and working-class women were trained as supervisors; Gilson also brought in college-educated women to be trained as executives. Given the proper set of wage inducements and promotion opportunities, Gilson argued, women made as reliable a set of employees as men. "All these women were competent and respected by management and workers," she claimed. "And all the predictions about high labor turnover among women and losing money training them did not come true .... The question of sex did not enter in when we were fine-combing our organization for able persons to take supervisory or other important positions. If a woman was chosen she was held as reponsible for capable performance as was a man."[63]

Gilson firmly believed that women had the best chance of holding their own in a system based on performance and merit, as long as that system was sexually unbiased. She thought that holding workers directly accountable was the key to creating such a system. Using other criteria would win the circumstantial or subjective argument for men every time: "a profit-making system involves using the best available worker for a job and not employing a man because he has a sick wife or because he wants to pay a mortgage." Gilson was infuriated by such arguments. She had once heard an industrial relations man tell at a conference "how his firm attempted to discover who was 'worthy' of the best jobs. He said they found that one of the girls in their offices lived in a very nice apartment, and they decided she was not in need of promotion!"[64] Women stood a better chance of gaining a place in industry by standing on their abilities and a system that judged workers completely on their merits. There were limits to Gilson's reforms in ending discrimination and opening opportunity, however. Although she rationalized wage rates and increased women's wages in general, women were still paid about half as much as men, on average, at Clothcraft, and union protocol guaranteed that management would never make women operatives into cutters.[65]

The service programs at Clothcraft were under Gilson's command as well. With a large contingent of women workers and a managerial style that emphasized personal interaction, Clothcraft had assumed the kind of in loco parentis role for its young women workers that often characterized enlightened firms. By 1915 Clothcraft had an employee cafeteria, a medical department (which provided free eye examinations and eyeglasses), a thrift bank, recreation facilities, a factory orchestra and a choral club, and a branch of the Cleveland Public Library. Workers were encouraged to attend night school or continue their education.

Service programs were not confined to the factory; Gilson and her staff used an extensive system of home visits to root out tardiness and absences, inappropriate dress, poor health habits (including sleeping at night with the windows closed), and "causes of dissatisfaction." These visits were, no doubt, both intrusive and maternalistic. But if Gilson's descriptions of them are analyzed more carefully, it is also clear that she saw them as an indispensable part of her feminist agenda. Reproving those who were tardy and absent had the same goal as a system that promoted piece rates and rapid, efficient production; it provided an atmosphere in which those who worked the hardest and were most able would be most rewarded. Home visits might reveal a problem with a foreman or a parent that a worker would be afraid to reveal on the job. No-nonsense dress and an absence of jewelry were both safer for the workplace and indicative of the seriousness of women's intentions there. A talk with parents might convince them that their daughter deserved to keep some of her own wages instead of handing them over to the family coffers every payday. Gilson found that daughters who had their own bank accounts worked harder and were more reliable.[66] Gilson was above all anxious to prove the critics of women workers wrong by demonstrating that women could take their jobs as seriously as men. And while she saw ending discrimination as one aspect of her campaign, she also saw creating new habits of industry and independence in her women workers as another:

> One thing is self evident,—women must cease regarding themselves and permitting themselves to be regarded as "cheap labor." This means that they must be exacting of themselves in living up to the requirements of the work they undertake. They must, in other words, "play the game" and their self respect must forbid them to expect or accept privileges on the grounds of sex. If they disregard the laws of health, if they are unsteady in attendance, if they are over sensitive and if they do not carry adequately the responsibilities with which they are entrusted they must expect to be rated accordingly.[67]

Gilson's plan for giving women more responsibility and self-confidence at Clothcraft depended on the cooperation of working-class women. Would they agree that every job, no matter how unimportant, was a test of women's reliability? Gilson's account of her days at Clothcraft was carefully tailored to prove the beneficience of scientific management. Low labor turnover at the plant probably indicated some degree of worker satisfaction with Gilson's policies and the better than average working conditions of Feiss's factory in Cleveland. But it is doubtful that women operatives always had the same goals Gilson did. It seems more likely that class perspective helped to shape feminist ambitions. Did women who looked forward to being married and having families want to assume the kind of rigorous self-accountability Gilson promoted if it meant giving up married life? Or were these largely the ideas of women managers, most of them single, like Gilson?

Gilson's policies included the firing of women upon marriage. She claimed that married women were "as a rule irregular in attendance and burdened with household duties" and often had husbands whom they supported. But behind this policy was another idea of Gilson's: urging young women to postpone marriage to a later date. She claimed that the "unwritten" marriage law at Clothcraft had "materially lessened the early, precipitate marriages in our factory."[68] She wanted women to become independent of fathers and husbands alike, not only because she thought they would be happier women, but also so that the sex of women could begin to prove its real worth.

Whatever the chord Gilson's ideas struck among women workers, her bid to offer managerial and executive positions to women generally fell on deaf ears at other corporations. But she was not alone in her determination to open supervisory and clerical positions to factory operatives. Her ideas about the development of internal labor markets were rapidly gaining acceptance and were perhaps an inevitable consequence of the growing complexity of large organizations. Most personnel management texts published after the war routinely discussed the need to provide not only training for workers but also the opportunity to advance to higher positions or transfer to other departments. Moving loyal and productive workers up to positions as forepersons, supervisors, or office staff had been practiced by many firms on an informal basis for years. Organizations with large numbers of male clerks, like railroads and insurance companies, had classification schemes and promotion plans in place at the turn of the century, and male clerks were recruited for managerial positions as the changes accompanied by cost accounting and the record-keeping revolution were instituted. Other manufacturing firms with strong links to welfare work, scientific management, and large numbers of women employees began experimenting with the training and transfer of factory workers to office work in the teens: the Scott Paper Company, Dennison Manufacturing, Curtis Publishing, and Cheney Brothers Silk Mills are four examples. The telephone company had similar policies, and the department stores encouraged training of saleswomen to develop heads of departments and buyers.[69] Civil services were also implementing policies of internal promotion.

During the war and the months immediately following it, the recruitment of large numbers of women for responsible positions in industry brought Gilson's work at Clothcraft some notoriety.[70] She used that public exposure to promote equal pay for equal work and access to promotions for women. A 1921 article in *Industrial Management*, except for its omission of the question of race, was forthright in its bid for equal treatment:

> As a mere matter of justice society must recognize the right of all normal adult workers (and this is generally taken to mean men and women over twenty-one) to a wage sufficient to support themselves and several dependents at a "comfort minimum," regardless of sex, age, religion . . . but with due regard to fitness for work and ability to accomplish a given task. Furthermore, society must also realize the right of every adult who qualifies for promotion by virtue of his or her personality and ability regardless of any of the aforementioned characteristics, to consider the sky the limit. When this attitude prevails there will be a reservoir, as yet untapped, of ambition, of incentive, of ability and pride in work among women.[71]

Feminist demands for equal treatment and opportunity were converging with the development of modernized personnel systems, which also emphasized merit and an end to personal favoritism. Personnel departments were on their way toward "the systematic dispensation" of rewards and benefits. Such "bureaucratic control" characterizes the most modern corporate structures and tends to undermine labor discontent by creating segmented labor hierarchies whose tiers are allegedly based on rational criteria of education, training, experience, and merit.[72] As Gilson's experiments demonstrated, the exclusion of women and people of color from upper-level jobs remained an irrational aspect of an increasingly rational system. "Rightly or wrongly," admitted a subcommittee of the Office Executives Division of the American Management Association in 1924, "most organizations . . . do not consider their female employees as timber for advancement in the same sense that the male employees are considered."[73] The continuation of practices that denied promotion to certain categories of workers undermined the validity of rationalized personnel management. In future years the continued refusal of managers in both government and private industry to consider promoting people beyond certain levels because of race, sex, or religion would often spark resentment in bureaucratic organizations. The most articulate feminist critique of such policies developed in the civil services, where promises of internal promotion through examination and job review provided employees with a rationale for challenging discrimination.

Civil Service Reform in
a Feminist Framework

Women had been seeking office positions in the federal civil service since the Civil War, and as will be shown in chapter 4, the recruitment of women by government offices to save labor costs began escalating in the 1880s. As municipal and state civil services expanded in the early twentieth century, they too began to recruit women. Civil service examinations promised the taxpayer competent employees, but also raised employee expectations for equitable treatment. Women and people of color were simply denied—by custom or law—access to examinations for huge categories of jobs. Even when allowed to take the tests, qualified women could often be passed over for men, even if they stood higher on the list and had been waiting longer for placement. While people of color, particularly African Americans, would have to wait until World War II to make much headway beyond menial positions in the civil service, white women successfully challenged some aspects of sex discrimination in hiring and promotion by World War I. The challenge was facilitated by the growing interest of civil services at every level of government in using modern personnel practice.

During the war feminists both inside and outside of government tried to seize the national spotlight to promote equality in civil service examinations, placements, and promotions. Women's successes in new positions, the shortage of labor in civil service jobs, and the organized ardor of the suffrage movement provided them a strong ideological position. A flurry of well-documented studies of women in the civil service appeared in 1918 and 1919, and an assembly of civil service commissions of the United States and Canada in 1919 resolved to investigate the whole matter of appointment on the basis of sex.[74] May B. Upshaw, assistant chief examiner of the Municipal Civil Service Commission of New York City and one of the highest-ranking women in civil service work, threw down the feminist gauntlet in 1919: "The suffrage is well established in many states, and it is, we believe, practically assured of nation-wide extension. But in one of the greatest fields of employment, the civil service, we still find the bonds of precedent and the fetters of tradition that have been so generally discarded elsewhere. Under many Commissions women are not permitted even to be examined for work of any but a subordinate character, and mainly in the old fields that have always been open to them, stenography, nursing, teaching, and institutional labor."[75]

Even more opprobrious to feminists was the fact that department heads in most commissions could still designate jobs for one sex or the other, even if those of the opposite sex had placed higher on the list of eligibles. "A woman might be first on the list ten times over," Anna Martin Crocker of the New York City Civil Service Commission declared indignantly in 1916, "and still not be appointed if the appointing officer so desires."[76]

A 1919 report on women in the federal civil service by Bertha Nienburg of the Women's Bureau underscored the validity of feminist grievances. Most of the 40 percent of all the civil service examinations open to women were for clerical positions. Women were especially likely to be barred from the professional, scientific, and managerial examinations leading to prestigious work and higher pay. "Chaotic salary conditions" characterized the federal civil service in general, with department heads given wide latitude to determine the salaries and sexes of new appointments. Women were overwhelmingly concentrated in the lowest salary ranges of $900 to $1,300 a year. Nearly half of the men made more than $1,300 a year, whereas only 5 percent of women did so. Nonetheless, the number of women who had qualifed by examination for employment was growing every year. Between 1915 and 1916 fewer than 10 percent of those eligible for appointment were women, but by 1917 and 1918, more than 23 percent were.[77] Women were waiting in line for civil service appointments to better positions.

The federal government, desperate for women workers during the war and about to grant suffrage to women, was also under pressure to expedite their recruitment. Within ten days of receiving Bertha Nienburg's Women's Bureau report on women in the civil service in October 1919, the Civil Service Commission issued a ruling opening all examinations to both women and men. Further liberalization came out of the recently appointed Joint Commission on Reclassification's milestone report in 1920. It documented "a bewildering array of titles and a jumble of salary rates for exactly the same kind of work." The commission recommended more equitable systems of payment and promotion, the organization of occupations into "classifications," and a more centralized personnel management structure.[78] One proponent of these more elaborate personnel management policies for the federal government argued that productivity and justice must be inextricably linked in a smoothly working civil service. Although taxpayers deserved the most efficient system that could be created, it was also true that "a democratic government must function in its dealings with its own employees democratically and according to the principles of justice. Generally speaking, it must provide equal pay for equal work, [and] equal opportunity for advancement."[79]

The Classification Act of 1924 continued both modernization and gestures toward equality. It created a federal Personnel Classification Board charged with establishing equal pay for the same positions, "irrespective of sex," and classifying positions according to their job descriptions so that more "scientific regulation of compensation" could be established. But the prerogative of a department head to designate jobs for males or females remained and fundamentally undermined efforts to end sex discrimination.[80] Nienburg's follow-up study for the Women's Bureau in 1926 showed that relatively few women had benefited from the 1924 act.[81]

Nonetheless, the ruling opening examinations to women and the establishment of a Personnel Classification Board were significant steps forward for those seeking fairer conditions for women workers. The changes created a psychology of rising expectations, legitimized notions of equality, and promoted the use of scientific research in personnel management both inside and outside government. The unfairness of refusing to appoint or promote someone who qualified through examination seemed irrefutable and may have fueled the determination of many women in the civil service to challenge discrimination. Anna Martin Crocker summed up the outrage of many: "It [is] . . . such an iniquitous system that I can hardly trust myself to speak judicially about it."[82]

The heightened expectations of the war made women push for greater opportunities. Many women were confident that they could prove themselves once the opportunities came. The perception that civil service employment had more clear-cut job descriptions than the private sector, examinations for appointments based on merit, and some opportunity for women to move upward may very well have accounted for the extent to which women moved into civil service in the teens and twenties. Once in the civil service, obstacles based on sex or political patronage seemed intolerable.

By the end of the 1920s, federal managers were thoroughly aware of women's discontent, with one investigator noting that "many of the more ambitious women" in government had the "feeling that they are being discriminated against, or that women in general are not accorded all the opportunities and privileges which would be given them if they were of the opposite sex." Although he questioned the validity of much of this feeling, the investigator did concede that the government had an "obligation to its women citizens to accelerate the tendency toward the provision of equal opportunity."[83] Although private employers would not make these kinds of gestures toward a system based on merit regardless of sex for many decades, they were adopting, through the guise of personnel management, many of the policies characteristic of modern civil service and employment systems: detailed job descriptions, job classifications, wage standardization policies, and at least limited opportunities to move ahead within the organization, even for women workers.

Objective qualifying examinations, more specific job descriptions and classifications, and internal promotion policies have an ambiguous effect in the workplace. Workers perceive them to be conditions of equitable employment. They are also characteristic of large, rationalized bureaucracies, where too much equity might be disadvantageous. While employers may believe that more rationalized personnel management policies will boost morale and reduce labor turnover, they also want to simplify the tasks of management by making hiring, promotion, and wage levels more efficient. The urgent need for a more efficient employment and placement system in the federal civil service made it a forerunner in the implementation of modernized personnel systems in the years surrounding the war, but the changes were also driven by demands for a fairer system. The civil service was one place where feminist demands were being explored and, to some extent, addressed through action. The war years also demonstrated the inherent connections among modern personnel management systems, feminist sensibilities, and the growing participation of women in employment management.

Women in Personnel Work: The War Years

In the years between Taylor's death in 1915 and the Federal Classification Act of 1924, personnel management had become a standard function in the administration of large bureaucratic enterprises. Internal promotion schemes were only one of the responsibilities assigned to the personnel office. Overseeing welfare work, analyzing jobs, rationalizing wage structures, keeping employee records, assuming responsibility for promotions and transfers, and overseeing company discipline and merit reviews all increased the size of the personnel office staff and its clerical operations.

Manufacturing establishments, banks, mail order houses, telephone companies, and civil services had all reorganized their personnel work. Some of the most elaborate employment programs were in the large department stores, public utilities, and insurance companies, with Metropolitan Life, Filene's and Macy's leading the way. These large employers sought to rationalize their employment policies by doing local wage studies, setting minimal education requirements (particularly for clerical and managerial positions), training hirees, and replacing the casual interview with application forms and testing. The comprehensiveness of and importance accorded to personnel work within individual firms varied a great deal, but nearly all large organizations had employment departments and systematic methods of hiring, training, and promotion.[84] Employment or personnel management had taken its place alongside cost accounting and engineering as an essential ingredient of scientific management, although there would continue to be a debate over whether the personnel manager should be as powerful as executive-level managers.[85]

Women made surprising strides in the new field, not just as researchers and psychologists, but also as employment and personnel workers. Some male employment managers tried to confine women's personnel management influence to female employees. "A large proportion of our employees are men," stated the director of welfare at the Corn Products Refining Company in Argo, Illinois, "and we do not feel that a woman is capable of keeping in touch with them. The men of foreign birth in particular will not take up their problems with a woman." An employment officer at the American Lithograph Company of New York thought that although some women might be suited to personnel work "most of them probably would be too sympathetic and idealistic."[86]

But male personnel experts also admitted that personnel work for both men and women required qualities which they thought women were especially likely to possess. One man thought these included "keen knowledge of human nature, infinite tact and patience, poise, firmness, coupled with high ideals and constructive sympathy." Another wrote that "[women] are character readers by intuition. This work requires a sort of motherly interest in the employee and a desire to place them in work best suited to their strength and ability." Said another, "Bright women are generally good readers of character; they have an understanding of human nature which men often lack. With proper backing they can do all that a man can do."[87] With the industrial and bureaucratic explosion of World War I on the horizon, women were poised to enter personnel work, and few real ideological barriers stood in their way.

Mary Gilson was well aware of the opportunities the oncoming war might provide to women in personnel work. In March of 1918 she confided to Emma Hirth that she had been "working on a scheme for training women employment managers." In contact with a woman instructor who taught courses in principles of factory management at Western Reserve University, she intended to take in six or seven women trainees at Clothcraft and was certain that she could find positions for more in other Cleveland factories. "In the fall," she continued, "these women will be expected to take at least a semester at Western Reserve and after that we shall attempt to place them in employment departments throughout the country." Having recently heard from Mary van Kleeck of the Women's Branch of the Army Ordnance Department's Industrial Service Section (ISS) about women's chances in the new field, Gilson was convinced that the "demand for women employment managers would be great in a very short time."[88] Nonetheless, as Gilson was to discover, the recruitment of women as wartime employment managers was not altogether smooth sailing.

During the war van Kleeck summoned Gilson to the War Industries Board in Washington to contribute expertise on employment management. Government planners were about to create emergency instruction programs to train personnel managers but envisioned separate courses for women. Gilson recalled the dramatic discussion this proposal set off: "Nine men sitting in a circle in a room of a government building in Washington were urging the establishment of a separate training school for women employment managers . . . . I told the gentlemen that there was as good a reason for a woman's ability to head an employment department where the majority of workers were men as for a man's ability to head a department where the workers were chiefly women . . . . I maintained that we ought to throw aside our fusty ideas and put capable persons, regardless of sex, into our munitions plants to handle employment functions."[89]

Fearful that if women were trained separately they would emerge as mere assistants to male employment directors and never go beyond employment work with women, Gilson insisted not only that women be given the same courses as men but also that the courses be coeducational. With van Kleeck's help, Gilson succeeded in her main objective. While women with no industrial experience were given instruction in plant operations in a separate course in Cleveland, the graduates of that course and other women with industrial experience were sent to "the classes already established for men at

Harvard, Rochester, on the Pacific coast, and in other parts of the country." Gilson agreed to be the associate director of the coeducational training course at Rochester and to recruit the twenty-five women to be admitted. She began a number of hectic months commuting on the sleeper train from Cleveland to Rochester; van Kleeck had also put her in charge of the Women's Division of the ISS for western Pennsylvania and northern Ohio. Her job for the ISS was to make sure that government regulations with regard to safety conditions, hours, and child labor were maintained in plants with government contracts.[90]

The course in employment management was to last for six weeks and to provide living expenses, books, and a weekly wage of $12. In looking over the "thousands of letters" from women which "poured in from every quarter of the country and from every class and occupation" for the trainee positions in employment managent, Gilson had clear criteria in mind as she made her selections. She was looking for single or widowed women out on their own; the minimum age requirement was twenty-five. Her years at Clothcraft had taught her that women of such circumstances were available and eager to work. She later described them, perhaps somewhat autobiographically, as "congenital old maids . . . without the traditional characteristics of this species, widows, . . . [or] the sort who more than gave us our money's worth before they married." Gilson would probably have agreed with her contemporary Ella V. Price, who said in 1918 that the ideal female employment manager was "a woman who you think could be married at any time if she chose but just for some reason does not."[91]

Although Gilson did not list any formal education requirements for admission, she obviously intended candidates to have at least high school preparation; she dismissed out of hand an application from "one poor illiterate" who claimed, "I need the money bad. I've been in bed with thirteen doctors and my husband is a Veteran of the Spanish War." In a more serious vein, she also tried to sort out those who were old-fashioned welfare workers from those who could be instilled with the principles of scientific management. She knew there were many of the latter lurking in employment departments throughout the country, and thought the former would only embarrass the program: "In my countless trips through plants in various part of the country I had seen instances of inefficient men lapping up kudos while efficient women behind the scenes were doing the work. Sometimes, too, I had seen a 'woman welfare worker' whose chief assets were a kind face and white hair. I was not interested in training women for the job of wiping tears and being motherly."[92]

Yet, as in her work at Clothcraft, Gilson's insistence on efficient women employment managers for her training program did not mute her Progressive sympathies or her desire for equitable employment. These positions were complementary and depended upon each other for their success as far as she was concerned. Relating with indignation twenty years later an episode in a munitions plant, she recalled encountering a male accountant turned employment manager who not only had employed more than a hundred children under fourteen and was intolerably rude to applicants, but had also refused to warn men who were at work near dangerous explosives of the risk involved or to advise them on how to prevent accidents. When he responded indignantly, "Do you think they'd go to work if they knew it was dangerous!" she intervened, interviewed the job-seekers herself, and left her woman employment manager trainee in charge, having "clinched that decision by going to the owner and manager of the plant and getting it in writing."[93]

Both middle-class women reformers and upwardly mobile working-class women were to be found as employment managers by the teens. Marjorie Sydney, an investigator of possible connections between working conditions in department store work and commercialized prostitution for New York City's Committee of Fourteen, was hired by Macy's in 1915 to help organize its new centralized employment department. A 1934 study uncovered the story of "Miss Lewis," who began her working career as a bookkeeping clerk about 1905. When her father died six years later she supported her mother and three younger siblings, working for a series of firms doing accounting, statistical, and auditing work. Sometime after taking a job with a new employer in 1915 she developed an "enlightened personnel" department, and a sympathetic employer allowed her "to attend conferences, and to organize work according to her own ideas."[94]

The 1918 Intercollegiate Bureau of Occupations study of nineteen welfare workers was accompanied by a sample of thirty-three women in employment management. More than a third of those surveyed in employment management had taken some college courses. While only seven were college graduates, just a handful had failed to complete high school. They all had worked elsewhere before taking up their current jobs as employment managers; there were former clerical workers, teachers, and social workers in significant numbers. Some had held jobs as welfare workers, and there

were saleswomen, librarians, a policewoman, and a suffrage orga-
nizer. Of the twenty-three women whose employment histories
could be ascertained, nineteen had obtained their personnel jobs
between 1916 and 1918, with the majority of these finding their
current employment during the war.[95] For example, Louise Moore
of Boone, Iowa, a Wellesley graduate and then a teacher for six
years, computed statistical data for the Iowa State Department of
Labor between 1914 and 1916 and then, in a whirlwind of public
agency employment, worked for the Children's Bureau, the Council of National Defense, and the Child Labor Division. After taking
the employment management course at Harvard in 1918 she was
hired as employment and service manager of the Dutchess Manufacturing Company of Poughkeepsie and from 1926 to 1930 served
on the board of councilors of the American Management
Association.[96]

Some women had begun their work much earlier. Heloise Arnold
went straight from normal school to Sears and Roebuck in 1905 as
employment manager for women and by 1917 was in charge of
more than eight thousand employees. Amelia H. Thompson, also a
former teacher, took a similar position at Eastman Kodak in 1908, a
firm that employed about 5,500 workers in 1918, more than two
thousand of whom were women. Jane C. Williams, whom Mary
Gilson later described as "the first woman to hold a position of
dignity and responsibility in industrial relations," was working at
Plimpton Press in Boston in 1912 as a cost clerk when efficiency
experts arrived and recommended that she be promoted to the job
of employment manager. A grammar-school-educated German
woman who began work at the telephone company as an operator
became chief operator of a large central office and then manager of
the operators' training department, where she was responsible for
both the selection and training of a force of twelve thousand. Several department store training managers had moved into similar
positions. But whatever their earlier history, the expansion in employment in the teens and during the war had increased the scopes
of these women's managerial responsibilities.[97]

A YWCA report on women in responsible positions in the
greater New York and New Jersey industrial region in 1919 and
1920 underscored this finding. The report found that in 250 factories employing a hundred or more women, women had been most
likely to achieve managerial status as forewomen and employment
workers. The authors concluded that "women have had easier access to personnel work because the work itself is an innovation, and

hence the frequent prejudice against women has failed to operate." The report stressed that women employment workers had successfully made the transition from welfare work to scientific management: "This work is relatively recent. In its beginning it was called 'welfare,' and was often a paternalistic attempt to make workers appreciate as a gift, conditions which should be theirs as a right. The women who entered factories in the early days of 'welfare' looked upon their work as uplift or charity . . . . It was soon recognized, however, that the welfare department was not attacking the problem of labor relations at its center. And so the emphasis shifted to employment and 'personnel,' with the activities of health, food-giving, and recreation in subordinate places."[98]

This assessment was probably correct. Women employment managers were well aware of the ideological debate over the differences between welfare work and personnel management and were quick to point out their alignment with the goals of scientific management. Many of them subscribed to the journals most engaged in promoting Taylorism: *System, Industrial Management, Annals of the American Academy of Political and Social Science,* and the *Bulletin of the Taylor Society.*[99] Gilson's feminist sentiments had clearly emerged in women personnel managers' circles as well. One personnel director interviewed by the YWCA proclaimed: "I regard it as my chief duty to waken the individual girl to the possibilities in her job. It is a mistake to suppose that all girls are simply looking for an interim job between school and marriage. We select women with ambition, and then see to it that they have stimulus and opportunity to rise." These early women employment managers did not see any fundamental contradiction between scientific management, feminism, and Progressive reform ideals.[100]

Under Suspicion: Women and Personnel Management in the 1920s

By the end of World War I, personnel management had emerged as a profession, complete with associations, journals, and conferences. That same year eight hundred employment workers met in Rochester to form the National Association of Employment Managers (by 1923 the American Management Association), an organization whose goal was to promote "modern" employment methods. The association's journal, *Personnel,* provided information on recent publications and offered a "placement" column for those looking for work, including women. Women wielded some influence in the formation and early practice of institutionalized personnel management. Jane C. Williams of Plimpton Press was on the first board of directors of the Association of Employment Managers, and in June of 1918 the Boston affiliate formally changed its constitution so women could be admitted.[101]

The government's growing interest in personnel management helped to foster the new profession, particularly as the country made the transition from a wartime economy and many industrial departments were demobilized. Having commissioned both army IQ and placement tests and new civil service examinations for many office jobs during the war, the government had a vested interest in the promotion of the new discipline, and industry was happy to learn what it could from government personnel work.[102] The sharing of information and research among government, business, and academic institutions was encouraged in 1921 when the National Research Council created the Personnel Research Federation at the request of the Engineering Foundation. One of the chief goals of another agency, the Bureau of Public Personnel Administration, created in 1922 to coordinate state, municipal, and federal civil service activities, was to promote an "interchange of ideas and experience between those men who are concerned with personnel in private industry, and those who deal with personnel in public service."[103]

The Personnel Research Federation's first constituents included many of those groups with an interest in more "scientific" personnel policies, including academic departments of applied psychology from Bryn Mawr and Carnegie, the Engineering Foundation, the American Federation of Labor, the country's leading business schools, vocational guidance groups, and the U.S. Bureau of Labor Statistics and the Civil Service Commission. The Personnel Research Federation held open room for a human relations approach to personnel management that often locked philosophical horns with the cost accounting approach of the American Management Association. Although women participated in both groups, the Personnel Research Federation generally promoted the "softer" side of personnel management.[104]

Feminist connections and voices in personnel management were strengthened by the work of the federation, where attempts in personnel work to merge notions of fairness, opportunity, and efficiency reached an apotheosis. Emma Hirth of the Bureau of Vocational Information attended the first meetings, was elected to the executive committee, and made the investigation of women in professional occupations like chemistry and banking an early topic of consideration. Information about women doing personnel research was frequently printed in the federation's *Journal of Personnel Research*, and women contributed original and influential work on labor turnover, absenteeism, training, and testing to its pages.

But whatever the influence of women researchers and vocational guidance experts in the Personnel Research Federation, the first rush of enthusiasm for women employment managers was dampened by the end of the war and the economic downturn of 1921. By late 1919 both men and women who had worked in government installations and war plants were out of work and advertising themselves for new positions. Women found it especially difficult to find jobs.[105]

Women's employment and welfare managers' positions were undermined by the widespread dismissal of women industrial workers after the war and the relatively small increase in manufacturing jobs for women in the 1920s. The pages of *Personnel* were now devoted almost entirely to the activities of men, although many women had placed themselves in "seeking work" columns for employment managers in 1919 and 1920. Most local personnel management associations tended to be, Mary Gilson claimed later, for men, with women's absence reenforced by their exclusion from Chambers of Commerce and Rotary Clubs. In this context both the Taylor Society and the Personnel Research Federation loomed large as forums where women in personnel management might find a voice. Gilson thought the Taylor Society was more receptive to women than the American Management Association.[106]

During the twenties, personnel management developed into a sophisticated and stratified occupation that more closely resembled the gender hierarchies of the other business professions. College-educated men were most likely to be "personnel officers," with real access to executive decision making and high salaries. Women and lower-ranking men were likely to be in charge of specific functions within personnel departments: employment, training, recreation, and health. The tasks of testing and employment became standardized within a few years and primarily consisted of record keeping and paperwork; the employment office was analogous in function and process to purchasing, billing, or payroll. As such, its director was often more an office manager than a personnel officer. A 1921 study by the Boston Women's Educational and Industrial Union of salaries for men and women in the employment management field cited a range of $2,000 to $5,000 per year, and an exceptional peak, for "men of real ability," reaching as much as $25,000 a year. Women were more likely to be assistants to employment managers than heads of departments, and in twenty-two firms with "unmistakable personnel departments," only five were directed by women. The median salary of women personnel workers in industry was only $1,846.[107]

Many personnel managers after 1925, including those who were men, complained that they were not taken as seriously as those they considered to be their equivalents—production engineers, sales managers, and accountants. In fact, the decade saw many firms back away from the idea that the personnel manager should have executive status.[108] The American Management Association viewed personnel managers with some suspicion and urged executives to keep them firmly in control. Sam Lewisohn, head of the planning committee at Miami Copper and president of the AMA in 1923, would declare four years later that although employment management in and of itself could accomplish nothing, the notion that "the personnel specialist should have jurisdiction co-ordinate with the man in charge of production or finance" was wrong. "In the few establishments in which this was tried it proved impractical from an administrative point of view .... The management of human relations must rest in the hands of line officials —the regular production executives." He urged managers to become more educated in personnel methods as an alternative to hiring personnel managers with real authority.[109]

Personnel managers and employment experts, whether male or female, were on the defensive in the 1920s. Their earlier associations with Progressive reform and "sentimental" values in general were an embarrassment to a business community that now prided itself on increases in productivity, the squelching of union activism, and a hard-nosed approach to keeping costs down.[110] Personnel managers tried to counteract their isolation from the more tough-minded business professions by insisting they had abandoned any pretense of welfare work and social reform. They were, instead, scientific managers organizing human materials in ways that would make them more efficient.

The more masculine field of business administration reinforced this point of view. In his widely used textbook on *Business Administration* (1921), L. C. Marshall of the University of Chicago contrasted the fancy that "attention to personnel problems in modern industry is justified as a means of improving human relationships" with the more concrete expectation that such attention was designed primarily to earn a profit. "It is highly important to utilize properly the persons who work with things in modern business .... It pays; ... it yields gains over and above the costs; and ... the manager should therefore engage in personnel activities as a business proposition." Government administration expert W. E. Mosher, a colleague and supporter of Mary Parker Follett, asserted that although the personnel manager should be "an executive clothed with real authority," he should not "be a 'welfare worker,' whose business it is to give expression to the humane and philanthropic instincts of management. Although he may do this in some organizations, this is not his proper calling .... He is a technical specialist, who has made a scientific study of the characteristics and capacities of the human part of the machinery of production. Where successful, he measures his success in terms of increased efficiency."[111]

But in 1929 Millicent Pond, employment manager at Scovill Manufacturing, continued to define personnel management quite differently and to incorporate the human relations school in her description: "the psychology of management must go beyond matters of job standardization, rate-setting, and the general welfare of employees .... It must ... set itself the goal of the maximum adjustment of human relations and utilization of human powers within its jurisdiction."[112] Pond's work at Scovill since 1923 had focused on developing training programs for tool makers and business machine operators. She had also devised tests that would measure aptitude and progress for internal promotion. She published her work in the *Journal of Personnel Research*. John Goss, Pond's employer, served as a vice president of the Personnel Research Federation in 1929. But Scovill never regained its World War I prosperity, and there was so little labor turnover at the brass factory by the late 1920s that Pond's internal promotion programs were of little help to employees. As the Great Depression approached and Scovill's profits declined, the training programs were scrapped, and Pond became, for all intents and purposes, the office manager of the employment office. In 1942 she left Scovill Manufacturing and went to work for the War Department and then the Connecticut State Department of Labor. Scovill was about to enter a rocky period with its manufacturing workers, who saw John Goss as the epitome of slave-driving management. When costs were too high, real attention to the human factor was out of the question—at least to management. In an atmosphere where the raw reality of the employer-employee relationship was all too clearly exposed, the techniques of personnel managers proved to be superfluous.

Nonetheless, the positions of Marshall and Pond continued to represent the confused debate within personnel management literature over how best to mobilize the human factor in industry. The "liberal" (read feminine) camp, drawing on psychology, welfare work, and the ideas of human relations thinkers like Mary Parker Follett and Elton Mayo, stressed tapping into the cooperative attitudes and psychological desires of workers to create more smoothly working and socially responsible bureaucracies. A more "conservative" (read masculine) camp, harking back to strict interpretations of Taylorism and the gospel of cost accounting, continued to see rationalization of the employment process, token welfare programs, and a straightforward wage-labor system as the only legitimate functions of personnel management.[113] The feminine tendencies of personnel management remained suspect. Not only were individual women considered to be polluters of masculine hegemony in the corporation, but ideas associated with women were also insidious and even life-threatening to the vitality of organizations dominated by men.[114]

In some sense the conservatives were right about the subversiveness, in both gender and class terms, of the liberal position. In turning "their attention to the attitudes and feelings of employees," Reinhard Bendix once observed, "American employers and managers ... were inadvertently questioning the basis of their own authority."[115] What kept the liberals in the game were the psychologists employed as personnel staff, a stable contingent of middle-aged personnel workers and academics who had formed their political views in the Progressive period, and the repeated failure of the conservatives to achieve success in their own terms. Elton Mayo's experiments with the effect of lighting on workers at the Hawthorne plant of the Western Electric Company in 1924 underscored how little managers really knew about human interaction in the workplace and its effect on production. The sense that there was "something more to it" hovers over most of the personnel management literature of the twenties. It was not until the Hawthorne experiments that the liberals finally had demonstrable proof of what that something more might be.[116]

As for women, many of those who succeeded in personnel management after 1921 did so as experts in office management. This is not surprising; personnel management was used most extensively and sophisticatedly in firms that employed large numbers of nonindustrial workers.[117] Both the numbers of clerical and sales workers and the proportion of these who were women were increasing in the 1920s. Some of these women office management experts remained committed to versions of personnel management with a feminist consciousness—providing vocational guidance, furthering upward mobility by promotion, and using management positions to open more responsible work to women. But these enthusiasms could rarely be advocated openly. The precarious position of the small numbers of women in higher levels of management, the falling from official favor of the liberal position in personnel management, and the escalating concern over the costs of employing "nonproductive" (clerical and administrative) workers were bound to mute the feminist platform.

It was not so much that women welfare and employment management workers in the 1920s differed significantly from those who had preceded them in the Progressive years as that the climate of reform and feminist consciousness that informed the earlier years was now gone. The precarious alliance between Taylorism and Progressive reform, the labor shortages of the war, and the intervention of the federal government had allowed someone like Mary Gilson to voice her feminist and reformist views in the teens; in the 1920s these circumstances had changed.

Gilson's fate after 1920 is all too instructive. In a burst of enthusiasm Richard Feiss decided to build a new factory in Cleveland to house the anticipated gains in demand for men's clothing during World War I. But by the time the plant opened in 1921 the men's clothing industry suffered a headlong decline. Plunged into near financial ruin, Feiss suffered a nervous breakdown in 1924. He was forced out by company directors, who now suspected his progressive methods of putting the business in jeopardy. He and Gilson both left Clothcraft, and many of Gilson's programs were dismantled. In a swan-song appearance before the Taylor Society in 1924, Gilson outlined the contributions Taylorism had made to personnel management, but insisted that it had never really been implemented fairly with regard to women: "Many people have applied scientific management methods as far as 'the efficient use of men and materials' is concerned, but I have yet to be overwhelmed with many evidences of a broad and generous viewpoint concerning the efficient use of women in the matter of training and opportunity for advancement. A reservoir of pride and competence in workmanship has yet to be tapped when 'equal opportunity' becomes more than a pretty phrase."

Gilson left management and entered the academy. She wanted to study economics at Harvard, but was told by Dean Donham of the Harvard Business School that she would have to attend sex-segregated classes at Radcliffe; even more insulting, it seemed, was the rule that men could study in the library until 10 P.M. but women had to leave by 6. She did her Ph.D. work at Columbia instead. In the late 1920s she became an expert on the effects of unemployment, contributed to the growing support for government legislation to provide unemployment benefits for workers, and in 1931 joined the faculty at the University of Chicago.[118]

Gilson wrote to Elton Mayo in 1940, recounted her own attempt to enter the Harvard Business School, and inquired whether women were still barred. About to review *Management and the Worker*, a book by Mayo's colleagues Roethlisberger and Dickson, and at work on her autobiography, Gilson could not resist a feminist jibe: "I can't help chuckling over the naive statement on p. 245 that men comment more than women about advancement. Knowing that women are not permitted to hold positions as forewomen at Western Electric and knowing a few things about the attitude toward a 'sky's the limit' policy for women it seems to me they would quite naturally refrain from commenting on the impossible."

In his reply, Mayo, who usually espoused the more feminine side of personnel management, demonstrated that position did not necessarily lead to support for women's equality. He confirmed Harvard's continued exclusion of women, but did admit that he had allowed his own daughter to serve tea at a graduate seminar and to stay for the discussion. He argued that women should continue to take separate classes at Radcliffe, partly because "I as a youngster would have found it exceedingly difficult to give close attention if there had been a very attractive girl seated anywhere near me." Gilson's emotional response indicated just how deeply the Harvard slight had been felt, and just how evocative the conjunction of the Roethlisberger and Dickson book and the old wound was. In this second letter she criticized the drafters of the Hawthorne experiments at Western Electric for their inattention to both women and organized labor and suggested that she might have, if asked, been able to expand the Harvard researchers' perspective, "much" of which she thought was "painfully obvious." It must have been apparent to her that if she had gone to Harvard in 1924, she might very well have participated in the Hawthorne experiments. The agreement between men of the academy and men of the corpora-

tion to exclude women—as workers, as managers, as theoreti-
cians—had never been more clear.[119]

Gilson's unequivocal feminism is appealing to those in the present looking back at her work. But she and other scientific management enthusiasts of the teens and twenties, both women and men,
had failed to see the darker possibilities of the drive to organize the
human factor in the American workplace and how it might evolve
when efficiency and cost accounting once again took the upper
hand. Because profit-making was the ultimate goal of American
business, and because male-dominated inner sanctums of business
managed the implementation of that goal, most middle-class
women would be as likely as working people to face exclusion.
Without a feminist movement that came from below as well as
from above, women like Gilson and Pond were likely to be stranded
on desert islands in a sea of male corporate culture.

NOTES

1. The 1918 survey was conducted by the Intercollegiate Bureau of Occupations (IBO), precursor of the Bureau of Vocational Information. These
quotes are from questionnaires returned to the IBO by employment managers and welfare workers. BVI, folders 203-8.

2. The first five requests for information were, in order of preference,
home economics, secretarial work, social service, teaching, and modern
language work. Several other categories, akin to personnel management,
were listed separately, including psychology, vocational work, economic
and commercial research, and the vaguest of all the categories, "industry."
BVI News Bulletin [*BVINB*], Oct. 1, 1922, 2, 4. This information was also
summarized in *Personnel Journal* [*PJ*] 1 (1922-23): 243.

3. An advice book by Agnes F. Perkins, *Vocations for the Trained
Woman: Opportunites other than Teaching* (New York: Longmans, Green,
1910) mentions welfare work but not employment management. After the
war, occupational advice books endorsed both fields for women. See
Elizabeth Kemper Adams, *Women Professional Workers: A Study made for
the Women's Educational and Industrial Union* (Chautauqua: Chautauqua
Press, 1921), 185-200; Miriam Simons Leuck, *Fields of Work for Women*
(New York: D. Appleton, 1929), 74-75; and Catharine Filene, ed., *Careers
for Women: New Ideas, New Methods, New Opportunities—to Fit a New
World* (Boston: Houghton Mifflin, 1934), 169-73.

4. Ida M. Tarbell, "The New Place of Women in Industry, III," *Industrial
Management* [*IM*] 60 (Dec. 1920): 65; BVI, folders 203-8.

5. Adams, *Women Professional Workers*, 185-86.

6. Janice Law Trecker, "Sex, Science and Education," *American Quarterly* 26 (1974): 352-66; Hamilton Cravens, *The Triumph of Evolution:*

American Scientists and the Heredity-Environment Controversy, 1900-1914 (Philadelphia: University of Pennsylvania Press, 1978), 56-86.

7. The definitive work on women and experimental psychology is Rosalind Rosenberg, *Beyond Separate Spheres: Intellectual Roots of Modern Feminism* (New Haven: Yale University Press, 1982), 55-83. The sympathy of the early experimental psychologists for women may have had deeper cultural roots in religion and philosophy. Most early psychology departments in universities and colleges emerged from philosophy and theology. William James's background as the son of an eccentric Swedenborgian transcendentalist is well known. James's original training was in philosophy, and he saw no inherent barriers between religion, philosophy, and psychology. Another founder of American psychology, Walter Dill Scott, trained to be a teacher and a missionary in China but decided to study psychology in Germany instead. Edmund C. Lynch, "Walter Dill Scott: Pioneer Industrial Psychologist," *Business History Review [BHR]* 42 (Summer 1968): 155-57, 162; Cravens, *Triumph of Evolution,* 59. The "feminization" of American religion had been noted since the early nineteenth century. Ministers were assumed to be both in league with women and abnormally under their influence. As twentieth-century heirs of religion, psychologists may have been perceived to have these same propensities. On the feminization of American religion, see Ann Douglas, *The Feminization of American Culture* (New York: Avon Books, 1978), 17-142, and Nancy F. Cott, *The Bonds of Womanhood: "Woman's Sphere" in New England* (New Haven: Yale University Press, 1977), 126-59.

8. Walter V. Bingham recalled that when he first went to Carnegie Institute of Technology the chief concerns of the program were vocational guidance and courses in psychology for women students in education and social work. "Psychology Applied," *Scientific Monthly* 16 (Feb. 1923): 141-59.

9. Thomas Woody, *A History of Women's Education in the United States* (New York: Octagon Books, 1966), 2: 334-38; "Vocational Aspects of Psychology," *BVINB,* April 1, 1923, 1-2, 6.

10. The implications of Thompson's and Stetter Hollingworth's work are carefully explored by Rosenberg, *Beyond Separate Spheres,* 55-113. For an analysis of the importance of their work for the women's movement of the teens, see Margaret W. Rossiter, *Women Scientists in America: Struggles and Strategies to 1940* (Baltimore: Johns Hopkins University Press, 1982), 100-115.

11. Leta Stetter Hollingworth, "The Vocational Aptitudes of Women," in H. L. Hollingworth, *Vocational Psychology: Its Problems and Methods,* (New York: D. Appleton, 1916), 244.

12. Alice Bryan and Edwin G. Boring, "Women in American Psychology: Prolegomenon," *Psychological Bulletin* 41 (1944): 447-48; Rossiter, *Women Scientists in America,* 136-37; Betty M. Vetter and Eleanor Babco, *Professional Women and Minorities: A Manpower Data Resource Service,*

5th ed. (Washington, D.C.: Scientific Manpower Commission, 1984), 250. On women with graduate degrees and their difficulties in obtaining academic positions, see Barbara Solomon, *In the Company of Educated Women: A History of Women and Higher Education in America* (New Haven: Yale University Press, 1985), 134-38. Although eighty-two women were members of the American Psychological Association in 1924, and despite the fact that membership required a Ph.D., published research, and active participation in psychological work, only thirty-three of the eighty-two taught in colleges and universities. See "Women Psychologists," *BVINB*, June 15, 1924, 92.

13. On the history of industrial psychology, see Morris S. Viteles, *Industrial Psychology* (New York: W.W. Norton, 1932), 44-48; Bingham, "Psychology Applied," 141-59; and Loren Baritz, *The Servants of Power: A History of the Use of Social Science in American Industry* (New York: John Wiley and Sons, 1965), 21-41.

14. This is, of course, only a partial list. See the *Journal of Personnel Research*, [*JPR*] *Annals*, *Personnel*, and publications of the American Management Association for more published research of women psychologists.

15. The best general account of mental testing remains Cravens, *The Triumph of Evolution*, 224-65. Also see Michael M. Sokal, ed., *Psychological Testing and American Society, 1890-1930* (New Brunswick: Rutgers University Press, 1987) although this book's essays completely ignore both Helen Bradford Thompson and Leta Stetter Hollingworth.

16. However, the work of a number of women psychologists and sociologists in the teens and twenties refuted the elitist and racist findings of early intelligence testers. Martha Maclear of Howard University tested African-American children in public schools in Washington, D.C., and claimed that IQ tests were "culture bound" and not a true measure of actual intelligence. Augusta Bronner studied juvenile girls and concluded that family and social experiences in childhood, not subnormal intelligence, were most clearly the causes of antisocial and deviant behavior. For these and other examples, see Cravens, *The Triumph of Evolution*, 237, 239, 243, 254, and Rosenberg, *Beyond Separate Spheres*, 82-88. Rosenberg reports that after her marriage, Helen Thompson Woolley did research with working-class children in Cincinnati and concluded that "native intelligence was but one factor in personal success; other factors, such as ambition, general appearance, manner, dress, social ease, and personal persistence . . . were also important." Woolley was an ardent suffragist and in 1921 "led an exodus from a professional meeting in a leading hotel when the admission of a black member was questioned."

17. For example, H. L. Hollingworth argued that "the employment of feeble-minded women as domestics, factory operatives, laundresses, clerks and nursemaids constitutes not only a nuisance to the general public, but a real source of inefficiency and danger to the community." *Vocational Psychology*, 77-78.

18. The classic text of the vocational guidance movement is Meyer Bloomfield, *The Vocational Guidance of Youth* (Boston: Houghton Mifflin, 1911); also see Cyril Curtis Ling, *The Management of Personnel Relations: History and Origins* (Homewood: Richard Irwin, 1965), 246-50, and Sanford M. Jacoby, *Employing Bureaucracy: Managers, Unions, and the Transformation of Work in American Industry, 1900-1945* (New York: Columbia University Press, 1985), 65-98.

19. What little printed information about Follett there is can be found in Henry C. Metcalf and Lyn Urwick, eds., *Dynamic Administration: The Collected Papers of Mary Parker Follett* (New York: Harper and Brothers, n.d. [1941]), 9-20, and Lyn Urwick, *The Golden Book of Management: A Historical Record of the Life and Work of Seventy Pioneers* (London: Newman Neame, 1956), 132-37. A full biography of Follett by Joan Tonn is forthcoming from Oxford University Press. Tonn graciously shared information from several of her chapters on Follett's work in Boston with me. The men of the Boston vocational guidance movement, Bloomfield in particular, have received most scholarly attention, and like so many of the women in the early history of personnel management Follett rarely gets credit for its formation. The development of an analysis that will allow for the inability of women to "lead" and "speak for" movements like vocational guidance but nonetheless to "influence" them significantly will have to be developed before Follett, Gilson, Bills, and other important women in personnel management become incorporated effectively.

20. Mary Parker Follett, "The Social Centre and the Democratic Ideal," unpublished speech delivered at the Boston Ford Hall Forum, Dec. 14, 1913, 10-11. The Vocational Guidance Bureau also invited those responsible for hiring employees to form the first employment managers' association in 1911. Metcalf and Urwick, eds., *Dynamic Administration*, 26.

21. Mary Parker Follett, "Midnight Oil in the Schools," *Boston Evening Transcript*, April 1, 1914, 20. Krug notes that vocational counselors in the Boston public schools dramatically increased the number of boys and girls applying to the commercial and vocational high schools. Edward A. Krug, *The Shaping of the American High School* (Madison: University of Wisconsin Press, 1969), 1: 241-43.

22. Mary Parker Follett, *The New State* (Boston: Longmans, Green, 1918); *Creative Experience* (Boston: Longmans, Green, 1924); and "The Illusion of Final Authority," *Bulletin of the Taylor Society* [TSB] 11 (Dec. 1926): 243-50. Metcalf published a number of Follett's lectures in his *Scientific Foundations of Business Administration* (Baltimore: Williams and Wilkins, 1925). Metcalf and Urwick, *Dynamic Administration*, 24, thought that Follett's influence had been far-reaching and put her work on a par "with the pioneering work of Frederick W. Taylor."

Dennison's 1929 speech referring to Follett and her lectures for Metcalf is entitled "Fundamental Objectives of Business Management," and can be found in the Henry S. Dennison Papers, carton 1, Library of the Harvard Business School.

Follett may have had more immediate influence on the actual practice of management in England than in the United States, although her emphasis on the psychology of management, individual motivation, and the dynamics of group interaction would eventually come to dominate formal theories of management and would gain new practical significance in the United States, mainly as a result of the Hawthorne experiments in the 1920s and the work of Elton Mayo at the Harvard Business School. Judith A. Merkle, *Management and Ideology: The Legacy of the International Scientific Management Movement* (Berkeley: University of California Press, 1980), 236-37. William Greaebner found frequent references to Follett's work in what he defines as the literature of social engineering and says that she was one of its "most influential theorists." *The Engineering of Consent: Democracy and Authority in Twentieth-Century America* (Madison: University of Wisconsin Press, 1987), 71.

Whether Elton Mayo was influenced by Follett's ideas is a topic for further exploration. Mayo knew Lyn Urwick, a promoter of Follett, personally, and had many connections in the "softer side" of the British and European personnel management community. Urwick was director of the International Management Bureau in Geneva, and his bureau was supported by E. A. Filene through 1932. Urwick published an early monograph on the Hawthorne experiments, and Mayo described his bureau as conducting "careful painstaking inquiry into the present facts of industrial organization" and contrasted it to the more mechanical kinds of scientific management practiced in England. Typewritten copy of memorandum, "Urwick, Orr and Partners," circa 1939, Elton Mayo Papers, folder 1.077, Library of the Harvard Business School.

23. *BVINB*, Oct. 1, 1922, 1, 4; also see "The Bureau of Vocational Information," *BVINB*, Aug. 15, 1923, 1-3, 6. Hirth presented a report on women in chemistry at the first meeting of the Personnel Research Federation in March 1921. *Monthly Labor Review [MLR]* 14 (June 1922): 50.

24. On the coevolution of welfare work and personnel management in industry, see Henry Eilburt, "The Development of Personnel Management in the United States," *Business History Review [BHR]* 33 (Autumn 1959): 345-64; Norman J. Wood, "Industrial Relations Policies of American Management, 1900-1933," *BHR* 34 (Winter 1960): 403-20; Ling, *Management of Personnel Relations*, 73-80; Daniel Nelson, *Managers and Workers: Origins of the New Factory System in the United States, 1880-1920* (Madison: University of Wisconsin Press, 1975), 101-22; and Jacoby, *Employing Bureaucracy*, 39-64. For a brief but interesting discussion of welfare capitalism and its connections to "scientific Progressivism," see David B. Danbom, *"The World of Hope": Progressives and the Struggle for an Ethical Public Life* (Philadelphia: Temple University Press, 1987), 164-71.

25. On Patterson, Dennison, and the Filene brothers, see Edward

Berkowitz and Kim McQuaid, eds., *Creating the Welfare State: The Political Economy of Twentieth-Century Reform* (New York: Praeger, 1980), 11-24. Dennison was one of the first manufacturers to institute unemployment insurance, and by 1908 had established a bonus plan for employee suggestions, a clinic, a cafeteria, a library, a social club, and a savings bank. In 1900, after Dennison visited Patterson's factory in Toledo, he concluded a handwritten set of observations by saying: "To my mind one of the soundest features of their plan is the absence of pure philanthropy. Wholesale, indiscriminate charity harms both giver and receiver . . . . Their Plan is founded on economy, an economy which looks ahead for returns, and this is the only principle which can accomplish anything." Memorandum by Henry S. Dennison, 7, Dennison Papers, carton 1, Library of the Harvard Business School.

26. For on-the-spot accounts of many of these early welfare programs see Budgett Meakin, *Model Factories and Villages: Ideal Conditions of Labour and Housing* (New York: Garland Publishing, 1985).

27. Scott's policies and the Seroco Mutual Benefit Association program of Sears and Roebuck are described in Louise Asher and Edith Heal, *Send No Money* (Chicago: Argus Books, 1942), 128-42 and Boris Emmet and John E. Jeuck, *Catalogues and Counters: A History of Sears, Roebuck and Company* (Chicago: University of Chicago Press, 1950), 141-46.

28. See Susan Porter Benson, *Counter Cultures: Saleswomen, Managers, and Customers in American Department Stores, 1890-1940* (Urbana: University of Illinois Press, 1986), 142-46 for a discussion of welfare work in department stores.

29. Walter J. Matherly cites the Lowell mill experiment as the first case of welfare work in America, "The Evolution of Personnel Management," *IM* 72 (Oct. 1926): 257. Daniel Nelson observes that welfare programs at the turn of the century often entailed different kinds of programs for male and female workers. *Managers and Workers*, 118-19.

30. Typewritten extract from "Welfare Work by a Big Flour Mill," *American Miller*, March 1, 1913, BVI, folder 203. The welfare work at Ballard and Ballard was particularly controlling and included a men's clubroom to substitute for the local saloon.

31. Eilburt, "Development of Personnel Management," 350; Nelson, *Managers and Workers*, 111. Nelson found more than twenty of these women in welfare departments by 1906.

32. Gertrude Beeks, "The New Profession," *National Civic Federation Review*, Feb. 1, 1905. On the importance of the National Civic Federation in welfare work, see Ling, *Management of Personnel Relations*, 362.

33. BVI, folders 203-8.

34. Author unknown, "Women as Labor Managers (about 1921)," typewritten manuscript, BVI, folder 199.

35. Letter from Urith Pope Galt to Emma P. Hirth, April 2, 1918, BVI, folder 203. Galt's questionnaire for the 1918 BVI study indicated that she

had been employed at Ballard and Ballard since 1895, making her the longest-employed welfare worker of the nineteen who replied.

36. BVI, folder 203.

37. Ibid.

38. Eleanor Gilbert (Ann Rosenblatt), *The Ambitious Woman in Business* (New York: Funk and Wagnalls, 1916), 365-66.

39. Miriam Simons Leuck, *Fields of Work for Women* (New York: D. Appleton, 1929), 75.

40. Richard Edwards calls these methods "bureaucratic control." *Contested Terrain: The Transformation of the Workplace in the Twentieth Century* (New York: Basic Books, 1979), 132-53; also see David Montgomery, *The Fall of the House of Labor: The Workplace, the State, and American Labor Activism, 1865-1925* (Cambridge: Cambridge University Press, 1987), 236-44.

41. For an account of Taylor's position on welfare work and personnel management, see Daniel Nelson, *Frederick W. Taylor and the Rise of Scientific Management* (Madison: University of Wisconsin Press, 1980), 44-45. On the separate and sometimes antagonistic development of welfare work and Taylorism, see Daniel Nelson and Stuart Campbell, "Taylorism vs. Welfare Work in American Industry: H. L. Gantt and the Bancrofts," *BHR* 46 (Spring 1972): 1-16.

42. M. M. Jones, formerly a director of personnel at Edison, underscored the overhead cost of the new techniques when he reviewed Eugene Benge's influential text *Standard Practice in Personnel Work*: "The aftereffect of reading the book is one of strong apprehension. To contemplate the mass of system and red tape which industry must struggle with in order to handle properly the administration of personnel work is disquieting. When we add to this the mass of system existing in other management functions we may well wonder if industry can stand the cost of so much overhead." *Management Engineering* 1 (July 1921): 62.

43. In an analysis of articles indexed in the *Reader's Guide to Periodical Literature* between 1905 and 1930, Hornell Hart found that those covering religion and philosophy were on the decline, and that scientific topics of all sorts were on the increase. While radio, aeronautics, automobiles, motion pictures, and electricity were heavily represented in the commercial application category, Hart found scientific management a significant enough topic to be listed separately in his table. Interest in scientific management peaked between 1915 and 1921, but the topic was still widely discussed at the end of the 1920s. Hornell Hart, "Changing Social Attitudes and Interests," in *Recent Social Trends in the United States: Report of the President's Research Committee on Social Trends* (York, Pa.: Whittlesey House, 1923), 381-402.

44. Ernest M. Hopkins, "The Supervisor of Personnel," *TSB* 1 (Jan. 1915): 9, 12. Also see Richard A. Feiss, "Personal Relationship as a Basis of Scientific Management," *TSB* 1 (Nov. 1915): 5. For an example of ways in

which the language of Hopkins and Feiss had entered the thinking of some business executives, see the summary of E. K. Hall's speech before the Pittsburgh Convention of the National Personnel Association in 1922. Hall was a vice president of American Telephone and Telegraph. "Management's Responsibility for and Opportunities in the Personnel Job," *JPR* 1 (1922-23): 462.

45. Eugene J. Benge, *Standard Practice in Personnel Work* (New York: H. W. Wilson, 1920), 4, 7.

46. Henry P. Kendall, "A Decade's Development in Management: Trends and Results of Scientific Management," *TSB* 9 (April 1924): 55.

47. Ida B. Tarbell, "Making the Most of Men," *TSB* 10 (Jan. 1925): 80, reprinted from *Saturday Review of Literature*, Oct. 25, 1924. Tarbell discusses her visits to factories between 1912 and 1916 and her perceptions of Taylorism in *All in the Day's Work: An Autobiography* (New York: Macmillan, 1939), 280-96.

48. Sue Ainslie Clark and Edith Wyatt, *Making Both Ends Meet: The Income and Outlay of New York Working Girls* (New York: Macmillan, 1911), 268.

49. Josephine Goldmark, *Fatigue and Efficiency: A Study in Industry* (1912, repr. New York: Survey Associates, 1913), 192, 200. Goldmark remained critical of what she saw as the worst propensities of applied Taylorism: speeded-up work and its attendant strain, monotony, and long hours.

50. "The Women's Industrial Conference," *TSB* 11 (Feb. 1926): 40-42.

51. The Industrial Code evolved from one imposed by the ordnance department of the army on its manufacturers during World War I. Still in the process of revision on the eve of the depression, it seems to have dropped out of sight completely in the 1930s. See "Industrial Employment Code," *TSB* 16 (Feb. 1931): 19-24.

52. "Industrial Employment Code," 30.

53. This account of Gilson's life is summarized from her lively autobiography, Mary Barnett Gilson, *What's Past Is Prologue: Reflections on My Industrial Experience* (New York: Harper and Brothers, 1940), 1-25.

54. Gilson, *What's Past Is Prologue*, 34-46.

55. Ibid., 53-57.

56. The evidence for connections among these individuals remains circumstantial, but Feiss's welfare programs bore such a resemblance to those of Filene and Dennison that the likelihood of their collaboration remains compelling. Compare Henry S. Dennison and John S. Kerr, "The Selection, Assignment and Training of Workers," *Personnel* 7 (Aug. 1930): 42-51 to Gilson's and Feiss's discriptions of employment management at Clothcraft.

As usual, Follett's influence, if there was any, appears in shadow, despite the striking similarity of Feiss's notions about "personal responsibility" to her ideas. Gilson had undoubtedly heard of both Henry Dennison and

Mary Parker Follett while she was in Boston, but it is unclear exactly when she first met them. In her autobiography she recalls but does not date "a thrilling weekend I spent with him [Henry Dennison] and Mrs. Dennison in their hospitable New England home. Mary Follett was there and we had a lively discussion of the new state which might evolve out of the current chaos, when healthy and creative industrial relations would be basic to a sound political organism." Henry Dennison was president of the Taylor Society in 1920, and he was succeeded by his vice president, Richard A. Feiss, in 1921. When Feiss left Clothcraft in 1925 he became a consultant for the Dennison Company in Boston.

57. For an account of Feiss's reforms and his collaboration with Gilson, see Charles D. Wrege and Bernice M. Lattanzio, "'The Human Side of Enterprise'—Forty-Five Years Before McGregor: The Work of Richard A. Feiss, Early Explorer in Human Relations," typewritten paper (Saugus, 1977), Feiss Papers, accession folder, Labor Management Documentation Center, Cornell University, Ithaca, N.Y.; and Bernice Lattanzio, "Mary B. Gilson: Personnel Management Pioneer from the 'Oaks of Wellesley,'" Feiss Papers, box 4, folder 16.

58. It will probably be impossible to determine exactly which changes instituted after Gilson came to Clothcraft were the result of her ideas, Feiss's ideas, or their joint collaboration. Surely Gilson deserves more in the history of scientific management than to be described as a mere appendage of Feiss. Although he quotes from her autobiography, *Managers and Workers*, 77, Nelson does not even refer to her by name; she is instead anonymously described as "a welfare secretary." Nelson also omits any mention of the feminist content of Gilson's work. Gilson receives more attention from Jacoby, *Employing Bureaucracy*, 50-51, but comes across as a welfare-worker busybody, and, again, the feminist intentions of some of her measures are ignored. All of Feiss's major speeches and essays on connections between scientific management and employee relations were made from 1913 to 1924 during the period he employed Gilson. Although Feiss did prepare several papers after 1925 they were more narrowly focused on the relationship between management and proper engineering methods.

59. Gilson charged that after World War I the director of the American Management Association "and others were responsible for turning the clock back a considerable distance in regard to the development of functionalization in the selection and training of workers as well as in safeguarding discharge, because of their blind zeal in defending what they called foremen's 'rights.' . . . But the American Management group at that time had few members who understood or cared to labor diligently to understand Taylor's ideas." *What's Past Is Prologue*, 101-2. Her ideas on the extension of Taylorism to personnel work were presented in Mary B. Gilson, "Scientific Management and Personnel Work," *TSB* 9 (Feb. 1924): 39-50.

60. The best descriptions of the Gilson employment and welfare programs are in Gilson, *What's Past Is Prologue*, 60-107, Feiss, "Personal Relationship as Basis of Scientific Management," and Mary Gilson, "The Relation of Home Conditions to Industrial Efficiency," *Annals* 65 (May 1916): 277-89. Feiss's elaborate statistics on reduced labor turnover at Clothcraft are analyzed in his "Personal Relationships as the Basis of Scientific Management," 13-14; also see Gilson, "Work of the Employment and Service Department of the Clothcraft Shops," Bureau of Labor Statistics Bulletin no. 227, Washington, D.C.: GPO, 1917, 1-14.

61. The correspondence between Taylor and Feiss is in the Taylor Collection at the Stevens Institute of Technology, Hoboken, N.J., and a summary of it, "Manuscript Material Relating to Richard A. Feiss on file in the Taylor Collection," can be found in the Feiss Papers, box 1, folder 2. In a letter to John Commons of Jan. 31, 1914, Taylor "states that of all the manufacturers: 'Mr. Feiss has the proper spirit of men who are making a success of Scientific Management.'"

Gilbreth was using conditions in the Feiss factory to oppose the Tavenner Bill at a 1916 Sagamore Sociological Conference, after a speech given by Feiss. Tavenner proposed to prohibit the use of scientific management techniques at government arsenals and workshops, where they had encountered stiff opposition. See Richard A. Feiss, "Personal Relationship in Business Administration," Sagamore Sociological Conference, Sagamore, N.Y., June 27-29, 1916, Feiss Papers, box 6, folder 4.

62. The Clothcraft guest book reads like a who's who of scientific management, personnel and office management, and women's social reform. Taylor visited shortly before his death in 1915. Other guests included Ida Tarbell, Lee Galloway, Morris L. Cooke, Walter Dill Scott, Henry S. Dennison, John R. Commons, Jane C. Williams of Plimpton Press, Florence Peterson, later head of the Women's Bureau but then a representative of Selby Shoe, Josephine Goldmark, and representatives of Equitable Life Insurance, the Industrial Commission of Ohio, Montgomery Ward, and Sears Roebuck. The guest book is in the Feiss Papers, box 6.

63. Gilson, *What's Past Is Prologue*, 99. Gilson discussed her program at Clothcraft to train women for supervisory positions in a letter to Emile J. Hutchinson, Oct. 23, 1917. BVI, folder 201.

64. Gilson, *What's Past Is Prologue*, 73-74.

65. John R. Commons thought Clothcraft's reform of its wage system was directly linked to lower labor turnover and greater job satisfaction among its women workers, but he also documented different pay rates for men and women at the firm. See "To the Men Who Sell Clothcraft Clothes," reprint of John R. Commons, *The Independent*, Nov. 6, 1920, Feiss papers, folder 7, box 4.

66. Gilson, "The Relation of Home Conditions to Industrial Efficiency."

67. Gilson, "Wages of Women in Industry (Part II)," *IM* 62 (July 1921): 41-42.

68. Gilson, "The Relation of Home Conditions to Industrial Efficiency," 284.

69. On internal promotion in department stores, see Benson, *Counter Cultures*, 163-65; Sarah Smith Malino, "Faces Across the Counter: A Social History of Female Department Store Employees, 1870-1920," Ph.D. diss., Columbia University, 1982, 225-36; and "Outline of Personnel Work at R.H. Macy and Co., Inc.," typewritten report, circa 1918. "The policy of the store," claimed this report, "is to develop from within." Originally in the BVI papers but evidently removed in the 1986-87 reorganization; copy in possession of the author. On life insurance firms, see Lawrence Washington, "Personnel Management of the Metropolitan Life Insurance Company," *IM* 62 (July 1921): 27-32.

For examples of training and promotion from factory to office work at Cheney Mills and Scovill Manufacturing, see "Employment Tests," *Scovill Bulletin [SB]*, Dec., 1926, 15-16; Millicent Pond, "The Value of Mental Tests," *SB*, Jan.-Feb. 1932, 11, 16-17, 20-21; and J. P. Lamb, "A Statistical Analysis of Personnel," American Management *Office Executive Series [AMAOES]* 21 (1926): 7. Pond began her article with the following "story": "'Mary's a darn good worker,' said the foreman of Mary's room in a modern factory. 'She's ambitious and faithful, always has her mind on her work, doesn't raise her head when people go by, is always on time, a good producer. Been with me a year. Now she says that she wants to do clerical work or typing, and by golly, I think she ought to have a chance!'"

70. "What Industry Means to Women," *IM* 60 (Nov. 1920): 4-5. See Gilson, "Wages of Women in Industry (Part I)," *IM* 62 (June 1921): 429-30. Gilson also defended piece rates, time and motion studies, and the Taylorist philosophy of a fair wage for a fair day's work.

71. Gilson, "Wages of Women in Industry," (Part II)," 39. Gilson did include race as a category in a similar statement in *Past Is Prologue*, 100.

72. See Edwards, *Contested Terrain*, especially 132-64.

73. Eugene J. Benge, "Transfer and Promotion Among Office Employees," AMAOES 1 (1924): 4.

74. Fannie M. Witherspoon and Anna Martin Crocker, *Opportunities for Women in the Municipal Civil Service of the City of New York* (New York: Intercollegiate Bureau of Occupations, 1918), and May B. Upshaw, *Woman's Place in Civil Service* (New York: Federation of Women's Civil Service Organizations, 1919), n.p. Upshaw's report contains summaries of the status of women employees in most civil service systems in the country in 1919.

75. Upshaw, *Woman's Place in Civil Service*.

76. Typewritten transcript of lecture by Anna Martin Crocker, March 28, 1916, 10, BVI, folder 21.

77. Bertha M. Nienberg, "Women in the Government Service," *Women's Bureau Bulletin [WBB]* 8 (1920).

78. W. E. Mosher, "A Federal Personnel Policy," *MLR* (July 1920): 11.

79. Herman Feldman, *A Personnel Program for the Federal Civil Service* (Washington, D.C.: GPO, 1931), 19.

80. Of course the ideal of a classification system with rationalized salary rates was easier to imagine than to establish. Follow-up legislation came in the form of the Welch Act of 1928, and Feldman concluded in 1931 that "while encouraging progress in personnel work has been made [in the federal civil service], a comprehensive program is still a matter of the future." *A Personnel Program for the Federal Civil Service*, 114.

81. Bertha M. Nienburg, "The Status of Women in the Government Service in 1925," *WBB* 53 (1926).

82. Lecture by Anna Martin Crocker, 10-11, BVI, folder 21.

83. Feldman, *A Personnel Program for the Federal Civil Service*, 237-38.

84. For example, in 1918 R. H. Macy had separate employment and training departments. While the employment department was in "full charge" of recruiting, testing and selecting employees, transfers, promotions, and dismissals, final authority was vested in a general manager, not a personnel director. New York Telephone, an employer of thirty-one thousand women in 1918, had an assistant to the vice president in charge of employment work at the New York City office but no welfare department. By 1921, the personnel management divison of Metropolitan Life Insurance was in charge of employment and placement, records of turnover, labor saving, position analyses, grades and salary increases, ratings, promotions, reductions, transfers, and dismissals. The company was also known for its elaborate welfare measures. Eugene Benge of the Atlantic Refining Company reported that employment functions for about a thousand salaried employees at that firm had been centralized in an Office Personnel Division in 1921 and that by 1925 there was no longer any question about its authority and efficiency. At Sears and Roebuck, while an efficient employment and training system had been set up in the teens at the main mail order plant in Chicago for clerks, there was no real personnel function at the top management level, and it was said that Julius Rosenwald "feared that a personnel department might become an autocratic agency exerting control over line departments as a result of the intimate relationship of the personnel department with employees." At Plimpton Press, on the other hand, a small book factory heavily influenced by Taylorist ideas, Jane C. Williams had the title of personnel manager and sat on the board of directors in a policymaking role. Robert Lovett's survey of sixty-seven firms in 1923 showed that the majority of personnel departments reported to managers or vice presidents and rarely to the president or board of directors. These personnel systems are discussed in "Outline of Personnel Work at R. H. Macy and Co., Inc.," typewritten report, circa 1918, and "Brief Report of Employment Departments of Local Companies and Manufacturers (NYC)," circa 1918, BVI, folder 200; Washington, "Personnel Management of the Metropolitan Life Insurance Company," 27-32; Eugene J. Benge,

"Selecting the Salaried Employee," *IM* 69 (May 1925): 279-83; Emmet and Jeuck, *Catalogues and Counters*, 547-48; Robert F. Lovett, "Present Tendencies in Personnel Practice," *IM* 65 (June 1923): 327-33; also see Magnus W. Alexander, "Hiring and Firing: Its Economic Waste and How to Avoid It," *Annals* 65 (May 1916): 128-44.

85. The evolution of personnel work in individual firms before 1925 is discussed by Daniel A. Wren, "The Origins of Industrial Psychology and Sociology," in *Classics of Personnel Management*, ed. Thomas H. Patten Jr. (Oak Park: Moore Publishing, 1979), 4-11; Nelson, *Managers and Workers*, 148-56; and Jacoby, *Employing Bureaucracy*, 199-206. An attempt to compare personnel management literature with personnel practice is made in Gerald E. Kahler and Alton C. Johnson, *The Development of Personnel Administration, 1923-1945*, monograph no. 3 (Madison: Graduate School of Business, 1971). Kahler and Johnson found (12) that centralized employment was the most common feature of personnel work in the 1920s.

One problem with these accounts is that they focus on manufacturing firms and exclude public utilities, department stores, insurance firms, mail order houses, and civil service employers. Although not based on a systematic comparison of individual firms, my own impression of personnel work in the 1920s is that personnel management made the largest strides in establishments with large numbers of clerks, salespeople, salaried employees, and, because these tended to coincide, in firms with large numbers of women workers. Not only does Jacoby not consider sectors in which many women worked, but he also does not consider women workers at all on the grounds that they "accounted for only a small fraction of the manufacturing labor force." *Employing Bureaucracy*, 10. Although this may be true of raw totals of workers in manufacturing, the importance of women workers in certain kinds of manufacturing can hardly be disputed. This exclusion seems even more curious given the possible link between the origins of welfare work, the presence of women workers in manufacturing establishments, and the growing number of clerks in manufacturing, many of whom were women.

86. Questionnaires returned by male employment and welfare workers in the 1918 IBO survey, BVI, folders 203-4. A "well-known industrial engineer" quoted in a YWCA report thought "that where women are employed to any extent, a well-equipped woman should be in charge of the personnel work for them, and I invariably make this recommendation to the firms I deal with." Young Women's Christian Association, "Executive and Technical Women in Industry: Survey of Factories, 1919-1920," microfilm, Schlesinger Library, Radcliffe College; also see Ida M. Wilson, unidentified newspaper clipping, circa 1918, BVI, folder 513.

87. BVI, folders 203-4.

88. Letter from Mary B. Gilson to Emma P. Hirth, March 28, 1918, BVI, folder 201. Maurine Wiener Greenwald describes the Ordnance Department as the "greatest single industrial organization in the United States"

during World War I. *Women, War, and Work: The Impact of World War I on Women Workers in the United States* (Westport: Greenwood Press, 1980), 58.

89. Gilson, *What's Past Is Prologue*, 167.

90. News of Gilson's employment course was released by the Committee on Public Information on July 19, 1918 with the headline, "War Work of Women," BVI, folder 513; also see a typewritten summary of the "War Emergency Courses in Employment Management" (1918). Originally in BVI collection but evidently discarded in 1986 reorganization; copy in posssession of the author. For a description of the employment course at Bryn Mawr, see "Bryn Mawr Asked to Train Women to Be Supervisors," *Bryn Mawr College News*, May 30, 1918.

A 1942 survey of women in personnel work concluded that World War I had played a significant role in creating opportunities for those currently holding jobs. Although one woman had been employed in personnel work since 1907, the median number of years of experience in the group was seventeen years, meaning most had taken their first jobs in the field in the teens and early twenties. One woman specifically stated that she had been assigned to her present work "because of experience with Mary Gilson twenty-five years ago." Marion E. Owens, "Women Personnel Executives," *PJ* 20 (March 1942): 298-316. Ida Tarbell reported on Gilson's role in wartime training programs in "The New Place of Women in Industry (VI): The New Industrial Professions," *IM* 62 (Aug. 1921): 106-8.

91. Ella V. Price, a former accountant and statistician, had become employment and service manager at Narrow Fabric and made this remark on a questionnaire returned in the IBO survey; she was also "a strong advocate of equal pay for equal work." BVI, folder 206.

92. Gilson, *What's Past Is Prologue*, 168-69.

93. Ibid., 172-73.

94. Ralph M. Hower, *History of Macy's of New York: Chapters in the Evolution of the Department Store* (Cambridge: Harvard University Press, 1943), 388; Anne Hendry Morrison, *Women and Their Careers: A Study of 306 Women in Business and the Professions* (New York: National Federation of Business and Professional Women's Clubs, 1934), 152.

95. There were twelve former clerical workers, eleven social workers, nine teachers, seven employment or welfare workers, three librarians, two accountants/auditors, and two sales workers (some had had more than one occupation). BVI, folders 203-8. A study of a group of fifteen women personnel workers questioned in the mail in 1930 found that "five entered their economic careers in clerical service, four in sales work, two as factory workers, and one as a telephone operator, while three earned their first wages as teacher, companion, and training assistant in a department store." Morrison, *Women and their Careers*, 149. This was a relatively older group, more than 80 percent being forty or older in 1930.

96. A profile of Louise Moore can be found in *Personnel* 2(Oct. 1920): 2.

97. BVI, folders 203-8.

98. YWCA, "Executive and Technical Women in Industry," 7-8. Mary van Kleeck, Lee Galloway, and Henry Metcalf worked on the preparation of this report.

99. The 1918 IBO survey asked employment managers to indicate the periodicals to which they subscribed.

100. YWCA, "Executive and Technical Women in Industry," 9.

101. "Women are Interested in Boston Association," *Personnel* 1 (Aug. 1919): 8.

102. Between June 1916 and June 1922, the federal executive civil service added 122,806 employees to its rolls, 100,000 of whom were "directly chargeable to the war." "News Notes," *JPR* 1 (1922-23): 245- 46. For the evolution of federal civil service testing, see Herbert A. Filer and L. J. O'Rourke, "Progress in Civil Service Tests," *PJ* 1 (1922-23): 484-520, and Samuel Kavruck, "Thirty-Three Years of Test Research: A Short History of Test Development in the U.S. Civil Service Commission," *American Psychologist* 11 (July 1956): 329-33.

103. As quoted by Herman Feldman, *A Personnel Program for the Federal Civil Service* (Washington, D.C.: GPO, 1931), 113-14; also see "Bureau of Public Personnel Administration," *JPR* 1 (1922-23): 522-25. Psychologist L. L. Thurstone said in 1923 that "there are few private firms that employ clerical help by methods as thoroughly studied in detail as those that are being used by the larger civil service commissions. For this reason I believe that private industry could profitably study and copy the civil service employment methods." "Psychology in the Civil Service," *Annals* 110 (Nov. 1923): 194-99. Also see Waldon Fawcett, "Uncle Sam Rates the Efficiency of His Office Workers," *Office Economist* [*OE*] 9 (May 1927): 3; Sadie A. Maxwell, "New Tests for Clerical Workers," *OE* 6 (April 1924): 5-6; and W. E. Mickey, "Rating the Government Employee," *OE* 11 (May, 1929): 6, 12.

104. Alfred D. Flinn, "Development of Personnel Research Federation," *JPR* 1 (1922-23): 7-13, and "Personnel Research Federation: Report of Annual Meeting," *JPR* 2 (1923-24): 19-29. Both the Personnel Research Federation and the Taylor Society have been described by Sanford Jacoby as "fringe groups" in the field of personnel management in the 1920s, *Employing Bureaucracy*, 184. For attempts to claim far more influence for the federation, see "Personnel Research Federation," *PJ* 18 (Nov. 1935): 193-5, and Ling, *Management of Personnel Relations*, 344, 372. Ling describes the *Journal of Personnel Research* as "the most important journal in the personnel area through the 1920's and 1930's."

105. For examples of experienced women employment managers seeking work see *Personnel* 1 (March 1919): 8 and (June 1919): 11. In July 1919, *Personnel* ran a boxed advertisement (4, 6) promoting its list of eligi-

ble women employment managers, but nearly all of the new positions listed as filled were taken by men. Ida Tarbell observed in 1921 that "in the present depressed state of industry in the country, it is inevitable that many women should be dropped from the new tasks, . . . that . . . many women who have prepared themselves and had held positions as employment managers, be out of employment." "The New Place of Women in Industry."

106. Gilson, *Past Is Prologue*, 122. A list of local association officers in 1919 turned up only one identifiable woman, Eleanor Good of Rochester, *Personnel* 1 (Feb. 1919): 8, and Jane Williams left the board of the association in 1920 to an all-male slate of officers.

107. Adams, *Women Professional Workers*, 191-94. Adams also provides (185-222) a useful summary of the development of personnel management training courses, the war's effect on the field, and women's emerging position in it.

108. These developments are discussed in depth in W. J. Donald and Edith King Donald, "Trends in Personnel Administration," *Harvard Business Review* 7 (Jan. 1929): 143-55.

109. Sam A. Lewisohn et. al., *Can Business Prevent Unemployment* (New York: Alfred A. Knopf, 1925), 88-89. Robert Lovett's analysis of seventy-four "prominent concerns" in 1923 showed an overall tendency toward centralization and a wide variety of organizational structures of personnel management. "Present Tendencies in Personnel Practice," 327-33; also see A. H. Young, "What's New in Personnel and Industrial Relations," *Personnel* 7 (Nov. 1930): 67-77.

110. For a discussion of the status of personnel managers after 1920, see Jacoby, *Employing Bureaucracy*, 168-205.

111. Leon Carroll Marshall, *Business Administration* (Chicago: University of Chicago Press, 1921), 115; Mosher, "A Federal Personnel Policy," 22.

112. Millicent Pond, "Some Managerial Prerequisites to Successful Placement," Industrial Conference Papers, Pennsylvania State College, 77, SM, case 58. Pond's test techniques and program are described in "Selective Placement of Metal Workers," *PJ* 6 (Jan. 1927): 345-66, and (Feb. 1927): 405; also see Pond, "The Value of Mental Tests," 11, 16-17, 21-22.

113. Of course the terms *masculine* and *feminine* do not indicate the sex of those who hold such views but rather the gender characteristics of those views; men could be in the "liberal" (feminine) camp and women in the "conservative" (masculine) camp. A detailed discussion of the vast body of personnel literature between 1920 and 1940 has to be beyond the scope of this book, but this summary is based on my persual of the major journals and textbook literature of the period.

114. If anything, these views appear to have become even more pronounced over time. See, for example, Peter Drucker, "Is Personnel Management Bankrupt?" in *Classics of Personnel Management*, ed. Patten, 59-68. Drucker claims that "Scientific Management . . . may well be the most

powerful as well as the most lasting contribution America has made to Western thought since the Federalist Papers," but describes personnel administration as "partly a file clerk's job, partly a housekeeping job, partly a social workers' job and partly 'firefighting' to head off union trouble or to settle it." In an article on human relations for *Look*, Oct. 28, 1958, 47, Malcolm P. McNair, a professor from the Harvard Business School, asserted that "frequently, business failure can be laid directly on the doorstep of human relations. I have seen executives exhibit such sentimentality and tender-mindedness, when they needed hardheadedness, that businesses have had to close down, putting a lot of people out of work." The gender associations in these statements are obvious.

115. Reinhard Bendix, *Work and Authority in Industry: Ideologies of Management in the Course of Industrialization* (New York: Wiley and Sons, 1956), 297-98.

116. The Hawthorne experiments made an immediate splash. A. H. Young, for instance, described Hawthorne as "the most challenging bit of scientific research in industrial human relationships yet undertaken." "What's New In Personnel and Industrial Relations," 77. In general, two major findings came out of Hawthorne. One was that any change in the workplace increased production ("the Hawthorne effect") and the other was that the worker was above all "a worker in a group" and that human interaction could be understood more clearly and tapped by management to increase production. A useful summary of Hawthorne is Ling, *The Management of Personnel Relations*, 411-15. For more complete accounts see Elton Mayo, *The Human Problems of an Industrial Civilization* (Boston: Harvard Graduate School of Business Administration, 1933), and F. J. Roethlisberger and W. J. Dickson, *Management and the Worker* (Cambridge: Harvard University Press, 1939).

117. Of course nonindustrial workers included the home offices and sales forces of manufacturing firms. Richard Edwards argues that systems of "bureaucratic control" were *most likely* to originate in office sectors of large corporations and *then* to spread to production work (my emphasis): "the new system transcended its white-collar origins and . . . came to organize manual as well as mental work." *Contested Terrain*, 132. Donald and Donald claimed in 1929 that while personnel work had first arisen around the organization of factory workers during World War I, it had found its most important niche in the organization of office-personnel and sales-personnel departments in the 1920s. "Trends in Personnel Administration," 146-48.

118. Gilson, "Scientific Management and Personnel Work," 46. Gilson describes her attempts to enter Harvard in *What's Past is Prologue*, 215.

119. Letter from Mary B. Gilson to Elton Mayo, March 8, 1940; Letter from Mayo to Gilson, March 12, 1940; Letter from Gilson to Mayo, March 14, 1940. Gilson did not mention Mayo by name in her autobiography (216) but said of her decision to attend Columbia and not Radcliffe that

"less of my energy would be drained off in kicking against medieval stone walls erected in a dead past when women were not people." Although Mayo did not, evidently, respond to Gilson's letter of March 14, the two did exchange letters in 1946 which indicated they maintained a friendly relationship. Letter from Gilson to Mayo, Oct. 10, 1946 and his reply, Nov. 4, 1946. These letters are all in the Elton Mayo Papers, folder 1.040, Harvard Business School Library.

4

"Light Manufacturing":
The Feminization of Clerical Work

Wᴴᴇɴ ᴇᴅɪᴛʜ ᴄʜᴀʀʟᴇѕ went to work as a comptometer operator at Brown and Sharpe in 1913, she found that the Providence machine tool manufacturer had implemented scientific management techniques on the factory floor and in the office. The labor of workers was now recorded on time cards, along with the materials they used. In the office, machine operators like Charles processed the cards to keep track of inventory, produce the payroll, and arrive at competitive prices. "It seemed like a very efficient system," Charles later explained. "When they got through, they had the labor and the material . . . (so) that they knew exactly what it cost to make that object." If Charles produced more computations than the norm, she received a bonus, and mistakes were deducted from her total number of pieces. A worker who produced too little or who made repeated mistakes could be fired: "the section I was in had to check requisitions, and then add them and get a total. Then you had to post them and check your total. And stamp your initials. If you made more than one mistake, you were called down."[1]

At Brown and Sharpe the bookkeeper and his counterpart on the factory floor, the foreman, had lost their traditional importance to a brigade of new office workers, managers, and professionals. Accountants, timekeepers, and purchasing, production, and invoice clerks, many of them machine operators like Edith Charles, were now the brain and nervous system of the corporate structure. They also had or soon would have counterparts in every large bureaucracy in the nation: insurance companies, department stores, mail order houses, city and state governments, and administrative departments of the United States government.

The accounting and record-keeping revolution at the turn of the century demanded a new hierarchy of workers and a more specialized division of labor. Opportunities for both men and women in the office hierarchy were greatly expanded, not only in the professional and managerial positions described in previous chapters, but also in a wide variety of new clerking occupations, many of which entailed machine work.

The surge in production in office machines and the search for a widely expanded labor force to operate them were thus both evoked by, and ran parallel to, the cost accounting and scientific management revolution. Historical treatments of office work have emphasized the conjunction of mechanization, scientific management, and the hiring of women as clerical workers. As a result, the connection between women and routine office work appears to be inevitable. Some economic historians have used human capital theory to postulate that although high school or business training gave women the general skills they needed to become suitable candidates for office work, they were less willing or able than men to invest in advanced education and were thus excluded from more specialized or "firm specific" jobs. Because both women and their employers expected women to leave the work force and eventually marry, it made no sense for their employers to train them for more responsible positions. Women were, therefore, especially suited to mechanized or rationalized jobs requiring only general levels of skill. One labor historian has argued that the new office machines—particularly the typewriter—were unassociated with either gender. The sudden demand for machine operators at the turn of the century created a kind of gender vacuum that women were thus available to fill. Those emphasizing proletarianization have associated women with the de-skilling of men's work.[2]

Although all of these views have merit, they do not get at the complexity of the process by which women entered the office to take up clerical work and what happened to them once they got there. Human capital theories do not explore the irrational as well as the rational motives that confined women to low-paying jobs. They assume that job titles and salaries truly reflect the work clerks perform. They assume women accept the logic of the marriage bar, and that few unmarried, or older, women remained in the work force. They do not account for the ways in which the marriage bar was used to protect the privileged status of many male workers and the extent to which discrimination was part of the picture. Scholars who emphasize the gender-neutral aspects of office machines underplay the historical connection between women and factory operative work, and scholars who emphasize proletarianization and feminization have overstated their case. Many jobs remained largely untouched by rationalization and mechanization, and men continued to work in offices in large numbers.

Business machines and rationalized office work were primarily adopted because they had the potential to dramatically increase office work productivity. The key to the successful installation of both new technology and new labor systems from a management point of view was, however, a competent, affordable labor supply. In this chapter I explore the process by which office employers arrived at the conclusion that women—rather than men or adolescent boys—met their labor requirements, and what impact that conclusion had on the sexual division of labor in the office. Employers were making a rational choice when they moved toward hiring women as clerks. Women had the "human capital" to perform office jobs; both high school- and college-educated women applied for them. Moreover, the human capital of women could be used differently than that of men; women could be treated as though they had no future in offices, and they could be paid less than men, whatever their jobs actually were.

The traditional association between women factory operatives and repetitive work also facilitated the identification of women with mechanized and routinized clerking. Dressed up with somewhere to go, the factory girl could be put to work doing assembly-line clerical work in the office. But only so many jobs could be routinized. Many tasks remained beyond the scope of scientific management, and privileged groups of workers (especially men) often successfully resisted the efficiency experts. Both employers and workers resisted the penetration of rationalization too far up the office hierarchy or too far into men's work.

Feminization was not nearly as complete by 1930 as previous accounts have implied, and a dual system of retention and promotion based on sex proved to be the key to the successful deployment of office labor. Employers needed a wide range of office workers, working and middle class, male and female. In an explosively growing occupation, especially during World War I, women could continue to be absorbed in what only thirty years before had been primarily a man's world without completely subverting men's place. Women and men worked alongside each other in the office, and large numbers of men continued to be attracted to clerking. But men and women were not treated in the same way. Men received higher salaries, access to promotion opportunities, and more prestigious job titles. Women were much more likely than men to be assigned to routine, rationalized work. On the other hand, whatever their salaries or job titles, women often performed the kinds of varied tasks that supposedly made men more valuable as long-term employees. Continued profitability in hiring women was far more dependent on discrimination than on women's so-called lack of "human capital."

Origins of the Sexual Division of Labor: Men and Women in Clerical Work

Clerical work emerged as a significant occupational category in the nineteenth century in both England and the United States. Many of these early clerical jobs were tedious and repetitive; ledger clerks entered figures and did elementary arithmetic, copyists copied documents all day long. Wages were rarely high enough to put clerks solidly into the middle class. Even job security was often out of reach. Clerks faced frequent layoffs from periodic business depressions and bankruptcies and were often hired as temporary workers to do copying, addressing, and posting jobs by the piece. Few of them realistically expected to rise to positions of executive rank. On the other hand, this apprentice system of on-the-job training was the way in which a selected group of future business managers were likely to be trained (long after the education of physicians and lawyers moved to professional schools). In short, significant opportunities existed for men to move up from clerical work in the unmechanized office, but no guarantee that all of them would.[3]

As more specialized skills in bookkeeping, stenography, and typing were developed and enhanced by mechanization at the end of the nineteenth century, and as larger economic and administrative entities required more managers, clerks were probably more secure in their jobs in many establishments than they had been in previous decades. For much of the middle class, increasingly losing its self-employed or entrepreneurial status, office work was a reasonable substitute. Some men augmented their economic status by rising through the clerical ranks to managerial or executive positions.[4]

But promotion opportunities were possibilities, not guarantees, and as tasks diversified and the layers of the office hierarchy thickened, reaching the top became more difficult for men without college educations. Vocational guidance reformer Bertha Stevens's study of boys and girls in Cleveland commercial work in 1916 gave some idea of promotion opportunities for men. It was still the policy of the railroads to promote office boys and male stenographers to more responsible and higher-paying positions as clerks, but there were clearly limits on how high they might expect to rise. The Cleveland railroads employed about seven thousand office employees, most of whom were men; about seventy clerks in a thousand could expect to become officials, specialists, managers, or heads of departments. Stevens interviewed an "unusually alert, intelligent youth of twenty-two" who had gone into the railroad office after completing a night-time commercial course. He said that while he had already received several promotions he could expect only three more in the forseeable future and a salary high of $80 a month: "And there I will stick! There will be about four other fellows doing different work but all on the same level and we will all be waiting for the chief clerk to die off. If he does, then somebody will jump to $125—but any one of us has only one chance in five of being that person." [5] Mary Schauffler, a sociologist who interviewed a male secretary at the New York Central Railroad in Cleveland ten years later, found much the same reaction: "[He] said he should leave at once if there were no future in it for him. His brother was promoted to a big sales position from a secretarial job and he expects to become a railroad executive by the same road."[6]

The Cleveland clerks' concern for their future was endemic to modern office work. Faced with the ongoing production of clerks in public schools and business colleges, male clerks could not throw up the kind of roadblocks to training and promotion that both the professions and the unionized trades could. The office was bound to become a place in American society where tension and competition among individuals would surface. These conditions were further complicated by the arrival of growing numbers of women.

The federal government first hired female clerical workers during the Civil War because not enough men were available to clip treasury bills and went on hiring them in the following decades to take over hand work usually done by men. Government managers had a simple motive for the continued hiring of women: they wanted to reduce labor costs. Stuck with stingy budgets fixed by congressional appropriation, they were nonetheless facing a growing body of work. Women not only were available in large numbers and desperate for work, but they also could be paid less than men.

Federal law had conveniently established a maximum salary for women of $900 a year in 1866, whereas maximum salaries for men ranged between $1,200 and $1,800.

The opposition to hiring women in low-level positions quickly fell away. Although women employees were initially concentrated in a few departments, most as copyists, a congressional survey of 1870 showed that "those having experience with women's work thought highly of it." Some were skeptical of women's capacities, but the Librarian of Congress succinctly stated a compelling reason for hiring women: "they could give good service for less pay than the men on his staff, thus resulting in economy." A new act in 1870 facilitated the hiring of women by opening some examinations to them and allowing but not requiring department heads to pay them more than $900 a year. As government offices expanded their duties and became responsible for producing more paperwork, the temptation to hire women at the minimum salary increased. By 1893 nearly one-third of all the employees in Washington offices of the federal government were women.[7]

At the end of the century most women clerical workers in the federal government were still being appointed as copyists, and most men as clerks. But since the pace of mechanization and rationalization was erratic, and clerks and copyists might both perform diverse tasks, these job title distinctions stood for little except a lower salary schedule for women. Nor were women necessarily assigned mechanical work when the government purchased greater numbers of machines. In the 1880s both men and women used typewriters, and as late as 1904 only 21 percent of government typists were women, indicating that both office supervisors and male clerks still thought typing to be appropriate for men. Men who used business machines, however, sometimes saw their wages fall or remain equivalent to those of women. And there was a tendency to hire women rather than men for jobs being subjected to specialization and routinization.[8]

More clerical examinations in the civil service were opened to women by the federal government after 1910, although women's salaries rarely climbed above $1,100 a year. Both professionals and manual workers in the federal civil service had better luck than clerks in excluding women from their workplaces. On the eve of civil service examination reform in 1919 women were still barred from 64 percent of the exams for scientific and professional positions and 87 percent of those for mechanical and manufacturing positions, but they were eligible for 85 percent of the clerical examinations. The influx of women into some government clerical jobs did not deter men from seeking similar employment. In fact, the number of clerical jobs held by men increased significantly over those held by women in this period. Many men were willing to take jobs at $900 a year or less, and hundreds of male applicants were turned away each year.[9]

One of the first pure installations of rationalized and mechanized work in federal government offices appeared with the tabulation of the census of 1890. With the help of punch card and sorting machines designed by Herman Hollerith, an engineering graduate from Columbia University, the United States hoped to usher in the new century with the most elaborate and quickly reported census in its history. The Census Bureau initially hired both men and women to operate Hollerith machines. Almost no one in the federal government had used these machines before, so no built-in constituency of male card punchers and tabulators were anxious to protect their domain. Unlike many other government offices, where typewriters and other office machines were still used to do varied tasks in relatively unstructured work situations, the Census Bureau was anxious to promote speed and efficiency by subdividing operations. The census jobs were also largely temporary and did not necessarily guarantee further work. Male employees, many of whom were law clerks or government employees working the night shift for extra pay, complained about the pace of work and the difficulty of using the machines and often quit after the first day. In contrast, the *New York Sun* reported that women on the day shift worked 50 percent faster than men and were "more exact in touch, more expeditious in handling the schedules, more at home in adjusting the delicate mechanisms of the electrical machines," and (perhaps a more perceptive observation) "apparently more anxious to make a good record." Eventually 80 percent of the census computers were women.[10] The census office scenario pointed up the gendered characteristics of mechanized and routinized work. Given their economic options and expectations of future work, women had to be less fussy than men about the jobs they took. Men could often afford to spurn factorylike work in the office; they had other choices.

Interlude: Office Machine Technology and Mechanization

By the mid-nineteenth century growing sophistication of the machine tool and die industry allowed precision parts to be manufactured and assembled into inexpensive mechanical products like the repeating rifle and the sewing machine. Most office machines were simple devices that could easily be produced on a mass basis once demand for them had arisen. The prototype of the mechanical calculator was developed by Pascal in 1642. Charles Babbage devised a computing engine in England in 1835, but only a handful of mathematicians saw any use for it. The typewriter had been devised in the 1830s, but did not receive sufficient capital financing for an improved mechanism until the 1870s; mass production, surging to meet growing demand, was underway a decade later.[11]

The more widespread use of pneumatic tubes, telephones, and typewriters by the 1890s made it possible to compile information quickly, communicate directly, and produce documents less laboriously. Installing machines often enabled employers to create more modern labor forces. Pneumatic tubes in department stores, for instance, allowed larger stores to centralize cashier departments and end the employment of children as messengers, an unpopular labor policy with Progressive social reformers.[12] Banks and insurance companies found similar uses for the new gadgets. In its 1905 catalog Sears and Roebuck boasted of the machines to be installed in its huge new warehouse and shipping depot under construction near Chicago, where clerks were to be linked in a factorylike setting to process a hundred thousand orders a day: "Miles of railroad tracks run lengthwise through, in and around this building for the receiving, moving and forwarding of merchandise; . . . pneumatic tubes and every known mechanical appliance for reducing labor, for the working out of economy and dispatch is to be utilized here in our great Works."[13] The dictaphone, which combined elements of the sewing machine, the phonograph, and the telephone, complemented the use of the typewriter and paved the way for the rationalization of stenography. The stencil and mimeograph machine allowed for the mass reproduction of paper documents.[14]

The development of computing machines to implement the new methods of scientific management and cost accounting was the most rapidly growing sector of office machine production after 1900. In 1899, eighteen establishments made calculators and adding machines valued at less than $6 million, but by 1919, sixty-five firms made more than $83 million worth of products. As early as 1899 the value of calculating machine products had outstripped typewriter products and in 1919 ran ahead by more than $30 million.[15]

Engineers and business-minded inventors in small machine tool and die shops developed most of the technology required for the production of bookkeeping and accounting machines. William Patterson made the first cash registers (adding machines on drawers) for use in his Dayton coal yard business in 1882, and later founded the National Cash Register Company. Joseph Burroughs, a former bank clerk from St. Louis, named his adding machine the American Arithometer but sold only 1,435 machines between 1895 and his untimely death three years later. After renaming the firm Burroughs, his successor sold nearly eight thousand machines in 1905 and was producing a hundred thousand calculating machines by 1930. Frank Baldwin's adding machines and calculators were adopted by the accounting department of the Pennsylvania Railroad and a leading life insurance company. A young college graduate and employee of the Western Electric Company, Jay Monroe, helped Baldwin develop more successful high-speed calculators and then named the machines after himself.[16]

Adding machines like those made by Burroughs and Monroe listed addends and their totals on a paper tape. Operating them required two motions: punching the keys and turning a crank. Electrified machines were not used very extensively until the 1930s, so any additional mathematical functions made the machines bulkier and more difficult to use. The fancier machines were still very large, expensive, and most likely to be used by accountants or statisticians. Business and government consumers wanted light and affordable machines for their bookkeepers and clerks. The comptometer, developed by Felt and Tarrant in Chicago, was often more popular than the calculator because it was key-driven, light in weight, inexpensive, and once a special system was learned, could also be used to for subtraction, multiplication, and division. It was non-listing; no printed tape showed each item entered, but a running total appeared in a window. Because the bulk of many businesses' financial record keeping required simple addition, the comptometer was suitable to a wide variety of purposes. Some of the first machines were ordered by the U.S. Treasury Department and a large public utility.[17]

Bookkeeping and billing machines, used to enter transactions and make up bills, invoices, and purchase orders, were simple combinations of typewriters and adding machines. The productivity of bookkeeping and typewriting machines was greatly enhanced if used in conjunction with addressing machines, which allowed for the mechanical reproduction of alphabetized names and addresses on mailings, bills, and statements. The addressograph, composed of detachable metal name and address plates linked together on a mimeographing device, was simultaneously invented by an Iowa mill superintendent and an editor seeking a more efficient way to prepare his bicycle magazine for mailing.[18]

Tabulating and key-punch machines became familiar to the general public during the compilation of the Census of 1890. Really a variation of the seventeenth-century Jacquard loom, the principle behind the machines was to key-punch individual pieces of data onto a small card and then use a sorter to compile the cards into different categories of results. Unlike typewriters and adding machines, tabulating machines were expensive and likely to be used only by very large corporations or government offices. Although any number of patents for such machines had been filed in the 1880s, Herman Hollerith was the first to receive assurances from the Bureau of the Census that his machines would be used once produced. A variety of agencies and corporations leased Hollerith's production models, including the surgeon general's office, the Baltimore Department of Health, and the New York Central Railroad.[19]

Most of the publicity about the use of tabulating machines concerned the compilation of vital statistics, but their cost accounting possibilities were equally as important to business and government. The New York Central could, after the installation of its Hollerith system, "tell on a nearly current basis how many hundreds of tons of freight were moving East-or-West, which of hundreds of stations along its lines were profitable; where freight cars should be sent or returned; which freight agents were being paid." All in all, it gave "the railroad a much firmer command of its far-flung business." At the 1902 hearings of the Interstate Commerce Commission some railroad officers predicted that the statistics demanded by the commission "would cost the roads millions," and would entail "a complete readjustment of their statistical processes." The New York Central comptroller remained unruffled, however, and said his road would make no objection to the commission's requests, "as he can simply run his figures through his electrical tabulator and the additional trouble and cost would be nominal." Hollerith devised a tabulating system for sales analysis and bookkeeping at the Marshall Field department stores, and tabulating machines were put into use at Pennsylvania Steel along with an accounting system that computed both labor and overhead costs. By 1907 Eastman-Kodak, American Sheet and Tin Plate,

Western Electric, and Yale and Towne were using the machines, and the Post Office was interested in a tabulating system for keeping track of its money orders. Seven years later the rental fees for Hollerith's machines from insurance companies alone amounted to more than $91,000. At the Watertown Arsenal, a Hollerith system allowed for one of the first systematic installations of Taylorism on a large scale in 1915.[20]

The tabulator was the most important of all the business machines. While other machines really sped the process of producing individual pieces of information, the tabulator could combine those pieces into a variety of categories. In many ways, especially when used in combination with other machines, it was the precursor of the digital computer, and its admirers tended to talk about it in ways that anticipate the claims that would later be made for computerized programming and data processing:

A business of huge proportions is today as incapable of functioning economically without a tabulated chart of operations as a ship on an uncharted sea without a compass. The tabulating machine is the last word in accountancy. It is the data analyzer par excellence. It brings figure-facts up to date so they become a dynamic force in the control and direction of business effort. They tabulate labor and material costs and thereby make it possible to determine the proper selling price. They eliminate guess work by fixing definite charges against particular effort. In the salesmanship field, they ... eliminate unprofitable areas, and they do all these things as rapidly as the facts are fed into the hopper so that the master mind in business is able to chart his course day by day.[21]

As early as 1900 Hollerith was at work on a standardized cost accounting machine to be used in conjunction with tickets filled out on the factory floor. He encountered his first real competition in 1910 when a newly named Russian immigrant, John Powers, was hired by the Bureau of the Census to supervise production of the bureau's census machines. Powers developed a keypunch machine that more closely resembled a typewriter keyboard and a method for printing tabulated information onto rolls of paper. The Powers statistical accounting machine, perfected in 1916, became known for its cost accounting uses. Hollerith's machines were distributed by the Computing Tabulating Recording Company (CTR), created in 1911. Under the guidance of Thomas J. Watson, a former salesman at the rapidly expanding National Cash Register Company, CTR became one of the big money-makers in the business machine field. CTR not only leased its machines rather than selling them, but also produced and sold the lucrative punch cards that the machines required. CTR netted a profit of nearly $3 million in 1918 and took on the less cumbersome name of its acquisition, the International Business Machine Corporation, in 1924. Powers's machine was eventually distributed by Remington-Rand.[22]

The business machine companies flourished in the four decades before 1920 and became an important sector of American manufacturing, but there were limits to which products they could market successfully. All the technology needed to create the mechanical digital computer was available by World War I, but neither the federal government, which had taken on such an important role in the development of the tabulating machine, or business, which rushed to use the machine once it was available, was willing to provide the kind of capitalization the development of such a computer would require.[23] Nor had the complexity of business and government really reached the point where digital computers were an imperative. Office machine technology responded to demand for machines more than inventions influenced demand. As C. Wright Mills later argued, machines were mass-manufactured as they complemented the changing social reorganization of the office.[24]

One goal of mechanization was to accomplish more tasks but to accomplish them with a smaller labor force than would have been possible without machines. However, mechanization and the new methods of clerical work could also facilitate systematic management and the integration of large-scale institutions. In some ways these goals were not always complementary. The possibilities of what the machines could do were bound to increase the number of tasks for which they might be put to use and to suggest other ways in which machines might be combined or improved to accomplish even more tasks. The introduction of machines usually increased the number of workers required in an office, despite their promoters' insistence that they would save labor costs. In an American economy characterized by economic growth and greater bureaucratic complexity, the tendency was to add more functions with the use of new machines, and therefore more workers. The International Labour Office observed in 1933 that mechanization almost always created greater office employment: "The number of office employees thus increases with mechanisation. The reason is simple enough; office machines make it possible to carry out profitably a whole series of operations which would be too expensive if they had to be done by hand. The growth of large administrative departments and the extension and concentration of undertakings have made it easier to install office machinery on a large scale and to increase supervisory and statistical work to an enormous extent, for the machine reduces the cost of each item to a minute figure."[25]

Mechanization, Gender, and the Question of Skill

Mechanization had the general effect of leading to a greater division of labor, the creation of more monotonous and tedious jobs, and an increase in the speed at which operations were performed. But machines could also facilitate the mental work of those who used them and permit the performance of more complicated operations. Machines themselves placed limits on how regimented their use could be. Some could be used continuously but were controlled by the operator. Others prompted the operator, who in a sense thus became a part of the machine. As the International Labour Organization concluded, "a typist is to some extent free to decide how to set out the type, but the operator of an addressing machine is, so to speak, merely a cog in the machine."[26]

Mechanization did not necessarily lead to the de-skilling of office work and might, in fact, create a new kind of task altogether or enhance the ability of the operator to perform a job previously done by hand. Workers who performed tasks on Hollerith machines to do census work were not "unskilled"; they had to combine a number of organizational, mechanical, and physical talents. Some kinds of mechanization, such as telephone operating, card punching, and check proofing, created jobs that had never existed before.

Both stenography and typing required special training and were dependent on human attributes not inherent in either the typewriter or stenographic languages. The clerk's familiarity with English grammar and spelling, and his or her speed and accuracy, were important components of success, qualities that might make her or him, not the notebook or the typewriter, indispensable to an employer.[27] Theoretically, a stenographer had the specific task of taking dictation and of typing it into reports and correspondence. But only in the most elaborately systematized establishments did stenographers stick to these duties alone or do their transcribing from machines.[28] There was a tendency, as other kinds of clerking were rationalized, to give to the stenographer (sometimes called a secretary) tasks that could not be systemized. Most frequently these tasks arose out of the administrative or supervisory functions of the stenographer's immediate boss; sometimes they were tasks that were of personal benefit to the boss, such as making coffee or sewing on buttons.

Managers and bosses who used the services of stenographers and secretaries wanted to assign them miscellaneous tasks that went beyond rationalized stenography and typing and frequently required other skills. Having one's own secretary became a measure of success as well as a real convenience. Advertisers of early stenographic phonographs were aware of managerial resistance to machine dictating and geared their advertising to convince executives that the machines would save time and labor costs. In 1910 the businessman was asked to "think of the advantage of dictating your mail without the embarrassing presence of the stenographer, waiting, pencil poised, to get your every word and sending your best thoughts sky high," but was still being urged in 1925 to "Dictate [to an Ediphone]: it's here to stay." Advertisements for typewriters and computing machines were, by contrast, far more self-assured about the penetration these machines had already made into the office market.[29]

Typewriters and stenographic languages, on balance, may not have threatened the traditional stenographer or secretarial worker with either the loss of a job or job de-skilling, and may, in fact, have made him or her more indispensable to an employer. Adding machines had more ominous possibilities for bookkeepers, who held relatively prestigious positions in traditional offices. They not only kept the books and performed transactions, but they also often managed other office employees. They had far more to lose than copyists as both mechanization and rationalization set in. Accountants and office managers often assumed the managerial and planning aspects of the bookkeeper's job; machine operators could perform the bookkeeper's computing tasks.[30]

On the other hand, calculating machines might very well enhance the bookkeeper's ability to produce specialized information, especially in the smaller firm. The new reverence for figures increased the overall importance of both bookkeeping and accounting so that bookkeepers hardly lost their importance in the new office systems; there were more bookkeepers than ever by 1930. Advertising reflected the ambivalent status of bookkeepers by depicting both men and women at work on machines. Men were usually depicted individually, using the machines to solve problems. Women were shown in groups, using machines to do repetitive work. But in reality, both women and men used bookkeeping machines for varied operations, and the number of women in book-keeping continued to climb (Table 2).

By the turn of the century, male bookkeepers began to see their occupation change as managers introduced new organizational techniques and machines as well as women. When the bookkeeping offices of a large New England textile manufacturer were reorganized between 1900 and 1910, a dozen men were replaced by adding machines, and then another dozen lost jobs after a more efficient bookkeeping system was installed. Younger men willing to work for less pay replaced older clerks, and men with seniority no longer received their traditional salary increases. When a dry goods jobber replaced bound ledger books with the more maneuverable loose leaf variety, carbon forms, and some computing machines at the turn of the century, he eliminated six male clerks and replaced them with one male billing clerk and a female compto-meter operator.[31]

When vocational experts Jeanette Eaton and Bertha Stevens studied the job of bookkeeping in Cleveland, they found that most computing machines and machine operators were introduced to expand operations, so most male clerks kept their jobs. But they did predict a general flattening of opportunity for some men as both rationalization and mechanization took hold: "the use of machines is preventing the firms from taking into their employ high priced bookkeepers and clerks skilled in rapid mental calculation. It is this advanced mental equipment that is no longer much in demand, and those who possess it will be displaced in the future by operators on the efficient machines."[32]

Adding machine manufacturers attempted to head off the issue of de-skilling men's work by insisting that their products would both lower the cost of bookkeeping and free male clerks for more interesting jobs. They explicitly tried to convey to managers the notion of a dual labor system based on gender and rationalization that would gain the cooperation of men rather than their enmity, as in the following excerpt from a 1905 guide to office machines:

> In many of the largest business houses in America the calculating machine is operated by girls, who not only are employed at a comparatively small compensation, but at the same time become so expert in the use of machines, that everything in the way of computations are given to them . . . . This method results in relieving the bookkeepers and accountants from any of the mental strain consequent to the add-

ing of long columns of figures or vast collections of cash or credit tickets, and allows them to devote their time and energies to other features where their abilities are of special value.[33]

Although the overall effect of mechanization on individual workers might remain ambiguous, the fact remained that its main purpose was to increase productivity, rationalize tasks, and require smaller training periods for clerking jobs. As machines became more specialized, those who used them did tend to perform more routine tasks. As establishments became larger, more and more tasks could be routinized. Routine clerical work, especially when performed on a large scale, whether mechanized or not, could be subjected to the principles of scientific management. Taylor immediately found disciples such as William Leffingwell and Lee Galloway, who asserted that there were no real differences between office and factory work; both could be managed like assembly lines. From filing to bookkeeping, systematization was the key to greater output with reduced labor costs. The office management expert George Frederick observed in 1920 that offices in the preceding ten years had seen a definite trend toward the application of "standardized methods" originally developed in factories. "Office work," he argued, "is simply production work of another kind, different only in its character, and not as different from factory work, as factory work differs between various factories. Indeed, it is 'light manufacturing,' and the principles are precisely similar."[34]

The consequences of standardized methods for the gender characteristics of office labor were, as a general rule, fairly predictable. Women were more likely than men to be assigned to routinized tasks, whether performed in conjunction with machines or not. It was suggested through advertising, job titles, and sex segregation in the office that the more interesting and varied jobs were reserved for men.

Women were more likely to be hired for office jobs that were being subjected to systemization, mechanization, or both. Employers had rational economic motives for doing so based on the actual characteristics of the female labor force: large numbers of working-class and middle-class women with English-language skills sought office jobs and could be paid less than men with comparable skills. But firmly implanted cultural notions about the gender characteristics of work helped all concerned make an easy association between women and mechanized, rationalized office work. Employers and workers often found it both "natural" (as in the natural order of things) to see women as likely candidates for routine work and, as a corollary, to assume that if women were doing office jobs, whatever the skills required, and whether or not the jobs were mechanized, pay and status should automatically be linked to operative status. Women's traditional association with light manufacturing in nineteenth-century industries that had pioneered in rationalization, such as textiles and paper-making, helped pave the way for their hiring in new manufacturing sectors like the electrical industry in the twentieth century and contributed to the notion that women would be suitable to light manufacturing in the office.[35] Both electrical factory assembly lines and simplified office jobs relied on what amounted to piecework systems, systems with which women were already associated and the installation of which scientific managers saw as the crux of breaking the hold of male craft workers. Although women were increasingly employed after the turn of the century in settings where new machinery was important, in these settings they frequently performed unmechanized hand operations that could be counted and subjected to speed-up. Such operations were also characteristic of office work.[36]

It was not so much that typewriters, tabulators, or comptometers were neutral machines and free to be gender-stereotyped that facilitated women's use of them. Rather, the association between women and light manufacturing was already an acceptable image upon which advertisers and employers could draw in establishing the wide-spread use of new machines and the employment of operators in offices. The nineteenth century had implanted firm notions of men and women in the industrial world; native-born men were associated with artisanry and craftsmanship, native-born women with light factory work, and immigrants and blacks with manual labor. In the new office, it was desirable to appropriate these notions in familiar but somewhat recast forms.[37]

As a powerful additional incentive, most office employers believed, as at the Census Bureau, that young women exhibited lower turnover rates than adolescent men in lower-level clerking positions. Boys had initially been hired as typists in some establishments, and the Pennsylvania Steel Company had employed boys to punch cards for an early Hollerith system. The Bell Telephone system experimented with the use of boys as operators for its first telephone system in the 1890s.[38] But juveniles in general had notoriously high rates of labor turnover and low levels of general training.[39] A growing discontent with their performance, as well as moral arguments against their employment, began to end the

possiblity of using youngsters under sixteen in offices and department stores and may have provided the first impetus to hire older
girls instead. Even had they been suitable to office work, not
enough juveniles were available to staff the mushrooming number
of new office jobs. In 1890 nearly 7 percent of all children between
the ages of ten and fifteen were employed in nonagricultural pursuits, but this figure had reportedly fallen to 1.4 percent by 1930.
The number of youngsters between the ages of ten and thirteen
listed as messengers and office boys and girls had declined dramatically by 1930; compared to their counterparts in agriculture, textiles, and newspaper selling their numbers had never been very
significant anyway.[40] During the Progressive period, the growing
consensus to abolish child labor led to raising the age for manda-
tory school attendance and directing more negative attention to
those industries that employed children regularly.[41]

High labor turnover among young male machine clerks, noticed
by 1910 in a variety of offices, gave employers an extra reason to
sex-stereotype machine jobs for women. Bertha Stevens reported
that boy billers in department stores "are not satisfied to remain at
billing. If they do not find promotion in a year or two they usually
leave the store." One railroad offical asserted during World War I
that he preferred young women clerks because "they are steadier
than boys. They are not so damn anxious to get out and rustle
around . . . . They never think of themselves as General Managers
of a railroad and are content to work along." Eugene Benge, an early
and influential personnel management expert, declared that "the
belief that there is less mobility among women workers, older men,
and married men, has definitely been proven," and claimed that
women were less hostile than men to taking up restructured jobs.
Marion Bills, a psychologist and office management expert, showed
in a 1923 study of insurance company clerks and their tenure
patterns that even when terminations for marriage were included,
young women made more permanent employees than young men.[42]

Many firms continued to hire some younger teenaged men as
messengers and all-purpose office boys, hiring that probably increased temporarily during World War I. But the general tendency
of employers was away from recruiting boys under sixteen for
lower-level clerking jobs and toward the hiring of young women
with some high school or business college training. The longer attendance rates of high-school-aged girls made them ideal for office
jobs that required literacy in English and competence in mathematics. Teenaged boys were more likely than girls to leave school before

1920, probably because their employment opportunities were far more diverse. The same opportunities made boys restless in jobs with no future and more likely than girls to shift around in search of better ones. Discrimination against women, in addition to their human capital (high school attendance rates) made them good candidates for office jobs.

Behind the Marriage Bar: The Meaning of Women's Labor Turnover

In addition to lower turnover rates than were typical of youthful men, women were desirable employees for another reason: they could be subjected to a "marriage bar." The marriage bar was both a cultural convention and an arbitrary workplace requirement. The cultural norm before World War II was to expect that when women married, they would retire to the home, especially if they had children. Organized labor emphasized the concept of a "family wage"; men were to be paid enough so that wives and mothers could remain out of the work force and attend to domestic labor. Most of the middle class assumed that work and motherhood were incompatible. Employers who chose to impose the marriage bar could do so easily because they were, in a sense, reenforcing societal expectations. The marriage bar had some highly desirable economic advantages for employers. It created a large population of workers who could be fired while their relatively low wages still made their labor profitable, and, if they kept working, a group of workers who could be considered automatically ineligible for promotion.[43]

The argument that employers benefited from hiring short-term workers in positions that required brief periods of initial training and in which seniority simply increased labor costs may seem to contradict the claim that women made ideal office employees because they had lower rates of labor turnover, and often more education, than men. But the contradiction is only apparent. Employers did not want what I would define as "permanently permanent" employees in clerking jobs but, rather, "temporarily permanent" employees. Tenures of five to ten years for female office workers satisfied managers and handsomely repaid their investment in job training, suited some women for positions requiring more responsibility and longevity, and at the same time did not obligate employers to promote or pay women wages comparable to those of men.[44]

Discrimination against women in employment and the use of the marriage bar made women captive in clerical work, if not in individual office jobs. Men had other alternatives. The sociologist Mary Schauffler's informal study of Cleveland companies in 1925 found male secretaries still in place at only the railroads and the electric company. "The prevailing opinion," reported Schauffler, "was that men good enough for efficient secretaries will not be satisfied in this work but will merely make it a stepping stone to better jobs." Schauffler immediately grasped the role discrimination played in making women more desirable as secretaries: "It seems that for men secretarial work is just a step in their progress to bigger positions; to most women it is the end of the road. It has been a little amazing to hear men say they hire women because ... [women] will stay and they offer no promotion because women will stay without the possibility of promotion."[45]

In the process of applying the marriage bar to women and sex-stereotyping some office jobs, employers were building different systems of employment for women and men. As the division of labor became more elaborate, employers tried to designate some jobs, particularly stenography, typing, and machine clerking, as unfit bases for promotion to managerial and executive positions. In many instances men were no longer considered for typing and stenography jobs, whether they wanted them or not. Employers needed a pool of promotable clerks, however, and stressed that they welcomed men with higher ambitions for certain kinds of positions. Interest in women reflected the opposite expectation. A high school principal reported to one commercial education expert that, "Generally if you can say a boy has pep and a girl is quiet, you have satisfied the business man."[46]

Because most people did eventually marry, the marriage bar guaranteed that women as a group would be unable to stay on to earn higher wages and agitate for more responsible positions; those single and married women who did continue to work into middle age could be ignored as anomalies, despite their growing numbers. The dictum that women could not be promoted because they might marry became a self-fulfilling prophecy. As the divison of labor in the office began to create new categories of managers and professions that required higher education and separate promotion tracks, discrimination in education and the professions guaranteed that most women would be unable to secure either the training or consideration for better jobs. They would remain available for clerical work.

The marriage bar was especially useful to employers in creating the office labor force they and their male workers desired: one segmented primarily by gender. Employers and male employees used the marriage bar, perhaps both consciously and unconsciously, to regulate women's employment and also to discredit women workers. Although women left jobs for a variety of reasons, employers insisted that women could not be counted upon because they married. This convenient cultural convention had important economic benefits. By firing most women upon marriage, employers helped to ensure that women would continue to "fail" to live up to the ideal male model of a "career," and thus make the convention a reality. Women who left jobs because they were restless and unsatisfied could be shunted into the "women leave jobs to get married" category, thus confirming predisposed prejudices. At the same time, male employees may have been happy to countenance a system that secured their breadwinner dominance in the culture at large and in their own specific families and eliminated an entire gender from the competition for better-paying and more rewarding jobs. Stylized discussions of labor turnover diverted attention from women's real grievances in the office and served to reenforce the application of the marriage bar.

What about the claim that women left jobs to marry? Closer examination of women's labor turnover in clerking jobs elicits a complicated picture in which quits or firings upon marriage were important but not the most statistically predominant variables. Aggregate studies of women office workers demonstrated the same principle: interchangeability of skills made most women clerks relatively mobile in the teens and twenties, a mobility that could be handily confused in employers' minds with quits for marriage.

Women's work cycles in clerical jobs followed fairly predictable patterns according to age. One of the double binds of the marriage bar was that it was likely to be applied to women just when youthful workers in general (male or female) were settling into more regular employment habits. The greatest rates of labor turnover for both boys and girls occurred when they first left school and entered the work force.[47] High juvenile turnover rates guaranteed women workers a bad reputation for long-term reliability, whether they married or not. Because women in the work force were generally younger than men, their overall turnover rates were bound to be higher than men's, even though teenaged women generally stayed at their jobs longer than teenaged men. Very young women, if they made it through the first few months of employment, often made reliable employees, partly because they had so few other options for employment. It was generally true however, that women clerical workers between the ages of twenty and twenty-five were, at least as far as employers were concerned, all too restless. The clerical worker who was twenty-one or twenty-two usually had enough experience to find herself another job. If she was approaching twenty-five, she might be able to move on to a secretarial, bookkeeping, or supervisory position, all of which paid significantly better than routine clerical work. Once over twenty-five, women clerical workers were much less apt to move or to quit. They were now likely to be making better money and have better positions; they also found it difficult to find new jobs that would pay as much as those they already had. Rampant discrimination existed against women clerical workers over thirty-five in initial hires, so once in her thirties a woman clerk was more or less stuck.[48]

Feminist social scientists and personnel managers tried to point out that a number of variables other than quits for marriage affected labor turnover rates, and they called for careful research of women's work cycles. They argued that labor turnover rates for both men and women varied according to their ages and the kinds of jobs they had. Anne Bezanson of the Industrial Research Department of the University of Pennsylvania studied manufacturing workers and established that when skills and job levels of male and female workers were held constant, turnover rates were about the same.[49] Marion Bills found similar evidence in an elaborate study of ten insurance companies, and also showed that turnover rates for women were lowest in companies that paid higher salaries to women and offered them promotions to better positions.[50] The implications of these studies were generally ignored; they led to the conclusion, perhaps impossible to absorb until recently, that women's work lives could parallel those of men and that gender inequalities in the workplace based on the marriage bar were largely irrational.[51]

Women left jobs for a variety of reasons, and, in fact, marriage was not the one most frequently given. In Minneapolis, about 20.5 percent of all labor quits were for marriage.[52] Marion Bills found that only 14 percent of quits at Aetna Insurance were for marriage, and she argued that "at least during the early years of employment marriage is not a predominating cause of turnover."[53] Most women left jobs to take other ones. Some disliked their current employers, some found better positions, and others saw the possibility of advancement at a new firm. Others became ill, moved to other cities, decided to return to school, or left because of personal reasons.[54]

How much differing rates of education affected labor turnover is not entirely clear. Women with better educations had more long-term success in clerical work but were also reputed to be especially restless in clerical work and likely to change jobs frequently. Women stenographers and secretaries polled by the Bureau of Vocational Information in 1924-25 were, on average, older and better educated than most clerical workers. Nonetheless, their responses were surprisingly similar to those found by researchers of high school-educated clerical workers. Ruth Shonle Cavan developed a comparison of "reasons for leaving business" from the employment records of the Chicago YWCA Employment Bureau and the Chicago Collegiate Bureau. It might be assumed that the YWCA Bureau was primarily used by grammar-school and high-school-educated women, whereas most college-educated women found jobs through the Collegiate Bureau. The figures showed the same tendencies in both groups, as well as some important differences in emphasis. Those who used the YWCA Bureau were more likely to work in marginal firms and to lose their jobs when business conditions changed. Women who used the Chicago Collegiate Bureau were more likely than the YWCA group to change their occupation, probably because they had some professional training and more job options. But both groups were equally inclined to leave jobs because they disliked them or to better their positions.[55]

Individual clerical workers had patterns of longevity ranging from stable to restless, with most changing jobs once or twice during their careers. The Bureau of Vocational Information's survey uncovered one woman who had held thirty jobs in four years, but such job switching was rare. Beatrice Doerschuk's analysis of the 2,480 BVI questionnaires showed that nearly 30 percent had held only one job, and another 25 percent had held only two jobs. Only 17.5 percent had more than four jobs. In the sample of 948 BVI questionnaires that I studied, longevity at any one job increased with age, but even most seventeen- to.twenty-four-year-olds stayed with their employers for more than a year. The sample of Rhode Island clerical workers from the Rhode Island Women's Biography Project and the Rhode Island Working Women Oral History Project had a similar work profile. Of the twenty-two women who eventually left the work force upon marriage or to take care of children, the median number of years spent working in offices was eight, with a low of two, a high of thirteen, and an average of 6.8. Most had more than one job during that time, but none had more than three. Ethel Erickson's sample of New York City's clerical workers showed that 80 percent had worked at two or more jobs, and 40 percent had worked at three or more.[56]

It made sound economic sense to change jobs in the early years of employment. Elliott and Manson's 1926 study of women who were members of the Business, Professional and Women's Club, 41 percent of whom were clerks, found that judicious job-shopping increased salaries. "Apparently it pays to change jobs," claimed the authors. "The women who have held two or more positions have consistently higher median earnings than those who have continued in their first position."[57] Mary Schauffler's study of typists, stenographers, and bookkeepers in Cleveland demonstrated that clerical workers who changed their jobs in the first three years of employment were able to increase their salaries over those of women who stayed put.[58] Some women used frequent job-changing to improve their working conditions or to stand up to unsatisfactory employers. In a flippant but bold example, a high school graduate with some college education quit her first job during the war when she was not given permission to see a Liberty Loan parade; she left her desk in mid-morning, gave notice, and went to see the parade. Despite frequent job changes in the intervening six years, she was making a respectable $40 a week by 1924.[59]

A variety of personal stories lay behind quits, including what contemporary observers would term "sexual harassment." Alice R. left her first job, as stypist and stenographer in a Providence cotton broker's office, because the man who dictated to her "would walk all around the room and look out the window, so it was very hard to take a letter . . . . And one day, he swore at me, so I left." Rene Gibbs left her job at a New York City magazine office in 1917 because her "employer made love to me."[60]

A remarkable example of frequent job-leaving surfaced in a detailed letter that accompanied Helen McGregor's BVI questionaire. McGregor explained the knot of motives that had compelled her to hold fourteen jobs in nineteen years. Her beginnings were humble. She left commercial high school in Grand Rapids, Michigan, after two years of study; her first job was as a cashier and bundle girl at a laundry in 1906. She continued in the bookkeeping line for some time, obtaining jobs as billing clerk, cashier, bookkeeper, and office manager. She studied both shorthand and bookkeeping in night school and was currently working as a secretary, making $34 a week. In the course of her career she moved to Detroit, on to Chicago, and finally to San Francisco, where she took courses in accounting through the University of California extension system. Along the way she had married but was evidently childless. She did not find her marriage to be a hindrance in finding a job but thought that her current age of thirty-five would begin to negatively affect her chances of new employment.

McGregor explained her work history, which, she feared, might appear to be that of a "floater." "Personally," she explained, "I do not feel this is true. My moving about has been a sort of seeking after the ideal. I have never been discharged from a position, and in some instances I have been the youngest and highest paid employee on the payroll." The desire to improve her position had prompted her quits, and the evident belief that she might be "able to connect with the type of establishment that believed in women's capabilities" someday. The "jobs just ahead," she claimed, "have nearly always been filled by men, and in some instances by women of mature years." She recounted her job-hunting experiences in Chicago, where, over the course of four days, she answered thirty-three job advertisements and received twenty-eight interviews. "I think the result of that experiment made a permanent impression upon me," she said, "for it imbedded in my consciousness the fact that an employee has the same right (tho' they seldom exercise it) to choose their position, as an employer has to choose his help."[61]

McGregor's manifesto revealed a significant truth about clerical work in the twentieth century except for the years of the Great Depression. In a labor market characterized by widely interchangeable skills and high labor turnover, changing jobs was one way in which clerical workers could protest against the system, strike back at an individual employer, and carve out a measure of self-determination and personal dignity. The option of moving may also have had a negative effect on organizing efforts and group job actions. "Voting with their feet" was a more likely route for most women clerical workers than organizing workplace resistance. Clerical workers, most of whom were under thirty, were relatively mobile if they wanted to be. At the same time, women's job quits reenforced employers' prejudices that women were inherently unreliable and could continue to be subjected to a different wage and promotion system than men. As the feminization and rationalization of office work proceded, employers had few qualms about the rationale of assigning women to low-level jobs and keeping them there indefinitely.

Patterns of Feminization in Clerical Work

Patterns of feminization varied considerably in offices before World War I. The Aetna Life Insurance Company, for example, continued to cling to male clerks well into the twentieth century and did not hire its first woman office worker, a telephone operator, until 1908. She was joined by thirty-five machine operators in 1911 for a study of mortality statistics. Three of these women stayed on as permanent employees but were asked to use the back elevators so they would not be seen by the company president, who did not approve of women working in the insurance business. Although the number of women working at Aetna had grown to 150 by 1916, they remained in sex-segregated typing, filing, and machine-operating departments. At Metropolitan Life Insurance Company, a larger insurance firm, nearly 60 percent of the labor force (who numbered more than a thousand) was female.[62]

Eaton and Stevens's survey of offices in Cleveland in 1913-14 found that women were more than half of all clerks in manufacturing offices and insurance companies. While men still predominated in municipal offices, Eaton and Stevens predicted recent civil service examination reform would open more of these public-sector jobs to women. Women had made the smallest inroads in railroads, banking, and accounting firms, but even in these offices women's recruitment for comptometer and Hollerith operations was beginning to change the sex ratio. Women dominated clerical work in small establishments, addressing firms, the telephone company, and retail stores.[63] Department store offices, where clerical workers did billing, pricing, inventory, and payroll computations, were highly feminized. The enormity of these operations, which were characterized by tedium and suitability to office management techniques, was obvious; the retail credit industry of New York City reported in 1924 that there were three and a half million charge customers at New York stores alone. By 1916 women office workers in stores in Cleveland outnumbered men four to one. A study of Ohio department stores showed that although the number of male clericals had remained nearly constant since the beginning of the decade, the number of women doing stenography, bookkeeping, and clerking had doubled.[64]

The railroad industry had large bureaucracies of male clerical workers by the late nineteenth century, many of whom used office machines, including typewriters and tabulators. As late as 1910, 92 percent of all railway clerks were male, and female membership in the Brotherhood of Railway Clerks was "negligible." Strong craft unions had enabled male railway clerks to maintain fairly high salaries and ladders of upward mobility. Female clerks began to be hired in the 1890s, most as stenographers and machine clerks. In Cleveland in 1914, the 23 percent of all railroad clerks who were women were most likely to be stenographers, to use adding machines, and to do card punching and sorting or statistical work on comptometers. Young women usually began with job titles differing from those of men, and they were not in line for promotion to higher ranks.[65]

Some women worked at the Calumet Repair Shop of the Pullman Company in Chicago before World War I, but as seamstresses or shop laborers, not as clerks. World War I saw the first significant inroads of female clerks, most of whom took positions as comptometer operators, timekeepers, and record clerks. These new hiring policies by Pullman's management were part of a strategy to create a two-tier labor system based on sex segmentation. Regular promotions were available to men in the middle levels of clerking, and women and juvenile boys were used as a reserve labor pool for low-paying machine jobs with no chance of promotion.[66]

The railroad industries were being forced to adopt new clerical systems to keep up with demands made on their management and cost accounting capabilities. Other kinds of firms were also acting on the assumption that office jobs were adaptable to Taylorist organization. New methods used at Sears and Roebuck are a good illustration of just how dramatic the large-scale implementation of scientific management could be in the organization of office clerking and how it had the general effect of furthering the segmentation of office workers according to sex.

Over a thirty-five year period the labor force at Sears, mostly composed of clerical workers, managers, and shipping clerks, grew from eighty to several thousand. In the 1890s the founding partners still ran all the office and administrative functions personally, with the assistance of a few female clerical employees. Effective advertising promotions in company catalogs had created such a huge volume of orders for merchandise that the office and shipping department could not process or complete them in an efficient and timely fashion. By 1904 express companies in Chicago were threatening to boycott Sears because the office was so confused that it frequently submitted claims for merchandise never shipped. Shoddy and inefficient office work practice was at the root of Sears's difficulties. Richard W. Sears, who often worked until midnight, expected his clerks to do the same for no extra pay, which led to frequent absenteeism and a high rate of walkouts; the clerical work itself was riddled with errors made by exhausted and confused employees. Although most Sears workers were hired through newspaper advertisements, the company sometimes had to resort to "barking" for applicants from a soapbox in the street.[67]

Sears's sales had grown from about $75,000 in 1895 to nearly $38 million by 1905. Drastic organizational changes were in order if these sales were to continue. When Sears moved into its elaborate new shipping plant in 1906 it had an employment office, a work force of nearly eight thousand, and the latest in mechanical devices. A handful of managers, one of them a former bicycle correspondent and another an office boy turned employment manager, began to institute the techniques of office management experts. The elaborate new technology at the shipping plant was heavily touted in the catalog, but an enormous amount of routine clerical work was still done by hand: stamping, dating, pricing, filing, and addressing. Thousands of catalogs and fliers, for instance, were still addressed in long-hand until the Elliott Company devised addressograph machines for Sears during World War I.

The key to the new "system" in the plant was not just mechanization but a rigid timetable built on time and motion labor studies, piecework and bonus plans, and more sophisticated hiring and promotion practices. The company goaded both individual workers and their departments into performing faster and more efficiently by holding the managerial staff personally responsible for output. To eliminate one traditional bottleneck and speed up the reponse to order time, all mail was opened by machines and sent to appropriate departments by a special shift of workers before the regular work day began. Departments that failed to supply their part of an order on time had to foot the bill for shipping it separately and were also fined. Department heads were judged almost entirely on the performance of their staffs; the output of each employee was measured daily and wages reduced for errors; promotions and wage increases were mainly based on output. After 1910 the company established a standard performance tied to unit labor cost for most tasks and paid a premium to those employees who could increase production and lower the unit labor cost. Some workers used these bonus plans to increase their wages by as much as $10 a week.

Correspondence, always the most time-consuming of the clerical labor processes at Sears, was handled in a variety of ways. Form letters were used whenever possible, but a huge volume of letter writing still required stenographic dictation, and Sears seems to have been one of the first large firms in the country to have used female stenography pools outfitted with dictating machines. Clerks in both stenographic pools and accounting departments, most of whom were women, were subjected to rules derived from Taylorist shop discipline: no talking to neighbors; only one person to the water cooler or bathroom at a time; the submission of all questions and comments about work to department heads; the deductions of errors from wages; the submission of daily records of output; and "instant dismissal" for tardiness or other rule infractions. By 1918 bundles of orders were being dispatched at ten minute intervals throughout the day and prepared for shipping within four hours. And while its employees had mushroomed to more than twenty-five thousand by 1919, Sears's profits reached nearly $19 million.

Although the "system" was given much of the credit for the mail order firm's flamboyant expansion, its success was also tied to a careful recruitment policy and wage schedule for men and women in different categories of clerking. A cost-of-living study in Chicago determined that Sears could pay a minimum wage of $8 a week to young women living away from their families, although the company was charged by both the Chicago Vice Commission and the Illinois Senate Committee on Vice with paying wages so low they might lead workers into prostitution. Most men earned higher salaries than women, but the wage system discriminated between younger men and those considered to be more mature; any unmarried man under twenty-one could be given a salary as low as $5 a week. There was a more complicated entry-wage schedule for women, with the $5 minimum going only to girls under sixteen; those between sixteen and eighteen began at $6 a week. Female typists and stenographers over eighteen received higher salaries than younger teenagers of both sexes. Sears attempted to curb turnover by promising salary increases to employees who had worked at Sears for five years; workers were given examinations to determine possible increases in salary and promotions. A few women reached salaries of more than $20 a week; in 1913 the highest-paid woman employee, a department head, received $35. But a male manager of a billing department (made up of 150 women) made $100.

Women were now more than half of all Sears employees, but thousands of new male employees had been hired as well. Women performed billing, typing, and stenography jobs; men dominated the more prestigious and less routinized position of typist-correspondent into the 1920s, but were rarely hired as machine operators. Instead, low-paid male clerks with minimal educations were messengers, order fillers, and packers. The large mail order house preferred women with some high school or business college training in clerical skills and was willing to pay somewhat more to those who had it. By 1920 at the Philadelphia Sears plant women typists began at $14 a week and stenographers at $18; male messengers earned $10 a week and male packers $12.

The labor policies of Sears were soon to appear elsewhere. World War I broke down whatever resistance there was to employing female clerks and made them a significant presence in offices everywhere. Businesses that had put off developing better bookkeeping systems and scientific management practices had to install them to keep control of their burgeoning enterprises. Government contracts demanded new cost accounting and auditing procedures.[68] The existing shortage of young men was heightened by army recruitment, the sudden surge in industrial expansion, and the demand of the United States government for clerical workers to staff its wartime agencies.[69]

An officer of the Lincoln Insurance Company recalled that office managers during the war "were called upon to organize . . . a rapidly increasing volume of business with male members of our staff leaving for the service in ever increasing numbers. We advanced junior clerks to positions of responsibility, and trained large groups of girls to perform duties formerly considered as strictly male jobs." Even at the hidebound Aetna Insurance Company women now worked in departments with men and by 1922 were 44 percent of the home office. The Women's Bureau found that the use of female bookkeeping machine operators in banks became general practice during the war, and by its end women were "entrenched as bookkeeping machine operators on customer accounts and other applications of listing and balancing." The Guarantee Trust Company of New York reported to the Bureau of Vocational Information that "due to the demand upon our men for Government Service, opportunities for Bookkeeping and clerical work . . . , Private Secretaryships and other junior clerical positions, formerly held by men, are now being filled by women." In early 1918 about sixty-one thousand women worked for the railroads, and by October, more than a hundred thousand, 72 percent of them in offices. More than three-quarters of these women worked in railroad accounting departments, where comptometers, card punches, and tabulators were in widespread use.[70]

The problem of finding an alternative labor supply was acute, and crystalized management's determination to make clerking jobs available to women: "There must be new workers to take the place of those who have gone. Already labor has become scarce, especially labor of good quality . . . . Where are these new workers to come from? There are no untapped resources among men. In 1910 as much as 96 percent of men in the ages of 21 to 44 years were engaged in gainful occupations, and even among the males from 14 to 20 years of age the proportion was as high as as 69 percent. Even if it were desirable to employ the younger workers in larger measure they are not available in sufficient numbers to supply the need."[71]

Recently fired from her job at Brown and Sharpe after marrying a fellow clerk and "tired of being home without any work," Edith Charles easily found a new job during the war through the comptometer placement bureau, despite her married status. Two young women friends from Scituate, Rhode Island, with business college training found that jobs were available for the asking: "You could get a job anywhere . . . . Another girl and I, we'd take a job in the morning, and if we didn't like it we'd quit at noontime and take another one in the afternoon."[72]

Office machine companies, perceiving a golden opportunity to sell new products, urged businesses to buy machines and avoid wartime labor supply problems by training women. They quickly made the link between women, routinized work, and machine operation that was helping to ease the transition of women workers into the office. A Dalton adding machine testimonial in *System* declared: "Uncle Sam took my experienced clerks. In their place I have willing workers but *inexperienced*. So I must have simple office machines . . . . inexperienced operators soon become lightening fast on the 10-*key Dalton*." The same machine promised to "substitute woman-power for man-power; . . . with little practice a girl . . . does the figure work of three or more experienced men." Burroughs announced that "anyone who can read can post ledgers with a Burroughs Automatic Bookkeeping machine."[73] Although many women hired for industrial jobs during World War I throughout the country were fired in 1919, women office workers often stayed on; the war had demanded more deep-rooted modernization, permanently increased the number of jobs in the office, and installed women in them for the forseeable future.[74]

The steady stream of women coming into railroad offices during the war heightened men's anxieties about their own positions. Women were given the most tedious jobs, and supervisors and co-workers tried to insist they not receive consideration for better ones. The rapid introduction of more modern accounting methods, scientific management techniques, and the sudden hiring of large numbers of female machine operators did provoke outbreaks of hostility toward women. Men unused to working with women on a daily basis sometimes responded with both verbal and physical harassment. The use of women as strikebreakers in the years before the war may have predisposed male clerks to view women with suspicion, believing that men's "status would be severely and perhaps irrevocably weakened" if women were hired.[75] They were, in fact, quite right; the mechanization and feminization of office work was part of a process that was bound to change the world and status of the traditional male clerk. There was little men could have done to prevent the hiring of women for clerking jobs, but the fact that men protested the initial appearance of significant numbers of women indicates their fear that women would either take their jobs, lower their wages, or that women's presence symbolized a turn by management to restructuring men's work.[76]

In sectors of employment outside the railroads and the post office, male clerks rarely had any semblance of union protection. They had virtually no recourse if employers decided to institute machines or hire youthful stenographers, bookkeepers, and machine operators, many of whom were women. The traditional strategy of craft unions was to control workers' access to the apprenticeship system to insure higher wages and a limited labor supply. But as public schools, business colleges, and corporation training schools provided free or cheap training for office work, bookkeepers and stenographers, despite foot-dragging and antipathy to the new systems, were relatively helpless in preventing the hiring of clerks that they no longer trained on the job.[77]

The American Federation of Labor organized some locals of bookkeepers, stenographers, and accountants after 1900.[78] These unions were attempting to define themselves in terms of the craft union movement and viewed the growing number of recently educated young stenographers, typists, and machine operators with alarm. Organized clerks blamed more readily available education in business skills for declining wages and worsening working conditions. As late as 1931, Maurice Rabinovitz, a male secretary from a bookkeepers, stenographers, and accountants' local, decried the "present system whereby thousands of young men and women are graduated annually from the high schools and business colleges and eagerly seek employment at low wages, thereby competing with the experienced workers who have achieved some measure of stability and prosperity as the result of years of endeavor." He was still proposing a three-year apprenticeship system managed by union members, an idea that was certainly hopeless by that point.[79]

Men and women office workers tended to organize in union locals separately, with men agitating for licensing of "professional" clerks, and women banding together in mutual associations that went on to agitate for higher wages and equal pay. This bifurcation represented, in fact, what was happening in the sexual division of labor in the office; women were more likely than men to be stuck in low-paying jobs with little possibility of promotion, and although male clerks tended to receive higher wages than women, their traditional status was being undermined by mechanization, feminization, and rationalization. The position of the male unionists was untenable, and the female unionists were faced with the same uphill slogging that other female locals in the AFL encountered before the depression and the rise of the Congress of Industrial Organizations. Men with the resources to pursue further education for managerial or professional positions were beginning to leave clerking work altogether, or were turning to other white-collar jobs less accessible to women: sales and managing in particular.[80]

The most effective organizing of women clerical workers took place in the railroad industry, among telephone operators, and in the federal civil service.[81] But declines in the railroad industry in the 1920s and the institution of the dial telephone system at the end of the decade undermined the strength of both unionized railroad and telephone workers. Male unionists in both sectors also did their best to isolate women and prevent them from having anything like equal access to jobs. In the federal civil service, despite continued discrimination against women, the concept of equal pay for equal work had been established as a union goal, legitimized ideologically by the opening of civil service examinations to women, the Classification Act of 1924, and new personnel management policies of the federal government. The National Federation of Federal Employees had two women on its executive board in 1924, and in the 1930s its offshoot, the United Federal Workers, would elect the first woman union president in the CIO.[82]

Wages, Job Titles, and Conditions of Office Work: The Limits of Rationalization

The unionization of women office workers before 1930 was probably undercut by relatively high wages and good working conditions in offices. Most observers in the teens and twenties agreed that the average wage-earning woman fared better in office work than in other kinds of nonprofessional employment. The hours were shorter, the pay better, and vacations and sick days were usually offered to workers whose tenure on the job was long enough.

While working conditions in small offices ran the gamut from exploitative to munificent, those in larger ones were more predictable. By 1930 C. Wright Mills estimated that more than half of all clerical workers were employed in offices of fifty or more people.[83]

A picture of working conditions in relatively large offices by the end of the 1920s was presented in an American Management Association (AMA) study of 304 firms, 80 percent of which employed fifty or more white-collar workers, and in Ethel Erickson's Women's Bureau mammoth study of large urban offices. Ethel Erickson's 1931-32 Women's Bureau survey profiled forty-three thousand women in 314 offices, most large ones with more than a hundred workers each, in seven cities with large concentrations of industries that required paperwork: New York, Philadelphia, Chicago, Atlanta, St. Louis, Hartford, and Des Moines. The establishments in both of these studies—large manufacturers, public utilities, department stores, insurance companies, banks, advertising agencies, and investment firms—had rationalized clerical work systems and were located in the some of the most rapidly growing urban centers of the country. "Compared with hours in trade and industry," Erickson noted, "office hours are short." The workday was usually seven and a half hours and four hours on Saturday, although almost all the firms admitted to at least occasional overtime. Erickson found that male clerks were more likely than female clerks to put in overtime, but nearly all firms occasionally had "emergency work" for women as well as men. Only 19 percent of the AMA firms paid extra for overtime, and most of these were larger firms trying to adhere to a regimented day; supper money was likely to be the only reward for working late. Most firms provided employees with two weeks a year of vacation with pay, and some paid sick time, ranging from one to four weeks a year. Erickson found that workers were almost never docked for being out sick during short illnesses. Large banks, insurance companies, and public utilities were most likely to offer organized welfare activities, and mid-sized to large firms were more likely than small firms to provide sitting rooms, athletic teams, and social clubs. More than two-thirds of the firms, regardless of size, gave periodic salary increases, with most granting increases once or twice a year.[84]

Clerical work had a wide range of salaries, with the possibility of making more money as time went by. Except for the lowest ranks of machine work, filing and typing, clerical work generally paid more money to women than all but the professional occupations. On average, women office workers consistently earned more than other women workers outside the professions, and clerical workers continued to make larger gains in salaries in the twenties than did their nearest counterparts, saleswomen.[85] Unlike many other kinds of women's work—especially in manufacturing or domestic service—years of experience in clerical work did usually lead to somewhat higher salaries and promotions to better positions.[86]

Women and men in clerical work, unlike most other occupations, still shared some job titles and did similar work. This fact had a different impact on incomes earned by women and men. Although men's clerical wages were not climbing after 1900 as rapidly as they once did, in part because women were now more likely to be clerical workers, women clerical workers were earning more than women in more "feminized" occupations partly because they were doing work that was still being done by men.

Feminization, however, was not the only factor, perhaps not even the most important factor, in lowering the overall wage levels of clerical work. Free commercial training in high school and inexpensive training in business colleges also helped to lower wage scales in clerical work and provided a larger pool of skilled labor. Combined with the entrance of more women into clerical work, such education led to a general erosion of men's wages. In his classic work on real wages in the United States between 1890 and 1926, the economist Paul Douglas showed that clerical wages, if tied to the cost of living, rose at their fastest rate between 1890 and 1898 and then leveled off after 1905. On average, salaried clerical employees were only slightly better off in 1926 than they had been in the 1890s. As Douglas observed, public schools were increasingly taking over the responsibility of training clerical workers for business, and in a larger sense, creating the impression that the appropriate thing to do with a high school education was to enter office work. As a result, "the high schools have primarily served to recruit juveniles for clerical work, and the vast numbers that have poured out of the high schools have served to keep wages down to a much lower point than would otherwise have been the case." Douglas argued that this massive recruitment of public-school trained men and women into clerical work would continue to stagnate clerical wages and narrow the gap between manufacturing and white-collar workers. Analyses of clerical and manufacturing wages between the late nineteenth century and the mid-twentieth centuries have confirmed his prediction. While male earnings in clerical work have consistently exceeded those for women, men's clerical wages were at their relative peak in the early twentieth century, after which the gap between manufacturing and clerical wages steadily narrowed.[87]

Between 1920 and 1931 there were some regional differences among salaries paid to clerks, but studies of clerical work showed remarkable uniformity in ranges of wages. The National Industrial Conference Board's 1925 survey investigated the salaries of 25,782 male and female clerical workers in eighteen major cities in 416 establishments with an average employment of sixty-four persons each. Like other wage surveys of the decade, it showed that most women clerks earned salaries of $16-$25 a week. "Women's jobs," particularly typing, stenography, filing, machine operating, and miscellaneous clerking, earned the least money. A significant exception to this general rule was secretarial work, which, in the upper ranges, paid considerably more than other jobs dominated by women. Jobs that retained fairly general titles and conveyed some sense of importance—"chief clerk," "head bookkeeper," or "junior clerk"—had the widest range of salaries and contained the most men; these were also the jobs in which women made the most money and probably had the most varied work. Jobs that conveyed "machine operator" in their titles were not as low-paying as some jobs like filing and mail-room work, which required no skills in machine work at all. Jobs that required bookkeeping or supervising were the jobs in which women tended to earn the most in comparison to men (Table 6).[88]

The NICB categories of office work made one thing clear: classification systems of jobs in office work were burgeoning. The office hierarchy was elaborate if not very precise. When job analysts tried to compare job titles from firm to firm, there was little guarantee that jobs and duties would be the same. Office management experts tried to devise classification schemes for clerks according to job title, job duties, sex, and levels of skill, and they wrote about these schemes extensively in books and periodicals.[89] But those who actually looked at clerical workers on the job usually found only the skeleton of a functioning classification system. Even in the largest firms, there was no guarantee that all typists would be typing, all stenographers taking dictation, or all ledger clerks doing ledger

Table 6.
Clerical Occupations and Salary Ranges, 1926

Occupation	Percent Women	Weekly Salary Range	Percent of Women in	
			Highest-Paid Group	Lowest-Paid Group
Chief clerks	12	below $40–over $75	1.0	69.8
Head bookkeepers	24	below $30–over $60	1.0	23.6
Secretarial stenographers	88	below $25–over $55	1.1	11.0
Senior clerk	43	below $20–over $50	0.5	11.4
Cost clerks	37	below $20–over $40	0.3	52.5
Shipping clerks	06	below $20–over $40	1.8	47.2
Senior stenographers	93	below $20–over $35	3.0	7.7
Junior clerks	41	below $18–over $32	1.5	42.0
Machine operators	81	below $15–over $30	4.9	10.0
General clerks	58	$10–over $30	1.8	8.8
Ledger clerks	27	$10–over $30	7.0	0.5
Experienced typists	94	below $17.50–over $27	7.1	23.2
Switchboard operators	95	$15–over $27.50	17.4	4.5
Junior stenographers	97	below $17.50–over $26.50	12.4	19.8
File clerks	84	below $10–over $25	12.1	8.4
Mail Clerks	35	below $10–over $25	7.0	0.4
Inexperienced typists	96	below $13.50–over $23	2.3	22.2

Source: National Industrial Conference Board, *Clerical Salaries in the United States* (New York: NICB, 1926), 11-21, 29.

work. Many office workers performed a variety of functions and used several different kinds of machines. One out of every eight women in offices, Erickson found, used a machine other than the typewriter. Women clerical workers understood this fact and built it into their job-seeking strategies. In looking at employment cards filled out by women who sought work through a private employment agency in Cleveland, Mary Schauffler uncovered similar data. A woman might seek work as a bookkeeper, typist, or a stenographer, but frequently listed abilities and experience in a half dozen or more kinds of clerical work. Most women outside the narrowest machine operative jobs were learning or using a variety of office skills that made them eligible for a variety of jobs, and, theoretically, should have made them eligible to go on to the higher levels of clerking.[90]

Whatever the duties a job entailed, job titles remained important, as every office worker knew. A secretary was usually paid more than a stenographer, a senior clerk more than an operative. Job titles were linked to prestige on the job and to self-esteem. Erickson found that although significant numbers of operatives were in the large firms she studied, most women clerical workers were not operatives. While about 36 percent of all women clerical workers had job titles that put them into the operative category (including typists, machine operators, telephone operators, and file clerks), another 12 percent were secretaries, bookkeepers, supervisors, and correspondents, and 49 percent were in the murky occupation categories of "general clerk" and "stenographer." Some of these clerks and stenographers performed rationalized work, but many did not (Table 7).[91]

The large proportion of women who were classified as clerks in Erickson's study reflected the census count as well and emphasized an important fact about the sexual division of labor in office work. Although by 1910 most office workers with the job titles of "typist," "stenographer," or "machine operator" were women, men and women were both increasing in the job categories of clerk and bookkeeper. When office work is assumed to be stenography and typing alone, it appears to be more feminized than it actually is. Certainly, many male clerks were actually doing typing, stenography, and bookkeeping, even if they were not given specialized job titles like "typist" or "stenographer"; conversely, many female typists, stenographers, and bookkeepers peformed varied tasks. More precise job titles were a signficant aspect of scientific management employment methods. The ability of many men (and some women) to hang on to amorphous job titles like "clerk" and bookkeeper" may indicate that both they and their employers sought to minimize the connection between men's clerking and operative status and to limit the effects of rationalization upon the gender hierarchy. At the same time, job titles did not necessarily reflect the work that men and women did or the skills they used on the job.[92]

The fundamental irrationality of the job classification system in clerical work undermines the reliability of human capital theory as an explanation for why women were increasingly hired as low-level

Table 7.
Percent Women Holding Specified Clerical Occupations in Offices

Occupations	Percent of All Women Workers in Category	Median Monthly Salary
General clerk	34.7	$ 90
Typist*	15.2	90–103
Stenographer	14.4	114
Machine operator	12.3	89–104
File clerk	6.0	81
Secretary	4.4	156
Supervisor	3.7	153
Bookkeeper	2.3	111
Telephone operator	2.1	109
Merchandising (mail order)	1.4	61
Cashier, teller	1.0	123
Correspondent	.9	105
Messenger	.9	55
Other[†]	.6	166

Source: Ethel Erickson, "The Employment of Women in Offices," *Women's Bureau Bulletin* 120 (1934): 6.

*Includes dictating machine transcribers, about 2.2 percent.

†Professional and semiprofessional women such as personnel directors and underwriters.

clerical workers after 1880. In the human capital view, employers were willing to absorb the cost of training people if they could reap the benefits of the training at a later date. More highly developed skills are said to coincide with prospects of long-term employment, promotion, and higher salary. Shorter careers for women supposedly made it unlikely that they would develop a wide range of firm-specific skills. But it cannot be argued that women who were graduates of commercial curricula in high schools, or who learned a variety of skills on the job, were, on the whole, less skilled than most male clerks. Job titles did not necessarily reflect what workers did all day; most women clerks acquired a variety of skills and could move beyond or integrate simple tasks. Women's job application strategies and work histories demonstrated that they often had a variety of office skills ranging from bookkeeping to stenography to general clerking. The notion that women willingly left the work force upon marriage has been assumed rather than established in fact. Moreover, there is no evidence that single and married women who worked continuously in clerical work, even with extensive training and skills, were "rewarded" for their "human capital" in the same ways that comparable men were. Rather, the gender of women was used as a rationalization for shunting them into sex-stereotyped occupations requiring specific skills but failing to pay adequately for them. Gender, as well as human capital investment, dictated the allocation of jobs and rate of payment.

Mechanization, feminization, and scientific management in the twentieth-century office, which came together most dramatically during World War I, had important implications for the gender characteristics of clerical work. The impact of machine technology had been ambiguous. While the use of machinery was associated with operative status and routinized work and therefore with women, office machine technology could enhance an employee's value and ability to perform specialized and independent tasks. Rationalization did not always accompany mechanization. Thus the division between men and women was not so much based on machine technology per se as it was on the kinds of tasks with which men and women were associated in the office, the wages they earned, and especially the future in office work they might expect.

The motives that had first prompted the hiring of women in office jobs in the federal government were certain to emerge in private industry as well. Employers wanted to find workers who could be paid less than traditional male clerks and who would have relatively low rates of turnover. They could pay women less than they could pay men with comparable education and skill levels; they would rarely have to promote women; and sex discrimination in a wide variety of other occupations was likely to force women to accept these conditions of employment for decades to come. The automatic exclusion of women from many categories of upper-level office jobs guaranteed they would be more likely than men to have to submit to tedious work, rationalization, and low wages. And, as a substantially beneficial side effect, as more women took jobs at depressed rates, the overall levels of wages for men might be reduced as well.

The growing presence of women clerks in both the federal government and large private bureaucracies like the railroads did not mean that men stopped looking for jobs in either sector. Rather, managers were retaining an older system of employment alongside a new one: in the older system, clerks (nearly all men) began in lowly positions but were promised access to promotions. In the new system, clerks (women and some young men) were expected to work with no expectation of promotion to management positions or significantly higher salaries.

Women did not take over or de-skill men's jobs so much as they took jobs created by the revolution in new methods of communicating, cost accounting, and record keeping. And without what the novelist Sinclair Lewis had described as a "revolution in the attitude" toward women, that is, an end to discrimination in hiring and promotion, the opening of other occupations to them, and the end of the marriage bar, women continued to make perfect candidates for these new jobs.[93] But the rise of sophisticated accounting methods, the new importance of bookkeeping, and the increased volume of sales, managing, and paperwork in general also guaranteed a huge surge in male white-collar employment after 1910. Rather than rushing to avoid taking jobs alongside women in so-called "feminized" offices, men sought office jobs nearly as frequently as women did. They had been guaranteed at least limited access to a separate hierarchy based on their gender. As more and more clerks filled new jobs, the business of managing them became a full-time occupation. In the next chapter I discuss the maturing of modern office work in the 1920s and the evolution of office management, where sexual difference showed up clearly and presented difficult contradictions for workers and managers alike.

NOTES

1. Interview with G. M. by Gail Gregory Sansbury, Feb. 6, 1983 (Edith Charles is a pseudonym), Rhode Island Working Women Oral History Project [RIWW], Special Collections, University of Rhode Island, Kingston.

2. The most explicit use of human capital theory with regard to clerical work is Elyce Jean Rotella, "The Transformation of the American Office," *Journal of Economic History* 41 (March 1981): 51-57. She emphasizes human capital theory less emphatically in her important Ph.D. dissertation, "Women's Labor Force Participation and the Growth of Clerical Employment in the United States, 1870-1930," University of Pennsylvania, 1977, 245-51. The most helpful critiques of human capital theory and clerical work are by sociologists Samuel Cohn, *The Process of Occupational Sex-Typing: The Feminization of Clerical Labor in Great Britain* (Philadelphia: Temple University Press, 1985), 5-13, and Graham S. Lowe, *Women in the Administrative Revolution: The Feminization of Clerical Work* (Toronto: University of Toronto Press, 1987), 21-22. Lowe (who studied the history of office work in Canada) and I were working on manuscripts simultaneously and, regrettably, did not know about each other or how much our work had in common. He comes to many of the same conclu-

sions that I do about the array of factors linking feminization, rationalization, and mechanization.

Economists who see sex discrimination as an important variable in both occupational sex-stereotyping and lower wages for women are: Mark Aldrich and Randy Albelda, "Determinants of Working Women's Wages during the Progressive Era," *Explorations in Economic History* 17 (1980): 323-41; Mary Corcoran, Greg J. Duncan, and Michael Ponza, "A Longitudinal Analysis of White Women's Wages," *Journal of Human Resources* 18 (Fall 1983): 497-520; Paula England, "The Failure of Human Capital Theory to Explain Occupational Sex Segregation," *Journal of Human Resources* 17 (Summer 1982): 358-70; Mary Huff Stevenson, *Determinants of Low Wages for Women Workers* (New York: Praeger, 1984), 50-57; and Mary Huff Stevenson, "Wage Differences betwen Men and Women: Economic Theories," in *Women Working*, ed. Ann H. Stromberg and Shirley Harkess (Palo Alto: Mayfield Publishing, 1986), 89-107.

Margery Davies suggests that typewriters began as a "gender-neutral" machine and could thus be associated with women's labor. *Woman's Place Is at the Typewriter: Office Work and Office Workers, 1870-1930* (Philadelphia: Temple University Press, 1982), 58. The most adamant proponent of the de-skilling of clerical work is Harry Braverman, *Labor and Monopoly Capital: The Degradation of Work in the Twentieth Century* (New York: Monthly Review Press, 1974), 293-358.

3. The classic accounts are C. Wright Mills, *White Collar: The American Middle Classes* (New York: Oxford University Press, 1951), 189-212, and David Lockwood, *The Blackcoated Worker: A Study in Class Consciousness* (London: George Allen and Unwin, 1958). Two accounts that stress the precariousness of male clerking in the nineteenth century in England are Cohn, *The Process of Occupational Sex-Typing*, 67-69, and Gregory Anderson, *Victorian Clerks* (Manchester: University of Manchester Press, 1976), 5-27. For an American clerk's account, see Francis R. Reed, *Experience of a New York Clerk* (New York: F. R. Reed, 1877).

4. For example, C. D. Palmer had been a bicycle manager until the depression of 1893-94 forced him into bankruptcy. He became a correspondent clerk at Sears and Roebuck, answering letters and complaints about bicycles, and developed a series of printed form letters to return to customers to save dictating time. He retired from Sears in 1928 as an office manager. Boris Emmet and John E. Jeuck, *Catalogues and Counters: A History of Sears, Roebuck and Company* (Chicago: University of Chicago Press, 1950), 131.

5. Bertha Stevens, *Boys and Girls in Commercial Work* (Cleveland: Survey Company of the Cleveland Foundation, 1916), 50.

6. Mary Schauffler, "Impressions on Secretarial Work," handwritten notes, 4, BVI, folder 494.

7. "Women in the Federal Service, 1923-1947," *Women's Bureau Bulletin* [WBB] 230-I (1949): 2; Cindy Sondik Aron, *Ladies and Gentlemen of*

the Civil Service: Middle-Class Workers in Victorian America (New York: Oxford University Press, 1987), 5.

8. Aron, *Ladies and Gentlemen of the Civil Service*, 65-91, is a careful analysis of these developments.

9. Bertha M. Nienburg, "Women in the Government Service," *WBB* 8 (1920): 10-11; Aron, *Ladies and Gentlemen of the Civil Service*, 96-115.

10. For a summary of the census of 1890, see Geoffrey D. Austrian, *Herman Hollerith: Forgotten Giant of Information Processing* (New York: Columbia University Press, 1982), 66-71. Aron observes that women had been hired as early as 1880 by the Census Office to tally census returns and without using machines. *Ladies and Gentlemen of the Civil Service*, 91.

11. For a brief history of the typewriter, see Davies, *Woman's Place Is at the Typewriter*, 31-38; Bruce Bliven Jr., *The Wonderful Writing Machine* (New York: Random House, 1954), 80-93; and Richard N. Current, *The Typewriter and the Men Who Made It* (Urbana: University of Illinois Press, 1954), 111-22.

Brian Randell, ed., *The Origins of Digital Computers: Selected Papers* (New York: Springer-Verlag, 1973) notes that the Babbage engine of 1835 embodied the concept of the "general purpose digital computer—consisting of a store, arithmetic unit, punched card input and output, and a card-controlled sequencing mechanism that provided iteration and conditional branching." In 1842 Augusta Ada (also known as Lady Lovelace, and a daughter of Lord Byron) developed what may have been the first "computer program" for use on the Babbage engine to compute Bernoulli numbers. Randell attributes the fact that Babbage's engines were not really produced in the nineteenth century to inadequate technology and also "to the fact that comparatively few of his contemporaries shared his beliefs in the need for such machines." Randell thinks the wide variety of calculating machines that appeared at the turn of the century, along with punched card machines and sorters, "led to the general acceptance of the idea of mechanical digital calculation, and so as the needs for greater speed and accuracy became apparent, helped to pave the way for the development of automatic computers," 1-14.

12. Susan Porter Benson, *Counter Cultures: Saleswomen, Managers, and Customers in American Department Stores, 1890-1940* (Urbana: University of Illinois Press, 1986), 19.

13. Emmet and Jeuck, *Catalogues and Counters*, 132-33.

14. C. King Woodbridge, *'Dictaphone' Electronic Genius of Voice and Typed Word* (Princeton: Princeton University Press, 1952); L. C. Stowell, "The Development of the Dictaphone, *Scovill Bulletin*, [*SB*] (March-April 1932): 14-18; and J. E. Sease, "Voice-Writing with the Ediphone," *SB* (July 1930): 1-3.

15. These figures are from U.S. Department of Commerce, *Census of Manufactures: 1921* (Washington, D.C.: GPO, 1924), 434, *1929*, 2: 1120. Production totals for calculating machines were reached despite the fact

that up until 1921 so-called bookeeping-typewriters were categorized with typewriters. Typewriters, of course, were also used extensively for the production of accounting and statistical documents. See, for example, E. H. Brown, *Statistical Typewriting* (New York: Ronald Press, 1924).

16. This account has been drawn from John S. Coleman, *The Business Machine—with Mention of William Seward Burroughs, Joseph Boyer, and Others—since 1880* (Princeton: Princeton University Press, 1949); Morgan Bryan, *Total to Date: The Evolution of the Adding Machine: The Story of Burroughs* (London: Burroughs Adding Machine, 1953); and Perley Morse, *Business Machines: Their Practical Application and Educational Requirements* (London: Longmans, Green, 1932). Also see William Henry Leffingwell, *The Office Appliance Manual* (n.p.: National Assocation of Office Appliance Manufacturers, 1926), 4-8.

17. Edwin Darby, *It All Adds Up: The Growth of Victor Comptometer Corporation* (n.p.: Victor Comptometer Corporation, 1968).

18. Morse, *Business Machines*, 57-60; George C. Brainard, *A Page in the Colorful History of Our Modern Machine Age* (Princeton: Princeton University Press, 1950), 14-15.

19. Austrian, *Herman Hollerith*, 58-141.

20. Ibid., 125, 140. For a detailed account of the Hollerith system and its importance to both Taylorism and cost accounting at Watertown, see Hugh G. J. Aitken, *Taylorism at Watertown Arsenal: Scientific Management in Action, 1908-1915* (Cambridge: Harvard University Press, 1960), 129-31.

21. Morse, *Business Machines*, 156-57.

22. Ibid., 128. Leffingwell recommended the use of the new accounting machines in his manual *Scientific Office Management* (Chicago: A. W. Shaw, 1917), 122-23. For accounts of the early history of IBM and Remington-Rand, see "International Business Machines," *Fortune* 5 (Jan. 1932): 34-40, and 21 (Jan. 1940): 36-44; and Edmund L. Van Deusen, "The Two Plus Two of Sperry Rand," *Fortune* 52 (Aug. 1955): 124; Ray W. McDonald, *Strategy for Growth: The Story of the Burroughs Corporation* (Princeton: Princeton University Press, 1978).

23. John T. Soma, *The Computer Industry: An Economic-Legal Analysis of Its Technology and Growth* (Lexington, Mass.: D. C. Heath, 1976), 15, fn. 54.

24. Mills, *White Collar*, 193.

25. International Labour Office, "The Use of Machinery and Its Influence on Conditions of Work for Staff," *International Labour Review* 35 (Oct. 1937): 515; also see Lockwood, *The Blackcoated Worker*, 36.

26. International Labour Office, "The Use of Machinery," 491.

27. For an important discussion of the skills involved in clerical work and a critique of the whole concept of de-skilling, see Cohn, *The Process of Occupational Sex-Typing*, 65-90.

28. Leffingwell argued in 1917 that good stenographers had both superior education and specific personal attributes, *Scientific Office Manage-*

ment, 125. For an examination of the private secretary and her or his functions, see "Objectives of Secretarial Training," BVI *News Bulletin,* April 14, 1924, 59, 61, 63; Davies, *Woman's Place Is at the Typewriter,* 129-62; and Rosabeth Moss Kanter, *Men and Women of the Corporation* (New York: Basic Books, 1977), 69-103.

Eaton and Stevens found only two firms in Cleveland using dictaphone operators in 1915, but one had twenty machines and another had forty. Jeanette Eaton and Bertha M. Stevens, *Commercial Work and Training for Girls* (New York: Macmillan, 1915), 215. The most frequent users of dictaphone machines before World War I were the large mail order houses, which had an extraordinary amount of routine correspondence. For a description of the stenographic department at Sears, see Lisa Michelle Fine, "'The Record Keepers of Property': The Making of the Female Clerical Labor Force in Chicago, 1870-1930," Ph.D. diss., University of Wisconsin at Madison, 1985, 115-17.

29. Advertisement for the "Edison Business Phonograph," *System* 18 (July 1910): n.p. and "Ediphone, Edison's New Dictating Machine," *System* 48 (Sept. 1925): 303; also see William Edward Ross, "Getting the Day's Work Done," *Office Economist* [*OE*] 2 (May 1920): 76. For a helpful discussion of the difficulty of scientific managers in instituting the dictaphone, see Adrian Forty, *Objects of Desire: Design and Society from Wedgewood to IBM* (New York: Pantheon Books, 1986), 137-39.

30. For a description of the traditional bookkeeper and his loss of status in the twentieth century, see Mills, *White Collar,* 191, 207; International Labour Office, "The Use of Machinery," 492-93; and Braverman, *Labor and Monopoly Capital,* 305.

31. Jurgen Kocka, *White Collar Workers in America, 1890-1940: A Socio-Political History in International Perspective* (London: Sage Publishers, 1980), 130-31; Edward Page, "The New Science of Business: Making an Office Efficient," *World's Work* 12 (June 1906): 7682-84. For other examples of the displacement of male computing clerks, see Kendall Banning, "Machines instead of Clerks," *Library of Office Management* (Chicago: A. W. Shaw, 1914), 1: 139-40; and W. B. Jadden, "Keeping Labor Records by Machinery," *Library of Office Management* (Chicago: A. W. Shaw, 1914), 4: 85.

32. Eaton and Stevens, *Commercial Work,* 217-18.

33. E. H. Beach, *Tools of Business: An Encyclopedia of Office Equipment and Labor Saving Devices* (Detroit: Bookkeeper Publishing, 1905), 8-9. Accounting experts commented on the resistance of bookkeepers to the new order. See, for example, T. H. Sanders, "The Present Status of Uniform Cost Accounting," *Harvard Business Review* [*HBR*] 1 (Jan. 1923): 172.

34. Leffingwell, *Scientific Office Management;* Galloway, *Office Management;* George Frederick, "Standards for the Office: Applying the Princi-

ples of Standardization of Factory Work to the Office," *OE* 2 (June 1920): 85.

35. For an important exploration of the gender construction of operative work in the eary nineteenth century, see Judith A. McGaw, *Most Wonderful Machine* (Princeton: Princeton University Press, 1987), 335-74. On women operatives in the electrical industry, see Ronald W. Schatz, *The Electrical Workers: A History of Labor at General Electric and Westinghouse, 1923-1960* (Urbana: University of Illinois Press, 1983), 30.

36. For the effect of rationalization and mass production on women's work, see Maureen Greenwald, *Women, War and Work: The Impact of World War I on Women Workers in the United States* (Westport: Greenwood Press, 1980), 6-7, and Alice Kessler-Harris, *Out to Work: A History of Wage-Earning Women in the United States* (New York: Oxford University Press, 1982), 142-55. Claudia Goldin found that women factory workers in 1890 were 3.5 times as likely to be employed on piece rates as men, and men were far more likely than women to work in teams under internal contractors. Pieceworkers in general tended to be easier to supervise and more productive than teams paid by a day rate. Therefore, "the ability of manufacturing enterprises both to use a technology with an intricate division of labor and to monitor the output of workers . . . fostered the employment of females." When this logic is extended to clerical work, as Goldin observes, it is not so much the mechanization itself that causes feminization as it is rationalization and the "reduced level of supervision needed to elicit some level of output." "Women's Employment and Technological Change: A Historical Perspective," in *Computer Chips and Papers Clips: Technology and Women's Employment*, ed. Heidi Hartmann (Washington D.C.: National Academy Press, 1987), 2: 212-13.

37. David Montgomery skillfully delineates these three categories of workers and their gender, racial, and ethnic connotations in *The Fall of the House of Labor: The Workplace, the State, and American Labor Activism, 1865-1925* (Cambridge: Cambridge University Press, 1987), 9-170.

38. Austrian, *Herman Hollerith*, 240; Greenwald, *Women, War and Work*, 190. Current makes the point that in the early days of typewriter use women typists "with training and experience . . . . had to be paid more than the mere boys but not so much as good men typists. In 1886, when top pay for women was fifteen dollars a week, most men were getting twenty." *The Typewriter*, 119.

39. Economists call this "low human capital attainment." Cohn argues that by the turn of the century employers were moving away from the hiring of juveniles for reasons of profit, not just morality: "Teenagers are hurt by their low human capital attainments. Not only do they lack formal training and job experience, but they often lack work discipline and show an extremely high natural propensity to turnover. The lack of these more social forms of human capital can be just as harmful as the lack of years of education." *The Process of Occupational Sex-Typing*, 195-96. Also see

Cohn's description (213–14) of the use of juvenile labor in the Great Western Railway and its replacement by women.

40. These figures—estimates to be sure—come from Alba M. Edwards, *Comparative Occupation Statistics for the United States, 1870-1940* (Washington, D.C.: GPO, 1943), 73-78, 97. Edwards warned (21) that the part-time nature of much of this employment for children complicated the census returns and made the results highly suspect.

41. The tendency to move away from juvenile labor was true of nearly all large-scale industries, even the ones that had traditionally exploited child labor. In 1906 Susan Kingsley reported to a special commission appointed by the Massachusetts legislature on the need for industrial and technical education in schools and found that although some textile mills were willing to hire fourteen and fifteen year olds, half of them preferred to hire young people sixteen to twenty. She concluded that most industries would no longer need child labor. *Report of the Massachusetts Commission on Industrial and Technical Education* (Boston: State of Massachusetts, 1906).

42. Stevens, *Boys and Girls in Commercial Work*, 67; Greenwald, *Women, War and Work*, 97; Eugene J. Benge, *Standard Practice in Personnel Work* (New York: H. W. Wilson, 1920), 54, 70; Marion A. Bills, "Permanence of Men and Women Office Workers," *Personnel Journal [PJ]* 5, no. 10 (1927): 402-4, and "Relative Permanency of Men and Women Office Workers," *Personnel* 5 (Aug. 1928): 207-8.

43. On the connection between "synthetic labor turnover" and discrimination against married women, see Cohn, *Process of Occupational Sex-Typing*, 93-97.

44. Ileen DeVault concludes that "early twentieth century authors all agreed that female clerical workers had a fairly rapid turnover rate, staying only a few years in any one job." "Sons and Daughters of Labor: Class and Clerical Work in Pittsburgh, 1870s-1910s," Ph.D. diss., Yale University, 1985, 315, fn. 11. Janice Weiss observes that "the fact that women employees usually left within a few years because they married, proved to be acceptable and to some extent even favorable to business. Clerical workers expected and usually received increased pay with increased seniority, so a faster turn-over rate could be profitable to an employer." "Educating for Clerical Work: A History of Commercial Education in the United States since 1850," Ed.D. diss., Harvard University, 1978, 71. Both Weiss and DeVault seem to base their conclusions on hearsay evidence (opinions of employers and writers). I would argue that they underestimate the average number of years most women clerical workers spent at their jobs. A statistical study by Marion Bills found that women hired at the age of seventeen at Aetna left for marriage, on average, at age 22.6. Bills, "Relative Permanency of Men and Women Office Workers," 208. An average of 5.6 years is considerably longer than "a few."

45. Schauffler, "Impressions on Secretarial Work," 4.

46. Leverett S. Lyon, *Education for Business* (Chicago: University of Chicago Press, 1923), 162.

47. One estimate of turnover for youths from sixteen to twenty years of age was about 400 percent; turnover for those older than twenty dropped to 40 percent. C. S. Yoakum, "Experimental Psychology in Personnel Problems," *Bulletin of the Taylor Society* [*TSB*] 10 (June 1925): 158.

48. For statistical summaries of clerical worker turnover and its relation to age, salary, and title, see Ethel L. Erickson, "The Employment of Women in Offices," *WBB* 120 (1934): 28-29; Mary Schauffler, "A Study of Three Clerical Occupations for Women," M.A. thesis, Western Reserve University, 1925, 16 and 35; M. C. Elmer, *A Study of Women in Clerical and Secretarial Work in Minneapolis, Minn.* (Minneapolis: Women's Occupational Bureau, 1925), 15-23; and Ruth Shonle Cavan, *Business Girls, A Study of their Problems* (Chicago: Religious Education Association, 1929), 59-62.

49. See Elizabeth Kemper Adams, *Women Professional Workers: A Study Made for the Women's Educational and Industrial Union* (Chautauqua: Chautauqua Press, 1921), 34; Marguerite B. Benson, "Labor Turnover of Working Women," *Annals* 143 (May 1929): 109-19; and Johanna Lobsenz, *The Older Woman in Industry* (New York: Charles Scribner's Sons, 1929), 159-66.

50. Marion A. Bills, "A Statistical Study of the Interrelation of Eight Items in Ten Life Insurance Companies," American Management Association *Office Executive Series* [AMAOES] 5(1925): 95-121. Bills, ever the scientific manager, was also interested in whether companies with large numbers of women employees were as efficient as those with relatively small proportions. She found a correlation among large numbers of women, low efficiency, and high turnover rates, but using one company as an example, showed that higher pay for women could eliminate both low efficiency and high turnover. "Would it be possible to have a company made up largely of women who were so selected and held by good pay that their efficiency would be high? That this is the case and that one must pay a fair wage for efficient work, be it man or woman, and that when that wage is paid good work is the result, would seem to be indicated by one company studied," 118. In the particularly oblique discussion by a group of male office managers that followed, Bills's findings were carefully ignored, except for an observation by Harry Hopf, who sabotaged her presentation by presenting statistics (123) from the Federal Reserve System showing that women had greater turnover rates than men in the first year of employment.

51. Bills's views were corroborated, for example, by Harold B. Bergen of the Henry L. Doherty Company. He found that when "better methods of personnel administration" were instituted, "which constituted improvements in the status of women workers," including "an organized attempt to eliminate prejudices against women employees, with a view to increasing the lines of promotion open to them" women made more reliable employ-

ees than men. Eliminating prejudice in this case included lifting the marriage bar. Harold B. Bergen, "Stability of Men and Women Office Workers," *PJ* 5 (July 1926): 71-73.

52. Elmer, "A Study of Women In Clerical and Secretarial Work," 22-23.

53. Marion A. Bills, "Relative Permanency of Men and Women Office Workers," *Personnel* 5 (Aug. 1928): 208; also see her "Stability of Office Workers and Age at Employment," *Personnel* (Jan. 1927): 475-77.

54. Women clerical workers who filled out more than 2,400 questionnaires distributed by the Bureau of Vocational Information in 1924 and 1925, most of whom were twenty-five to thirty-four years old, were asked to give their work histories and reasons for leaving jobs. I examined 948 of these, and of the 870 women who responded, there were 1,754 job terminations. Of reasons listed for termination, 344 were involuntary; in these cases the women were fired, their positions eliminated, or their places of employment closed. Another 137 terminations were for either taking a temporary war job or leaving a war job once it ended. Another 500 were for personal or miscellaneous reasons, including illness, taking time to travel, moving to a new location, or returning to school. The remaining 773 leavings reflected the search for better employment. Of these, 380 leavings were to obtain a better position, 195 were due to dislike of employer or working conditions, 101 were attributed to "no advancement," and 91 were because salaries were too low. Another seventy quits were put into a "miscellaneous" category. A very small number were specific enough to list "sexual harassment" (two) and machine work (four) as reasons for leaving jobs. (I devised these categories and sorted the responses into them.)

Elmer's respondents in Minneapolis also listed advancement, "no future," and "desired change" as prominent categories. In New York, Erickson found that 35 percent of all women left jobs for advancement, another 20 percent gave personal reasons, and 45 percent gave "business reasons." Because this was 1931, the effects of the depression were beginning to be felt, leading to more involuntary terminations. Elmer, "Women in Clerical and Secretarial Work," 23, and Erickson, "The Employment of Women in Offices," 28.

55. Why Women Said They Left Positions

Reasons for Leaving	YWCA (1929)	Percent	Collegiate Bureau (1924–25)	Percent
Business reasons (involuntary terminations)	204	39.2	121	25.3
Moving or traveling	87	16.7	80	16.7
Lack of salary or advancement	83	15.9	83	17.3
Dissatisfaction with employment	53	10.2	30	6.3

Illness	38	7.3	21	4.4
Home conditions	22	4.2	19	4.0
Change of occupation	29	5.6	107	22.3
Misc.	4	.7	18	3.8

Source: YWCA material is from Cavan, *Business Girls*, 63. I have abbreviated the description of the categories and in one instance combined "internal conditions of business" and "laid off."

56. Erickson, "The Employment of Women in Offices," 28.

57. Margaret Elliott and Grace E. Manson, "Earnings of Women in Business and the Professions," *Michigan Business Studies* 3 (Sept. 1930): 94.

58. Schauffler, "A Study of Three Clerical Occupations," 19.

59. Bureau of Vocational Information Woman Secretary Survey [BVIWS], 420 (1891), New York, Schlesinger Library, Radcliffe College.

60. Interview with L. P. by Gail Gregory Sansbury, Nov. 8, 1972, RIWW; BVIWS 102 (1508), New York.

61. BVIWS 572 (170), California, with Letter from Helene McGregor to Winifred Hausam, July 10, 1925.

62. Priscilla Murolo, "White-Collar Women: The Feminization of the Aetna Life Insurance Company, 1910-1930," unpublished paper, American Studies Program, Yale Univerity, 1982, 9; Joan Wallach Scott, "The Mechanization of Women's Work," *Scientific American* 249 (Sept. 1983): 171.

63. Office Workers in Cleveland , 1913-14

	Percent Women Clerical Workers	Offices Surveyed
Small offices (doctor, dentist, law, real estate)	100	17
Addressing	83	5
Retail	79	7
Telephone	71	1
Manufacturing	57	34
Insurance and printing	50	10
Municipal-city hall	33	1
Telegraph	31	2
Railroad	23	2
Accountancy	16	1
Banking	15	5

Source: Eaton and Stevens, *Commercial Work and Training for Girls*, 186-88.

For a breakdown of women in clerical work by specific sector throughout the United States, see Rotella, "Women's Labor Force Participation," 213.

64. In 1908 the Cleveland shopping district was half the size it was eight years later. By 1916 one store employed two thousand, another three thou-

sand, and ten stores had work forces of more than a hundred. As many as one in six department store employees was an office clerk by the mid-teens. See Stevens, *Boys and Girls in Commercial Work*, 62, and the "organization of a retail dry goods house" in F. V. Thompson, *Commercial Education in Public Secondary Schools* (New York: World Book, 1916), 109; also see John H. MacDonald, "The Records of the Credit and Collection Department," *OE* 7 (June 1925): 5. A 1927 survey of Massachusetts offices noted that women made up 93.5 percent of the office clerks in department stores. "Wages and Hours of Labor: Salaries of Office Employees in Massachusetts," *Monthly Labor Review [MLR]* 24 (Jan. 1927): 142. Also see the canvass of department store workers in eight American cities in the "Preliminary Report on the Senior Commercial Occupations Survey Giving the Data on 2590 Commercial Workers 18-30 Years of Age," prepared by the Federal Board for Vocational Education, April 5, 1922, BVI, folder 499.

65. DeVault, "Sons and Daughters of Labor," 119; Greenwald, *Women, War and Work*, 93-98. Stevens found that most men who graduated from high school commercial courses in Cleveland sought work at the railroad offices as stenographers, expecting to be promoted regularly. *Boys and Girls in Commercial Work*, 48-49.

66. Susan Hirsch, "Rethinking the Sexual Division of Labor," *Radical History Review* 35 (April 1986): 32.

67. This account of Sears summarized from Emmet and Jeuck, *Catalogues and Counters*, 136-292; also see Fine, "Record Keepers of Property," 115-17.

68. For a summary of these changes see Alfred D. Chandler Jr., *The Visible Hand: The Managerial Revolution in American Business* (Cambridge: Harvard University Press, 1977), 455.

69. For example, the Bureau of War Risk Insurance was created in 1914 as a unit of the Treasury Department, and by 1918 had nearly seven thousand employees. A year later the staff had more than doubled and was moved to a new eleven-story building. Gustavus A. Weber and Laurence F. Schmeckebier, *The Veterans' Administration: Its History, Activities and Organization*, Institute for Government Research, Service Monographs of the United States Government, no. 66 (Washington, D.C.: Brookings Institution, 1934), 215-25.

70. F. W. Rowland, "Present Status and Probable Trends in Office Management," AMAOES 61 (1933): 3; Murolo, "White-Collar Women," 8-11; Erickson, "The Employment of Women in Offices," 16; typewritten letter from C. P. Simpson to Emma P. Hirth, June 21, 1918, BVI, folder 203; Greenwald, *Women, War and Work*, 93. A survey of more than a thousand offices and twenty-two thousand office employees in 1927 by the Massachusetts Department of Labor showed that 63.5 percent of the office clerks in that state were women, and that "women were now nearly half of all the clerks in banks and trust companies." "Wages and Hours of Labor," 141.

71. *Women in Industry* (New York: Alexander Hamilton Institute, 1918), 3.

72. Interview with G. M., RIWW.

73. *System* 3 (July and Nov. 1918), advertisement endpieces. The office machine industry, like most others, was victim of a sharp drop in demand in 1921, but had regained and then passed its prewar totals as early as 1923. See Department of Commerce, *Census of Manufactures, 1929,* 2: 1120-21 and 1182-83 for periodic figures on office machine products and their value.

74. For examples from the railroad industry, see Greenwald, *Women, War and Work,* 87-138, 185-232; also see Hirsch, "Rethinking the Sexual Division of Labor."

75. Ibid., 33-34; Greenwald, *Women, War and Work,* 98-102.

76. Based on the evidence presented by scholars of railroad clerking in particular, male unions slowed down the pace of feminization and even retained the best positions for men in return for labor peace, but once labor shortages occurred or management perceived the hiring of women to be economically advantageous and was forced to consider ways of cutting costs, protests of male workers were simply ignored. See the discussion of "exclusion by organized labor," in Cohn, *The Process of Occupational Sex-Typing,* 136-72.

77. This point is made by Susan B. Carter and Mark Prus, "The Labor Market and the American High School Girl, 1890-1928," *Journal of Economic History* 42 (March 1982): 166.

78. Roslyn L. Feldberg, "'Union Fever': Organizing among Clerical Workers, 1900-1930," *Radical America* 14 (May-June 1980): 54-55.

79. Maurice Rabinovitz, "The Trade Union and Office Workers," *American Federationist* 38 (Nov. 1931): 1386-87. The sexism of the AFL and its harmful consequences for both women workers and American unionism have been elaborately documented. See in particular, Alice Kessler Harris, "Where Are the Organized Women Workers?" *Feminist Studies* 3 (Fall 1975): 91-110, and Martha May, "Bread Before Roses: American Workingmen, Labor Unions and the Family Wage," in *Women, Work and Protest: A Century of U.S. Women's Labor History,* ed. Ruth Milkman (Boston: Routledge and Kegan Paul, 1985), 1-22.

80. Feldberg, "'Union Fever,'" 55-58; Fine, "Record Keepers of Property," 190.

81. Theresa Wolfson listed women office workers in unions in 1924: three thousand in the National Post Office Clerks, ten thousand in the Brotherhood of Railway and Steamship Workers, and nine thousand in the National Federation of Federal Employees. *The Woman Worker and the Trade Unions* (New York: International Publishers, 1926), 127. Phillip Foner found 1,654 women members of the Bookkeepers, Stenographers and Accountants' Union, most of whom worked in the offices of unions af-

filiated with the AFL. *Women and the American Labor Movement: From the First Trade Unions to the Present* (New York: Free Press, 1979), 294.

82. Eleanor Nelson, president of the United Federal Workers, was the first woman president of a CIO union. See Sharon Hartman Strom, "'We're No Kitty Foyles': Organizing Office Workers for the Congress of Industrial Organizations," in *Women, Work and Protest*, ed. Milkman, 220 and 232, fn. 48.

83. Mills, *White Collar*, 198.

84. The Office Executives Committee of the AMA sent out 650 questionnaires and received 350 back, 304 of which gave specific information on the number of office workers in their employ. (These firms probably had the most progressive personnel and employment policies in the country.) The study covered a total of 174,053 office workers, 72,833 of whom were women. The committee divided the respondent firms according to size. There were sixty-two offices in Group 1 (1-50 employees), ninety-six in Group 2 (51-200), sixty-eight in Group 3 (201-500), and seventy-eight in Group 4 (500 or more). Firms reporting represented a wide range of industries, including insurance, manufacturing, banks, and educational institutions. H. J. Taylor, "Office Working Conditions and Extra Compensation Plans," AMAOES 30 (1928).

Erickson's study profiled working conditions in 314 offices, mostly employing a hundred or more workers each in New York, Philadelphia, Chicago, Atlanta, St. Louis, Hartford, and Des Moines. "The Employment of Women in Offices," 13-15.

85. The definitive comparison of women's wages in different fields of employment is in Benson, *Counter Cultures*, Appendix C. Rotella found that urban women's clerical wages were 1.8 times as high as those for the average in manufacturing in 1890 and had only fallen to 1.3 times as high as those in manufacturing by 1930. "Women's Labor Force Participation and the Growth of Clerical Employment," 281. In examining the wage report of the Ohio Industrial Commission in 1915 Stevens concluded that "for women, . . . clerical occupations pay best; . . . salesmanship ranks second, and all the industries have a considerably lower rank." *Boys and Girls in Commercial Work*, 113. Also see Carter and Prus, "The Labor Market and the American High School Girl," 165-66, and Louise Marion Bosworth, *The Living Wage of Women Workers: A Study of Incomes and Expenditures of 450 Women in the City of Boston* (London: Longmans, Green, 1911), 37.

86. See, for example, Eleanor Martin and Margaret Post, *Vocations for the Trained Woman* (London: Longmans, Green, 1914), 128-29; and Schauffler, "A Study of Three Clerical Occupations," 27, 34-35, 41-42. While a 1927 Massachusetts study of office workers showed that more than half the women machine operators earned less than $20 a week, jobs in bookkeeping and accounting (usually held by older workers) were the

best paying, with a significant number earning as much as $40 a week. "Wages and Hours of Labor," 143.

87. Paul H. Douglas, *Real Wages in the United States, 1890-1926* (Cambridge: Harvard University Press: 1930), 366 and "What Is Happening to the White-Collar-Job Market?" *System* 50 (Dec. 1926): 719-21, 782, 874. The most comprehensive comparison of men's and women's clerical wages over time is Albert Niemi, Jr., "The Male-Female Earnings Differential: A Historical Overview of the Clerical Occupations from the 1880s to the 1970s," *Social Science History* 7 (Winter 1983): 97-101.

88. National Industrial Conference Board, *Clerical Salaries in the United States* (New York: NICB, 1926).

89. For some examples, see Galloway, *Office Management*, 447-63; Committee on Salary Standardization, "Salary Administration," AMAOES 5 (1925); E. O. Griffenhagen, "Classification and Compensation Plans as Tools in Personnel Administration," AMAOES 17 (1926); Sterling B. Cramer, "Job Analysis: The Technique of Job Analysis as Applied to Office Workers," AMAOES 25 (1927); R. C. Nyman, "A Method of Evaluating Clerical Jobs and Employes [*sic*]," *TSB* 13 (Aug. 1928): 170-72; Roy R. Marguardt, "Scientific Classification of Trust Department Personnel," *Personnel*, 7 (Nov. 1930): 77-81.

90. NICB, *Clerical Salaries*, 4; also see Nichols, "A New Conception of Office Practice, 73-75. Nichols's table (71) of the frequency with which office workers performed duties not reflected in job titles is particularly interesting. "Regardless of what the payroll name for a clerk's job," Nichols observed, "almost any combination of duties may be listed." Erickson's Women's Bureau study of 1931-32 came to the same conclusion. "The Employment of Women in Offices," 5.

91. While Erickson's study was conducted after the stock market crash of 1929 and no doubt reflects some of the early stringencies of the Great Depression, I think it should be seen as a study of the 1920s. Unemployment had not, by 1931, hit office workers with full force. In fact, some of the kinds of firms in Erickson's study— notably insurance companies and public utilites—did not fire large numbers of workers during the depression. Somewhat flattened wage levels did show up in Erickson's study, reflecting the fact that many firms were already cutting back on overhead and lowering wages by 1928 or 1929. The study stands, then, as a kind of benchmark for the decade from 1920 to 1930, at least for proportions of women holding kinds of office occupations, conditions of work, and the extent of office mechanization.

Useful information on clerical worker wages in the 1920s can also be found in Elmer, "A Study of Women in Clerical and Secretarial Work." The Elmer study was conducted in 1924 and 1925 and included data from 191 establishments employing five or more, for a total of 4,734 women. Elmer probably combined some of those Erickson considered typists with stenographers and did not attempt to sort out machine operators. The firms

Elmer examined were considerably smaller, on average, than those in Erickson's sample. Minneapolis was not a center of paperwork industries (insurance, mail order, corporate headquarters) and had lower salaries, on average, than many of the cities in Erickson's sample. However, it is interesting to see how comparable many of the salary categories are.

Also see "Wage and Hours of Labor," 141-43; Henry E. Niles, "Rents and Salaries in Ninety-Six Cities," *HBR* 6 (Jan. 1928): 194-97; Cavan, *Business Girls*, 57; Sophonisba P. Breckinridge, *Women in the Twentieth Century: A Study of their Political, Social and Economic Activities* (New York: McGraw-Hill, 1933), 181-82; Amy G. Maher, "Bookkeepers, Stenographers and Office Clerks in Ohio, 1914-1929," *WBB* 95 (1932).

92. In summarizing the findings of a 1922 report on commercial education and opportunities, one expert concluded that the essence of a general clerk was his overall knowledge and promotability, not his separation from machine work: "he helps everywhere in the office so . . . he has the opportunity to rise, to become a supervisor, an office manager, or, in time perhaps, an even higher executive . . . . His training must give him familiarity with all the usual . . . business papers, orders, invoices, statements . . . ; he must also have a knowledge of arithemetic extending from the work of a billing clerk to that of a payroll or statistical clerk . . . . such a clerk must be familiar with the typewriter, adding machines . . . and the whole world of common office appliances." The use of male subjects and pronouns was obviously deliberate here. Lyon, *Education for Business*, 1523.

93. Sinclair Lewis, *The Job: An American Novel* (New York: Grosset and Dunlap, 1917), 235.

5

Managers, Clerks, and the Question of Gender

W ORLD WAR I BROUGHT unprecedented industrial production to the United States and ended just as more sophisticated manufacturing and administrative systems peaked. During the war, American firms accumulated staggering profits, working people found jobs for the asking, and women, blacks, and others who had previously been excluded took up some new occupations. Flexing their wartime muscle, workers, including New England women telephone operators and Scovill factory employees, staged massive strikes in 1919. While union recognition was a major goal of workers, so was an attempt to keep wages in pace with inflation. Through early 1920 the economy continued to boom. Pent-up demand for housing, electrical power, gasoline, and consumer goods contributed to steadily rising prices. Many businesses, large and small, continued to produce goods nonstop, to stock large inventories, and to assume that the bubble would never burst.[1]

By 1921, recession had arrived. Federal government spending declined, prices fell sharply, unemployment rose to nearly 12 percent, and corporations faced drastic drops in demand. A wave of union busting, backed up by court injunctions, lock-outs, and "company union" plans, dramatically reduced the ranks of independent organized labor and gave management more power in the workplace.[2] Administrative reforms and stricter cost accounting procedures followed, continuing the revolution in accounting and management that had begun early in the century.[3]

Corporations were spending more on office costs than they ever had before because profitable growth was heavily dependent on more elaborate accounting, paperwork, and advertising. It was also true that many of the areas where the economy grew most in the 1920s employed large numbers of clerical workers and salespeople. These firms—which included the electrical products industries, oil companies, public utilities, life insurance firms, banks, department stores, and automobile plants—relied heavily on sophisticated personnel management procedures, used consumer advertising extensively, and were in the forefront of new office methods.[4]

By 1923 better-organized American corporations were ready to take advantage of weakened unions and new opportunities for expanded consumer markets. Although some traditional sectors of the economy, notably agriculture, coal, and the railroads, suffered continued declines, others made dramatic gains. A burst of mergers and vertical integrations, aimed at controlling wholesaling and retailing, gave many firms more rationalized methods for predicting demand and desirable rates of production. Diversification, or acquiring subsidiary firms making different products, made corporations less reliant on the success of one line and allowed them to find new consumers. A more consolidated and predictable banking system provided credit for construction and commercial growth.[5] Home offices in cities and suburbs plotted new advertising methods and training plans for brigades of sales personnel. By 1929 advertising expenditures in the United States stood at about $1.78 billion, or about 2 percent of the country's national income.[6]

Governments were subject to the same trends. The federal government's expenditures declined immediately after the war, but total spending on civil administrative functions was still 2.37 times as high in 1930 as it had been in 1915. Despite the Republican party's faith in minimal government, many of the federal government's functions became more intricate over the course of the decade. The Veterans' Bureau and the Internal Revenue Service were large bureaucratic enterprises. Government activity included the enforcement of Prohibition, the pursuit of antitrust cases, procedures of the Interstate Commerce Commission, and regulation of the public utility industry. The Bureau of the Budget, the General Accounting Office, and the Personnel Classification Board signaled the federal government's turn to more thorough administration of its own business and the need for more clerks to keep track of it. The departments of the Interior, Treasury, and Agriculture received major organizational overhauls. One budget expert estimated that about 50 percent of all government expenditures were for personnel, and by 1930 the federal executive civil service employed about 610,000 people, 225,000 more than it had employed in 1910. The General Accounting Office alone employed two thousand and spent about $4 million a year.[7]

State governments, especially in the Northeast and Midwest, were especially likely to grow during the twenties; municipal governments continued to institute accounting and administrative efficiency measures.[8] By 1926 the budget of the City of New York was $437 million, about 12.5 percent of the federal budget, and the city's civil service commission employed 116,000.[9] More modern office work systems allowed cities to develop continuous meter-reading and billing for water and other city services.[10] More accountable administrative and financial systems meant more government employees; by 1930 New York state had thirteen thousand more employees than in 1920.[11]

A surge in public utility use was one of the chief features of the 1920s. Electrical light and power consumption increased threefold, and gas consumption by half. Intense consolidation accompanied increased use. By 1930 ten electric companies distributed 75 percent of the power in the United States, and sixteen gas companies produced 45 percent of the gas. The Pacific Gas and Electric Company, which served more than half the population of California, maintained executive offices in San Francisco and employed more than five thousand. Although industrial use accounted for much of the increase in utility consumption, gains were also made in residential use. The Philadephia Electric Company's "Wire Your Home" campaign accompanied its electrification of seventy-nine thousand homes, and by 1927 the Philadelphia utility had nearly a half million customers making purchases of appliances on the installment plan. The giant electrical products companies, General Electric and Westinghouse, also turned to the promotion of home electrification and appliances in the twenties. The number of radios sold, for example, went from about 100,000 in 1922 to 4,980,000 by 1929.[12] The twenties saw a 70 percent increase in telephone use, dominated by the huge American Telephone and Telegraph Company, which by 1930 had a payroll of 324,000.[13]

In the financial industry, stock and bond market investment and the sale of stock to finance corporate investment created new business for banks and securities firms. The growing importance of the Federal Reserve System and banking regulation at both the state and federal levels increased pressure on banks to install modern accounting systems. Installment buying and home mortgages, the growth of checking accounts and savings plans, and commercial loans to business all stimulated growth in banking. While many banks failed in the twenties, especially small country ones, mergers and consolidations increased, making urban banks bigger and far more powerful. The larger banks established branches in cities and suburbs; between 1920 and 1929 the number of branch banks increased sevenfold.[14] Personal finance companies, electric companies, and automobile dealers offered consumers short-term loans, and by 1925 retail installment sales had risen to about $5 billion. By the end of the decade it was estimated that about half of all retail sales were made on credit.[15] A flood of statements, payments, and checks processed by clerical workers accompanied the surge in credit.

The life insurance business grew dramatically. After the regulations that followed the Armstrong hearings of 1905, more restrained advertising established the legitimacy of life insurance as a savings mechanism and widened its appeal to the middle class. Life insurance in force in the United States rose from $40,540 million in 1920 to $106,403 million in 1930. The Metropolitan Life Insurance Company moved past its competitor, the Prudential Company, by providing insurance to the armed forces through the Bureau of War Risk Insurance. By 1921 Metropolitan, "gigantic, highly bureaucratized, yet projecting an image of corporate beneficience," had six thousand clerical workers. Monthly billing systems for life insurance had been avoided by most insurance companies because of the clerical work costs involved, but by 1926 Metropolitan had developed a system to make the costs of monthly payments by mail "manageable." Enormous urban home offices were required to maintain insurance policies and sales. In 1924, for instance, the Equitable Life Insurance Company moved two thousand home office employees and 940 van loads of office furnishings and records to a new twenty-two-story building on Seventh Avenue in New York City opposite the Pennsylvania Railroad Station.[16]

By 1920 almost 10 percent of the population of the United States lived in New York, Chicago, or Philadelphia, and these major cities grew by more than a third in the next decade. New York City went from 1.5 million to 7 million. By 1930 Chicago had 3.5 million, and Detroit and Los Angeles 1.5 million each. Dozens of smaller cities also grew substantially, and by 1930 nearly four hundred buildings of more than twenty stories—"skyscrapers"—had been added to the American landscape. The growth of cities—especially in the

Northeast, along the Pacific Coast, across the Great Lakes region, and in southern commercial centers—was in part a result of the increased importance of cities as regional centers of trade and finance and their expanding paperwork industries.[17]

Skyscrapers were harbingers of the future. The largest of them symbolized the corporation's reliance on elaborate systems of office work and centralized planning. The New York City Standard Oil Building at 26 Broadway was completed in the mid-twenties. Designed in "a free adaptation of Italian Renaissance architecture," the twenty-eight-story building of steel and concrete commanded a stunning view of New York Harbor at Battery Park and was topped by a tower complete with a two-thousand-watt light to direct ships in the harbor. Standard Oil's promotional literature claimed that "thousands of men and women" passed daily on their way to work through its forty-foot-high vaulted foyer of marble. Macy's Department Store sales increased from about $36 million in 1919 to nearly $99 million by 1930, and a twenty-story building completed in 1924 made Macy's "the tallest and largest store premises in the world."[18] Hundreds of thousands of office workers poured into these urban paperwork factories every day, and a growing body of office management experts offered their advice on how they might best be managed.

Scientific Management, Bureaucratic Control, and the Sexual Politics of Office Work

As personnel management emerged after 1910 and matured during World War I, office supervision became one of its most sophisticated subspecialties and a major focus of employers. As much as they heralded the application of scientific management and cost accounting to the world of work, managers were not always prepared psychologically for the increase in office staffs that the new methods required. The rise in the sheer numbers of office workers and the shrinking profit margins of the 1920s clearly fueled interest in office management and the pursuit of more productive methods. Some of the most rapidly developing industries in the twenties— insurance companies, banks, public utilities, and civil services— did not really "produce" goods at all and found the growth in administrative and clerical labor inescapable. The fact that numbers of what managers called "nonproductive" labor (clerks, managers, and executives) were rising at much faster rates than the industrial labor census alarmed many old-fashioned business leaders. Modern business leaders who understood the necessity for larger office staffs were less alarmed but still concerned about the rate of office growth and the uncharted territory such growth represented. Several generations of businessmen and managers raised on the notion that such labor was inherently wasteful were perpetually anxious about the overhead costs of clerical work. These anxieties coincided with managers' fears that the hordes of women pouring into offices might permanently change the way the nation did its business. Controlling overhead, in other words, also meant controlling women.

The influx of women into what had often been male preserves only twenty years earlier raised important issues about men's work and masculine privilege. In places where men and women worked alongside each other the sexual division of labor required elaborate ideological and structural bolstering to ensure its preservation. The "control of women" was often a clearly articulated aspect of the new methods of bureaucratic management. The desire to control women went beyond the desire to supervise their work; it extended to the containment of both the female body and the feminine influence. "The general run of office help," said one office manager, "had if anything a maximum of everything peculiarly feminine. Their sex attributes are more exaggerated than they ever will be again, and to organize them for work is a task calling for some things unknown to managers of men."[19]

Pure Taylorism, as its Progressive women advocates such as Ida Tarbell and Mary Gilson maintained, could potentially ignore gender in its drive toward total efficiency. Some women office management experts, most notably Marion Bills and Millicent Pond, tried to suggest the possibilities for office management. But there were limits to the neutral application of Taylorism. Most male managers and workers sought to protect the sexual division of labor and the gendered social relationships it preserved from the rationality of scientific management. This tendency runs through the work of the "father" of office management, William Henry Leffingwell. Leffingwell believed passionately in the tenets of scientific management, but also viewed the arrival of women in office work with alarm. His patronizing—even patriarchal—vision of women in the workplace made his use of Taylorism anything but even-handed.

Although he liked to refer to himself as a "management engineer," Leffingwell, the son of a woodworker, had in fact been trained as a stenographer. After graduating from Grand Rapids High School in the 1890s he went to work alongside another man, a bookkeeper, in a small manufacturer's office where he took dictation and filed letters in a copy press. After working his way up from stenographer to office manager at a small New York publishing house in 1910, Leffingwell began to develop management techniques, and in 1918 founded his own consulting firm.[20] Taylor could not have had a more devoted disciple than Leffingwell, who took up the real engineer's ideas with a vengeance. There was a disciplinary tone to Leffingwell's work that mirrored Taylor's incessant concern with "soldiering" (attempts by workers to avoid work and resist the "one best way"). And in an interesting twist of Taylorism, Leffingwell added gendered references to suit the growing sexual division of labor in the clerical work army, whose foot soldiers (and most likely "soldierers"), in his opinion, were women. Leffingwell's managerial experiments with stenographers and machine operators performing repetitive tasks heightened his realization that clerking was increasingly being done by women and contributed to his determination to keep clerical workers under control.

It was Leffingwell's conviction that "new clerks" (that is, women) were not as skilled or responsible as "old clerks" (men) like himself. His derision of women had nativist overtones as well; he paralleled the recruitment of hundreds of thousands of clerks with the "great hordes of immigrants" who arrived in America in the 1890s to seek factory work and who had replaced "workmen who knew only the trades and crafts." Like their factory counterparts, clerks, Leffingwell harped repeatedly, were not being properly managed, and, in fact, because of their lower quality, needed especially strict supervision: "We are diluting the original fund of good clerks by rearing a horde of parasites whose ideal is to avoid work, and who regard it as cruelty that they should be asked to work." There was no doubt in Leffingwell's mind that the prototypical office loafer was a woman. He liked to tell the story about a woman clerk who had been transferred from one department to another and then asked to return to her original job. "'Why do you wish to be transferred?' asked the manager. 'Is the work too hard for you? Don't you like the man you work for?' 'Oh, no,' replied the girl; 'The man I work for is very nice and the work is not so hard. But on the other job I used to have a couple of hours a day to myself, and down there I have to work all day.'"[21]

Leffingwell was not alone in presenting the growing number of clerical workers, especially women clerks, as a potential menace to American society. Here was a segment of the American population that had grown seventeenfold in a mere forty years and that produced nothing more tangible than piles of paper. If this "sinister growth" continued, overhead would rise until it erased already shrinking profits completely. Wallace Clark lamented that despite "the twenty years' campaign for so-called efficiency which has been carried on in this country, each year it becomes harder to get the office work done." The war took qualified men from the office, most did not return, and "in none of the large cities are there enough office boys to go around." Men were departing, women were taking their places, and something was amiss: "The majority of office workers have not been taking the same interest in their work that they used to take. When things go wrong they shrug their shoulders and let someone else worry. These familiar things and others less general have lowered the standards of accomplishment and caused a general slowing down of work."[22]

Leffingwell was even more hysterical in his association between the alleged decline of clerical work standards and the arrival of large numbers of women workers. Implicit in Leffingwell's critique was the assumption that women's sexuality was both distracting and dangerous to corporate discipline. The "vast host" of office workers was allowed to assemble "weekly for its pay envelopes," he claimed, despite the fact that, as in the Biblical scripture, they "'toil not, neither do they spin, yet Solomon in all his glory was not arrayed,'— in white collars, silk stockings or furs." The "neglected Cinderella" of office work, Leffingwell warned, might very well become a "Frankenstein ... which will eventually devour its makers."[23] The irrationality of gender politics permeated the construction of the "rational" systems that office managers developed in the 1920s.

Office Management and its History

There were real limits to what office management could accomplish in the 1920s. But there were also immediate benefits to installing its techniques, particularly those of employee selection and the rationalization of office work tasks. Potential clerical workers, as both the federal government and large corporations had found, could be easily tested before hiring and then placed where they would work most effectively. Clerical workers tended to come from a fairly homogeneous population that had some high school education; in that context, the selection process, although really confirming choices already being made, appeared to be entirely efficient.

In the office itself, scientific management was largely aimed at finding ways to make clerks produce more in ways that cost less and to pay clerks less in order to reduce the cost of "nonproductive" labor. The nearly total absence of labor unions among clerical workers gave managers a fairly free hand in arranging methods of work, although notions about the special characteristics of white-collar workers continued to limit the expansion of the drive system in office work in the 1920s, and, in turn, to inhibit unionism. Managers were committed, for the time-being, to keeping "white-collar" workers loyal by maintaining distinctions between office and industrial workers through the use of different methods of compensation, job titles, and workplace facilities. The nature of clerical work itself may have spurred the application of these techniques to office management; while some clerks could be handled like factory workers through direct supervision and driving methods, many others performed idiosyncratic tasks that were difficult to rationalize. In these cases, internalized appeals to loyalty, efficiency for the firm's sake, and dedication to managers had to be substituted for the drive system. The economist Richard Edwards describes this phenomenon as bureaucratic control, a characteristic of modern capitalist enterprises, and suggests that bureaucratic control was first applied to office staffs.

Ideas about women as inherent operatives were helpful to the experts in their application of pure Taylorism (chapter 4). Office managers were, in general, far more willing to apply Taylorism to women clerks than to men clerks. They continued to see young women, especially from the working class, as potential light-manufacturing operatives in the office. The discussions of office management experts like William Leffingwell and Wallace Clark cast clerks in gendered terms that legitimized the sexual division of labor and different notions of men's and women's work. Office management experts who attempted to critique this gendered interpretation faced hostility and censorship.

A prolific body of management literature had already appeared by 1915, and office mangement consulting firms like Leffingwell-Ream offered their services to employers. Textbooks that applied Taylorist ideas to the office were widely available, and management periodicals such as *System* and *Industrial Management* presented the advice of office management specialists. In 1924 the American Management Association formed an Office Executives

Group, whose members met periodically to exchange ideas and present research. The papers presented at these meetings, along with the discussions that followed, were published in pamphlet form and sold to subscribers. Office methods were also discussed at meetings of the Taylor Society and published in its bulletin. Employers in similar fields, such as life insurance companies and department stores, established their own research bureaus to develop office management techniques.[24]

The firms most likely to present the results of their office management applications in print and to join management organizations can be put into several categories. Conspicuously absent were the railroads, and among the most prominent were life insurance companies, banks, electrical products industries, public utilities, department stores, and oil and rubber companies. Size was not an absolute predictor of participation; although some of the largest corporations in the nation were active, others were not. Ford, General Motors, and U.S. Steel, for instance, were not represented, but U.S. Rubber and Standard Oil were. Some relatively small firms were very active. These were often businesses, like Cheney Mills, Dennison Manufacturing, Gillette Razor, and Curtis Publishing, which had called in consultants to institute scientific management in their factories in the teens and saw its extension to the office as logical. There were no doubt some executives, like John Mitchell of General Electric and John Patterson of National Cash Register, who supported the development of office management to ensure that their firms had access to the most up-to-date methods. They were modernists in their approach to almost everything.

The development of office management ideas between 1910 and 1930 incorporated the same debates that characterized the early history of personnel management, with strict Taylorism and psychology as the frames of opposing but sometimes overlapping arguments. Early office management techniques, discussed in print most systematically by William Henry Leffingwell, reflected the mechanistic ideas of early scientific management. Leffingwell argued that if office work was properly laid out, if tasks were divided into simple units and measured, if workers were paid decent salaries and bonuses for producing more than the minimum, and if machines were incorporated wherever possible, workers could be made to produce more. But as experience with the implementation of these methods was gained, office managers felt the pull of pyschological approaches as well; pure Taylorism (or pure Leffingwellism) tended to ignore the human factor, was costly to supervise, did not allow for flexibility in office routine, and evoked resentment in workers. Managers continued to propose an amalgam of Taylorism and bureaucratic control. The basic principles of office systemization still in use today were developed before 1930 by Leffingwell and several others, notably Lee Galloway, Wallace Clark, and Marion A. Bills.[25]

Most business managers agreed with Leffingwell's concerns about the unprecedented growth of clerical work after 1910. The cost of clerical work was a staggering element of business overhead. By 1930 it was estimated that the ratio of office expense to general overhead stood at 41 percent for department stores, 52 percent for manufacturers, 59 percent for railroads, 60 percent for banks, and 61 percent for insurance companies. Office management expert Eugene Benge reported that office labor cost per life insurance policy had grown from $1.91 in 1908 to $2.76 by 1928.[26]

Office managers and efficiency experts almost always responded to these facts in the same way. They were, unlike Leffingwell, convinced that a great deal of the growth of clerical work was inevitable when larger organizations and more complicated demands for recordkeeping and cost accounting began to appear. "No one who has studied the matter can doubt," said Marion Bills of Aetna Life Insurance, "that the actual clerical work necessary in performing any operation, increases as the size of the business units increase." While this was partly a defensive posture, it also helped to establish the efficiency experts' main goal: to call attention to both their own indispensibility and the urgency of applying scientific management techniques. The traditional view that clerical work, in Bills's words, was "a by-product of the important elements of business, a necessary evil, which like an incurable disease, it was best to bear with as little thought and discussion as possible," had to go out the window. A new spotlight had to be shone on the office in order to reduce the unit cost of clerical operations; it was crucial "to introduce easier methods, to standardize practices, and to obtain from the clerical force their best efforts."[27]

In considering how to take up Bills's charges in the 1920s, managers faced a number of worries. The seemingly unstoppable growth of clerical personnel was one. The problem of "bigness" in large companies was another. How could operations be systematized effectively so that repetitions, lost time, and errors could be kept to a minimum? In one growing insurance company Bills had studied, for example, it took thirteen people just to look for lost filing cards.[28] Eugene Benge observed that mergers and consolidations had made many organizations top-heavy with middle managers and executives, created intricate problems in combining records, and overloaded many firms with simple business machines while, at the same time, leaving them without sophisticated machine installations for more complicated recordkeeping necessary for larger enterprises. Lower margins of profit and rising salaries and wages in the 1920s meant that firms could no longer simply wait for the money to roll in; steps had to be taken to reduce costs.

While the mechanization of office work was one solution to a growing volume of work, mechanization in and of itself was never a total solution.[29] The machines themselves were costly—one estimate put the cost of equipping a hundred-worker office in 1920 at $36,000—and without proper supervision many were not used efficiently.[30] "These appliances have helped a great deal in increasing the amount of work done," Clark concluded, "but they have not enabled offices to keep up with the progress in production. In many offices you will see these labor-saving machines standing idle, although there is a great deal of work ready to be done on them. Managers are beginning to realize that the use of equipment is vastly more important than its ownership."[31] Like the workers who used them, machines had to be held to some system of measurement.

Other problems loomed as well. Like production managers who saw foremen on the factory floor as obstacles to better management, office managers frequently viewed department supervisors as major roadblocks to streamlining. Supervisors liked to do things their own way, whether efficient or not, saw large staffs as a reflection of their own glory, kept inefficent workers on because they liked them, and refused to promote their most valuable workers to better positions so their services would not be lost. When warned that they had exceeded their budgets, they claimed there was nothing to be done, and management had little recourse but to acquiesce. Methods had to be found for penetrating the mysteries of how work was done in individual departments.

Another costly problem for managers was the unspoken convention that clerical workers would receive automatic salary increases as rewards for continued employment. A 1928 survey of 350 firms, most with two hundred employees or more, established that 21 percent gave salary increases every six months, and 44 percent gave increases every twelve months.[32] The practice of giving periodic increases was partly a holdover from a system dominated by male clerks and also a response to a still tight white-collar labor market in the years after the war. But it had created a significant group of workers, most of them men, whose performance, in the opinion of managers, had not kept pace with their "inflated" salaries. A manager of office workers at the Hawthorne Works of Western Electric commented: "The general basis of increase had been, of course, that employees usually become more valuable with increased service, but when an actual measuring stick was applied, many were found lacking. Those who are grossly overpaid are, of course, special problems to worry over."[33] A personnel manager from a large bank in New York that employed 2,500 people in 1929 was concerned about the "lack of uniformity in . . . determining salaries and promotion of the 'white collar' workers." Merit for a job well done should be the basis of salary increases, not seniority. "[I]f this were a factory instead of a bank, we would pay employees on a basis of work content, instead of for length of service."[34]

Office managers were thinking about three kinds of solutions to their problems. One was to incorporate office management more effectively into the cost accounting strategies of organizations and to compel department heads to adhere to strict budget restraints. As the decade drew to a close and the depression approached, this view became more dominant. However he or she had to do it, the manager had to stick to a predetermined budget. Rewards for managers should be based on how well they kept down costs. This method had its advantages; it kept the efficiency expert and time and motion supervisor out of the office as much as possible, and it supposedly made lower-level managers allies rather than enemies of "progress."[35]

A second approach stressed centralizing clerical operations and using up-to-date machinery. Functions such as payroll, timekeeping, and handling purchase orders should be extracted from factory departments and moved to a central location, as should stenography, typing, and duplicating services. Centralized accounting and bookkeeping departments could make effective use of expensive calculating and tabulating machinery as well as provide integrated summaries to comptrollers. Centralization could also remove a fairly large number of employees from the supervision of foremen or individual bosses and make them more accountable to higher-level management.[36]

Once larger categories of office workers were in one department, they could be subjected to a third management solution, the rationalization, measurement, and monitoring of tasks. Most managers believed, as Leffingwell insisted, that office management had to break jobs down into smaller pieces and organize procedures efficiently to gain "real" control. Many were also committed to measuring output and paying workers on the basis of how much they produced. Measurement and standardization swatted a number of flies with one blow. Theoretically, managers could learn about how much workers could actually do and thus eliminate loafing, lay off the least efficient workers, and invest in fewer machines. A more rational basis was provided for retention, salaries, and promotion; by rewarding workers who produced the most with wage bonuses—a form of the piece rate—salary increases could be tied to efficiency instead of seniority. When employees reached their maximum output, their salaries would stay fixed. When vacancies occurred in other departments or when internal promotions were in order, the most efficient workers could be identified immediately. Clerical workers could be made to perform a full day's work for a full day's pay.

By his own admission, Leffingwell was "obsessed with the idea" that these efficiency techniques could be applied to any office, large or small, to any clerical job, no matter how complicated. He continued to claim that 95 percent of all clerical work could be subjected to measurement, and, not surprisingly, to insist that the able office manager—not the personnel manager or the accountant— was the key to a successful business. Most clerical work could become "routine work."

There was a correlation in most managers' minds between "women" and "routine." Managers had no difficulty with imposing factorylike conditions on young female typists, stenographers, billing operators, and other machine workers. They were consciously drawing on parallel constructions of women as operatives in factory work, women as operatives in clerical work, and the idea that all working women were, therefore, operatives. A number of manufacturers made this connection clear by training factory women and promoting them to clerical work machine departments. Gillette Razor Blade Company of Boston, for instance, moved from a "Point Plan" incentive program in its factory in 1922 to similar methods in its office in 1925, where "rates were excessive and increases were granted to a great degree on length of service." Gillette sent some of its women factory operatives to train at the Burroughs calculator and comptometer school and then installed them as timekeepers in the office: "They had never been office workers, but they had the Point Plan idea after working on the system for two and a half years in the plant." Gillette used these ex-factory workers to set higher rates of production and undercut "inflated" salaries in its offices; the old automatic increases were a thing of the past, the inefficient were fired, and favoritism was "no more."[37]

Many of the inefficient whose salaries were inflated were men. Setting up new operative departments often helped management convert from departments staffed with higher-paid male clerks and female clerks to all-female, lower-paid departments. Managers believed young women to be more pliant and more capable machine workers than men of any age. Cultural conventions about women's alleged dexterity and patience were a part of these beliefs. After Public Service Electric and Gas Company of Newark installed its efficiency plans in 1928 in its billing and bookkeeping departments it fired many of the remaining men and hired only women as new employees because "girls are more adept at this work than men."[38] John Mitchell's AMA survey of results from 152 firms with measurement and incentive departments in 1928 showed that 90 percent of operatives were women, and 95 percent of the operatives were under the age of twenty-five.[39] A survey of office work in Chicago in 1931 showed that only 1.2 percent of the city's male clerks were bookkeeping and billing machine operators, and only 2.2 percent were calculating machine operators.[40]

Men, Women, and the Limits of Scientific Management in Office Work

Male employees were far less likely than women to have to accept efficiency measures. Although some men were fired and replaced by women, until 1931 or so, men had other employment options. Some successfully resisted the efficiency experts, some walked out on jobs being rationalized, and some were either moved to other departments or put in charge of women. Herbert Carey, a young man who went to work in the sales and shipping office of telephone equipment of Western Electric in 1922, recalled that efficiency experts were sent in to do time and motion studies shortly after he came to work. In an office where women were confined to typing and filing and men did the clerical work, he and his male co-workers were able to resist attempts to rationalize their work for the moment. Carey, who was a college graduate and disliked the routine—whether rationalized or not—of clerical work, went over his immediate boss's head to the personnel office, where he landed a new job as assistant to the personnel director.[41]

The resistance that male clerks made to efficiency techniques was rarely discussed in much detail by management experts, but now and then an example surfaced. When Lewis Meriam went to work at the Census Bureau in 1905 new efficiency techniques were being applied and production records were used to evaluate employees. The male clerk with the lowest record in the group "first accused the other employees of falsifying their production records." His next defense was to accuse Meriam of being "a slave driver . . . . The employee then announced that he would not work in any organization which used such methods; he would resign first." It turned out that this clerk had attempted to spark a rebellion against the new methods among other clerks by deliberately producing a low output. Meriam was happy to see the clerk follow through on his threat to quit.[42]

As more routine and mechanized clerical jobs were handed to women, rationalization continued apace. Office management literature was full of stories of the successful application of the rationalization of clerical work in the 1920s. When the Metropolitan Life Insurance Company decided in 1919 to establish a dictaphone bureau it had 176 stenographers, some in a stenography pool but most scattered around the firm. Phonograph operators were recruited from among both stenographers and typists and trained in a company "dictaphone school." The company paid a bonus of 5 cents a typed line over the minimum, allowing workers to average a salary of $29.47 per week. The average dictaphone operator could type 476 pieces of correspondence (the equivalent of 5,925 lines) a week. The dictating labor force had been cut to fifty-three workers by 1924.[43] At the much smaller firm of Holeproof Hosiery, the office manager could not do a time study of his own because "there was a certain amount of lack of cooperation on the part of our people, who were fearful of a cut in pay." Holeproof consulted with a billing machine maker instead, "who had one of his expert operators make a test run for us." The results were "remarkable." Billing clerks were cut by a third, and those who remained gradually increased from a rate of twenty-five bills an hour to as many as seventy an hour; mistakes had to be corrected on the operator's own time.[44]

Women's responses to the efficiency methods sometimes broke through these rosy descriptions. In 1927 Roxanna Petroleum put all of its accounting, transcribing, filing, and typing work on the twelfth floor of its office building in St. Louis, despite resistance from both department heads and workers. While managers "carried the subconscious notion that their particular type of work was sacred to their jurisdiction," "the girls were reluctant to give up their places near the department staff, [and] . . . seemed to think the work might be more humdrum and difficult all in one department. They felt in some cases they might not be able to measure up to the standard and quality of work expected, that they might lose some freedom, that their chances for promotion would not be so good." These objections were firmly ignored and the new system put into effect. The results, from management's point of view, were impressive. The calculating workers put out 70 percent more work, and the 50 percent of the stenographers who kept their jobs produced 33 to 50 percent more work. Savings on salaries, even after accounting for bonus payments, came to $32,000 a year. Roxanna claimed that the workers who had survived the efficiency tests liked the new system.[45] This claim was echoed by many efficiency experts in the 1920s, who argued that workers would initially resist their techniques but would take to and even extoll the virtues of the system once it was installed. "People like to break records," claimed an office manager at Purina Mills. "We have in our department such a fever of competition in bringing records up, such a frenzy that there is no longer any disciplinary or production problem."[46]

Some of the most ambitious efficiency systems were installed at mail order houses and public utilities, where there was a large volume of routine stenography, comptometer, and bookkeeping machine work. Milwaukee Light and Power began its measurement and bonus plans in 1919 and by 1930 had more than a thousand workers on what it called "mutual gain sharing plans." The utility thought it had increased production by about 50 percent in its clerical departments but also set aside 20 percent of the gross savings for "development cost, the cost of reporting the work, the cost of keeping the records, and the cost of computing the bonuses." The remaining 80 percent was divided between the company and the workers in the form of incentive payments, some of which were, by company fiat, put into an employees' savings and building and loan association. Workers at Milwaukee Light and Power had no scheduled rest periods, but could be excused to go to the rest room on their own time. In an eight-hour day machine billers produced an average of "1,600 bills per day, which is equivalent to 200 bills per hour." In a description of the actual machine process involved, it was clear these clerks were working very hard: "Each bill necessitates about 35 key and motor bar strokes which means that in addition to striking 116 keys per minute, the operator must insert and remove the bill, insert and remove proof sheets, turn meter records, obtain and return stacks of bills as well as take personal time. The best operator averages 4 1/2 bills per minute, about one bill every 13 seconds, 8 hours a day, 5 1/2 days per week."[47]

Efficiency experts kept up a line of happy talk about how much female operatives liked measurement and bonus plans ("the squarest deal they have ever had").[48] Metropolitan Life Insurance and Holeproof Hosiery both claimed their clerks were enthusiastic about efficiency. "Clerical work is cheerfully done," asserted Holeproof's manager, "and there is no loafing or stalling on premium work. The supervision required on this work is very slight, for the operator feels that she is working for herself at the same time she is working for the Holeproof Hosiery Company." Metropolitan reported that its dictaphone operators were "a happy, healthy group of clerks with a mental attitude toward their work which is unquestionably induced by the knowledge that . . . conscientious application is rewarded by full compensation for meritorious achievement." There did seem to be some workers who, as management frequently claimed, preferred clear rules and standards for output to the older subjective methods of measuring performance. A manager at Western Electric told of a typist who had been considered rather average until the introduction of an efficiency plan, under which she "blossomed" into a remarkable worker. She was discovered inserting two forms simultaneously into her typewriter in order to double her output. When asked why she had not developed this method under the old system, she replied that she had been the coworker for two years of two other typists who had received the same automatic small raises as she. One "she described as 'beautiful but dumb,'" and the other one whose "attitude was that it did not pay to over-exert yourself for any big corporation because it never got you anything." Now she felt her extra efforts would really be rewarded. The story had a chilling conclusion; although the typist's initiative won her a salary bonus, the other two women were laid off because of lack of work.[49]

Such an example was relatively rare. The truth was that many women clerks protested the transition to new ways of doing the work or resisted them once established. If they had other options, women clerks, like their male counterparts, left machine work and found different jobs. "Clerical personnel," admitted one manager, "the same as factory personnel, object to a time study engineer or clerk sitting at their elbow at first. They feel the speeding up of work is merely part of the management's idea of driving."[50] Lateness and absenteeism were such problems in operative departments that some offices either deducted from salaries and wages for these or gave bonuses for being on time or for perfect attendance. Cyclometers (meters to count typewritten lines) were developed in the 1920s to prevent false self-reporting. Many managers feared that without relentless supervision all sorts of devious schemes for beating the system would proliferate.

Women who had done operative work complained about its speed, its monotony, and its dehumanization. Like repetitive assembly-line factory jobs, clerical work on the efficiency plan created mental tension and physical strain. A dictaphone operator interviewed by Eaton and Stevens in Cleveland in 1915 said that she had had "no initial prejudice at all against the machine and recognized that she made a higher salary by its use," but with experience found it "a great nervous strain and that on, some days, she feels 'just ready to fly.'" She hoped to leave her position and return to taking shorthand dictation instead. A biller who worked an eight-and-an-half hour day thought the work "heavy and tiresome, and that the slight overtime work . . . is especially difficult to endure."[51] Grace Coyle cited studies done in England in the twenties which attributed high rates of sickness and absenteeism among office machine operatives to the speed, intensity, and monotony of the work.[52]

Called in to investigate punch card operating in the Census Bureau in 1920, the Women's Bureau found that the piece rate of 840 cards per day induced ill health in operators: "All persons interviewed referred to the strain either from excessive physical exertion or intense nervous strain or both." Some operators quit because they could not keep up the pace, others fainted on the job, and "one girl had returned home the afternoon preceding the interview in a hysterical condition." In order to meet their quota, some operators came to work early to punch cards, because working overtime after the quitting hour of 4 P.M. was not allowed. Some operators complained that when the census forms profiled the foreign-born it took longer to punch cards and slowed their rate. Some operators accused supervisors of channeling the forms of native-born respondent forms to favored workers and punishing others with data on the foreign-born. The punch release on the operators' machines tended to crumple cards as they were being removed and thus delay work. Cards incorrectly punched were not counted in the piece-rate totals, and as workers' speed improved they received disproportionately lower bonuses for work completed.[53] The Women's Bureau urged the Census Department to abandon the piece rate to make punch card work more humane.

Stenographers and secretaries who were questioned by the Bureau of Vocation Information in 1924 sometimes volunteered information about their experiences with operative work. They were most likely to be women older than twenty, with a wide range of educational backgrounds, who had successfully made a transition from machine work. What the women disliked most about operative work was its pace and the boring routine. A woman who had left four jobs within a year had finally found one she liked: "only decent office where one does not have to work like a factory hand." Another had landed a secretarial job in which "the work, while entailing more responsibility, seems easier to me than the routine boiler factory work of mere fast typing and endless stenography." Another frequent job-changer had left her last position because the firm "installed a dictaphone which I refused to operate all day long." In a manufacturing firm a secretary who had first worked for Travelers' Insurance in Hartford described it as "a huge concern in which she felt like a cog in a great machine—very impersonal and routine." An older woman who began as a railroad clerk in Maine and worked as waitress when she moved to California in 1908 had worked herself up to a secretary-stenographer in a bank that employed 1,500. She left the firm and found another job when "machinations of a so-called efficiency expert stirred up entire general office." Her own superior was "supplanted, my work changed for a year, and I was unhappy over . . . continual unrest in all the offices." A woman in her thirties who had been at Western Electric since 1903 had managed to become a private secretary to the general manager but had put in her time for years in the stenographic department and "did not like it." Another woman in her forties summed up her years of work experience by concluding: "I am far from being a pessimist but it seems to me lately that everything is being sacrificed to *speed*, with inadequate pay."[54]

In the long run, women clerks could do little to stop the efficiency process. By attacking relatively small groups of workers within firms or offices, managers effectively isolated them from other clerks; without any tradition of solidarity around walkouts or work stoppages it was unlikely that job actions could be successful. By playing men against women, and often older workers against younger ones, managers helped to promote individualism and competitiveness.[55]

Nonetheless, cooperative attempts by workers to help each other keep up with or set reasonable paces of work were probably frequent responses to efficiency measures. May, who worked in the information department of a large bank in Providence, found the work to be easy. When a co-worker had trouble going fast enough, however, other workers pitched in and covered up her incompetence. "Everyone was awfully nice to her. We all helped her so she'd get out at five o-clock . . . . On every section of the alphabet, she always claimed . . . she had . . . the heaviest. She couldn't help it . . . , but I guess she was nervous, just couldn't cope with things . . . . She said to me one day, 'You know I've been here so long; I've never gotten a raise.' . . . She never was able to take on more and if anything you're supposed to become more efficient."[56]

Another example of operative cooperation surfaced in Lewis Meriam's recollections of his days as a civil service manager for the federal government. He set up a system in one department "that he thought fool-proof," but the individual production results were not even close to the standards set. Of particular concern was the fact that "the employee he regarded as the ablest in the unit had the lowest production, whereas the poorest employee had the highest." When the section chief was assigned to do some detective work while pretending to work at a desk in the corner of the room, she saw what was wrong immediately. Her own assistant, the subsection chief, "had a difficult individual assignment." Not wanting to bother her, the clerks took their problems to the clerk "regarded as the best in the group." Moreover, "the poorest clerk sat next to the best clerk, and simply laid all her hard schedules on the desk of the best clerk." The best clerk, then, by doing the work of several others in the room, had the lowest production score in the room, and the poorest clerk had successfully disguised her inefficiency. The women's attempts to cover for each other were, in this case, thwarted; the subsection chief was relieved of her supervisory duties, the best clerk was made the supervisor, and the poorest clerk was fired.[57]

As ongoing resistance to them continued, Leffingwell's ideas were no longer the panacea that they originally appeared to be. Their application to straightforward machine and repetitive work obviously paid off in the short run, but they also required a large initial investment in efficiency experts and new systems, as well as ongoing built-in costs for measurement. A number of thorny issues were connected with measuring. Should employers measure by the minute, the hour, the day, or the week? Should they measure individuals, small groups, or whole departments? Should they deduct pay for errors, lateness, and absences? Efficiency techniques seemed to work well when first installed, but routines broke down over time, and sloth and lethargy crept in; workers were frequently unable to sustain their early records. As John Mitchell of General Electric said, "if they remain on the same type of work they lose their enthusiasm, and their efficiency drops." Clerical workers with youthful endurance and few other employment options were the best candidates for efficiency plans; workers reached a performance peak after one or two years of experience and were close to the maximum salary rates. What should be done with them then? Could efficiency techniques be extended to departments where neither routine work nor routine workers were the norm? Could male clerks be forced to accept routine work? And how did one define routine?[58]

Most managers continued to believe, however subconsciously, that methods of work should reflect a person's class and gender status. Extending efficiency measures to large numbers of male clerks, to college-educated clerical workers, or even to older women workers, continued to be problematical all through the 1920s. The rationale for not doing so continued to be the alleged "nonroutine" nature of most clerical work. There was no doubt that many clerks still performed complicated tasks requiring a variety of skills. Office management experts, despite Leffingwell's assertions to the contrary, continued to claim that, for the moment anyway, many kinds of office work could not be subjected to scientific management. "On most clerical jobs," Erickson's study of 1931 concluded, "it has seemed to be difficult to set standards of output and efficiency to serve as a direct basis of remuneration."[59] But there was enormous resistance to having the work of certain classifications of clerks labeled "routine," even if it already was or could be. For the moment, the division between "skilled" and "unskilled" was too important a boundary to be blurred by extending measurement plans too far up the gender and class hierarchy.

Those who did try to extend scientific management beyond the operative level ran into trouble. Marion Bills, who had a Ph.D. in psychology from Bryn Mawr and had worked with the applied psychologist Walter Bingham at the Carnegie Institute of Technology, managed office systems at Aetna Life Insurance and did consulting for many other firms. She took seriously the notion that most clerical work, including that of men, could be standardized. She had been horrified to learn in a study of the personnel employed by three insurance companies that 50 percent had been on the payroll since 1908 and that 30 percent of those received "greatly" excessive salaries. She hoped, eventually, to put 60 percent of Aetna Life

Insurance's employees on measurement and incentive plans and to establish maximum wages for each job, "above which we cannot afford to pay, no matter how well the work is done." But by 1929 only about 10 percent of all workers at Aetna were on such plans, including dictaphone operators, typists, file clerks, Hollerith card punchers, tabulators, and policy loan calculators. Bills's methods were resisted by supervisors and workers outside the all-female departments, and, most tellingly, management acquiesced to that resistance. By the mid-1930s, in fact, Aetna had moved to another approach for the nonroutine departments, in which both women and men worked. Aetna agreed to ban time and motion efficiency experts and to use cost accounting controls as an incentive to department heads to keep costs down.[60]

Bills's experience at Aetna was evidently typical. When the AMA Research Committee on Measuring Office Output gathered its findings on the extent of office work measurement from seventy-nine responding member firms (and these might be assumed to be among the most modern in the nation), only twenty-five reported systems in place that measured operatives' work and paid them on a bonus plan; thirty-nine reported no measuring systems at all.[61] A 1931 survey of fifty-two firms in New York City found only five that paid workers, mostly dictating and billing machine operators, according to output. Most businesses, Bills thought, not only remained convinced that many tasks could not be defined carefully enough to be measured, but were also afraid that most workers would simply refuse to allow the installation of efficiency and bonus plan techniques. Office managers were well aware that "the average office employee . . . . likes variety in his work. Some like monotonous tasks, but most do not."[62] At least until the advent of the depression, many business firms were unwilling or unable to attack the varied routines of the general clerks, about half of whom were men.

It was also increasingly clear that Taylorism often backfired, creating an overblown system of controls that failed to achieve the desired result. By the mid-1920s technocrats like Leffingwell had fallen into disfavor among the more sophisticated office management theorists. "Most of us remember the 'Efficiency Expert' of a few years ago," said a manager from Western Electric, "and the ridicule to which he was subjected. He had an idea but was unfortunate in his presentation or application of it."[63] Lewis Meriam, who had been with the federal civil service since 1905, commented in 1938 that efficiency systems were "too frequently designed so that they will fit everything, with the result that often they do not really fit anything."[64] While office managers agreed it was theoretically possible to systematize any clerical job, it might not be beneficial from a cost basis to do so. Moreover, attention had to be paid to clerical workers as human beings. Elton Mayo's studies on fatigue had begun to show that "loafing" was a complicated psychological process involving the worker's "total situation" at home and at work, and that the fatigue that usually accompanied monotonous work led to high labor turnover, absenteeism, tardiness, and even mental disorder. People had to be motivated, or manipulated, not just compelled, into doing their best.[65] Office management consultant Harry Hopf put the changing consensus clearly: "You may set up mechanisms . . . . and deal with figures to your heart's content, but the result comes through proper motivation of the human factors. The stage may be set, the measuring instruments may be applied, but some force must be used to get better results from the workers."[66]

Experiments with more psychological approaches to clerical work, including self-measurement, group production teams, rest periods, the incorporation of "wasted time," combinations of measured and unmeasured work, and plans for rewarding employees with limited promotions, all took place in the 1920s. Marion Bills developed the use of these at Aetna and other insurance companies. She was convinced that a group spirit of cooperation had to be developed and that workers needed to be told how they were doing and when they were doing well, not just in comparison with each other, but when their efforts were saving the company money. She did not believe that workers were inherent "soldierers." In a rebuke to Leffingwellism in 1928 she observed that operations could be reduced to lightning speed, but "the great loss of time is . . . in the time wasted between operations, that is, in stacking papers, in fumbling for cards, in asking questions, in visiting with neighbors, in getting the machine adjusted. In nine of ten cases all these items of waste are, we believe, totally unconscious on the part of the worker."[67] In a review of Leffingwell's 1925 edition of *Office Management* she poked fun at "its ponderousness—850 pages, two and a quarter inches thick . . . . One begins to feel that managing clerical activities is really a technical job . . . . Some discussions in the book are fundamental; others concern the smallest details; and the latter follow the former with no warning." By the time the reader reached the advice that the pages of reports "'should be numbered in the middle at the bottom 3/4 inch up,' one resents the mental drop." In a later effort Bills continued her jibes at Leffingwell by arguing that although time and motion studies were "a lot of fun" and made the office expert feel "superior," they were of limited usefulness. She had, for example, through a minute analysis of the handling of carbon paper by typists, been able to cut the number of necessary motions from twenty-five to seven, but because the operators spent only 1.5 percent of their time each day handling carbon paper, the experiment was hardly a real contribution to profit-saving or efficiency.[68]

Bills experimented with a wide variety of management techniques, even as she continued to incorporate time and motion studies. By 1929 she already knew of the Hawthorne experiments and had immediately grasped the essence of their importance for office efficiency experts: "Any change . . . produces an increase in efficiency. That is, if management expends time and energy enough to make a change, no matter whether that change is for better or the worse, immediately the workers pep up and do better work . . . . If this is true, . . . then one of our criterions of success has just fallen from under us."[69] She continued to follow the Hawthorne literature with interest.

Bills, who had begun her career developing clerical work employment tests, advocated the view that good selection techniques and measurement plans made a powerful team. It had long been known that clerks who scored in the middle ranges of general clerical ability and IQ tests made the best operatives; those who were "too intelligent" often grew bored with operative work and became inefficient. These findings fit neatly with preconceived notions about correlations between class, gender, and intelligence. Testing new hires helped to confirm what some employers had found through experimentation: young and relatively inexperienced working-class women made the best (and perhaps only) candidates for operatives in clerical work. They had the lowest rates of labor turnover and were least likely to complain about routine work. Employers were well aware that the paucity of other employment options for these women made them more reliable operators. The Curtis Publishing Company purposely set out to hire inexperienced working-class women who were not high school graduates for ledger clerking, a "repetitive routine" job that was "subject to standardization of methods." Curtis looked for young women "who have some economic incentive to work, . . . that is the girl who is partially or wholly dependent on her earnings for her livelihood, . . . who has the inclination and ambition to get into clerical work in our company." If they had never worked before, Curtis claimed, they were less likely to have "bad habits" and more likely to develop a "sense of loyalty."[70] A popular business writer who visited a large New York City bank ledger room filled with young women and machines corroborated the Curtis plan when he was told by the bank manager, "These girls come to the business world from a social stratum that would surprise you. Of course they need the money or they wouldn't go into business."[71]

The grammar school- or partially high school-educated working-class woman could be trained in a few days, hired at wages just slightly higher than those in factories or department stores, and then induced to work in an assembly-line setting. Without a high school diploma or experience in stenography and bookkeeping, the youthful woman operator found it relatively difficult to move into a better position in the first few years of employment. One manager explained the logic of these hiring methods clearly:

> We have found it disadvantageous to hire a professional trained bookkeeping machine operator . . . . In the first place, she knows more than our work requires and consequently can command a higher rate of wage than we need to pay . . . . In the second place, this training places us in a competitive position with other concerns whose work is not so finely subdivided . . . and who consequently require higher and more diversified training in the operator. Therefore, we train our own girls, and we find if we train a girl in the precise details that concern our job and pay her the market rate of wage in our community . . . , we have a much more permanent employee . . . for the reason that she is not sought after by other concerns.[72]

Factories also employed working-class women for clerical jobs. Both Scovill Manufacturing and Gillette Razor, for example, found it useful to recruit factory workers for machine departments. Cheney Brothers, a New England silk producer and one of the first textile mills to Taylorize, more than doubled its clerical staff between 1899 and 1923. Clerical workers were recruited from mill employees, and by 1923 nearly three-quarters of the office staff had been "promoted" from factory positions. More than half of Cheney's office workers were children of foreign-born parents and included both southern and eastern Europeans.[73] Several factories in New York and New Jersey told YWCA interviewers during World War I that they had similar policies: "Office workers were recruited from the ranks, the social standing and easier conditions making up for the difference in pay." The implication was that beginning salaries in some of these clerking jobs were even lower than salaries in manufacturing, but that working-class women were "grateful" for the chance to move up to office work.[74]

Firms that generated heavy paperwork also turned to the employment of working-class women. Marion Bills conducted statistical tests that showed that daughters of working-class men were least likely to leave their jobs; "the chance of the person remaining with you increased as the social standing of the fathers' occupations decreased."[75] Aetna's first women employees had been from Yankee, English, or Irish families. By the mid-twenties, however, Italians, Poles, East European Jews, Germans, and French Canadians all worked at Aetna; one sample shows that more than half of all women clerks at Aetna were daughters of blue-collar men. In Hartford, home base of Aetna and other life insurance companies, more than half of male workers were employed in manufacturing, but most women workers were clerks.[76]

As management had discovered, younger working-class women often had no other option than to take operative jobs in the office if they wanted to "move up" to clerical work. Their response to operative work may well have been that typing or preparing bills on an assembly line was preferable to an assembly line in factories. Their perspective on what constituted "suitable work" was probably different than that of middle-class high school graduates, and they may not have felt "degraded" by operative work per se. When compared with factory work, clerical operative jobs were cleaner, more pleasant, and usually required more skills.

A sample of Rhode Island women who held clerical jobs in the teens and twenties included several women who performed operative work in offices. They were the most likely in the sample to be daughters of working-class fathers, and the least likely to have graduated from high school. They seemed to accept the rigid rules and production requirements of operative work but also took great pride in the jobs they had done. Ellen recalled that her telephone operating work landed her a spot in training school to learn toll directory assistance and machine switching. She liked "the mechanical aspects of the job, handling equipment." Edith, who worked at Brown and Sharpe, had two fifteen-minute breaks and an hour for lunch. She and her friends used the breaks to go to the rest room because "it was a little walk over to the ladies' room," and if "you had to go to the bathroom in between, you had to ask him [the supervisor] . . . [and] that was kind of embarrassing." There was to be no talking during working hours. "But, of course," Edith remembered, "there was always a way." Notes and candy, for instance, could be passed around the room in a wastepaper basket. Edith and other comptometer operators developed keyboard methods to increase their speed. By keeping their fingers at the bottom of the machine they could avoid changing the position of their hand, so "we never used . . . an eight, we'd just press four twice . . . . You could divide and subtract, and everything, on those things . . . . If you made a mistake you were called down; I suppose if you made more than one, you'd get fired . . . . If you didn't work a day, you didn't get your pay. But I built up a lot of speed there, because we had to."[77]

Some workers thought firms with scientific management policies delineated work responsibilities more clearly and provided a set of rules that supposedly applied to everyone. One of the consistent complaints of both managers and stenographers in traditional offices was the tendency of dictators to bunch letter writing at the end of the day, leading to slow periods in the morning and then hectic work or overtime in the afternoon. Some bosses worked their stenographers hard, others did not, and many assigned personal errands to their "girls." A spokesman for Roxanna Petroleum reflected on these concerns in describing his firm's changeover to an efficiency system and claimed they were alleviated. Under the old method, workers were "doing considerable office and errand boy work for members of the staff . . . and . . . department idiosyncrasies reflected too much upon their work." With the newly established centralized clerical services department "they like uniform supervision."[78] An insurance clerk who worked in Providence in the teens and twenties seemed to confirm this assessment. She preferred her second job, at Amica Insurance, to her first job, where she had a co-worker who left right at 5 P.M. in order to catch her train. "She would leave some of the work that had to be done that night, . . . so I'd get stuck with her work. I had to stay overtime and I didn't think that was fair at all." At Amica, by contrast, "everybody was treated alike," and a worker who insisted on coming in late was fired.[79]

Women Supervise Women: The Woman Office Manager

While office systems were often designed for large firms by personnel management experts, their execution required a host of lower-level managers and supervisers. Many of these were women, especially when the work was machine operating, stenography, or typing. In small firms, the woman secretary or bookkeeper might supervise the rest of the office staff. At a motion picture firm in Los

Angeles, for example, a bookkeeper supervised a stenographer, a telephone operator, and an office boy. She did the hiring and firing for these positions as well.[80]

The woman office manager of large machine departments was almost always older than twenty-five, and usually older than thirty; she had often begun her working life as a schoolteacher and then moved into stenography. She had most likely shown herself to be useful in training other employees.[81] She had usually demonstrated loyalty to the firm by remaining with her employer for a number of years but was also not "too old": a woman filing specialist listed as rejects for office supervision "flappers who didn't seem to be worth more than a few dollars a week, [and] women too old to be considered."[82] The office supervisor's job security depended directly on how well and quickly she could get her workers to perform. She might be responsible for checking mistakes, assigning fines and bonuses, issuing efficiency ratings, checking on lateness and absenteeism, and making certain desk tops were free of clutter or personal decorations. Like their counterparts in factories, clerical assembly-line workers were engaged in constant guerilla warfare against what they perceived as petty rules. They went to considerable lengths to shorten the time they spent on tedious work by coming in late, leaving early, getting up from their desks whenever possible, chatting with neighbors, and taking as many sick days as possible.[83] Seemingly straightforward actions like going to the rest room became the focus of employer-employee power struggles. In short, supervisors of clericals on scientific management plans might be viewed as the enemy in the office, even though they were women.

The young office woman might see the office supervisor as a reincarnation of her school teachers, a kind of female ogre who was her most immediate link with company discipline and the rigors of working life. The office supervisor, rather than the company, might appear to be the source of workplace oppression. Rose became the supervisor of the card department at Amica Insurance in 1928. Although she tried to divide the work evenly among "the girls, . . . some would be quicker than others." One slow employee had taken to hiding her unfinished work in her desk. When the cards couldn't be found, Rose had to send for the woman personnel manager, who came downstairs and searched the employee's desk, "and there they were." As often happened, the "personnel manager" in this instance was also the head office manager for women employees and responsible for firing slackers; "the problems would all go to her and she had to solve them ... once in a while she'd have to let somebody go."[84] A female chain of command clearly disciplined female clerks at Amica.

It was commonly understood that most women preferred male supervisors to female ones, and it is easy to see why. Men were more likely to be in charge of departments doing varied work, they were often moving on an upward track to higher positions, and their destinies did not probably ride so heavily on the performance of their underlings. All of this was said to make them more easygoing and tolerant as bosses. "Men give orders that appear to be requests," said one observer. "Girls obey—they know they are dismissed if they do not. Women give orders to be commands—and antagonize. Superior women will work under inferior men supervisors, not under women who are equals or inferiors."[85] Men had patriarchal authority on their side as well; if they were tyrants, women employees could do little except quit. The woman office supervisor was in a much more vulnerable position. She was likely to be in her position for years, she could probably only move laterally to another department or another firm, and as a woman her authority was likely to be inherently more in question and subject to manipulation by other women. Mary Gilson commented on what kind of behavior this might produce: "I have sometimes seen a hard, uncompromising, petty-minded woman supervising an office; but find the man in charge of her and you will see he is driving her or afraid to be frank with her, and neither attitude is conducive to the development of a good supervisor."[86] The precarious position of the woman office manager often caused her to range between extremes of "over-leniency or nagging; or because of her personal likes and dislikes, resulting in either the appearance or the actuality of playing favorites."[87]

Office management, like teaching, produced psychological strains for women supervisors. It meant being cooped up with mostly younger workers in an authoritarian situation where arbitrary rules had to be imposed and control maintained. The tendency for the supervisor to distance herself from the supervised as a "parent" or a "teacher" was one way of handling this relationship. An office manager of a legal firm positioned her desk where she could "settle quarrels, repress chatter, train green children just as when I was called a teacher .... Well-trained children," she contended, "can do almost anything if there is an adult in the background."[88] The chief stenographer of the Western Union Telegraph Company in Chicago, another ex-teacher, reaffirmed that "teachers' training [is] very valuable in conducting [the] work of girls."[89] Many supervisors were keenly aware of the age differences between them and their charges and of the likelihood that work, to their dismay, might be only one of several priorities of their youthful employees.[90]

Some women office managers took to the task of supervision with enthusiasm and found in scientific management a way around any "personal" question. The YWCA survey encountered a young college woman during the war who was directing a large office staff at a firm where she had begun as a statistical clerk. She had studied the system already in use and then compared it with others she had read about or seen in action. In a detailed report, she "showed the possibilities" she saw for "efficiency and economy." She was put in charge of a few clerks, was invited to reorganize other functions, and had recently moved on to "a system for branch offices."[91] Eleanor Gilbert's description of Miss E. M. Hull was enough to strike terror in the heart of any file clerk: "she trained girls to maintain the high standards she initiated in each office, so that there would be no return to slipshod methods of filing."[92]

Some women clerks refused to become supervisors because they knew they would be placed in an ambivalent position with their sister workers. Personnel management expert Lewis Meriam cited the example of an efficient woman clerk in a federal government office who at first refused to take a supervisory position. One of her first jobs in the civil service, it turned out, had been with a "supervisor who was, first and foremost, a tartar for routine discipline." She had rebelled, encountered a lot of trouble with her boss, and "developed a contempt for supervisors and did not want to be one herself and 'have all the girls despise me.'"[93] "Practically ordered" to take the job, she did so with the understanding that she would not perform it with the dictatorial methods of her old boss. Other women took supervisory jobs because they were the best jobs they could hope to have. A woman who had begun as a stenographer in Chicago in 1905 for a public utility was supervising ninety-five people in the equipment service department of Western Electric at the Hawthorne works by 1925. She thought she had obtained her current position, which netted her $60 a week, "through attentiveness to duty and ambition." Although she didn't think secretarial work was as difficult as supervisory work, she became a supervisor because "one must assume responsibility if they expect to advance."[94]

Once in a managerial job, the effective supervisor often had personal qualities that disguised real power relationships in the office.

Galloway stressed that a woman with a "tactful personality" who was able "to influence others to do their best" made the best head of a centralized department. Lewis Meriam preferred "depending practically entirely on the sense of responsibility and of fair play that most government employees possess" rather than on strict enforcement of rules. While frequently stuck managing scientific management-style departments, some women supervisors were allowed to use more cooperative methods of supervision. In describing the work of the woman who feared becoming supervisor because she would lose all her friends in the office, Meriam noted that she had been allowed to handle the discipline of her department "in her own way. In her section there was practically no routine discipline, and no need for it ever developed. Incidentally, all the girls liked her." There were never any "problem" cases reported to the personnel officer from her department, "and yet the work was excellent."[95]

Human relations techniques were inherent in skillful office management, and they did not come easily to everyone. A manager of a credit department in a manufacturing firm confirmed this. Her job required "the arrangement of the work so that all the people . . . have sufficient work to do without overloading one or slighting the other. Handling individuals is the most difficult, getting them to do what you want done, and preserving their good will at the same time. Only an expert can accomplish this."[96] A relatively young woman in her mid-twenties with two years of high school education was made chief stenographer of a department of fourteen women at a Los Angeles telephone company. Managing a group of women, "most of them older than I, requires tact and judgment," she reported, "but is most interesting." She thought further promotion would depend on her "ability to keep harmony in the department, and turn out work satisfactory to everyone concerned."[97]

In a lengthy letter to the BVI, Anna Raymond, an office manager who was a former teacher, agreed that regulating the flow of work to avoid unequal distribution of work to individuals and to continue group morale were among her most difficult tasks. "Things will go along smoothly for a few days and then there is a surge. The supervisor must know how to meet this, how to marshal her forces to produce at the appointed hour, the bulk of the work." "Proper selection" of employees could lessen attention to discipline, but cases requiring discipline were bound to arise, and the supervisor would have to meet them "in positive terms." Empathy with her workers, which Raymond thought included the ability of the supervisor to perform office work tasks herself, was also "advisable." "If she does not know what it means to be a stenographer and be expected to get out a large quantity of work in a limited time and have it right; if she does not know . . . the demon which now and then seems to possess a mimeograph, she is likely to fall short."[98] These office managers had understood the essence of why strict scientific management techniques often had to be replaced with more internalized initiatives; workers frequently performed the best when allowed to develop group strategies for getting the work done. In this kind of setting, the woman office manager might be viewed as "one of the girls," or as a sympathetic older presence in the office.

Office Management, Labor Segmentation, and Some Thoughts on the Great Depression

Many of the dilemmas faced by office managers in the 1920s were resolved once the stock market crashed, smaller firms went out of business, and unemployment increased dramatically. The cost accounting approach to office management abruptly took precedence in office management literature. Clerical departments with "inefficient" production records were pushed to improve these at all costs, and given the difficulty most clerks had in finding work, managers could impose whatever conditions of employment they desired. The urgent need to cut overhead costs and the abrupt reversal of a tight labor market gave employers every incentive to use measurement plans to impose more factorylike conditions in offices, with or without bonus payments, and even on men. The results were the conditions that office worker unions began to describe so dramatically after about 1933: flattened wages, the firing of older workers, and the breakdown, at least to some extent, of protections for men of their less routinized work methods. Business machine companies reported a surge in sales, and more sophisticated combinations of machinery run by electricity allowed corporate employers to systematize and centralize the work of more employees. A survey of large offices in 1931 noted "a growing interest in salary standardization for clerical workers and in incentive systems of payment as the routine and repetitive type of work has increased." Bonus and efficiency plans were definitely on the upswing.[99]

These developments meant that some of the differences between clerical workers based on gender and class were temporarily, at least, given less attention, and similarities in the work of women and men could be underlined rather than differences stressed. Middle-class professionals who had studied to be teachers or social workers, both women and men, now found themselves in the same kinds of jobs as working-class clerks with partial high school educations. Given the paucity of jobs for adolescents, more and more working-class youngsters were graduating from high school and seeking clerical work. With European immigration at a new low, more young people than ever had the English-language skills required of clerks and helped to expand the ranks of the white-collar unemployed. Fewer men had the options they had in the 1920s for moving out of clerical work and into managerial or professional jobs.[100] Common experiences produced some common workplace efforts, and to the extent that they were encouraged by the AFL and CIO, far greater numbers of clerical workers turned to union organizing than had in the 1920s.[101]

Perhaps because of the new self-consciousness of clerical workers in the 1930s, office management experts were never as revealing about their methods in widely circulated print as they were up to 1933. But there is no reason to believe that the basic principles of office management changed much after their maturation in the 1920s. The women workers who thronged the city streets and skyscraper lobbies on their way to and from work were facing increasingly rationalized techniques at work in an ongoing irrational system based on the sexual division of labor. In the last three chapters of this book, I explain who these women were and describe the office worker culture of which they were a part.

NOTES

1. For summaries of economic changes in the 1920s, see Edwin F. Gay and Leo Wolman, "Trends in Economic Organization," in President's Research Committee on Social Trends, *Recent Social Trends in the United States* (New York: McGraw-Hill, 1934), 218-67; George Soule, *Prosperity Decade: From War to Depression: 1917-1929* (New York: Rinehart, 1947), 121-84; Robert Aaron Gordon, *Economic Instability and Growth: The American Record* (New York: Harper and Row, 1974), 17-23; and Jim Potter, *The American Economy Between the World Wars* (New York: John Wiley and Sons, 1974), 17-56.

2. On General Motors and Sears, see Alfred D. Chandler, Jr., *Strategy and Structure: Chapters in the History of the Industrial Enterprise* (Cambridge: MIT Press, 1962), 138-52, 231-79. On department stores, see Edward A. Filene, *The Model Stock Plan* (New York: McGraw-Hill, 1930), 62-63; Edward A. Filene, Werner K. Gabler, and Percy S. Brown, *Next Steps Forward in Retailing* (New York: Harper and Brothers, 1937), 9; and Ralph

M. Hower, *History of Macy's of New York, 1858-1919: Chapters in the Evolution of the Department Store* (Cambridge: Harvard University Press, 1943), 372. On Standard Oil, see George Sweet Gibb and Evelyn Knowlton, *The History of the Standard Oil Company of New Jersey*, vol. 1: *The Resurgent Years, 1911-1927* (New York: Harper and Row, 1956), 600-627; and Henrietta Larson, Evelyn H. Knowlton, and Charles S. Popple, *The History of the Standard Oil Company of New Jersey*, vol. 3: *New Horizons, 1927-1950* (New York: Harper and Row, 1971), 12-20.

3. David Montgomery, *Workers' Control in America: Studies in the History of Work, Technology and Labor Struggles* (Cambridge: Cambridge University Press), 91-112, and *The Fall of the House of Labor: The Workplace, the State, and American Labor Activism, 1865-1925* (Cambridge: Cambridge University Press, 1987), 370-464.

4. For two discussions of the importance of sophisticated cost accounting in the 1920s, even for small firms, see T. H. Sanders, "Present Status of Uniform Cost Accounting," *Harvard Business Review* [HBR] 1 (Jan. 1923): 167-74; and George H. Koskey, "The Relation of Cost Control to the Evolution of System," *Industrial Management* [IM] 72 (July 1926), 34-38. A useful summary of these changes and their connection to growing offices can be found in Dewey H. Anderson and Percy E. Davidson, *Occupational Trends in the United States* (Stanford: Stanford University Press, 1940), 586-92.

5. John H. MacDonald, "Records of the Purchasing Department," *Office Economist* [OE] 7 (April 1925): 3; Alfred D. Chandler Jr., *The Visible Hand: The Managerial Revolution in American Business* (Cambridge: Harvard University Press, 1977), 458-59 and *Strategy and Structure*, 66-67, 90-98.

6. Robert S. Lynd and Alice C. Hansen, "The People as Consumers," in *Recent Social Trends*, 871-72.

7. Carroll H. Wooddy, "The Growth of Governmental Functions," in *Recent Social Trends*, 1278-92; Leonard D. White, "Public Administration," *Recent Social Trends*, 1410; A. E. Buck, *Public Budgeting: A Discussion of Budgetary Practice in the National, State and Local Governments of the United States* (New York: Harper and Brothers, 1929), 539-40, 553; Frederick C. Mosher, *The GAO: The Quest for Accountability in American Government* (Boulder: Westview Press, 1979), 65-71; Leonard D. White, *Trends in Public Administration* (New York: McGraw-Hill, 1933), 156-63; Thomas K. McCraw, *Prophets of Regulation: Charles Francis Adams, Louis D. Brandeis, James J. Landis, Alfred E. Kahn* (Cambridge: Harvard University Press, 1984), 145-51.

8. White, *Trends in Public Administration*, 9.

9. Lloyd Morey, "Uniform Accounting Classification for Illinois Cities," *American City* [AC] 25 (July 1921): 57-59; "Buffalo's New Accounting System," *AC* 42 (Sept. 1929): 177; Buck, *Public Budgeting*, 2, 245; Frank Mann Stewart, *A Half-Century of Municipal Reform: The History of the*

National Municipal League (Berkeley: University of California Press, 1950), 129.

10. Stephen B. Story, "A Commendable Meter-Reading and Billing System," *AC* 32 (Jan. 1925): 40-42; V. Bernard Siems, "Meter Reading and Billing of Metered Water Accounts in Baltimore," *AC* 35 (Dec. 1926): 793-95.

11. Wooddy, "The Growth of Government Functions," 1292-315; White, "Public Administration," 1411.

12. Soule, *Prosperity Decade*, 182-86; Nicholas B. Wainwright, *History of the Philadelphia Electric Company, 1881-1961* (Philadelphia: Philadelphia Electric Company, 1961), 148-204; Charles W. Geiger, "Administrative Methods of the Second Largest Gas and Electric Company in the Country," *IM* 72 (Sept. 1926): 196-98; Ronald W. Schatz, *The Electrical Workers: A History of Labor at General Electric and Westinghouse, 1923-1960* (Urbana: University of Illinois Press, 1983), 6; also See Barbara H. Brock, *The Development of Public Utility Accounting in New York* (East Lansing: Graduate School of Business, Michigan State University, 1981), 95, and Forrest McDonald, *Let There Be Light: The Electric Utility Industry in Wisconsin, 1881-1955* (Madison: American History Research Center, 1957), 186, 270.

13. N. R. Danielian, *A.T.&T.: The Story of Industrial Conquest* (New York: Vanguard Press, 1939), 14-15.

14. On banking, see Paul B. Trescott, *Financing American Enterprise: The Story of Commercial Banking* (New York: Harper and Row, 1963), 185; Gay and Woolman, "Trends in Economic Organization," 244; Eugene Nelson White, *The Regulation and Reform of the American Banking System, 1920-1929* (Princeton: Princeton University Press, 1983), 160; Soule, *Prosperity Decade*, 152-53.

15. On consumer spending, see Lynd and Hansen, "The People as Consumers," 857-71.

16. Keller, *The Life Insurance Enterprise*, 285-91; Marquis James, *The Metropolitan Life: A Study in Business Growth* (New York: Viking Press, 1947), 199-270; Lawrence Washington, "Personnel Management of the Metropolitan Life Insurance Company," *IM* 62 (July 1921): 27.

17. Warren S. Thompson and P. K. Whelpton, "The Population of the Nation," in *Recent Social Trends*, 15-16; Potter, *The American Economy Between the World Wars*, 21, 53.

18. *The Lamp* 3 (Dec. 1921): cover, 5; "26 Broadway of Today," *The Lamp* 6 (July 1924): 23-25; Hower, *History of Macy's*, 399.

19. Edith Padelford Cochrane, "Successful Managing of Women Office Employees," *OE* 7 (March 1925): 14.

20. Lyn Urwick, *The Golden Book of Management: A Historical Record of the Life and Work of Seventy Pioneers* (London: Newman Neame, 1956), 188-91. Leffingwell described his first job in "The Present State of the Art of Office Management," *Bulletin of the Taylor Society* [*TSB*] 10 (April 1925): 96. In a comment at an American Management Association meeting

in 1926 he used language that claimed for himself the identity of engineer and of evangelizer of the gospel of scientific managment: "There is only a very small percentage of the organizations in the United States, even in the factories, who have any degree of scientific management, although we engineers have been preaching it for many years." Discussion following Marion A. Bills, Wallace Clark, A. S. Donaldson, and B. Eugenia Lies, "Measuring Office Output," American Management *Office Executive Series* [AMAOES] 16 (1926): 38.

21. Leffingwell, "Present State of the Art of Office Management," 96-97.

22. Wallace Clark, "Getting the Office Work Done," pt. 1, *IM* 60 (July 1920): 13.

23. William H. Leffingwell, "Waste in Office Work," *TSB* 9 (Feb. 1924): 4.

24. Members of the office management department of the American Management Assocation began to issue reports and hold meetings in 1924. The publications of the group listed individual participants and their firms. In tallying the number of times representatives from particular firms served on committees, gave speeches, and participated in question and answer periods from 1924 to 1939, I found that the most frequent participants were General Electric (21), Henry L. Doherty and Co. (15), Chicago Mail Order (13), Ralston Purina (13), Atlantic Refining Co. (13), Eastman Kodak (12), Westinghouse Electric (12), Northwestern National Life (11), Jewel Tea Co. (11), Western Electric (11), Liberty Mutual Life (11), R. H. Macy (10), Metropolitan Life (10), Commonwealth Edison (9), Aetna Life (9), Prudential Life (8), Illinois Merchants Trust (7), American Telephone and Telegraph (7), Federal Reserve Bank of New York (6), Philadelphia Electric Co. (6), and People's Gas, Light and Coke Co. (5). U.S. Rubber, White Motor Co., E. I. Du Pont, Scovill Manufacturing, Union Carbide, Armour and Co., National Cash Register, Tidewater Oil, B. F. Goodrich, American Rolling Mill, Proctor and Gamble, RCA-Victor, Sears and Roebuck, and Standard Oil all participated from three to four times each. Compiled from AMAOES 1-89 (1924-39).

Fourteen of the industrial corporations on this list were among the top hundred in the country by 1929. Metropolitan Life and Prudential were the two leading insurance firms, R. H. Macy the largest department store, and Sears and Roebuck the leading mail order firm. AT&T had a virtual monopoly on nationwide telephone service. People's Gas, Light and Coke was one of the Insull holding company systems, and Henry Doherty's utilities controlled utility service to a thousand communities in twenty different states by 1930. A. D. H. Kaplan, *Big Enterprise in a Competitive System* (Washington, D.C.: Brookings Institution, 1964); Keller, *The Life Insurance Enterprise*, 285; Soule, *Prosperity Decade*, 185-86.

25. For Leffingwell's work of the teens, see "My Plan for Applying 'Scientific Managment' in an Office," *System* 30 (Oct. 1916): 373-79; "This

Plan More than Doubled Our Typists' Output," *System* 30 (Nov. 1916): 461-68; "What 'Scientific Management' Did for My Office," *System* 30 (Dec. 1916): 613-21; and 31 (Jan. 1917): 68-74. His series of manuals on office management and office machines appeared between 1917 and 1932, including the influential *Scientific Office Management* (Chicago: A. W. Shaw, 1917), updated and expanded in a 1925 edition. Leffingwell also wrote frequently for the *TSB*.

Wallace Clark was an industrial engineer who worked with H. L. Gantt's staff in installing scientific management techniques in factories and later became an expert on stenography department organization. He did his early office management work at Remington Typewriter and established his own consulting firm, which specialized in "office methods for manufacturing and distributing organizations." "Getting the Office Work Done," pts.1 and 2, *IM* 60 (July 1920): 13, and (Aug. 1920): 116.

Lee Galloway was a Ph.D. and taught at New York University, where he was head of the department of business management and professor of commerce and industry. He was a specialist on the teaching of retail selling and director of the National Commercial Gas Association. See title page of Lee Galloway, *Office Management[:] Its Principles and Practice* (New York: Ronald Press, 1919); for information on Bills see the discussion that follows and chapter 3.

26. John H. MacDonald, *Office Management* (New York: Prentice Hall, 1942), 5-6; Eugene J. Benge, *Cutting Clerical Costs* (New York: McGraw-Hill), 2-3.

27. Marion A. Bills, "Measuring, Standardizing and Compensating for Office Operations," AMAOES 44 (1929): 3-4.

28. Bills, "Measuring, Standardizing and Compensating for Office Operations," 8.

29. Benge, *Cutting Clerical Costs*, 4-5.

30. Estimate cited by Ethel L. Erickson, "The Employment of Women in Offices", *Women's Bureau Bulletin* [WBB] 120 (1934): 15.

31. Clark, "Getting the Office Work Done," pt. 1, 14.

32. H. J. Taylor, "Office Working Conditions and Extra Compensation Plans," AMAOES 30 (1928): 20.

33. W. M. Smith, "Measuring Shop Clerical Work," AMAOES 38 (1929): 19.

34. Dirk P. DeYoung, "Simplifying Employee Salary Administration," *OE* 11 (April 1929): 3-4.

35. George Frederick, "Office Cost or Administrative Overhead," *OE* 2 (Dec. 1920): 169; E. M. Hicok, "Budgeting Office Expenses," AMAOES 12 (1925); Hadar Ortman, "Budgeting Office Expense," AMAOES 52 (1930); H. V. Browne, "Recent Office Economies," AMAOES 56 (1932). Especially important are the comments of Frank W. Rowland, "Extra Incentive Wage Plans for Office Workers," AMAOES 11 (1925): 4. Rowland suggested that less attention be paid to measuring individual clerical workers and more to

treating department heads like foremen, holding them responsble for production and cost control.

36. For examples of the extensive literature on centralized clerical services, see Harry B. Horwitz, Harry A. Wembridge, and Herman J. Hutkin, "Statistical Compilation: Some of its Uses as a Function of Scientific Management," *TSB* 8 (Feb. 1923): 3-11; Maurice T. Fleisher, "We Cut our Expenses by Adding a Department," *System* 41 (March 1922): 281-82; Clark, "Getting the Office Work Done," pt. 2, 116-20; J. H. MacDonald, "Executive Control of Office Details," *OE* 10 (July-Aug. 1928): 3-4, 12; Paul F. Bourscheidt, "A Central Stenographic and Typing Department," *OE* 12 (Aug.-Sept. 1930): 3-4, 12.

37. John F. Cronin, "Discussion," AMAOES 44 (1929): 26-33.

38. John. L. Conover, "Management as Applied to Public Utility Billing Problems," AMAOES 43(1929), 15.

39. John Mitchell, "Measuring Office Output," AMAOES 35 (1928).

40. Erickson, "The Employment of Women in Offices," 75. Erickson commented (16) that "where bookkeeping machines had been introduced in the last 5 years, a change from men to women was reported in some of the instances. . . .As far as women are concerned, bookkeeping machines in the past have perhaps opened as many fields of employment as they have restricted. Men have been more adversely affected."

41. Interview with Phillip Herbert Carey by Sharon Hartman Strom, July 20, 1984, Middlefield, Connecticut.

42. Lewis Meriam, *Public Personnel Problems: From the Standpoint of the Operating Officer* (Washington, D.C.: Brookings Institution, 1938), 53.

43. William J. Harper, "Extra Incentive Wage Plan—Central Dictaphone Bureau of the Metropolitan Life Insurance Company," AMAOES 11 (1925): 8-10.

44. Paul T. Tobey, "This Wage-Making Plan Has Cut Our Office Costs for Three Years," *System* 48 (Oct. 1925): 405-8.

45. W. Franklin Jones, "Centralization Means Economy," *OE* 10 (Nov. 1928): 5-6, 13.

46. John Mitchell, Gertrude M. Ballsieper, and R. M. Blakelock, "Measuring Office Output," AMAOES 24 (1927): 19.

47. L. F. Seybold, "Measuring and Compensating Office Performance," AMAOES 54 (1930): 1-11.

48. Smith, "Measuring Shop Clerical Work," 20.

49. Harper, "Extra Incentive Wage Plan," 9; Tobey, "This Wage-Making Plan," 407; Smith, "Measuring Shop Clerical Work," 23.

50. Comment by A. C. Farrell of Dennison Manufacturing in "Incentives for Office Workers," AMAOES 42 (1929): 19-20.

51. Jeanette Eaton and Bertha M. Stevens, *Commercial Work and Training for Girls* (New York: Macmillan, 1915), 222, 223, 119.

52. Grace L. Coyle, "Women in the Clerical Occupations," *Annals* 143 (May 1929): 186.

53. Typewritten memo from the Women's Bureau, U.S. Department of Labor, to Sam L. Rogers, director of the Bureau of the Census, Oct. 19, 1920, folder: "Census Investigation—Punching Machines (Strain of Using)—1920," RG 86, Women's Bureau, Division of Research, Unpublished Studies and Materials, 1919-72, National Archives, Washington, D.C. I am indebted to Susan Porter Benson for this material.

54. Bureau of Vocational Information Women's Survey [BVIWS], 558 (1639), New York; 316 (197), California; 45 (1557), New York; 651 (304), Connecticut; 387 (437), California; 14 (1597), Massachusetts; 330 (141), California.

55. For a particularly helpful exploration of this idea, see Priscilla Murolo, "Gender, Skill and the Rationalization of Clerical Work: The Aetna Life Insurance Company in the 1920s," paper presented at the American Historical Association, Dec. 29, 1985, New York.

56. Interview with M. C. by Valerie Raleigh Yow, Oct. 25, 1982, Rhode Island Working Women Oral History Project [RIWW], Special Collections, University of Rhode Island, Kingston.

57. Meriam, *Public Personnel Problems*, 27.

58. This was the pivotal question Marion Bills put to Leffingwell in her paper "The Status of Measuring Office Work" for the AMA in 1926: "I asked Mr. Leffingwell and Mr. [Wallace] Clark, authorities on office management, what they considered a clerical position and where they drew the line between clerical, technical and executive positions. I judge from Mr. Leffingwell's reply that he draws the line of demarcation between routine jobs and other jobs. I will give Mr. Leffingwell a chance to interpret whether I am right, but I read his letter four or five times . . . . So far as I am concerned, if you say you draw the line at routine jobs, it leaves me in the dark still, because then you have to define a routine job." AMAOES 16 (1926): 6.

59. Erickson, "Employment of Women in Offices," 49.

60. Bills, "Measuring, Standardizing and Compensating for Office Operations," 18. Bills was the secretary of the ongoing AMA Research Committee on Measuring Office Output, chaired by John Mitchell of General Electric. The best secondary account of Bills and her work is Priscilla Murolo, "White-Collar Women: The Feminization of the Aetna Life Insurance Company, 1910-1930," unpub. paper, Yale University, 1982.

61. Bills, "The Status of Measuring Office Work," 3; Erickson, "Employment of Women in Offices," 32.

62. Wallace Clark, "The Control of Output in Offices," AMAOES 9 (1925): 8. Clark, who had been so dismissive of women clerks right after the war, was more flexible than Leffingwell in his ability to respond to a changing situation. He noted in this same essay that while nearly all young men in the office were ambitious, young women who worked "for a few

years seem to be most interested in their present incomes and in pleasant working conditions," but that "those [women] who are in business permanently may be appealed to on the same grounds as men." Like Bills, he argued (3) that "if a man does not do a fair day's work, it is not due to anything inherent in his nature, but to some other influence."

63. W. M. Beers, "Development of Office Methods," AMAOES 49 (1930): 5.

64. Meriam, *Public Personnel Problems*, 49.

65. See, in particular, Elton Mayo, "The Irrational Factor in Society," *Personnel Journal [PJ]* 1 (1922-23): 419-26; "Revery and Industrial Fatigue," *PJ* 3 (1924-25): 273-83; and "The Basis of Industrial Psychology," *TSB* 9 (Dec. 1924): 249-59.

66. Comment by H. A. Hopf in discussion following Hicok, "Budgeting Office Expenses," 12. Hopf ran an office management consulting firm and participated frequently in the AMAOES meetings.

67. Marion A. Bills, "Time Study as a Basis of Measuring Office Output," AMAOES 32 (1928): 3.

68. Marion A. Bills, review of W.H. Leffingwell, *Office Management: Principles and Practice* in *Journal of Personnel Research* 3 (1924-25): 463-64, and "Examples of Research Work Valuable to the Insurance Executive," *Proceedings of the 1934 Special Conferences of the Life Office Management Association* (New York: LOMA, 1934), 98-99.

69. Bills, "Measuring, Standardizing and Compensating for Office Operations," 17.

70. Earl B. Morgan, "Training Office Employees," AMAOES 6 (1925): 9-10.

71. Perley Morse, *Business Machines: Their Practical Application and Educational Requirements* (London: Longmans, Green, 1932), 90-91.

72. Comment by Mr. Stone (company affiliation unidentified) in discussion following Morgan, "Training Office Employees," 16.

73. J. P. Lamb, "A Statistical Analysis of Personnel," AMAOES 21 (1926).

74. YWCA, "Executive and Technical Women in Industry: Survey of Factories, 1919-1920," 10, pamphlet no. 8661, Schlesinger Library, Radcliffe College.

75. Bills, "Measuring, Standardizing and Compensating for Office Operations," 17.

76. Murolo, "White-Collar Women," 11-12.

77. RIWBP 24 and 281; RIWW interview with G. M. by Gail Sansbury, Feb. 6, 1983; names used are fictitious.

78. Jones, "Centralization Means Economy," 13. Both Alice Kessler-Harris and Maureen Greenwald agree that turn-of-the-century working women might have improved their occupational situations by working in jobs governed by scientific management. Alice Kessler-Harris, *Out to Work: A History of Wage-Earning Women in the United States* (New York: Oxford University Press, 1982), 146; Maureen Wiener Greenwald,

Women, War and Work: The Impact of World War I on Women Workers in the United States (Westport: Greenwood Press, 1980), 6-7.

79. RIWW interview with R. S. by Gail Sansbury, Nov. 6, 1982. 80. Galloway listed four characteristics necessary to the head stenographer: "1) character and personality; 2)knowledge of the concern's policies and organization; 3)skill as a stenographer; 4)ability to teach." He suggested that an appropriate person (later in the text referred to as "she") could be found within the firm. *Office Management*, 179. Another reference to women as natural supervisors of typing and stenography departments can be found in Clark, "Getting the Office Work Done," pt. 2, 118.

80. BVIWS 270 (1902), New York.

81. I identified at least nineteen women from the 1924-25 BVI study of stenographers and secretaries who were clearly department heads or office supervisors. Fifteen gave exit dates for leaving high school, ranging from 1887 to 1919. Of these, the median year for leaving high school was 1903, so more than half of these women were thirty-five and older, and only one, an office manager in a small manufacturing firm, was under twenty-five. Five of the nineteen were former school teachers, but most were former stenographers. Of seventeen who gave information about their level of education, only one had not attended high school, eight had attended some high school, eight graduated from high school, and of these, three had been graduated from college.

82. Ethel Scholfield, "Selecting a File Supervisor," *OE* 7 (Nov. 1925): 5.

83. Galloway emphasized that methods for achieving "strict accountability for time lost, i.e., holding employees to account by means of reports of daily attendance, showing the time they reach their desk" were a crucial part of the head stenographer's job. Breakdowns in discipline were to be reported immediately to the office manager, who was encouraged to take prompt action. *Office Management*, 183.

84. RIWW interview with R.S.

85. BVI handwritten notes, "Brief Investigation of Girls in Commercial Work." BVI, folder 72.

86. Mary Barnett Gilson, *What's Past Is Prologue: Reflections on My Industrial Experience* (New York: Harper and Brothers, 1940), 100.

87. Cochrane, "Successful Managing of Women Office Employees," 14.

88. BVIWS 35 (1914), New York.

89. BVIWS 672 (538), Illinois.

90. Cochrane, "Successful Managing," 7.

91. YWCA, "Executive and Technical Women," 12.

92. Eleanor Gilbert, "Woman's Value in Business," *OE* 3 (April-May 1921): 3-4.

93. Lewis Meriam described as "curious . . . the highly competent individual workers who are afraid of supervisory positions with larger responsibilities." *Public Personnel Problems*, 18.

94. BVIWS 591 (592), New York.

95. Meriam, *Personnel Problems*, 19.

96. BVIWS 662 (584), New York.

97. BVIWS 499 (100), California.

98. Anna A. Raymond to Emma Hirth, July 17, 1925. BVI, folder 471.

99. Erickson, "Employment of Women in Offices," 86. On mechanization and rationalization, see, for example, George C. Scott, "Mechanical Budgetary Control Accounting for Municipalities and Other Public Bodies," *AC* 40 (Aug. 1929): 154-55; H. H. Allen, "Economies in the Insurance Office," AMAOES 56 (1932); C. L. Stivers, "Office Incentive Plans—Then and Now," AMAOES 76 (1936); "Analysis and Forecast," *OE* 3 (Jan. 1936): 32, 83. Also see Sharon Hartman Strom, "'Machines Instead of Clerks': Technology and the Feminization of Bookkeeping, 1910-1950," in *Computer Chips and Papers Clips: Technology and Women's Employment*, ed. Heidi I. Hartmann (Washington, D.C.: National Academy Press, 1987), 2:77-78.

100. A significant exception to this general rule is the field of accounting, which experienced a relative surge in the 1930s due to more elaborate cost accounting methods and the increased paperwork required by government programs affecting employees, including unemployment insurance, social security payments, and expanded withholding taxes.

101. Sharon Hartman Strom, "'We're No Kitty Foyles': Organizing Office Workers for the CIO," in *Women, Work and Protest: A Century of Women's Labor History*, ed. Ruth Milkman (New York: Routledge and Keagan Paul, 1985).

At the Narragansett Electric Lighting Company in Providence, R.I., in 1897, the bookkeepers and their bound ledgers dominated the office. In this all-male workplace, even the typist (to the right) was a man. (Rhode Island Historical Society)

Just before World War I the main offices of the Royal Weaving Mill in Pawtucket, R.I., included both women and men clerks and some calculating machines. (Rhode Island Historical Society)

A pioneer in scientific management techniques, the National Cash Register Company in Dayton had already pooled its typists in a factorylike setting by the turn of the century. (Library of Congress)

At Scovill Manufacturing Company new timekeeping and cost accounting methods in the teens put women clerical workers into the rolling and casting mills for the first time. In this 1926 photograph of North Mill workers the women, from left to right, are Mae Dwyer, Margaret Travers, Nora Fitzgerald, Elizabeth Mulhern, Gertrude Holian, and Margaret Shelley. Irish-American women took up clerical work in large numbers by the early twentieth century. (Scovill Manufacturing Company Papers, Baker Library, Harvard Business School)

At the Veterans' Administration building in Washington, D.C., in the mid-1920s, banks of calculating machine operators, nearly all women, computed veterans' bonus payments, while office managers, both male and female, supervised. (Library of Congress)

At an unidentified firm in Providence, R.I., male excutives meet in an inner office to consider company business. Not even a woman secretary is present at this intimate session; most upper-level managers excluded women from strategic planning and administration. (Photograph by John R. Hess, courtesy of the Rhode Island Historical Society)

Mary E. Barnes, supervisor of mailing operations, confers with her superior, Major F. A. Awal, in the mail room of the Veterans' Administration. Barnes's charges were said to handle the correspondence of 500,000 veterans a day. By the 1920s, women managers such as Barnes often supervised the work of younger women clerks but reported to a male superior. (Library of Congress)

Hazel Gibson Bookman lived in Columbia, S.C., where she was photographed in the late 1920s. Bookman was a graduate of Benedict College and worked as a secretary for the National Benefits Life Insurance Company and then as bookkeeper for Waverly Hospital. Barred from white offices, African-American clerks found limited employment in their own communities and helped to anchor the growing black middle class in the 1920s. (Richard S. Roberts Collection, courtesy of Gerald E. Roberts and the South Caroliniana Library, University of South Carolina)

The tower and clock of the Metropolitan Life Insurance Company on Madison Avenue in New York City was completed in 1909. City skyscrapers drew thousands of office workers through their doors every day. (Library of Congress)

On Westminster Street in downtown Providence, retail establishments and eateries provided noon-time and evening shopping and entertainment for the city's office workers. (Photograph by John R. Hess, courtesy of the Rhode Island Historical Society)

An urban transportation system of subways, trolleys, and buses carried office workers downtown from outlying towns and suburbs. Young workers could attend business colleges like the Rhode Island Commercial School (upper right) and then find office jobs in the business district. (Photograph by John R. Hess, courtesy of the Rhode Island Historical Society)

These women office workers at the Hamilton Beach Company of Racine, Wis., were photographed in 1926. Most had marcelled hair, which kept bobbed cuts neat and corresponded to the latest fashions. The problem of what to wear and how to dress confronted all women clerks. The Clara Bow look-alike in the front center is Marjorie Koening, a dictaphone operator in the Credit Department. (Scovill Manufacturing Company Papers, Baker Library, Harvard Business School)

PART II

The Office and the World Beyond: Office Workers and Office Work Culture

6

High School, Office Work, and Female Ambition: Race, Class, and the Limits of Personal Choice

Dᴜʀɪɴɢ ᴡᴏʀʟᴅ ᴡᴀʀ ɪ, Rose Chernin, a young Russian Jew, went to work in a Waterbury factory making ammunition shells. She attended special high school continuation classes for working teenagers in the mornings and then rushed to work in the afternoon. She was expected to contribute most of her paycheck to the family wage. When she related this experience many years later to her daughter, she remembered why she tenaciously held to the hope of completing high school:

> Do you know what it's like, ten hours a day, looking at shells in a noisy, dirty plant? You take over a shell, this way, that way, until your mind goes blank. And always you're waiting for the break, the five-minute break to go to the toilet. This became the one meaningful thing in the ten hours of the day. You felt that there had to be another way. I thought, with the naivete of a child, that to get an education, a high-school education, would give me a job in an office. In an office! When we crossed the yard into the factory, we passed the offices. I looked at those girls, sitting there, cleanly dressed at their desks. And I thought, There is another world.[1]

A few years later in Chicago, "May," daughter of an "old-fashioned" German immigrant, entered that world. "An unusually able pupil," May had been encouraged by her teachers to finish high school. Her father protested, arguing that high school education was unnecessary "for a girl." May left school when she was sixteen and found a job as a stenographer in an office downtown. For three years her mother collected her salary and picked out her clothes. Then May rebelled. She negotiated a $9 a week payment of room and board to her mother and continued to help out with the housework. But her role as a submissive daughter had been permanently altered. She "bobbed her hair, dressed more fashionably and joined a YMCA club and began to go to movies with her girlfriends. The climax came when May wished to spend her vacation away from home."[2]

To a youthful Kate Simon, an immigrant who had come to America at the age of four, high school beckoned as a place where she might study literature, the subject she adored. Graduating from elementary school, she recalled, "was a rite of passage that would call for light rejoicing, especially in the houses of immigrants, to whom eight years in . . . school meant a long and broad education." But her father insisted that she enter a commercial high school, study typing and stenography for a year, and find a job. She was rescued by an extraordinary event, "a miracle worked by exalted personages. My father received a letter. . . . It said that a girl of my interests and capabilities should be offered the broader education of a general high school which might prepare her for college. No one could deny the authority of a high school principal and my father agreed."[3]

For Rose Chernin, May, and Kate Simon, all working-class women and daughters of immigrants, clerical work loomed as a composite of glorious opportunity, a route to independence, or a life of monotonous drudgery. Their parents expected them to leave school shortly after elementary school graduation to go to work to help support the family. The most promising avenue of work for daughters of immigrants was a clerical job. By World War I, office managers wanted to hire young women who had some high school education. They preferred young women for many of the new stenography and machine work jobs partly because women could be paid significantly lower wages than men with equivalent levels of education. Young women were less restless in these jobs than young men, and the marriage bar convention insured most women would leave clerical jobs before they could command higher salaries. But this analysis of the demand side of clerical employment does not explain why so many young women wanted to take clerical jobs. In preferring office work to other kinds of employment women and their parents were not simply pawns on an economic chessboard. Many had strategies for their lives as working people which made clerical work a logical choice.

A web of connecting threads bound working-class women to clerical work. Educators and vocational guidance experts encouraged working-class youngsters to take commercial courses in school. They saw clerical work as a suitable occupation for women and one that was preferable to factory or domestic work; commercial education might also bolster the future of secondary education if it kept children in school. Parents saw training for clerical work, offered free in public high school or inexpensively in commercial colleges, as an affordable investment in their daughters' futures. While these threads structured women's labor force participation, they were criss-crossed by finer strands of personal desire. Clerical work demanded facility in English, and performing it symbolized being American. Learning to operate typewriters and comptometers or to take dictation in stenographic languages required going to school and acquiring new skills. Self-respect and parental pride accompanied mastery of these trades. Completing two years of high school, graduating from high school, or attending a business college implied a family and an individual's investment in education and a new way of thinking about daughters' contributions to the family wage. Working in an office usually meant cleaner, safer, steadier work, and a middle-class environment appropriate for native-born status. Most significantly, clerical work paid more than other women's occupations and might provide limited upward mobility.

Women's choices of work in the early twentieth century were limited by a narrow labor market that left little room for flamboyant decisions. As a coalition between educators and the business class shaped the direction of the American high school, businessmen could encourage the production of the kinds of workers they needed at the expense of the state. The coalition between business and education helped make commercial training freely available— and to some extent inescapable—for many high-school-aged girls. Nonetheless, while women were being claimed as office workers, women and their parents were claiming office work as well.

"Not Merely Compulsory, But Compelling": Public Schools and the Rise of Commercial Education

Commercial demand for high-school-educated office workers expanded rapidly just at the point when the role of the public schools in American life was under intense public scrutiny. A sense of crisis pervaded the discussion of public schools, especially in cities where European immigrants and native-born rural migrants were testing educators' traditional teaching methods. Of particular concern was the public school system's inability to convince teenagers to remain in school. Many fourteen- and fifteen-year-olds, especially immigrant and working-class children, never got past the third or fourth grade. Compulsory education laws in most states were raising the legal minimum for leaving school, but it remained impossible for educators to retain children over fourteen who decided to quit. Nearly all states had work permit provisions that allowed youngsters to leave school legally, and many others simply disappeared.

In Massachusetts, for example, tougher enforcement of compulsory school attendance and a decline in demand for child labor had virtually eliminated truancy in the elementary grades. But while the average attendance rate at school for children under fourteen in 1895 ranged from 95 to 98 percent in Massachusetts's biggest cities, fewer than 10 percent of all teenaged children were in high school. More than one-half of all pupils failed to reach the last year of grammar school because they had started school late or repeated grades. When the Commission on Industrial and Technical Education issued its influential report in 1906 it included a special survey of school-aged workers and their drop-out rates. The survey's chief investigator, Susan Kingsbury, found that most of the state's twenty-five thousand fourteen- and fifteen-year-olds who were not in school were at work, "largely in jobs without prospect of future advancement." She termed the years from fourteen to sixteen "the 'wasted years' of the child's life" and argued that the question of keeping these children in school until sixteen "is the most important question which faces the educational world today." Kingsbury argued that employers, even textile mill managers, were not particularly anxious to hire children as workers. Nor were their parents responsible for forcing them to leave school. Except for what she termed the "lower foreign element," she found that most parents wanted their children to stay in school, and that it was the children themselves, lured by the immediate gratification of a job, however low-paying, who decided to leave the classroom. Not only were children being corrupted and exploited by such early employment, but business was suffering as well because the level of "industrial intelligence" of youthful employees remained far too low. Adolescent workers were inefficient and unproductive. The public school system had to find a way to sell school to children over the age of fourteen.[4]

Kingsbury's findings provided important ammunition for both educational experts and businessmen. Educators were engaged in an active battle in the early years of the twentieth century to modify the traditional curriculum of the public high school so that it would "be not merely free, but enlightening; not merely compulsory, but compelling." Many thought the solution to low high school attendance was vocational education: by providing practical skills in commercial subjects, the manual trades, and home economics, the schools would help children secure jobs later and thus keep them in school now. The agitation for vocational education, including business education, rested on what reformers viewed as the need for a "better adaptation of the curriculum to the needs of the rank and file, reduction of school 'mortality', and promotion of national industrial efficiency."[5]

Educational reformers, who supported the growing professionalization and employment of experts in the schools, tended to have values that allied them with the scientific management movement and made them, to some extent, naive spokespersons for the interests of business and the existing social order.[6] But educators were not simply serving as a front for the self-interests of the business class. Vocational curricula were not necessarily *intended* as a way of reenforcing class differences, although that was often the result of their implementation. Educators above all wanted to keep children in school because they thought the school and its experts could play "a potentially important role in reducing the strains and tensions that . . . society was undergoing at the turn of the century."[7]

Educators genuinely hoped to create better opportunities for working-class children, but they also believed that extended schooling would Americanize immigrants, produce better citizens, and sort people into categories according to their abilities and avocations. Working people had mixed reactions to these ideas. In Chicago, for instance, many labor leaders saw manual arts education and intelligence testing as systems for diverting working-class children away from classical education and into dead-end vocational training.[8]

Working-class parents had every reason to be suspicious. Whatever altruistic motives lay behind vocational education, what happened in reality was often denigrating to students. Educators tended to direct immigrant and black children into home economics and manual training programs, to use IQ testing and other measures to perpetuate racial and ethnic segregation, and to steer the "better sorts" into a pre-college curriculum. By the 1920s a body of respectable psychological literature argued that the very students found to be problematical—usually immigrants, blacks, and the poor—were inferior in intelligence to native-born whites and could be assigned to vocational training programs for their own good. Salvageable working-class students (likely to be English-speaking, white, and native-born) could be given a chance to improve themselves by taking commercial courses.[9]

These tendencies of vocational education dovetailed nicely with the ideas of the business class, whose influence in public schools was at a peak. In Massachusetts and Illinois they had promoted manual education since the early nineteenth century. The Massachusetts Commission on Industrial Education of 1906 was appointed by Governor William Douglas, a leading shoe manufacturer, who announced that "cheap and efficient production depended upon a trained labor supply." Douglas packed the commission with manufacturers and businessmen, and its members heard witnesses advocate vocational education because "the skilled and semi-skilled labor pool was inadequate." Urged on by Frederick Fish, president of American Bell Telephone, and A. L. Filene of Filene's Department Store, the commission tried to take control of vocational education from the board of education. While vocational education remained under the board of education's jurisdiction, business leaders gained an important victory; public education in Massachusetts now included vocational curricula as a permanent feature. Similar attempts by business interests to control vocational education took place in Chicago, where members of the Commercial Club promoted the city's first manual education schools and served on their boards.[10]

Given their power and prestige in the community, the viewpoints of business people were likely to be heard. A 1917 report showed that most city school boards were dominated by the business and professional class and that fewer than 10 percent of all board members could be loosely defined as "workers." Most educators saw the partnership between business and the public schools as entirely desirable, even natural. As one superintendent in 1913 told his colleagues at the National Education Association, "Since the school is maintained at public expense or at the expense of the business interests, and really exists for the sole purpose of developing the business men and women of the future, it is evident that there should be perfect harmony between the school authorities and the business interests." Elwood P. Cubberly, an expert on public school administration, saw the link between business and the public school as the dominant theme of public education in the twentieth century. "Our schools are, in a sense," said Cubberly, "factories in which the raw products (children) are to be shaped and fashioned into products to meet the various demands of life. The specifications for manufacturing come from the demands of the twentieth-century civilization, and it is the business of the school to build its pupils to the specifications laid down."[11]

"Specifications laid down" by the corporate economy pushed public schools toward providing commercial education. The growing demand for high-school-educated clerks made educators hope that schools could both meet the needs of business and the needs of children simultaneously. Indeed, public school educators settled on commercial education as the best drawing card of the American high school. In Poughkeepsie, New York, a pamphlet on "choosing an occupation" pitched its advice around the idea that staying in school could get students good jobs in offices and stores: "The greatest need and one that is growing greater all the time is for a good general education. To write and speak correctly, to be wide-awake and well informed, to be able to understand and follow instructions exactly . . . these are things a school cannot teach in one or a few years."[12] Girls who left school at fourteen or fifteen, warned Poughkeepsie educators, might never find a good job.

Another educator, F. V. Thompson, agreed that the introduction of commercial education could connect the classroom with the real world and convince children to remain in school:

> In the present order of society, the career motive is bound to be a dominant incentive to boys and girls in high schools. . . . The influence of the press, the hum of the streets, the multiplication of inventions, the increase in machinery, the stir and bustle of life in the city and in the country, all serve to turn the thoughts of our boys and girls toward the practical activities which are the genius of our age. The academic quietness of school halls cannot and should not resist these influences. . . . Our boys and girls must soon join the ranks of active

workers; they are eager to take their places, which is the chief reason why they leave school so early. Every investigation into the causes for leaving school shows that not necessity, but desire, has been the impelling motive. Our pupils will stay more willingly if they realize that they are being better prepared for future vocational needs.[13]

Commercial education programs were a smashing success as far as educators were concerned—if success was measured by official school attendance rates. In Cleveland, "the hope of prolonging the schooling of children destined to become wage earners early" had been the main motive behind the creation of a separate high school of commerce. The average number of elementary students who entered the Cleveland School of Commerce and went on to graduate increased from 14 percent in 1903 to 45 percent by 1913. In Boston, where vocational guidance counselors were meeting with students as early as 1908, twice as many graduates of elementary schools applied to commercial high schools as could be admitted two years later.[14] While the overall enrollment in Chicago's high schools increased by 53 percent between 1913 and 1918, the number of commercial students increased by 115 percent. Although most youths seeking office jobs at the turn of the century in Albany had attended private commercial colleges, the high school offered both two-year and four-year business courses by 1905. By 1918 nearly half of the city's commercial students, about evenly divided between the sexes, were receiving training in the public school system, and free tuition and books were offered in night school courses. Popular everywhere, these evening courses allowed young people to work full time and study for a new trade at night.[15]

The provision of commercial education did seem to produce higher attendance rates in high school. Fewer than 4 percent of all American children between the ages of fourteen and seventeen were in grades nine through twelve in 1890, but nearly 13 percent were by 1910; over the next twenty years the high school attendance of this age group increased to more than 44 percent. The number of students enrolled in commercial courses in the public schools increased from fifteen thousand in 1890 to nearly three hundred thousand by 1920.[16] Commercial curricula were particularly popular in the Northeast, where demand for office workers was highest, and they were popular with both boys and girls. While high school attendance for girls tended to outnumber that of boys by four to one among whites and by three to two among blacks, girls outnumbered boys in typing and stenography courses by only two to one, and in bookkeeping classes three to two, an indication that when boys did stay in school they tended to take commercial courses, particularly bookkeeping.[17]

Educators and social reformers had different ideas about how commercial education would benefit men and women. In looking at the future of girls, they were worried about the moral environment of the factory, the effects of hard physical labor and noxious working conditions on women's child-bearing, and the links between low wages, seasonal work, and prostitution. Boys were often expected to learn skills that would ensure them access to permanent jobs and opportunities for promotion. Girls, on the other hand, were expected "to earn a livelihood during the three, six, or eight years after leaving school" and then to make the inevitable transition to marriage and motherhood. Most educators assumed that the ultimate destiny of high school girls was to be "the wives and mothers of the next generation" and the "future homemakers of our cities."[18]

Initially, home economics and sewing were seen as the ideal vocational subjects for girls, but there was no evidence that instruction in either would lead to promising employment. In Worcester, for instance, the girls' trade school developed a skilled dressmaking program just as the garment industry in Massachusetts was being mechanized and recruiting male immigrant workers; one Boston merchant declared that skilled dressmaking was virtually a "dead industry" for women by 1915.[19] Commercial education held out far better hopes for future employment. Office jobs also seemed to be the perfect solution to the working girl's dilemma.[20] Such jobs were relatively untaxing, clean, generally full-time, and there were plenty of them. The required technical and English-language skills could be taught in high school. As clerical work expanded, educators happily seized on office work opportunities as proof that staying in school paid off for girls and got them jobs suitable to their gender.[21]

Commercial education was theoretically open to both boys and girls, but many educators agreed that women should be steered toward two-year courses in stenography and typing while men should complete four-year courses in general business, including bookkeeping. High school principals surveyed in 1917 thought businessmen wanted training for boys and girls to differ, with boys requiring "preparation for careers in administration and management," and women needing "training for relatively short-term employment as secretaries and typists."[22] Some large urban school systems developed separate high schools of commerce for boys and girls, and these schools were particularly directive in channeling the two sexes into gendered categories of commercial work. In Boston, the Boys' High School of Commerce opened in 1906 and offered electives in accounting, auditing, banking, and even international law, all designed to develop "business leadership." A related school called the High School of Practical Arts for Girls emphasized typing and stenography and also offered courses in sales and telephone operating. An advice book by two high school teachers published in 1913 contained chapters on "women's occupations" such as nursing, teaching, sales, telephone operating, and domestic service; the chapter on office work did not mention bookkeeping or the use of office machines other than the typewriter. A preliminary report on commercial occupations prepared for the Federal Board for Vocational Education in 1922 urged boys to prepare for bookkeeping and girls for stenography.[23] But most statistical surveys on wages showed that young women who had education in bookkeeping and were high school graduates earned the highest wages and held the best positions in clerical work, facts that educators often ignored.

While many youngsters were learning commercial skills in high school, business college education remained an important complement to public schooling. Business colleges had grown in a spectacular way between 1880 and 1890, and although they faced growing competition from secondary schools after 1900, they continued to increase their numbers of students up to 1920. By 1924 commercial students in public school outnumbered those in business college two to one. Despite claims by educators that commercial colleges were preying on young teenagers duped into leaving public school early, statistics showed that most commercial college students were between the ages of seventeen and twenty. Students often combined high school with a few months of commercial college training, partly because employers frequently recruited workers from business colleges, which were employment agencies as well as schools.[24] In Homestead, Pennsylvania, daughters of English-speaking immigrant steel-mill workers refused to go into domestic service. Most of them found jobs in Pittsburgh department stores or at the Westinghouse Electric plant across the river. Some, however, took commercial courses in high school or at Pittsburgh business colleges, "the extra expense" of which was "considered to be justified by the fact that the colleges assured positions on graduation. As one woman said of her young business school daughter, 'We are poor, and we must consider how she can get to work soonest.'"[25]

While the number of women attending business college continued to increase, men still comprised more than half of the students as late as 1910 and more than a third of them in 1925. These trends paralleled increasing attendance and graduation rates by men at public high schools. By 1930 nearly half of all fourteen- to seventeen-year-olds of both sexes were in high school, but only a third of the commercial students were boys. Both boys and girls were preparing for office employment by remaining in school, but girls were especially likely to be in commercial courses.[26]

Office Work and the High School Graduate: Business Says What It Needs

By 1910 a variety of institutions provided training in commercial skills. In some cities employers worked with the public schools to provide teenaged workers with supplementary education in "continuation schools." The Boston Board of Education established compulsory continuation classes for children under sixteen, and employers paid children to attend school four hours weekly. The Chicago Board of Education furnished instruction in commercial education for teenaged male employees at Swift Company, and Goodyear Rubber's ambitious "Industrial University" allegedly served five thousand employees with classes in salesmanship, home economics, factory costs and accounting, typing, and shorthand.[27] Employers hoped, with the cooperation of the public schools, to upgrade the skills and work discipline of teenaged workers.

Typing, comptometer operating, and shorthand skills could easily be tested before clerks were hired, and specialized machine operations could be taught on the job. Some firms relied on office machine manufacturers' schools for recruits who could operate specific kinds of business machines, and clerks who thought a particular machine skill might be required often took a crash course to prepare themselves for a new job. Eleanor Gilbert was surprised to find that few business schools taught the use of all types of business machines and that most clerks learned how to use them "from the manufacturers, who are always glad to teach any one to operate their devices."[28] Agnes L. Peterson of the Women's Bureau reported in 1929 that two weeks of study at a business college or the machine school in Washington, D.C. adequately prepared some women to pass the civil service examination in comptometer operation. A 1907 graduate of the Rhode Island Commercial School later recalled that she secured her position at the Waldorf Lunch Company through the Remington Typewriter Company. By 1925 Remington's placement bureaus found employment for twenty-five thousand. Comptometer bureaus of the Felt and Tarrant Company placed 27,500 operators in the United States and Canada in 1930 alone.[29]

Some corporations established vestibule or corporation schools to train workers for specific procedures in their own establishments.[30] The Federal Reserve Bank of New York reported in 1924 that it had created a successful training program for transit work (the sorting, proofing, and listing of checks). The bank estimated that it could train women with some bookkeeping machine experience to use the Burroughs adding machine, the Ellis bookkeeping machine, and the addressograph in three or four days; those without office machine experience could be trained in an average time of just fifteen days. Nearly 75 percent of the trainees went on to perform competent transit work. The Women's Bureau reported similar success in the rapid teaching of calculating machines and the relative ease of transferring competency from one kind of machine to another.[31]

More teenagers were attending high school, machine school or business college, but business employers were not always pleased with the results. In Chicago, more than 86 percent of employers interviewed in one survey said they had trouble finding "suitable" employees.[32] While machine skills were easy to teach young people, juveniles with elementary school educations did not have the other skills, job stability, and social polish required for most office jobs. Businessmen hoped that a variety of education programs, most funded by the state, would provide the workers they needed and that longer stays in high school would produce more desirable workers. Working-class children could be trained for jobs that required English-language skills and middle-class manners. A vague quality often described as "personality" began to creep into employers' demands for the ideal clerk. Working-class children had to be made over in public schools before they could take up most office jobs.

Some employers argued that it was particularly difficult to get working-class boys to stay in school long enough to qualify for office work. The director of the Swift Company's continuation school was reported as saying that "our greatest turnover consists of the rougher types of boys from poorer homes. We make a persistent effort to civilize them, but they almost invariably drift over to the trades when they become old enough to get factory employment." Boys with immigrant parents were often good at mathematics and accounting, but had deficiencies in English language and personality that made them "uncongenial members of office forces."[33]

Office management expert William Leffingwell made similar complaints about girls from the "wrong background" who attempted to use typing as an entree to stenography or secretarial work. "To be a good stenographer," Leffingwell said, "requires a much higher grade of education that [sic] many of them possess. The stenographer must be able not only to run a typewriter, but also to spell and use the English language better, as a rule, than her employer. . . . She must have tact and diplomacy." Poughkeepsie educators reported that employers claimed "girls less than seventeen or eighteen are practically useless, that before that age they cannot take up any kind of difficult work or work requiring judgment."[34]

Demands for intangible attributes such as middle-class manners and the ability to think more abstractly were especially likely to surface in discussions of stenography and secretarial work. Leffingwell admitted that not everyone could do stenography successfully, even when they had the proper training: "Good stenographers," he wrote, "are worthy of their hire and they are often underpaid, considering what is expected of them." A businessman interviewed in the mid-teens explained, "We want a girl who is old enough to grow in her work and sufficiently developed to really grasp what she is doing."[35] Another elaborated on the skills Leffingwell had assumed were so important:

If a girl comes into the office as a stenographer, it is of little importance to us whether she can write sixty words a minute on the typewriter, and take down her notes at one hundred words per minute and transcribe everything you dictate, and transcribe it exactly as you dictate it. It is far more important if she has a capacity for quick comprehension about our business, . . . and whether she has good judgment of the construction of a letter, so that . . . as she gets worked into the organization and some man dictates a letter hurriedly, she can . . . suggest that the letter is not clear and should be rephrased in certain particulars. The other day I turned a letter over to a new girl in our office . . . and asked her what she thought of . . . a letter some other firm had turned out, and she said that the letter looked neat, and was a very nice letter. I said: "I don't care how it looks, is it clear, do you understand it, is it a good forcible letter?" That is the idea which is typical of the capacity which we want in all kinds of people.[36]

Employers wanted the best of all possible worlds. They expected clerks, especially women clerks, to accept jobs in the office that paid minimal wages and to perform routine work with no complaint. But because most office jobs required sophisticated skills in thinking, organization, and written English, they wanted public schools to train people in these as though they were "natural" traits. Business people also thought that women and men who were graduates of high school made better candidates for office positions that required everyday contact with executives and office professionals. It was not just more education that employers were after, but also the class characteristics that investment in longer educations implied. In other words, business people were in support of systems of education that would produce larger numbers of skilled, white, native-born workers at relatively low cost. The state's assumption of responsibility for the production of these workers allowed employers to argue that their skills were inherent. As requirements for entry-level positions they need not be rewarded with job titles or salaries reflecting skilled work.

In the long run, the growing incidence of free commercial training in high school and the rise in the average number of years spent in school limited the ability of the working class to control the labor supply of potential clerical workers and helped to keep clerical wages low. As the English historian David Lockwood has said, the continuous growth of secondary education in the first half of the twentieth century resulted in the near interchangeability of most workers; "universal public education meant that every literate person became a potential clerk."[37]

Parents and Children: The Appeal of Commercial Training and Office Work Wages

Business people and educational experts combined forces to offer commercial training in the public schools. Offering the programs was not enough; students had to respond by taking them and staying in school. Students eagerly took advantage of the new courses, often urged to do so by their parents. Parents in the early twentieth century played an important role in making decisions about their children's lives, including how long they stayed in school, what they studied, and occupations they chose. Working-class parents planning the lives of their children saw office employment for both boys and girls as a step foward. Commercial skills could be obtained easily and at relatively low cost. Acquiring these skills might warrant staying in school when classical education in Latin, biology, or literature would not.

Working-class families often preferred commercial education to other kinds of public school curricula. In Pittsburgh skilled workers were actively involved in their children's school systems, agitated for commercial courses, and enrolled their children in them. While skilled workers in Pittsburgh made up only 19 percent of the city's population, their children made up 35 percent of the enrollees in high school commercial courses; unskilled workers, now 72 percent of the population, still managed to populate 19 percent of the student places in commercial subjects. Skilled workers were losing ground to new immigrants and seeing their jobs eroded by the institution of scientific management in factories. They saw office jobs as a way for their children to continue their status as "labor aristocrats." In cities like Seattle, St. Louis, Bridgeport, and Mt. Vernon, sons and daughters of labor aristocrats flocked to commercial courses in the high schools. In Bridgeport, Connecticut, for instance, evening courses in high school were most likely to be taken by children of working men in the machine and other skilled trades.[38]

As more immigrant parents sent their native-born children out into the work force in the teens and twenties, high school educations and clerical jobs were a sign of families' success in the new world. Mary Gilson recalled how pervasive this ideal was among garment workers at the Clothcraft shops in Cleveland: "The ambition of uneducated parents to give their children opportunities for an education is one of the most touching things encountered in intimate contact with workers. The faces of pressers, treading their pressing machines day in and day out, used to light up with pride as they told me of their sons and daughters in high school. They were willing to make any sacrifice for their children, hoping to ensure for them entrance into the enviable rank of the white collared."[39]

Before 1930 about equal numbers of women and men entered office work. But why didn't men take office jobs in even larger numbers? Why did women tend to be so heavily concentrated in them? One reason was that men, especially native-born white men, had many more opportunities for other kinds of work than women. Although manufacturing work grew at a slower pace after 1910, it did grow, especially for men. New trades in telephone installation, electrical work, plumbing, and steel building took their place alongside carpentry, machine work, and brick-laying. Some working-class men were able to move into the growing professional occupations. Sales and managerial positions for men with high school educations expanded considerably. As a result, clerical work was not nearly as important a sector of employment for men as it was for women. While 5.5 percent of all employed men worked as clerks in 1930, 21 percent of all employed women did, even though nearly equal numbers of men and women were clerks.[40]

Women continued to face a more limited list when they selected jobs than did men. The ongoing labor crisis of too few occupations for too many women was still severe by the turn of the century. The newer professions of social work, library science, home economics, and psychology provided more variety, but they usually demanded a four-year college education, beyond the reach of most working-class and many middle-class families. Nursing and normal school were less costly and took less time, and some working-class women became nurses and teachers. Jobs in retail sales were expanding but might also be part-time or seasonal. By 1900, most working-class women were still confined to domestic work, the sewing trades, and light manufacturing. New plants built by Westinghouse Electric, Heinz, and National Cash Register in such cities like Dayton and Pittsburgh were run on the principles of scientific management and hired many women workers. But in contrast to clerical work and retail sales, jobs in manufacturing for women at the turn of the century were not expanding rapidly. While about 24 percent of all employed women nationwide worked as operatives and kindred workers in 1900, by 1930 only about 17 percent did. Even in Chicago, where more women worked, on average, than in most other parts of the country, the percentage of women workers employed in manufacturing hovered around 30 percent between 1900 and 1910, and had fallen below 25 percent by 1920, when nearly 32 percent of Chicago's working women were in clerical work. The same trends were developing nationwide. While slightly more women still worked in manufacturing than in clerical work by 1920, the balance had shifted the other way ten years later and the gap would continue to widen (Table 3).[41]

In some ways young men faced a more perplexing situation than women when they considered attending high school and finding employment. They no longer found all the clerical occupations available to them; many firms refused to hire men as typists, stenographers, or machine operators. Men were, however, more likely than women to be hired as office boys, messengers, and shippers. In these jobs young men without high school diplomas might even begin at lower wage levels than young women, who were being recruited for jobs that required more specialized skills.[42] Yet in general men could expect more rapid raises and promotions than women in clerical work. Men who began at about the same wage levels as women in bookkeeping and general clerking tended to make substantially more than women after three to five years of experience.[43]

High school education did not predict increased wages for boys as well as it did for girls. The Cleveland employment expert Bertha Stevens conceded the more erratic possibilities for men when she concluded that "wage success in the case of boys may, at present, be attributable to neither education nor training but to certain other qualities, such as, perhaps, personal qualities or experience."[44] Perhaps partly because of the relatively low correlation between education and success, men, particularly those in the working class, were more likely to seek apprenticeships in traditional trades or businesses and to drop out of school. Girls did not have this option; they were excluded from apprenticeships on the basis of their gender.[45]

Young women and their parents could see a definite connection between high school education, clerical employment, and good wages. Two to four years of free public education might land a woman one of the best-paid jobs in her community. Women who graduated from high school commercial programs and remained in jobs for several years were candidates for salaries comparable to those of women in teaching, an occupation that required not only some high school education but also normal school or college training.

Clerical work also had a fairly wide range of salaries, with the possibility of making more money as time went by.[46] The work histories of bookkeepers and secretaries indicated that years of work experience could culminate in larger salaries and more responsibility; factory jobs could offer no such range of compensation or hope for future advancement.[47] When relatively high wages were added to the other advantages of clerical jobs—steady work, periodic vacations, and clean and safe working conditions—it is not difficult to see why so many parents thought that sending daughters to public high school was the best investment that could be made in their training for future work.

Women and their parents chose clerical work despite the fact that women consistently earned 25 to 45 percent less than men in clerical jobs.[48] It was still a foregone conclusion that the two sexes were connected to separate wage systems, each with their own rules of logic. Employers found these separate systems to be extremely useful in segmenting workers in the twentieth century. Although some bold feminists were raising the banner of equal pay for equal work, their rhetoric was nearly impossible to execute in the workplace without the help of strong unions and state or federal equal pay acts. However great the disparity between men's and women's wages, earnings in clerical work compared favorably to those in other kinds of occupations available to women—and this comparison was really the critical one.

As young men and women entered the work force between 1900 and 1930, they and their families were, consciously or not, weighing the gender division of labor and its varying consequences. The histories of a group of women and men who entered the job market in these years show how the process of choosing an occupation played out. These histories come from interviews with a group of twenty-eight former clerical workers in their old age.[49] The women were native-born and mostly from New England; they took up office work (including some telephone operating) between 1910 and 1930. Their families were likely to be from the upper levels of the working class or the lower levels of the middle class; their male parents were most likely to be artisans, skilled craftsmen and foremen, clerks, civil service employees, or owners of small businesses. Most had native-born parents; none of their parents appeared to be Italian or Greek, although several appeared to be Irish, German, Scandinavian, East European, or French Canadian.[50] Only seven of the women had parents on the extreme ends of the economic scale; four of these came from professional or business elite families and three came from families in which fathers were factory workers. Three came from households disrupted by death, divorce, and desertion and had been raised by relatives, usually grandparents.

Because most of the interviews included information about the subjects' siblings, they yielded data on the working lives of twenty-seven men and fifty-eight women of the same generation.[51] The girls and their female siblings were likely to attend high school longer than their brothers but were limited to a much smaller range of occupations. The boys became farmers, entered skilled trades, or worked in public utilities or business establishments. Those who did enter office work were unlikely to remain clerks and instead ended up in advertising and personnel management; some began their own businesses. A few of the men from more elite families went to college and entered the professions. None of the young women attended four-year colleges, although a few went to normal school and many attended business college. More than half of the women, thirty-six in all, became clerks, stenographers, secretaries, or bookkeepers. Another five became telephone operators. Of the remaining seventeen, six worked in factories, five became teachers, three went into nursing and sales, and two others became a nanny and a professional writer.

A few examples illustrate the differing possibilities for boys and girls. An Irish railroad agent from upstate New York and his wife, who took in homework for extra money, had four children between 1886 and 1892. All completed high school, and while the son became a personnel manager, the three girls found work as a secretary, cost accountant, and payroll clerk. A printer from Providence fathered five children between 1894 and 1905. The three boys left school early to become printers and a plumber; the girls finished several years of high school and then went to business college to prepare for clerical jobs. Two daughters from a farm family in upstate New York, born in 1901 and 1902, both went to high school. One went on to business college and worked in a doctor's office, the other went to normal school and became a teacher. An electrical welder from North Adams, Massachusetts, and his wife had five children between 1912 and 1919. All the children went to high school, and the last child, a boy, went to college and became a teacher. Three other sons became a prison guard, a bartender, and a telephone lineman supervisor, all occupations that would be closed to women for decades. The one daughter joined her brother at the telephone company, but as an operator.[52]

When the women talked about why they decided to take up clerical work, a subtle interweaving of advice from parents, siblings, and friends mingled with their own aspirations. Some entered clerical work with enthusiasm and a sense of accomplishment, some with ambivalence over other options lost. Florence graduated with honors from high school in 1918 and excelled in mathematics and science, although her father, who trained apprentice machinists, criticized her for studying "inappropriate" subjects for women. He insisted she take up stenography, and she changed her academic major from the classical course to a commercial one in her last years of public school. Dorothy wanted to become a certified public accountant, only to find that her father would refuse to send her to college. But the bookkeeping instruction she had received as a girl from an uncle helped her find a job, and she eventually became an office manager. Rachael's immigrant parents stressed education for their children, and she was able to graduate from high school and to attend the City College of New York for free at nights while she worked as a secretary in a jewelry-importing firm by day.[53]

Several of the women wanted to be something entirely different than office workers but could not convince their parents and guardians of the virtue of their choices. Jane was proud of the thirteen As and perfect attendance record on her last report card from grammar school. She had been in high school for six months when her grandmother decided she should leave and attend Child's Business College. Not entirely happy with her grandmother's decision, she went to work in the office of a Providence department store and saved money weekly so that she could attend nursing school in New Jersey. [Then] "I received the biggest disappointment of my life," she recalled. "I was told by my grandmother that I could not go because it was not proper for young ladies to leave home." Betty also wanted to be a nurse, "but Mama had been in the Providence hospital in 1906 and the nurses, all they did was empty bedpans and wash the floor. . . . They probably studied too but mama didn't see that. She said my health couldn't stand it. It would have." Since her father was a mail carrier in a beach resort community, she took the civil service examination in 1914 and worked summers in the post office.[54]

Others eagerly took up clerical work because it was what they wanted to do or because friends or relatives had already paved the way. Ida's father worked in an office, and her parents wanted her to go to college. But she had always wanted to be a secretary and landed a job as assistant to a purchasing agent. Edith, the daughter of an English immigrant who was an overseer in a textile mill, recalled that she had only attended high school for a year when she took up business: "I wanted to be a bookkeeper. . . . one of my personal friends, she went to Rhode Island Commercial School, and when I saw what it was like, that's all I wanted to do, was to go there." Two sisters who were raised by a "cultured aunt" after their parents died went through the commercial course at the high school and then on to a Katharine Gibbs business college, where, May recalled, there "were a few Roman Catholics," but everyone else was native-born and Protestant. Her aunt didn't think proper young ladies should work but expected the two sisters to survive on allowances of $5 a week. They went to work in the downtown branch of Rhode Island Hospital Trust Bank without the approval of their aunt, and May became the first woman information clerk in the bank's history.[55]

The women who had the least public school education tended to begin in factory or sales work and then make a transition to clerical work in their mid-teens. They were the most likely to be found doing machine operating or telephone work. Edith began work as a cashier after school and on Saturdays in the eighth grade. After leaving elementary school she attended business college for a year and learned how to use the comptometer in the office of a small manufacturer. After building up her speed she went to work in the cost accounting office at Brown and Sharpe, the Providence tool and die manufacturer, where scientific management policies had established a five-day work week. Edith and her co-workers had energy to spare; they took jobs in downtown department stores on Saturdays to supplement their $10 a week office salaries. Molly began her working life as a cashier in a grocery store while she was still in school and then got a full-time job at the telephone company. Enid, the daughter of East European immigrants, began working at Woolworth's after school when she was thirteen. She learned stenography in high school and got work at the offices of the Boston Store in the 1920s. Harriet's sisters had all left school in their early teens and gone into the mills, but she was the youngest child and allowed to complete one year of high school. She had worked in a factory during the summers and preferred the telephone operating work she took up at sixteen but found "it still had its drawbacks. . . . I always wanted to be a nurse but mother could never spare me." She became the secretary of her union and led a picket line in a summer telephone operators' strike for higher wages in 1923.[56]

The transition from factory to clerical work was happily made by Martha Ashness Doyle. Her father had once worked as a machinist but was chronically ill and unable to hold a steady job. The eldest of thirteen children, Martha went to work part-time at fifteen and left school a year later upon completing the eighth grade because "I had to help my mother." Her first full-time job in 1916 was at the Davol Rubber Company in Providence, where she repaired holes in rubber dolls. The fumes from the powerful glue overcame her, however, and she collapsed. She next tried work at a jewelry firm, producing pins at piece rates. "That just wasn't the kind of work I was interested in," she recalled. She heard of a temporary job in the order department at Brown and Sharpe and worked there "until the orders were caught up to date. Then a friend and neighbor of mine

said they needed a clerk to close accounts in the Rhode Island Insurance Company in Providence. I went in and filled out an application." She enjoyed her job, in which she added and posted
insurance premiums on a Burroughs bookkeeping machine. She
had always loved arithmetic, and "it seemed to come to me easy."
She postponed marriage for five years after becoming engaged in
1919 because her $6.50 a week wage was needed at home, although
she saved enough to rent her own telephone, have a tooth repaired
on the installment plan, and bring her mother a small present of
candy, cheese, or sausage every week.[57]

Class, Race, and the Limits of Opportunity

Before 1930, when a minority of all teenaged children attended
high school, employers who demanded high school education for
clerical jobs expected more than the ability to perform specific
commercial skills like typing and machine bookkeeping. Although
they rarely said so explicitly, office employers were also searching
for native-born white workers from English-speaking homes. They
could assume that most high school attendees would come from
middle-class families or from the most prosperous elements of the
working class. While public high school was free, children who
were older than fourteen or fifteen were also potential wage
earners, and poorer families were usually unable or unwilling to
cramp family income by allowing youngsters to remain in school
past the eighth grade. Some teenagers and young adults were able to
circumvent the problem of leaving school by working during the
day and attending commercial courses in the evening. Public high
schools found commercial night classes to be among their most
popular offerings.

Staying in high school or attending night classes were not options for many children, especially those from immigrant households. Often their school careers had already been badly affected by
absenteeism, repeated grades, and poor English skills. Leaving
school was a short-term family decision that often had to be made
so that children could begin making money, helping their mothers
at home, or working in a family enterprise, even when remaining in
school would produce more income in the long-run. The economist
Elsie C. Persons, who examined the wage histories of a hundred
thousand women collected by the Bureau of Labor in 1910, found a
definite correlation among levels of public school eduction, wages
earned, and immigrant status. Newer immigrants were the most

likely to leave school early, to earn the lowest wages, and to reach their peak in earnings at an early age. "Youth and low earning capacity are found together," Persons concluded. Most women wage earners seventeen years of age and under received wages of less than $7.50 a week, even though Persons pegged a minimum "living wage" at $8 a week. She disagreed with analysts such as Susan Kingsbury who had argued that children were making the decision to quit school. Persons claimed the primary culprit was the economic need of poor families: "The father's wage is insufficient for the family needs at the customary standard. . . . Since the family must maintain all its members in any case, it takes stock of its available labor and sells at the market rate. . . . The wage may be less than the necessary cost of the daughter's support. But that support is part of the irreducible 'fixed charges' of the family treasury, and if the labor of the child will yield any contribution to the hard pressed exchequer of the family, it is accounted worth while—even necessary."[58]

Mills, homework sweatshops, and small factories continued to offer fourteen-year-old school dropouts casual employment in most large cities. In the textile mill community of Fall River, Massachusetts, one of the targets of the Kingsbury study, and a place where large numbers of recent immigrants were employed, high school attendance of eligible teenagers stood at less than 6 percent.[59] For many, English-language and literacy requirements presented insurmountable barriers to remaining in school or finding commercial jobs. A 1925 study of two thousand working immigrant women in Philadelphia and the nearby Lehigh Valley showed that between 75 and 90 percent could not read English and that all were non-English-speaking. Even those who arrived with educations comparable to those of American clerks were likely to be found in factory jobs. If these women were in school they were likely to be studying English and would not be prepared to do commercial work until they mastered the language.[60]

Most non-Yankee clerical workers before World War I were German, Canadian, English, or Irish. These groups arrived in the United States with somewhat more education on average than other immigrant groups, faced fewer language and cultural barriers, or had been in the United States somewhat longer than the most recent arrivals. Education and desire might not be enough to obtain jobs, however; it was well known that some businesses, particularly banks and insurance firms, refused to hire Jews or Catholics.[61] These kinds of religious exclusions were erratically enforced in many urban settings, and some large employers of typists, stenographers, and machine clerks probably abandoned such exclusions as counterproductive. Irish-American women, who were often Catholic, for instance, often made desirable clerical workers. They were one of the few immigrant groups to come to America in greater numbers than men, and they married later, on average, than any other ethnic group in the country, if they married at all. Contemporary observers felt that second-generation Irish women faced less anti-Irish prejudice than Irish men and had made more progress moving into white-collar jobs by 1910.[62] The sociologist Edward Ross, in comparing Irish employment figures for 1880 and 1910, observed that both daughters and sons of Irish immigrants had moved into such work and that daughters in particular had poured "out of the kitchen, into the factory, the store, the office and the school." A Chicago labor leader claimed, with some exaggeration, that factory owners "can't get Irish-American girls any longer. . . . The girls of Irish descent are working, but they aren't working in factories."[63]

Some ethnic groups were more interested than others in high school education for teenagers. In Providence, Rhode Island, where there were substantial communities of Jews and Italians, boys from both groups were more likely than girls to be out of school at age fifteen, but Jewish girls stayed in school longer, on average, than Italian girls. Jews tended to come to the United States with higher levels of education and histories of being self-employed. Jewish parents seemed to place greater value on education and could sometimes offer employment opportunities to bookkeepers and stenographers in family businesses.[64] For example, an East European man who arrived in Buffalo in the mid-1920s with his wife and five children went to work for his brother-in-law. A daughter and a son also went to work for the uncle as office workers, and a cousin hired a second son in his office.[65]

Immigrant children could be victimized by unscrupulous trade schools. Vocational education experts claimed that substantial numbers of fourteen- and fifteen-year-old public school dropouts, often children of immigrant parents, were being lured by false advertising into fly-by-night business colleges, where they failed to learn the real skills required for office work. It was true that teenagers with elementary school educations often found themselves in low-level clerking jobs as messengers and machine clerks and were less likely than those with high school diplomas to move into stenographic and bookkeeping positions. They seemed to pro-

vide office firms with a floating labor pool of temporary or relatively unskilled workers and were the most likely to fall back into
sales, domestic, or factory work. This was not, however, the inevitable scenario; a full 54 percent of young people who had only completed grammar school in Cleveland were still holding clerical jobs
three years later, although they were less likely than high school
graduates to receive promotions and earn a weekly wage of more
than $7.[66] Wages in this range were really comparable to those in
factory work.

As immigrant parents became more economically secure, they
tried to prolong the time their daughters spent in public school, and
many of these girls, especially those born in America, began to
enter better-paid categories of clerical work. Indeed, clerical work
was the occupation of choice for native-born daughters with immigrant parents. There were more native-born women with foreign-
born parents in clerical work than in other kinds of nonagricultural
occupations, including manufacturing. By 1910, while more than
50 percent of all women clerical workers in the United States were
native-born women with native-born parents, 41 percent were the
daughters of the foreign-born and about 7 percent were immigrants. In cities where there were large populations of immigrants,
the tendency of immigrant families to place daughters in clerical
jobs was even more dramatic. Nearly 60 percent of all women clerical workers in Chicago in 1910 were the daughters of immigrants,
and 10 percent were foreign born.[67]

Although daughters of white immigrants made substantial progress in gaining access to office work, African-American young people were largely excluded. Few black teenagers ever reached high
school; by 1930 only 3 percent of all students in American public
high schools were African American. There were no public high
schools available to black students in the largely rural counties of
the southern states where most African Americans lived. In some
northern and midwestern industrial cities where blacks found
manufacturing work during World War I and where teenagers were
more likely to be attending school during the 1920s, white animosity toward black students—perpetuated by school personnel, parents, and student peers—made it difficult and sometimes impossible for black youngsters to receive academic or commercial
training. Bolstered in their racist predispositions by crude and misleading intelligence testing, most psychologists and educators automatically assigned blacks to manual training or home economics
programs.[68] Problems of discrimination were exacerbated by the

fact that many African Americans were recent arrivals in major cities. The poor or sporadic elementary school educations that most black children had received in rural southern communities meant that many had to repeat grades and were often as behind in school as immigrant children.

Chicago's 1922 study of race relations revealed how racism flourished in the city's public high schools. Those children in poorer neighborhoods who attempted to transfer to better high schools in the teens were frequently classified as academic failures and returned to their original schools. When asked about the transfer policy one teacher complained that "All this transferring is nonsense, anyway. . . . Children should be made to go to school in the district where they live and that would end the trouble." But the same teacher reported that when sixty black male students enrolled at one of three technical high schools in Chicago they were harassed so badly that most withdrew. A similar incident occurred in Gary, Indiana, when a vocational guidance counselor helped black students from the "colored trade school" transfer to the regular high school. White students went on strike to protest the presence of black classmates in 1927. The mayor intervened and forced most of the black students to attend a "temporary school for Negroes" until a new segregated high school could be built. Segregated high schools might or might not provide commercial education: Sumner, a segregated high school in St. Louis, did provide commercial training to black children, and about the same proportion of African Americans in St. Louis pursued the commercial course in their high school as whites did in theirs.[69]

Securing access to a commercial course in high school was one hurdle, but securing office work was even more difficult. When asked whether she planned to attend high school a young black woman from Buffalo replied: "What's the use of going to high school? I know plenty of girls who have had four years of commercial courses in high school, who are doing domestic work in the Z———Hotel, and working out by day." In Boston, Addie W. Hunter graduated from Cambridge Latin High School but could not find a job. She filed a lawsuit in the teens charging both private and civil service employers with racial discrimination but lost her case and had to work in a factory. Even during the war, when clerical workers were in sharp demand and African-American employment levels outside domestic work and agriculture reached new highs, researchers found that "colored women in the industries of New York City" tended to have far more education than white women in the same jobs. Most black women with high school educations had no hope of becoming clerical workers. "One would have to wait in an employment bureau many days to hear of even one request for a Colored bookkeeper or stenographer" investigators observed. Black women who had trained as stenographers gave up their search for office work and "finally entered factories doing unskilled, monotonous work—their spirits broken and hopes blasted because they had been obliged to forfeit their training on account of race prejudice."[70]

Employment discrimination against black Americans in offices run and staffed by whites remained systematic. Researchers of economic opportunities for blacks in Buffalo documented extensive racial discrimination in employment; in Chicago there was "a strong tendency to bar Negroes from employment in banks, except as porters or in some unskilled capacity."[71] Unlike Jews or white Catholics, most African Americans could not simply misrepresent their identity on application blanks, although some probably did and thus passed for white.[72] An exploration of short stories written by twentieth-century black women writers reveals discrimination in the workplace as a major theme. Pauline Hopkins's heroine Sappho Clark, for example, recounted a dreary tale of searching for clerical work: "the first place that I visited was all right until the man found I was colored. . . . At the second place where I ventured to intrude the proprietor said: "'Yes: we want a stenographer, but we've no work for your kind.'" A minister finally helps her to secure a job, but with the proviso that she do her work at home "so the proprietor runs no risk of being bothered with complaints" from the other clerks.[73]

White business people insisted that co-workers and customers would never tolerate the presence of blacks in clerical and managerial positions. Others simply mouthed popular prejudices of the times: "have found that a Negro will appear to be strictly honest for a period of years and then turn around and prove not to be."[74] Blacks routinely reported that businesses owned by whites would not hire them except as janitors and messengers, even when the businesses were in the black community. Large city banks opened branches in black neighborhoods but rarely hired neighborhood residents for desk jobs. The literary critic Mary Helen Washington recalls that "in the 1920s my mother and my five aunts migrated to Cleveland, Ohio, from Indianapolis and, in spite of their many talents, they found every door except the kitchen door closed to them. My youngest aunt was trained as a bookkeeper and was so good at her work that her white employer at Guardian Savings of Indianapolis allowed her to work at the branch in a black area. The Cleveland Trust Company was not so liberal, however, so in Cleveland (as Toni Morrison asks, 'What could go wrong in Ohio?') she went to work in what is known in the black community as 'private family.'"[75]

Despite the norm of racial exclusion, the number of black Americans employed as clerks rose between 1910 and 1930 and by 1930, about .5 percent of all women at work in offices were African American. By 1940 1.4 percent of female and 2.2 percent of male workers in the gainfully employed African-American population were clerks and kindred workers.[76] But clerking was a more important aspect of black gainful employment than these meager proportions would indicate. In large cities of the Northeast, Midwest, and South, where industries that required quantities of paperwork were growing rapidly, where black communities were large and prosperous enough to support black businesses, and where blacks were present in large enough numbers to demand positions in civil services, small but significant gains took place.[77] Some northeastern cities showed much higher percentages of growth; one estimate of clerical employment in New York in 1920 put 4,708 men and 1,104 women in offices and stores—8.3 percent of all employed black men and 2.7 percent of all black women. Discrimination in employment evidently varied from city to city. Black women had as much trouble finding clerical work in white offices in Philadelphia and Los Angeles as they did in Atlanta, Baltimore, and New Orleans, but had relatively better luck in New York.[78]

Black men were more likely to be clerks than black women, and the proportion of female black clerks did not rise as rapidly as the proportion of women clerks in the census figures of office workers overall. This was partly due to the overriding importance of the post office in providing clerical employment to black men. A survey of the most frequently held occupations of fathers of students in the segregated black high school in St. Louis from 1919 to 1922 showed that clerical work ranked a surprisingly high fourth place, behind personal service, common labor, and the machine trades. But three-quarters of these male parents who held clerical jobs worked at the post office. The federal postal service employed more than three thousand blacks in Chicago in 1930, 1,800 of whom were clerks, most of them men; blacks employed by the city's public service agencies as clerks were also likely to be men. Discrimination against black men in the economy at large probably strengthened their hold on clerical jobs in their own communities and worked against the employment of women. Overall, four times as many black men held clerical jobs as black women in Chicago by 1930. A Women's Bureau study of 1931 showed that black women who did find clerical jobs were, on average, better educated than their white counterparts but received lower wages. Like black women in other occupations they were also older than the average woman worker and more likely to be married.[79]

A growing number of black businesses were appearing in African-American neighborhoods of cities like Detroit, Chicago, New York, and Atlanta, although most were small retail or service establishments that did not employ many clerks. Banks and insurance companies owned by blacks provided the most substantial clerking employment for black men and women. A report of the National Negro Insurance Association in 1927 listed twenty-eight companies with nearly $11 million in assets and employment for more than nine thousand persons.[80] A 1931 Women's Bureau study of offices in Chicago and Atlanta found not a single incident of white women working with black women in a white office. There were, however, five insurance companies and one publishing firm in Chicago, all owned by blacks, which employed African-American women.[81]

Race pride movements among blacks in major cities in the teens and twenties produced calls for an end to discrimination in white businesses and the employment of blacks in black businesses. Jesse Binga, a former Pullman porter who owned one of two African-American banks in Chicago, announced in 1928 that between them the banks had four million dollars on deposit; seven insurance firms "managed by colored people for colored policy-holders" issued a million dollars in premiums a year. He thought one of the priorities of "controlling the Negro market" should be providing jobs for young men and women of the race as sales clerks, office workers, cashiers, and managers. But his bank had to close down, along with many others, in the run on banks that ushered in the Great Depression.[82]

Here and there exceptions were made to the general rule of excluding blacks from desk jobs in white offices. Researchers in Buffalo in 1927 found two interesting examples of African-American clerks who had overcome the usual hiring barriers. One man had attended high school bookkeeping courses at night while working as a bill collector for a large manufacturer by day. He was sometimes allowed to fill in at office work. When the company bookkeeper suddenly left, he was asked "if he could take over the books . . . and after a time he was put in charge of the firm's accounting." A young woman, also born and raised in Buffalo, prepared to be a school teacher but initially took up clerking instead. After a stint of teaching in the South, she was invited to return to her old job, which now required "two girls to do her work." Largely through luck and the chance to demonstrate their abilities, these token blacks were "allowed" to work in offices.[83]

The labor shortages of World War I provided other African-American women with their first real opportunities to pursue clerical work outside the black community. In Chicago, where, as Fannie Barrier Williams had written in 1905, "the color line is quite rigidly drawn against the colored girl in almost every direction," both Sears and Roebuck and Montgomery Ward hired hundreds of black women as addressers, bookkeeping machine operators, sorters, and checkers. Some were still at work in 1920, even though complaints from restaurants in the Loop about "the sudden influx of Negro girls" forced one company to open a segregated cafeteria. Better educated on the average than their white counterparts at the mail order houses, 75 percent of the black women workers at one firm were high school graduates and 12 percent had two or more years of college. White managers praised their performance and compared it favorably with that of immigrant women. Despite the fact that exceptionally well qualified and educated African-American women were clamoring for these kinds of jobs, strict segregationist policies continued in the mail order houses and the all black departments did not survive the economic downturn of 1921-22.[84] A spokesman for one firm tried to provide a rationalization for the exclusion of blacks at the main warehouse:

There has never been any necessity or any reason to seriously consider bringing colored girls in with the white girls. . . . Another thing to consider there would be the type of girl that we employ. They [the white girls] are all . . . mostly under twenty-five years, and they don't think for themselves. . . . You take one girl in an office of that size who was very anti-colored, and it wouldn't be long until her sentiment would spread. . . . If a colored girl should want to obtain employment in that part of our concern where we now employ all white girls, even if she were very competent she would undoubtedly have some trouble in securing employment in that department.[85]

Whether managers were perceiving real or imagined threats of racial animosity is not very clear. But the protests against blacks using

Loop neighborhood restaurants and the 1919 race riots in Chicago must have been fresh in managers' minds and outweighed the evidence that blacks worked effectively with white supervisors. It was simply too fantastic to imagine a racially integrated office in 1920, and the decline in mail order business by 1921 meant that employers could lay to rest the question of black employment for some time. This small taste of office work, even though segregated, proved exhilarating for many of the black women who worked at mail order house jobs. Some evidently hoped for even better possibilities and were disappointed when they did not materialize. A welfare worker at one office thought "the best type of colored girl we have in business is very ambitious. This is her first opportunity, and she feels that she is really a pioneer making history for her race." Nearly all of the workers who were interviewed said they enjoyed the work, and "seemed to take pride in the fact that they had succeeded in 'making good' in a new and attractive field of work."[86]

Although the numbers of black Americans working as clerks remained small, their importance should not be underestimated. Many of these individuals played important social and economic roles in their families and communities. They were viewed as pioneers in the world of work, demonstrating the fact that, like ministers and teachers, education might lift the race out of degrading jobs. They helped to develop a black middle class and to articulate demands for better education and more respectable employment for their children and grandchildren. In Columbia, South Carolina, Hazel Gibson Bookman attended local Benedict College and became a secretary-cashier at the National Benefits Life Insurance Company and then a bookkeeper at Waverley Hospital. A member of Columbia's black middle class, she entertained the singer Marion Anderson when she visited the city in the late 1920s.[87] The Chicago Commission on Race Relations uncovered Mr. L., who had attended Carbondale High School and the Southern Illinois State Normal School and was employed as a railway mail clerk in Chicago. In 1921 he lived in his own home and participated in such typical middle-class activities as tennis playing, church going, concert and movie attendance, and a neighborhood improvement association. He had already envisioned integration as a political goal: "Contact," he said, "is the only thing that will help to make conditions better."[88]

Most high-school-educated women of the teens and twenties, whether black or white, took up clerical work with enthusiasm. Parents, siblings, friends, and teachers all conveyed the idea that doing clerical work was both suitable for women and, for working-class women, a step forward in personal status. Awareness that apprenticeships in the skilled trades were closed to women reinforced the choice of clerical work and the faith that it would offer some space for individual ambition. The educational system and parental decision making structured the choice of clerical work for young women, but in the long run office jobs were preferable to other occupations that working-class women could expect to enter, with the possible exception of nursing and teaching. The choice of clerical work was rational, not just inevitable. For a woman like Martha Ashness, posting insurance bills was preferable to producing pins or inspecting rubber dolls, even though all three occupations were assembly-line operations. Ashness and her contemporaries sought the new clerical jobs in record numbers, and by 1930 large numbers of working-class women had become not only machine clerks and typists, but also stenographers and bookkeepers. Women were eager to work, to contribute to the family wage, and carve out a measure of self-esteem in the workplace. They were anxious to learn and use the skills that office jobs required. Office work, as Kessler-Harris has stated so aptly, was part of "an evolving labor market in which women were chosen, but in which they also chose."[89]

NOTES

1. Kim Chernin, *In My Mother's House* (New York: Harper and Row, 1984), 47-48.

2. "May" is a composite biography composed by Ruth Shonle Cavan, *Business Girls, A Study of Their Problems* (Chicago: Religious Education Association, 1929), 2-3.

3. Kate Simon, *A Wider World: Portraits in an Adolescence* (New York: Harper and Row, 1987), 8.

4. Marvin Lazerson, *Origins of the Urban School: Public Education in Massachusetts, 1870-1915* (Cambridge: Harvard University Press, 1971), 137-40; Susan Kingsbury, "Report of the Sub-Committee on the Relation of Children to Industries," in *American Education and Vocationalism: A Documentary History, 1870-1970*, ed. Marvin Lazerson and W. Norton Grubb (New York: Columbia Teachers' College Press, 1974), 76; Edward A. Krug, *The Shaping of the American High School, 1880-1920* (Madison: University of Wisconsin Press, 1969), 218-21.

5. National Education Association, "Report of the Committee on the Place of Industries in Public Education" (1910), in *American Education and Vocationalism*, ed. Lazerson and Grubb, 81-84.

6. For an especially convincing exposition of this argument, see Raymond E. Callahan, *Education and the Cult of Efficiency: A Study of the Social Forces That Have Shaped the Administration of the Public Schools* (Chicago: University of Chicago Press, 1972), 9-14, 95-178. Also see David K. Cohen and Marvin Lazerson, "Education and the Corporate Order, *Socialist Revolution* 2 (March-April 1972): 47-72; Janice Weiss, "Educating for Clerical Work: A History of Commercial Education in the United States since 1850," Ed.D. diss., Harvard University, 1978, 114; and John Rury, "Vocationalism for Home and Work: Women's Education in the United States, 1880-1930," *History of Education Quarterly* 24 (Spring, 1984): 23.

7. Weiss, "Educating for Clerical Work," 139-48.

8. Julia Wrigley, *Class Politics and Public Schools: Chicago, 1900-1950* (New Brunswick: Rutgers University Press, 1982), 48-90, 167-74.

9. For a description of home economics programs in urban schools for immigrant women—and students' lukewarm reaction to them—see Maxine Seller, "The Education of the Immigrant Woman, 1900-1935," *Journal of Urban History* 4 (May 1978): 307-30. On psychological testing see Callahan, *Education and the Cult of Efficiency*, 100-101; Edward A. Krug, *The Shaping of the American High School, 1920-1941*, (Madison: University of Wisconsin Press, 1972), 127; and Hamilton Cravens, *The Triumph of Evolution: American Scientists and the Heredity-Environment Controversy, 1900-1914* (Philadelphia: University of Pennsylvania Press, 1978), 114-65.

10. Lazerson, *Origins of the Urban School*, 148-58; Wrigley, *Class Politics and Public Schools*, 50-54, 67-78.

11. Callahan, *Education and the Cult of Efficiency*, 7, 150, 227-28, 152. Cubberly was author of *Public School Administration*, first published in 1916 and commonly regarded as the "most widely read and influential book on school administration" of his generation. While cost accounting was used to prepare financial budgets for public schools after 1910, "child accounting" was used to record school attendance, perhaps a more revealing term than its originators realized (96, 153).

12. Florence M. Brewer, *Choosing an Occupation: The Kinds of Work That Are Open to Women in Poughkeepsie* (Poughkeepsie: Board of Education [1911]), 9-10.

13. F. V. Thompson, *Commercial Education in Public Secondary Schools* (New York: World Book, 1916), 38.

14. Bertha Stevens, *Boys and Girls in Commercial Work* (Cleveland: Survey Company of the Cleveland Foundation, 1916), 133-34; Lazerson, *Origins of the Urban School*, 190.

15. Lisa Michelle Fine, "'The Record-Keepers of Property': The Making of the Female Clerical Labor Force in Chicago, 1870-1930," Ph.D. diss., University of Wisconsin at Madison, 1985, 167-69; Anita J. Rapone, "Clerical Labor Force Formation: The Office Woman in Albany, 1970-1930,"

Ph.D. diss., New York University, 1981, 124-25. Rapone concludes (7) that women's enrollment in such courses after working hours suggests their willingness "to relinquish a traditional and restrictive occupational sphere, to put aside less satisfactory work options in favor of a rationally calculated investment of their time and education in new occupational directions."

16. Rury says that the demand for commercial education rose in "all different types of urban settings, independently of the type of labor markets they confronted." "Vocationalism for Home and Work," 42. On the evolution of the public high school and growing student attendance, see Krug, *The Shaping of the American High School, 1920-1941*, 4, 7, 42, 120. Also see summaries of commercial education by Leverett S. Lyon, *Education for Business* (Chicago: University of Chicago Press, 1923), 3-16 and Thompson, *Commercial Education in Public Secondary Schools*, 1-6.

17. Weiss, "Educating for Clerical Work," 76; Rury, "Vocationalism for Home and Work," 30.

18. National Education Association, "The Vocational Education of Females," in *American Education and Vocationalism*, ed. Lazerson and Grubb, 114-15.

19. Lazerson, *Origins of the Urban School*, 172-74.

20. This is the theme of moralist Dorothy Richardson's 1905 novella, "The Long Day: The Story of a New York Working Girl," reprinted in *Women at Work*, ed. William L. O'Neill (Chicago: University of Chicago Press, 1972).

21. National Education Association, "The Vocational Education of Females," 115.

22. Rury makes this argument effectively, "Vocationalism for Home and Work," 22, 33.

23. Ibid., 34; Weiss, "Educating for Clerical Work," 137; Mary A. Laselle and Katharine E. Wiley, *Vocations for Girls* (Boston: Houghton Mifflin, 1913); Federal Board for Vocational Education, "A Preliminary Report on the Senior Commercial Occupations Survey . . . ," Washington, D.C., April 5, 1922, 10, BVI, folder 499.

24. Janice Weiss, "Educating for Clerical Work: The Nineteenth-Century Private Commercial School," *Journal of Social History* (Spring 1981): 410-11, 417; Weiss, "Educating for Clerical Work," (diss.) 136; Krug, *The Shaping of the American High School, 1920-1941*, 120.

25. Margaret Byington, *Homestead: The Households of a Mill Town* (Pittsburgh: University Center for International Studies, 1974), 125.

26. Weiss, "Educating for Clerical Work," 410-11; Weiss, "Educating for Clerical Work," (diss.), 174. By 1917-18 the percentage of high school students enrolled in commercial courses in large urban school systems in the United States ranged from 11 percent in Cleveland to 50 percent in Boston. Lyon, *Education for Business*, 11.

27. Lazerson, *Origins of the Urban School*, 176; Fine, "'The Record-

Keepers of Property,'" 170-71; Krug, *The Shaping of the American High School, 1920-1941*, 54-55; "Rubber Plant College Has 5,000 Enrolled," *Personnel* 2 (June 1920): 4, 215.

28. Eleanor Gilbert, *The Ambitious Woman in Business*, (New York: Funk and Wagnalls, 1916), 232.

29. Typewritten copy of letter from Agnes L. Peterson to Mary R. Patton, Sept. 11, 1929, folder: "Correspondence," RG 86, box 104, Women's Bureau, Division of Research, Unpublished Studies and Materials, 1919-72, National Archives, Washington, D.C. I am indebted to Susan Porter Benson for this reference. See also interview with R. S. by Gail Sansbury, Nov. 6, 1982, Rhode Island Working Women Oral History Project [RIWW], Special Collections, University of Rhode Island, Kingston; Ileen DeVault, "Sons and Daughters of Labor: Class and Clerical Work in Pittsburgh, 1870s-1910s," Ph.D. diss., Yale University, New Haven, 1985, 63; and Perley Morse, *Business Machines: Their Practical Application and Educational Requirements* (London: Longmans, Green, 1932), 78.

30. Gilbert mentions such schools as early as 1916. *The Ambitious Woman in Business*, 98. For a general summary, see Lyon, *Education for Business*, 328-45; also see *Women in Industry* (New York: Alexander Hamilton Institute, 1918), 22.

31. H. M. Jefferson, "Training Office Employees," American Management *Office Executive Series* [AMAOES] 6 (1925): 3-8.

32. Albert H. Leake, *The Vocational Education of Girls and Women* (New York: Macmillan, 1918), 339.

33. Krug, *Shaping of the American High School, 1920-1941*, 55.

34. William Henry Leffingwell, *Scientific Office Management* (Chicago: A. W. Shaw, 1917), 125; Brewer, *Choosing an Occupation*, 9-10.

35. Leffingwell, *Scientific Office Management*, 125; Jeanette Eaton and Bertha M. Stevens, *Commercial Work and Training for Girls* (New York: Macmillan, 1915), 48.

36. C. R. Dooley, *Fifth Annual Proceedings of the National Association of Corporation Schools* (1917), in Lyon, *Education for Business*, 93.

37. David Lockwood, *The Blackcoated Worker: A Study in Class Consciousness* (London: George Allen and Unwin, 1958), 37.

38. DeVault, "Sons and Daughters of Labor," 205-6, 304-5; George S. Counts, *The Selective Character of American Secondary Education* (1922, repr. New York: Arno Press, 1969), 26-35.

39. Mary Barnett Gilson, *What's Past Is Prologue: Reflections on My Industrial Experience* (New York: Harper and Brothers, 1940), 149.

40. In 1930 the census counted 2,090,476 men and 2,245,824 women in the clerical and kindred workers category. David L. Kaplan and M. Claire Casey, "Occupational Trends in the United States, 1900-1950," Bureau of the Census Working Paper no. 5, Washington, D.C.: Department of Commerce, 1958, 7, 17, 23 (Table 2).

41. Kaplan and Casey, "Occupational Trends," 7, 23-24; Fine, "'The

Record-Keepers of Property,'" 32. For an overall summary of women's employment opportunities at the turn of the century and the importance of the new scientific management industries, see Alice Kessler-Harris, *Out to Work: A History of Wage-Earning Women in the United States* (New York: Oxford University Press, 1982), 108-41.

42. Lyon, *Education for Business*, 118-19, 126-36, 139-40; also see the previous discussion of labor segmentation according to sex at Sears and Roebuck in chapter 4.

43. Thompson, *Commercial Education in Public Secondary Schools*, 63, 69-70; Eaton and Stevens, *Commercial Work and Training for Girls*, 12-13. While more than 32 percent of all male clerical workers in Massachusetts in 1926 made $40 or more a week, only 2 percent of the women did; 70 percent of the women earned less than $25 a week, but so did 25 percent of the men. "Salaries of Office Employees in Massachusetts," *Monthly Labor Review [MLR]* 24 (Jan. 1927): 143.

44. Stevens, *Boys and Girls in Commercial Work*, 119; also see Rury, "Vocationalism for Home and Work," 21-44, and Susan B. Carter and Mark Prus, "The Labor Market and the American High School Girl, 1890-1928," *Journal of Economic History* 42 (March 1982): 163-71.

45. Rapone, "Clerical Labor Force Formation," 68-69. For a discussion of skilled male workers' exclusion of women from apprenticeships and male craft unions and its connection to the concept of a family wage, see Alice Kessler-Harris, "Where are the Organized Women Workers?" *Feminist Studies* 3 (Fall 1973): 92-110.

Claudia Goldin argues that higher wages for women in the twentieth century in general were related to rising levels of high school education. "Women's Employment and Technological Change: A Historical Perspective," in *Computer Chips and Paper Clips*, ed. Heidi I. Hartmann (Washington, D.C.: National Academy Press, 1987), 2: 208-9. For an important but earlier study that corroborates Goldin's argument, see Margaret Elliott and Grace E. Manson, "Earnings of Women in Business and the Professions," *Michigan Business Studies* 3 (Sept. 1930): especially 49-91.

Economists have demonstrated a significant correlation between advanced levels of education for women and both higher earnings and greater employment participation. This was especially true of the cohort of women born between 1900 and 1910, which entered the work force between 1915 and 1930 and was increasingly likely to attend high school. Boys of this generation, on the other hand, tended to gain access to good jobs through on-the-job training; "schooling was much more critical for girls' future life work than for boys.'" Carter and Prus, "The Labor Market and the American High School Girl," 64.

46. Sharon Hartman Strom, "'Machines Instead of Clerks': Technology and the Feminization of Bookkeeping," in *Computer Chips and Paper Clips*, ed. Hartmann, 2: 87-89; also see the analysis of wages for typists, stenographers, and bookkeepers in Cleveland by Mary Schauffler, "A Study

of Three Clerical Occupations for Women," M.A. thesis, Western Reserve University, 1927.

47. See, for example, Eleanor Martin and Margaret Post, *Vocations for the Trained Woman* (London: Longmans, Green, 1914), 128-29.

48. The most comprehensive comparison of men's and women's clerical wages over time is Albert Niemi, Jr., "The Male-Female Earnings Differential: A Historical Overview of the Clerical Occupations from the 1880s to the 1970s," *Social Science History* 7 (Winter 1983): 97-101.

49. I conducted one of these interviews in 1986, and the others come from two oral history projects conducted in Rhode Island: the Rhode Island Women's Biography Project [RIWBP], consisting of biographies of the mothers and grandmothers of young women and men who studied women's history at the University of Rhode Island between 1972 and 1985, and the Rhode Island Working Women's Oral History Project [RIWW], consisting of taped and transcribed interviews with former clerical workers conducted by Rhode Island Working Women in 1982 and 1983. Both projects can be found in the special collections of the University of Rhode Island Library at Kingston.

50. The women were born between 1888 and 1910 in New England and the mid-Atlantic states; one was born in Cincinnati. Thirty-eight of their parents were native-born, twelve were foreign-born, and places of birth for six parents could not be determined. I have used the word appeared with ethnicity because I determined ethnicity from parents' last names. The foreign-born parents included two each from Ireland, England, Germany, and Austria and one each from Sweden, Poland, Canada, and Russia. Occupations of the fathers included skilled work (electrical welder, toolmaker, printer, jewelry designer, machinist, foreman, overseer, harness maker, cabinetmaker, and apprentice trainer); clerical and small business (draftsman, shipping clerk, mill office clerk, railroad agent, rural teacher-deputy warden, postman, tailor-contractor, grocery-hotel business, and baker-farmer); professional and business (physician, industrial engineer, farmer, and businessman); and factory (mill worker, machine worker, and tanning factory worker). There was insufficient evidence to determine the mothers' occupations before their marriages.

51. The fifty-eight women constitute the twenty-eight interviewees and their female siblings; the twenty-eight men constitute the male siblings of the interviewees. The careers, and often the sexes, of thirty siblings could not be determined.

52. RIWBP 348, 303, 662, and 24.

53. RIWBP 281, 156, and 635.

54. RIWBP 200 and 444.

55. RIWBP 491; interview with R. S. by Gail Sansbury, Nov. 6, 1982; interview with M.C. by Valerie Raleigh Yow, Oct. 25, 1982, both RIWW.

56. Interview with G. M. by Gail Sansbury, Feb. 6, 1983, RIWW; RIWBP 706, 288, and 324.

57. From the unpublished autobiography of Martha Ashness Doyle and an interview with her by Sharon Hartman Strom, June 5, 1986, Providence, Rhode Island.

58. Elsie C. Persons, "Women's Work and Wages in the United States," *Quarterly Journal of Economics* 29, no. 2 (1915): 213, 227.

59. Lazerson, *Origins of the Urban School*, 139. Lazerson is also critical of Kingsbury's assumption that the income of teenagers was "disposable" in many of these communities and posits (147) that most of their wages were necessary in providing a decent family income. When the number of widows with dependent children in communities like Fall River are considered, the importance of working teenagers for family survival becomes even more significant.

60. Caroline Manning, *The Immigrant Woman and Her Job* (1930, repr. New York: Arno Press, 1970), 27-32.

61. Niles Carpenter et al., "Nationality, Color, and Economic Opportunity in the City of Buffalo," University of Buffalo Studies 5 (June 1927), Monographs in Sociology no. 2., 131-54; Olivier Zunz, *The Changing Face of Inequality: Urbanization, Industrial Development, and Immigrants in Detroit, 1880-1920* (Chicago: University of Chicago Press, 1982), 339. For one study documenting the relative difficulty of Jewish and Catholic women in gaining clerical employment, see Schauffler, "A Study of Three Clerical Occupations for Women," 10-11.

62. On Irish-American women and their employment patterns, see Hasia R. Diner, *Erin's Daughters in America: Irish Immigrant Women in the Nineteenth Century* (Baltimore: Johns Hopkins University Press, 1983), 45-51, 71, 95.

63. Edward Alsworth Ross, *The Old World in the New: The Significance of Past and Present Immigration to the American People* (New York: Century, 1914), 36, and as quoted by Diner, *Erin's Daughters in America*, 95.

64. Judith E. Smith, *Family Connections: A History of Italian and Jewish Immigrant Lives in Providence, Rhode Island, 1900-1940* (Albany: State University of New York Press, 1985), 58-60. In 1915 in Providence 95 percent of Italian sons and 78 percent of the daughters older than fifteen and still living at home were "recorded as working." The comparable figures for Jews were 67 percent and 58 percent. Miriam Cohen, "Italian-American Women in New York City, 1900-1950: Work and School," in *Class, Sex and The Woman Worker*, ed. Milton Cantor and Bruce Laurie (Westport: Greenwood Press, 1977), found similar statistics for Italian school attendance in New York City, as did Manning in Philadelphia, *The Immigrant Woman and Her Job*, 27-30.

65. Carpenter et al., "Nationality, Color, and Economic Opportunity in the City of Buffalo," 123.

66. Eaton and Stevens, *Commercial Work and Training for Girls*, 22, 32, 118. Also see Gilbert, *The Ambitious Woman in Business*, 248-51. DeVault found that while graduates of the commercial high school course

in Pittsburgh were the most likely to find clerical employment, 66 percent of the dropouts were also able to find office work jobs. "Sons and Daughters of Labor," 314.

67. Elyce Jean Rotella, "Women's Labor Force Participation and the Growth of Clerical Employment in the United States, 1870-1930," Ph.D. diss., University of Pennsylvania, 1977, 188; Fine, "'The Record-Keepers of Property,'" 60-62. In Albany, New York, "second generation women did almost as well as Yankee women in moving into the clerical sector" by 1915. Rapone, "Clerical Labor Force Formation," 165. The statistics on male clerical workers from immigrant families are more difficult to read. In Chicago, a higher percentage of foreign-born men worked as clerks than did foreign-born women, a slightly greater proportion of native-born men with native-born parents than native-born women with native-born parents, and a smaller proportion of native-born men with foreign-born parents than native-born women with foreign-born parents. This pattern may reflect what was also true of African-American clerical employment; where larger numbers of men in a particular group sought limited kinds of employment, feminization of clerical work was delayed. On the other hand, the greater economic opportunities for native-born boys than for girls may explain the somewhat lower numbers of native-born men with foreign-born parents in clerical work. Roughly half of the "ordinary" female office workers in selected firms surveyed in Buffalo in 1925 were daughters of foreign-born parents, and these, the surveyors claimed, were far more dependent upon office work for employment than their brothers, who were distributed more evenly among a greater variety of Buffalo's employment categories. Carpenter et al., "Nationality, Color, and Economic Opportunity in the City of Buffalo," 147, 151.

68. Krug, The Shaping of the American High School, 1920-1941, 126-29.

69. Chicago Commission on Race Relations, The Negro in Chicago: A Study of Race Relations and a Race Riot (Chicago: University of Chicago Press, 1922), 253-54; Krug, The Shaping of the American High School, 1920-1941, 126, 127, 135; Counts, The Selective Character of American Secondary Education, 119.

70. Carpenter et al., "Nationality, Color, and Economic Opportunity in the City of Buffalo," 117; Jacqueline Jones, Labor of Love, Labor of Sorrow: Black Women, Work, and the Family from Slavery to the Present (New York: Basic Books, 1985), 179 181; Consumers' League of New York City, "A New Day for the Colored Woman Worker: A Study of Colored Women in Industry in New York City," March 1, 1919, 10-11.

71. Commission on Race Relations, Negro in Chicago, 229-30; also see Carpenter, "Nationality, Color, and Economic Opportunity in the City of Buffalo," 162-69.

72. Carpenter et al., claimed that the "'Native American' group . . . is probably overstated, as there seems to be a disposition on the part of certain workers of foreign stock to claim American birth and parentage, in the

hope of gaining preference in employment or promotion." Carpenter found only one female African-American clerk in a study of gainfully employed adults in fifty black families, and she had "passed for white." However, an informal survey of businesses in Buffalo also uncovered a black rate estimator and an information clerk in a bank, both of whom had presumably found work in offices without disguising their race. "Nationality, Color, and Economic Opportunity in the City of Buffalo," 132, 166, 168.

73. Mary Helen Washington, ed., *Invented Lives: Narratives of Black Women, 1860-1960* (Garden City: Anchor Press, 1987), 117-18.

74. Commission on Race Relations, *Negro in Chicago*, 229.

75. Washington, ed., *Invented Lives*, xx.

76. Alba M. Edwards, *Comparative Occupation Statistics for the United States, 1870-1940* (Washington, D.C.: GPO, 1943), 189. These figures are discussed by Jones, *Labor of Love, Labor of Sorrow*, 166. Rotella estimates a range of growth in the proportion of women office workers who were African American (and "other") from 0.48 in 1910 to 0.70 in 1930, "Women's Labor Force Participation," 188. Dutcher's tables show that of those black women employed in nonagricultural occupations, 0.6 percent were clerks and kindred workers (including sales clerks) in 1910 and 1.5 percent were in 1920; comparable figures for men were 2.3 percent in 1910 and 2.8 percent in 1920. Dean Dutcher, *The Negro in Modern Industrial Society: An Analysis of Changes in the Occupations of Negro Workers, 1910-1920* (Lancaster: Science Press, 1930), 102.

77. Dutcher, *The Negro in Modern Industrial Society*, 102. Figures on black employment before 1940 should be used with caution. The census figures of blacks in middle-class occupations before 1950, at least, were probably *artificially low* because the categories and instructions devised by census directors tended to put both women and racial minorities where census-takers thought they should be, not where they necessarily were. Census director Alba Edwards, for instance, remained suspicious of blacks who represented their labor as "non-manual." For a discussion of racial, class, and sexual biases in the census, see Margo Anderson Conk, *The United States Census and Labor Force Change, 1870-1940* (Ann Arbor: UMI Research Press, 1978), 139-44.

78. See Dutcher, *The Negro in Modern Industrial Society*, 96-97, for figures on clerical employment in New York and a wide range of other American cities. A survey of office employment in the South made by the Urban League showed that "clerical opportunities for Negro women and girls" were found "almost entirely among members of their own racial group." "Negro Girls in Clerical Occupations," *Woman's Press* 23 (July 1929): 475.

79. St. Claire Drake and Horace R. Cayton, *Black Metropolis: A Study of Negro Life in a Northern City* (New York: Harper, 1962), 1: 295; Jones, *Labor of Love, Labor of Sorrow*, 181; Counts, *The Selective Character of American Education*, 115; Ethel Erickson, "The Employment of Women in

Offices," *Women's Bureau Bulletin* 120 (1934): 92; also see the report in "Women in Industry," *Monthly Labor Review* 33 (Oct. 1931): 1231.

80. For information on African-American banks and insurance companies, see Monroe N. Work, "The Negro in Business and the Professions," *Annals* 140 (Nov. 1928): 138-44. For a survey of black businesses in Atlanta, see Robert J. Alexander, "Negro Business in Atlanta," *Southern Economic Journal* 17 (April 1951): 451-64; and Alexa Benson Henderson, "Heman E. Perry and Black Enterprise in Atlanta, 1908-1925," *Business History Review* 61 (Summer 1987): 216-42.

81. Erickson, "Employment of Women in Offices," 92; Drake and Cayton, *Black Metropolis*, 1: 82-83, 436.

82. Ibid., 2: 436.

83. Carpenter et al., "Nationality, Color, and Economic Opportunity," 168.

84. Fannie Barrier Williams, "The Colored Girl," in *Invented Lives*, ed. Washington, 150. This discussion of the mail order houses in Chicago is drawn from Commission on Race Relations, *Negro in Chicago*, 380-83. Also see Joanne J. Meyerowitz, *Women Adrift: Independent Wage Earners in Chicago, 1880-1930* (Chicago: University of Chicago Press, 1988), 157, fn. 56.

85. Commission on Race Relations, *Negro in Chicago*, 382.

86. Ibid., 381, 383.

87. Thomas L. Johnson and Phillip C. Dunn, *A True Likeness: The Black South of Richard Samuel Roberts, 1920-1936* (Columbia: Bruccoli Clark, 1986), 117.

88. Commission on Race Relations, *Negro in Chicago*, 173-74.

89. Kessler-Harris, *Out to Work*, 109.

7

Falling into Clerical Work: Middle-Class Women in the Office

Lois Stapleton studied physics and Latin in a Providence high school just before World War I and graduated with honors. Her parents, a toolmaker and a former school teacher, could afford to send their children to the state college, and her brother enrolled there to study metallurgy. But Lois and her sister went to business school and took up stenography. Lois, whose real vocation was church organist, later explained why she did not want to attend college and became a clerk instead: "I figured I couldn't go to college and keep my music up . . . . At that time, about the only thing you could do if you went to college was to become a school teacher, which I would have hated . . . . So I went to Katharine Gibbs and got an office job." Yet Lois also realized her ambitions had been shaped by her family's economic status and the limited choices it produced for women. "If my family had been wealthy," she surmised, "I would have liked to have gone to Bryn Mawr or Wellesley . . . and I had no end for what I would do after college, except I didn't want to be a teacher. In fact, the choice for college girls at that time was very poor."[1]

A woman described by a Bureau of Vocational Information interviewer in 1925 as a "quiet, earnest, conscientious worker" explained why she was working as an office manager at a bank in Pasadena. After graduating from high school in 1911 in mathematics and science, she abandoned the idea of teaching kindergarten and instead studied stenography and bookkeeping. In 1920, "tired of unpleasant conditions," she left her fourth clerical job and visited classes at Stanford for a year. "I hoped to find some new occupation," she recalled, "more remunerative and distinctive, but did not have an opportunity to find anything without too much special training, that I could afford to take, so went back to banking." She thought her brief flirtation with university training "was valuable in a general way, making me more independent, self-confident, etc.," and she hoped, eventually, to earn a law degree. But she could only afford to study part-time on her clerk's salary.[2]

A study of youthful business women in Chicago in 1927 uncovered a nineteen-year-old whose family lived in a pleasant residential neighborhood of Chicago and employed a chauffeur. Although her father was planning to send a younger brother to college, he thought two years of high school was enough for his daughter. After changing jobs four times in three years, the young woman was earning an average salary for Chicago stenographers, $25 a week, out of which she gave her parents $8 for room and board. Escaping this arrangement except through marriage appeared to be impossible: "She is accustomed to good clothes and recreation and finds herself unable to save much money to use for college . . . . Her father cannot imagine her living anywhere than at home."[3]

Middle-class women, or women with middle-class aspirations, were likely to find themselves in clerical jobs after 1910 for a variety of reasons. Like their working-class counterparts, middle-class parents hoped to shape daughters' choices of occupations. The professions most open to women—social work, library science, teaching, and home economics—usually required some education beyond high school. Middle-class status did not guarantee middle-class daughters college training. Many families—including small business owners, professionals, farmers, and white-collar workers—could not afford college educations for their children. Even parents who could afford education for daughters were not always willing to pay for it; extensive education beyond high school for girls might be seen as a waste of time, and family resources might be directed to the education of sons. Convinced that their daughters would eventually marry and leave the labor force, many middle-class parents placed less emphasis on the long-term career possibilities of jobs for their daughters and more on easy access to training for a skilled job. Clerical work seemed ideal: Training for it was brief, inexpensive, or even free in the public schools.

More women were going to college by 1910, but college was still the exception rather than the rule for the middle-class woman. The college-educated woman was supposedly in the best position to find interesting and high-paying employment. On average, the college woman did earn more than the woman who had only attended high school. But when compared to her male counterparts the college-educated woman faced many more obstacles to establishing herself in a meaningful and financially rewarding occupation. Discrimination was, if anything, intensifying in the professions and occupations that men thought desirable. Women were still being socialized to enter teaching and the other "women's professions," where pay was at the low end of the scale for college graduates. Clerical work was an option, as long as a few months of business training were added to the academic program. The college woman was absorbing an outpouring of vocational advice in magazines, books, and at school, most of which described clerical work as the potential solution to the educated woman's dilemma: finding meaningful work other than teaching and a way into the material world of corporate business. Even if she had chosen a woman's profession originally, clerical work was a viable career change. Many teachers sought to leave a profession they had never really wanted or enjoyed and found clerical work to be a reasonable alternative.

As urbanization and industrialization continued to undermine the economic position of families in rural communities and small towns, many native-born daughters with middle-class identities and very slim pocketbooks poured into the cities to seek respectable work. There they had to rub elbows with daughters of immigrants and working-class women. High school education and business college training gave women from different classes, ethnic groups, and parts of the country a common set of experiences and expectations before they entered offices. The new mass culture of dance halls, movies, amusement parks, and ready-made clothing stores offered an urban milieu in which it was no longer unrespectable for middle-class women to mingle with English-speaking working-class women in their leisure time. Jobs in offices required clothes and manners that blurred class lines and disguised the degree to which different social classes interacted, making the office a suitable environment for middle-class women while the factory was not. The middle-class woman found a clerical job easy to obtain because she was so likely to have attended high school. In fact, without additional education in college, there was likely to be no other occupation for which she was suited.[4]

The office, while hardly eradicating class differences, did create a new social environment in which middle- and working-class women worked alongside each other and even intermingled socially. The dramatic slowing of immigration after World War I, the rising number of native-born daughters, and the growing numbers of teenaged children attending high school contributed to this mingling and further blurring of class lines. A social movement of such enormous proportions quite naturally produced a public discourse aimed at processing the new phenomenon.

The Secretary and the Stenographer: Class and Representation

As women entered clerical work in increasing numbers, writings intended for popular consumption took up the image of the woman clerical worker and tried to fix her in the public's imagination. Representations of the woman clerical worker varied according to their intended audience and authorship, most often differentiated on the basis of class. In education publications high school educators and vocational guidance experts portrayed her as a satisfied youthful clerk. Feminist social scientists described her as an exploited machine worker in government reports and scholarly articles. The popular advice literature in books, newspapers, and magazines cast her as a genteel worker in a workplace suited to the feminine temperament, an upwardly mobile, self-made woman or a professional similar to a teacher or lawyer. The working-class stenographer and the middle-class secretary were the dominant symbols of these discussions.

Vocational guidance literature was directed at youthful working-class women and their public school counselors. By staying in school, teenaged working-class women might study commercial skills, find office jobs, and even rise to become stenographers or bookkeepers. Public high schools and business colleges were places to obtain the veneer of middle-class manners that business managers expected clerks to have. The secondary school vocational guidance movement talked about office work as a way for working-class women to secure modest social mobility before marrying and leaving the work force.

A mode of advice aimed at more ambitious women and somewhat older women (including working-class women who had high school diplomas and who aspired to middle-class life-styles) urged them to adopt much loftier goals. This advice, mainly published in popular books and magazine articles, portrayed the office as a suitable locale for genteel women, but also implied that ambition could catapult a woman beyond the lower levels of clerical work and into secretarial jobs and beyond. For the most part, popular advice writers tried to ignore the issue of class origins by assuming that women with high school diplomas were, whatever the economic status of parents, part of the middle class and therefore both cultured and potentially ambitious.

Although evidence collected by economists and sociologists pointed to the growing number of dead-end jobs in clerical work, popular advice books and articles pitched to high school graduates were generally upbeat and downplayed such bad news. They often made expansive assumptions about the kinds of jobs that could be obtained and the promotions that might result. Promotion was important because the object of the ambitious clerical worker was to separate herself from "mere clerks," who were implied to be of humbler origins. Popular advice writers tried to guide readers into lines of office work thought to be socially respectable for the middle class, such as private secretaryship. The finer clothing, manners, and social polish of the middle-class woman could confirm her status and essential difference from the working-class woman clerk. In giving advice on appropriate dress, one author pictured the separate and posh physical world in which the private secretary might be found: "If she is the confidential secretary to a captain of industry, and her office hours are spent amid mahogany or walnut furniture, richly-toned leather upholstery and handsome rugs, her costume should harmonize quietly and inconspicuously with her background. As her salary . . . is a generous one, she is able to dress smartly. Her employer expects her to present an excellent appearance." Her dress and environment would set her apart from her social inferiors in the outer office, who if "bookkeepers or stenographers . . . need not dress in a style other than that of other women of their class."[5]

The continued insistence of popular advice literature that middle-class and career-minded women should become private secretaries remains difficult to explain in terms of monetary rewards alone. The secretary did not always make the highest wages in office work. The office manager, the upper-level bookkeeper, the personnel worker, and the accountant often made more money. But the gender and class connotations of these occupations were more ambiguous than those of secretarial work. The personnel manager might have to work in a factory with working-class employees as her clients; the bookkeeper might work alongside men or do timekeeping adjacent to the factory floor. The office manager had to supervise stenographers, typists, or machine operators who might be working class. The accountant would have to compete in a "man's" occupation.[6] In asking whether it was wise for a woman to study certified public accounting, the writer Miriam Simons Leuck gave only a qualified yes: "A brilliant, exceptional woman, possessing plenty of the competitive instinct, and willing to spend her first few years in active combat, will find it worth while, and decidedly so, in the long run . . . . Prejudice against women is strong."[7] In theory secretaries remained the most isolated from proletarian workers, had the best access to the glamor of corporate surroundings, and would not be forced to engage in competition with men. For those who were tradition-minded, it could be argued that secretaries did "feminine" work like attending to details, assisting men in important work, and ensuring domestic tranquility in the office. And for those seeking careers for women, it was easy to incorporate the illusion that as right-hand assistant to a powerful person, the secretary could someday become powerful as well.

Popular advice literature helped to perpetuate a myth by creating the secretary as an ideal social type, without warning that there were relatively few secretarial positions. It was generally true that secretaries made more money and enjoyed better working conditions than other kinds of clerical workers, but their numbers were small. A Women's Bureau study of fifty-two large offices in New York City showed that of 14,006 women who worked in them only 5.4 percent were secretaries. Outside big cities such as New York and Chicago the proportion of secretaries was even smaller; a Minneapolis survey of four thousand office workers in 1925 found that only 2.5 percent were secretaries.[8]

In some sense, of course, the scarcity of the secretarial job was part of its charm for the self-made woman. Those who became secretaries could bask in the knowledge that they had proved themselves worthy of more interesting and responsible work. The advice literature worked to convey the idea that the woman who was seriously committed to her career could achieve success through sheer effort and desire. The competent and well-educated stenographer, regardless of her social class, could separate herself from the vast horde of mediocre clerks if she cared enough and tried hard enough to become a private secretary. Once she became a secretary, her clear superiority had been proven.

Eleanor Gilbert admitted that "office work, taken as a whole, is usually overcrowded and underpaid" but blamed these conditions on the "large proportion of grammar-school girls . . . who have been railroaded through a . . . so-called 'business school' and then foisted on a luckless business office." It was thus inevitable that such "inefficient workers in large numbers have dragged down the wage standards of the field as a whole." To become a secretary, a stenographer needed to study "the business as thoroughly and carefully as she could," be "full of 'commercial curiosity,' eager to absorb every available bit of information" and "become a veritable second mind to her employer." An ambitious woman had to distinguish herself from other women in order to get what she deserved. It "is only the worker who has recognizable ability, plus the ability to sell her services well, who is really paid the sum that intelligently performed office work is worth . . . . 'Private secretary,'" Gilbert declared, "is the title which every stenographer covets."[9]

Other advice writers echoed Gilbert's call to make the jump from stenographer to secretary through zealous effort. Sarah Louise Arnold of Simmons College implied that the stenographer-secretary could either write her own ticket or fall into a life of routine drudgery: "The so-called secretary may address envelopes all day or she may dictate original letters to a score of clerks. She may do one thing exactly as she is told . . . or she may organize, control, and initiate. Her immediate task, then, may demand only a limited experience and training or it may make use of the broadest possible culture, the finest personality, and the utmost executive ability." Helen M. Kelsey, a manager on Fifth Avenue in New York, claimed that ambition could carry a clerk far, no matter what her background. "Promotion in the business world is not a matter of routine; it goes to the one who deserves it, be she an old or a new employee, a college girl or 'self-made.'"[10] Miriam Leuck, whose book was intended for girls with some high school education, emphasized that "stenography is an occupation in which your competition will be almost entirely with other women . . . . It has come to be considered the entrance door to almost every other post in business, particularly to the executive desk. If there are more recent indications that it is also a very effective blind alley, they fail to prove the rule either way."[11]

The advice literature warned that although ambition and education were always required for success in secretarial work, they were not in themselves sufficient. The secretary must also have certain qualities of personality, most of them characteristic of feminine middle-class graciousness and domesticity. In combination with ambition and intelligence they were supposed to lead not only to a secretarial position, but also to the big payoff, promotion to an "executive" position. Stressing a nearly universal theme, Emma Carey, private secretary to a Washington judge, said "the constant observation of, and working with, men of high executive ability in many instances qualifies a private secretary for advancement to a position of executive capacity . . . . Promotion . . . is frequently the reward for those who apply themselves conscientiously to their duties." But she also made clear that manners and personal charm were necessary qualities as well. The secretary must be "energetic, . . . courteous, patient, tactful, loyal, and possess a gracious manner."[12] Sarah Louise Arnold defined the secretarial personality in a 1910 essay in a way that showed up frequently in the advice books:

> By *personality* we mean all the gracious gifts which home, school, friends and other great factors of environment have bestowed upon fortunate individuals . . . . The ability to deal easily and pleasantly with the various persons with whom one is brought in contact is indispensable to the secretary. Invariably courteous, gentle, cheerful, tactful, sunny, courageous, optimistic, she creates the atmosphere of the office . . . . While serving as stenographer, she is merely the channel for the message, and her own personality for the time being is lost in the impersonal act. At the same time she never fails to perceive anything which would add to the convenience of her employer, never forgets appointments or other items of business interest, brings order out of disorder, and in general makes good deficiencies without seeming to notice them.[13]

Here was the domestic manager in the office writ large: like good housekeepers and mothers, private secretaries were to submerge their personalities into an all-encompassing pleasantness, accommodation, and attention to detail. The secretary in these assessments became a kind of natural force, like the weather ("the atmosphere of the office"). However hard she actually worked, the result should appear to be effortless; to the extent that she served as a mere conduit for her boss's activities, she was successful. The advice literature posed a difficult and seemingly impossible task: combining ambition with obsequiousness. The secretary's role embodied an age-old difficulty for the traditional woman with higher ambition. To gain access to power, she had to practice the womanly arts of manipulation, domestic charm, and seduction. The combination of determined ambition, usually a masculine trait, with traditional feminine qualities of self-effacement and accommodation to others, was a central contradiction in the advice literature, and indeed, in the life of the typical secretary.

On rare occasions a popular critic attacked the way in which "feminine" characteristics had been built into office-work jobs and dismissed secretarial jobs for that reason. The journalist Dorothy Dunbar Bromley thought it was "doubtful whether big business could have become as big as it is if women were not there to do the monotonous exacting jobs for which young men would never have had the patience." Women made "ideal private secretaries" because they had "an instinctive solicitude for the welfare of some one person" and could be relied upon, "no less than the old-fashioned wife . . . [to] live by the motto, 'His ambitions shall be my ambitions.'" The secretary became a shadowy force behind the throne, doing most of the work and receiving little of the credit. Bromley's disgust with women who were willing to accept such conditions of employment was apparent: "these women have been martyrs either to their sense of loyalty or to their own fear and lack of initiative." But, as she admitted, the possibilities of finding alternatives remained dim, especially with the marriage bar still firmly in place and widespread discrimination against women the norm.[14]

The romance of the stenographer's rise to power and influence, high salaries, and glamorous surroundings was the stock-in-trade of optimistic advice publications. They also frequently emphasized that while class was not necessarily a barrier to success, part of the secretary's payoff would be access to a secluded environment with middle-class, perhaps even upper-class, pretensions. Enough women had this experience to warrant its retelling; the inner sancta of large offices, banks, and insurance companies, were, after all, designed to replicate upper-class parlors and provide bosses with domestic servants. The work histories of secretaries interviewed by the Bureau of Vocational Information in 1924 and 1925 provided ample evidence that the right combination of education, luck, and ambition could advance some stenographers and clerks to more responsible and glamorous positions. However unattainable for most, the dream of the successful secretary was not just a myth, and served as a kind of Horatio Alger discourse for women readers in the teens and twenties.

An Atlanta high school graduate who had taught mathematics from 1915 to 1917 found her career switch to office work rewarding for a number of reasons. By 1925 she was working as a private secretary and office manager in a real estate firm and earning $77 a week (plus periodic bonsues), or more than $4,000 a year, an exceptionally high salary for a woman. Her BVI interviewer described her as a "'keen' type of person," with a "great deal of self-confidence." She was "very well dressed, and evidently gave a good deal of attention to this, and to creating a certain atmosphere in the office." Her office was "really elegant and luxurious," furnished with mahogany and handsome rugs and set "on the seventeenth floor of one of the buildings owned by the corporation with a magnificent view over the city." She was left in charge of the office whenever her boss was out of the office and seemed equally at ease with male and female clients.[15]

This kind of success story was not unique. A woman whose father died while she was in high school was left with six brothers and sisters to support. She switched to the commercial course so that she could quickly find a job. Beginning as a $6 a week typist at a publishing firm, she studied commercial subjects at New York University at night and quickly moved up to stenographer, secretary, and then assistant to the director. Changing jobs during the war, she got a "huge raise" and was by 1924 working for the New York Tuberculosis Association and earning $62 a week. A 1916 graduate of Simmons moved through ten different jobs in New York City before settling down in the ideal secretarial position: as a receptionist and bond saleswoman at an investment firm she made $40 a week and a $1,000 a year bonus. She thought that secretarial work was "a stepping stone to anything that a girl wants." A woman who had graduated from high school in 1916 entered office work but left her job with a law firm in Seattle in 1922 "to go to Hollywood." There she became the secretary to Ouida Bergere, who wrote scenarios for Associated Pictures, and began to write screenplays herself. When Bergere retired, her secretary was summoned to New York to develop ideas for the movies. Reflecting on her success, she was more realistic than most about why she had done so well: "You will notice that my present position is not a secretarial one, yet it is the direct result of a former secretarial position in which I had demonstrated certain ability. However, I might be inclined to give 'fate' the credit. I might have combed New York to find such a position and would have been unable to do so."[16]

A researcher who conducted in-depth interviews with middle-aged women members of Business and Professional Women's Clubs at the end of the 1920s agreed that ambition and circumstance both played a role in the lives of her subjects who had carved out more responsible positions and higher salaries: "those who have attained the larger measures of success have done so in curious and indirect ways with expenditure of tremendous effort and persistence."[17] Clearly, some women had made the transition from stenographer to secretary and from secretary to more powerful positions, but whether the average clerical worker could replicate these transitions was a matter of dispute. Popular advice literature, largely written by self-made women, was countered by a body of research published by feminist social scientists.

Grace Coyle, an economist at Barnard College, published the results of her investigation of clerical work in 1929. In an attempt to put her statistical data into its cultural context, Coyle observed that the importance of clerical work for women could not "be rated in numerical terms only." Because, Coyle thought, the "feeling for social status" was more "pronounced" among women (presumably she meant in comparison to men), they were likely to choose clerical work, despite its steady proletarianization, infrequency of promotion, and discrimination based on the marriage bar.

Coyle was not entirely sympathetic with this choice. In listing the advantages of clerical work, she agreed that office jobs were clean, did not require heavy manual labor, had "comparatively short" hours, produced regular income, and often included vacations and sick leave. But she thought the chief attraction of clerical work was the glitter of false ambition: "Most important of all for many workers is the opportunity which clerical positions are believed to offer for a rise to business success so highly and universally esteemed among us .... However specious some of these advantages may seem," Coyle concluded, "they have combined to win for clerical work its relatively high place in the occupational hierarchy." She believed that women in "professional" jobs had made more intelligent choices in their occupations than those who chose clerical work. These women had begun, she asserted, to "move toward work after marriage." They were being motivated not so much by "economic reasons" as by "an attitude of mind related to the desire for independence, self expression and the use of expert skill."

Coyle did not think many of these qualities could be claimed for clerical work. Office workers had been lured to clerical work by the empty promises of middle-class status and better working conditions only to find that they were being subjected to the same conditions as existed in other menial occupations for women. The emphasis in Coyle's article was on the growing mechanization of office work and its low-paying salaries. "Comparatively few women are found in the higher wage groups which contain the best of the office positions," Coyle concluded. "It seems fair to say that at present the clerical worker can have little assurance that advancement is possible beyond the limits of the stenographic, comptometer, or dictaphone positions, and that if she is a woman she must have very unusual ability to attain one of the few positions which combine the opportunity for skill and initiative with higher pay and responsibility."[18]

Feminist social scientists such as Coyle and her colleagues— Ethel Erickson, a researcher for the Women's Bureau; Sophonisba P. Breckenridge, professor at the School of Social Service Administration of the University of Chicago; and Mary Schauffler, an Ohio sociologist who had studied office workers in Cleveland—wanted to show what clerical work was like in the aggregate, not the particular. They were contributing their results to the impressive body of data on the workplace that emphasized the growing degradation of work in an industrialized society. They were genuinely perturbed about the application of rationalization to office work and the exploitative conditions it created for women clerks.

Feminist social scientists tried to deflate the myth of secretarial success and hammered away at a different theme: most women would find only limited job satisfaction and mobility in clerical work. Ethel Erickson emphasized that while "systematic salary increases with regular pay-roll reviews" had been the norm in most corporations in the 1920s, they had been accompanied by "little job progression . . . . Many of the office jobs are routine in nature, afford little training and . . . belong to the blind-alley class." Mary Schauffler reported in 1925 that the number of "real secretarial positions" in Cleveland were "limited," and that "with a few exceptions, the salaries were much less than I thought they would be." Coyle concluded that "comparatively few women are found in the higher wage groups which contain the best of the office positions," and Breckenridge agreed that upward movement in office work was more an exception than the norm.[19] College-educated professionals themselves, these women social scientists were not really speaking to machine operators in offices; they were speaking to women in college on the verge of choosing careers. Coyle made the message explicit; she argued that college women would be fooling themselves if they thought working in an office would substitute for a real profession.

The work of women social scientists added a healthy note of realism to the optimistic excesses of the advice literature. The social scientists failed to grapple effectively, however, with a point their own data elucidated. Whatever the dead-end characteristics of clerical work for most or the extraordinary opportunities for a few, women who stayed at work in the office after their twenty-fifth birthdays had better jobs and made more money than most other women in the American work force. Whatever the exploitative aspects of clerical work, it was still true that it paid relatively well compared to other occupations for women. The crucial comparison for women was not what men made, but what other women made, and that was as important to the college woman as the public-school-educated woman. In that light clerical worker jobs would continue to be attractive not only to working-class women, but also to middle-class women, including those who attended college.

College Women and Vocational Guidance

The increasing employment of women in clerical jobs coincided with the expansion of college educations for women. Between 1900 and 1916 the number of men attending colleges tripled and the number of women quadrupled; by 1910 women were nearly 40 percent of all those in institutions of higher learning, and by 1920 more than 47 percent. Much of this growth of opportunity for women was in coeducational institutions; about 75 percent of all those women in college in 1915 and 1916 were in institutions that admitted both men and women. College education was still an unusual experience for American women, nonetheless. By 1930 about 10.5 percent of all eighteen to twenty-one-year-old women were in college, up from 2.8 percent in 1900.[20]

Once women got to college they most often studied liberal arts subjects and entered the "women's" professions, particularly teaching, home economics, and social work. Most women emerged from higher education to teach. A study of women who had graduated from eleven different institutions in 1903 showed that seven of ten who were gainfully employed in 1922 were teachers.[21] The proportions of women graduates who became teachers began to decrease somewhat as other occupations for middle-class women appeared. A 1932 study of 6,665 women graduates of land grant colleges showed that of those at work, about 58 percent were teachers, 18 percent worked in offices, stores, and business, 15 percent were other professionals, and about 8 percent were in home economics. Librarians, social workers, and home economists far outnumbered the handful of women in law, medicine, and engineering.[22]

Women's choices of college curricula and of occupations have usually been attributed to personal preference or the vagaries of "socialization," explanations that underscore the idea that women are primarily to blame for their own inferior economic standing and for occupational sex segregation. Economic and cultural realities probably have had more to do with these choices. By choosing to attend liberal arts colleges women were not rejecting the study of science; as undergraduates women were nearly as likely as men to study both the natural and social sciences. Nor did taking liberal arts courses necessarily preclude either vocationalism or professionalism. Most men who became doctors, lawyers, and businessmen had liberal arts degrees.[23]

The main obstacle to success for college-educated women was exclusion from the professions dominated by men. Discrimination against women was one of the hallmarks of male professionalism after 1910 (chapter 2). Whether they wanted to be teachers or not, women turned to teaching because teacher training was open to them and because they could get teaching jobs. Vassar educator Mabel Newcomer made the perceptive observation that "while teaching is high on the list of occupations when seniors are asked what they plan to do after graduation, it is low on the list when freshmen are asked the same question. The seniors are facing reality." Newcomer recalled her own anxiety when she realized that she was about to earn a graduate degree but had no real means of earning a living. She enrolled in both a secretarial and an education course.[24] The teaching profession was full of women who could find little else to do with their education.

Most college women needed to find paying jobs. The typical college woman was not upper class. She and her parents were likely to view college education as a financial burden requiring careful planning, self-sacrifice, and the prospect of a real job after graduation. Many women students had to work summers and during the school year, even those attending the elite women's schools.[25] Although college-educated women did begin to marry nearly as frequently and as early as the general population by the 1920s, they did not necessarily enter a life of middle-class leisure and homemaking. Research suggests that on average they were more likely than women without college educations to remain in the work force after marriage and to postpone child-bearing.[26] Those college women who chose not to marry had to support themselves and, frequently, to contribute to the support of aging parents. Whatever jobs they dreamed of having, as the historian Barbara Solomon has observed, most women "could not attend college without taking into account what they would do afterward; they knew they had to be gainfully employed."[27]

Expanding opportunities in office work appeared just as college educators and vocational guidance experts were overwhelmed by a rising number of college women seeking jobs. College guidance officers remained ambivalent over how to describe opportunities in office work. But faced with the discrimination against women in most professions, they were forced to consider the business world as a possible option for women students. Ideally, said the Bureau of Vocational Information, "the growing political importance of business, its scientific development as applied economics, its increasing professional aspects, all challenge the best intelligence, organizing and executive ability, and sound judgment." Both college men and women were being attracted to business, the BVI continued. The ideal business occupation should mean "working among live issues of immediate concern," offer "wide contacts," and have "the steady lure of developing responsibility and important service ahead."[28] If so, it would be appropriate for college women.

Women's schools and most coeducational institutions offered secretarial training, and women students often added business courses as an afterthought to their liberal arts training. The more prestigious women's colleges made connections with genteel business colleges like the Katharine Gibbs establishments for postgraduate commercial study. In some colleges with business departments, "secretarial science" courses were offered, some of which lead to a bachelor's degree. Women's schools like Simmons College built their reputations by offering thoroughgoing instruction of this sort.[29] But however well their graduates eventually did in the world of work, secretarial science programs did nothing to disrupt the gendered order of the business world and in fact probably helped to divert talented women away from the serious pursuit of business administration and accounting by complicitly accepting discrimination as a given. Secretarial instruction, as the elite women's schools insisted, would never substitute for enrollment in professional business schools. The BVI noted with some alarm in 1925 that "Various leading graduate and collegiate schools of business are not yet admitting women students. In secretarial courses, filing courses, and the like, however, women form the bulk of all students. This means, of course, that women are training for the business positions in which women today predominate, but it also means that they do not secure the type of training which prepares for undertaking the primary responsibilities in production, in transportation, in commerce."[30]

The BVI's concern about access to professional business schools was part of a heightened desire to find new vocational opportunities for middle-class women and for them to compete more openly with men. Feminist educators mobilized to use vocational counseling to advance the movement of women into the professions, the business world, academia, and the civil service. They promoted lecture series, wrote advice books, and established employment bureaus to woo college women to occupations other than teaching, including business. "There has never been," said Elizabeth Kemper Adams, "so much talk of 'professional opportunities' in the commercial world, nor so lively an inclination among educated women 'to go into business.'"[31]

College placement bureaus were designed "to give vocational guidance to the at-that-time bewildered and floundering young college graduate."[32] Between 1910 and 1923 fifteen such bureaus were established by college administrators and alumnae. The most important was the Intercollegiate Bureau of Occupations (IBO), founded in New York in 1911 by the alumnae of nine leading eastern colleges for women. The IBO's first information pamphlet, "Opportunities in Occupations other than Teaching," appeared in 1915. By 1917 the IBO had registered nearly 4,200 applicants, two-thirds of whom were college graduates, and had placed more than half of all the applicants in jobs. It had also answered ten thousand calls for vocational information and advice.[33]

When demand for college-trained women for federal jobs was high during World War I, the job placement tasks of the IBO were taken over by the U.S. Employment Bureau, and many clients took jobs in various departments and wartime agencies of the U.S. government. The IBO itself was replaced by the Bureau of Vocational Information, with Emma Hirth as its director. The BVI abandoned actual placement and devoted itself to studying "the facts governing the work of trained women in the various occupations and professions."[34]

The BVI described popular advice literature's discussion of women's employment as "exaggerated and one-sided" and worked to set the record straight. Hirth and other leaders of the BVI declared their belief "in the ability of mature women to choose their proper work when given adequate fundamental information."[35] Along with Catharine A. Filene's Institute of Women's Professions and Elizabeth Kemper Adams's Women's Educational and Industrial Union, the BVI worked toward presenting a more balanced analysis of occupational opportunities. All three groups completed guides to women's occupations following World War I. Before going bankrupt in 1926, the BVI issued a series of well-researched reports on women in statistical work, the law, chemistry, and "responsible" positions in department stores and also carried out an ambitious but never published survey of secretarial work. Its massive reference work *Training for the Professions and the Allied Occupations* (1924) listed hundreds of occupations, their educational prerequisites, where training for them could be obtained, and what job duties they entailed.[36] BVI publications in particular managed to describe the success some women had achieved in unusual or relatively unknown occupations and also portrayed realistically the barriers most occupations presented to training, hiring, and promotion.

The college vocational guidance movement was just one indication of the enthusiasm of middle-class women for occupations other than teaching. Another was the founding of middle-class working women's associations like the National Federation of Business and Professional Women's Clubs, which emerged in 1919 at a conference of businesswomen called by the YWCA.[37] "Career women" wanted to consolidate their group identity and give working women a new sense of legitimacy. Many had benefited from the war, particularly those who had been at work for a few years before the conflict began, because they were drafted to fill technical, managerial, and secretarial positions left vacant by men or newly created in the burgeoning corporate and government economy. Research showed that matriculants from 1909 to 1912 changed jobs more frequently than two earlier generations of college women and were earning higher salaries, especially if they were not in the classroom.[38]

Yet as the BVI frequently warned its readers, this success was clouded by the reality that most new jobs for college women were in clerical work, not the better paying male-dominated professions. Despite the brave efforts of small numbers of pioneers in accounting, actuarial work, and chemistry, women were making the most headway in office work, personnel work, and office management. As early as 1917 the Intercollegiate Bureau of Occupations reported that of those women it had placed in occupations other than teaching, 69 percent had gone into clerical work. "If further opportunities are not presented" to college women, two Columbia alumnae warned, "stenography and clerical training will rapidly replace teaching as an obvious method of earning a livelihood; and both the fit and the unfit will take it up. Secretarial positions offer big opportunity sometimes, but often they lead into backwaters stultifying to the ambitious girl."[39] Nonetheless, the temptation to put the college women into office work and call them professionals was irresistable. The notion that secretarial or clerical work would somehow get women into an executive or managerial position became a central artifice of the the college vocational guidance office.

The Flight from Teaching

Not only were more college women taking up office work instead of teaching, but many teachers were also becoming clerical workers.[40] Of 949 women who filled out questionnaires for the BVI's secretarial survey, 141 were former teachers. Of those who gave reasons for leaving teaching, most said that they did not care for the occupation or that clerical work offered better positions. But significant numbers also said that teaching was stressful or a strain on their health, or that they were unhappy with their salaries.[41] Interviews conducted late in the decade with 306 members of Business and Professional Women's Clubs turned up ex-teachers in a variety of clerical jobs, office management positions, and other women's professions. The interviewer concluded that "many teachers . . . gave up their original calling to experiment in other lines, because of irritations arising within the work itself."[42] These complaints reflected growing dissatisfaction with both the working conditions and wages of teaching and the attempt to find alternative employment.

The teaching profession was characterized by a gendered hierarchy of educational levels and salaries. To the extent that men worked in education, they held the best jobs. They dominated school administration and supervision, and comprised 48 percent of high school teachers; they made up only 12 percent of the nation's elementary school teachers.[43] Teachers with four-year degrees got the best jobs, but demand for college graduates was still relatively new, a phenomenon of the expansion of high school teaching and the wave of upgraded qualifications that characterized the professions after 1900. Many older teachers with high school or normal school training were finding it difficult to secure better jobs, and many younger women with limited financial resources simply could not afford to attend a real college or stay in school for four years. Daughters of small farmers, immigrants, African Americans, and working-class parents were especially likely to enter teaching with only normal school certificates.[44] Normal school

Table 8.
Women's Education and Annual Median Salaries
for Three Occupations, 1926

Educational Level	Salaries (and Median Years Experience)		
	Clerical Work	Teaching	Personnel Work
Grade school	$1,501(16.3)	$1,560(20.9)	—
High school	1,403(12.0)	1,436(16.6)	$2,167(18.8)
Normal school	1,490(14.2)	1,424(14.2)	—
College, nongraduate	1,454(10.3)	1,394(12.8)	—
College, graduate	1,621(10.6)	1,773(12.8)	2,450(12.9)

Source: Margaret Elliott and Grace E. Manson, "Earnings of Women in Business and the Professions," *Michigan Business Studies* 3 (Sept. 1930): 77.

graduates, who had one or two years of post-high school education, were concentrated in elementary schools, rural areas, and smaller towns and cities. Salaries for teachers were lowest in the South and rural Midwest, and highest in the urban Northeast, where women teachers in high schools made as much as $35 a week in 1926. The National Education Association reported in the same year that 168,000 one- or two-room schoolhouses were still in existence, with a median income for their teachers of $15 a week, equivalent to a lower-than-average clerical salary.[45]

Salaries in clerical work continued to be comparable to or higher than incomes in teaching through 1930. A former teacher with some education beyond high school but no four-year degree was most likely to benefit from the switch to clerical work. She made, according to one study, about $300 a year less in 1926 as a teacher than her colleague with a four-year degree. But if she became a clerical worker, she could earn $60 a year more than the average teacher. Women who moved beyond entry-level clerical work into private secretaryship, office managing, personnel work, head bookkeeping, accounting, or insurance brokerage made significantly more than did teachers. There were also higher salaries at the upper end of the scale in office work than in teaching; while 17.5 percent of office managers and 4.5 percent of secretaries made $3,000 or more a year, only 2.3 percent of high school teachers did and none of the elementary school teachers did (Tables 8 and 9.)[46]

Clerical work was more appealing than teaching for other reasons. The marriage bar was more rigidly applied in teaching than in clerical work, and teachers who married faced automatic firings in most school districts. A handful of judicial decisions in the District

Table 9.
Women's Median Earnings for Selected Occupations
and Percent Earning $3,000 or More, 1926

Occupation	Number Reporting	Median Earnings per Year	Percent Earning $3,000 or More
Business:			
Personnel	75	$2,066	21.6
Office manager	285	1,881	17.5
Finance	609	1,864	16.9
Welfare	315	1,911	7.0
Private secretary	534	1,733	4.5
Bookkeeper	752	1,317	0.8
Stenographer	1,029	1,295	0.2
Education:			
Supervisor	102	1,907	8.7
Principal	216	1,700	5.1
Teacher, high school	649	1,615	2.3
Teacher, elementary	925	1,289	0.0
Others:			
Proprietor	446	2,023	28.9
Library	140	1,595	6.4
Nurse	270	1,783	0.4

Source: Margaret Eliott and Grace Manson, "Earnings of Women in Business and the Professions," *Michigan Business Studies* 3 (Sept. 1930): 22.

of Columbia and elsewhere had ruled that teachers under contract or a tenure system could not be fired when they married, but tenure systems were still rare and nothing prevented schools from refusing to hire married women, even if they did not fire those who married while on the job.[47] Clerical work might be the only reasonable alternative for a married teacher who wanted to continue working. A woman who had taken a bachelor's degree from Ohio State University in 1918 and taught until 1921 could not find a comparable job when she moved with her husband to Pasadena. "I elected my college course for various good reasons, one being that I intended *teaching*," she declared. "*That* is my real vocation, but being barred in Pasadena, because I was a 'married woman living with my husband' I entered this secretarial field."[48]

Some teachers who switched to office work cited the stress of teaching for doing so. Some found teaching in urban schools, where there were higher proportions of immigrants, working-class children, and people of color, to be distasteful. A Hunter graduate who had taught from 1907 to 1912 and was now a secretary reported that she "disliked teaching intensely because of the very difficult position I filled, teaching in a crowded city school with a more than half negro [sic] attendance."[49] Former teachers claimed that clerical work was "much less nerve wracking work than teaching," that it was "not as exhausting," and that in general there was "not so much nervous strain . . . . When you leave [the] office, work is over. In teaching you are never through."[50] The "once every five years nervous breakdown" was a kind of inside joke in the profession.[51]

The lives of teachers were also under constant moral scrutiny in small communities, where they were expected to set a good example for their students and maintain propriety. The city required no such full-time decorum, with its growing numbers of "women adrift" seeking both employment and the new entertainments of movies, restaurants, cafeterias, downtown shopping, and women's clubs.[52] Office work might also bring women into a heterosocial work culture, which more fully reflected the new leisure activities and culturally prescribed sexuality for young women.[53] One secretary informed her BVI interviewer that "secretaries are happier in their work than teachers. There is more satisfaction in being in contact with men of unusual minds than the immature mind of a child. [She] thinks it is [a] more natural existence to be working for and among men than with women and children, as teachers do."[54]

One of the major attractions of clerical work for teachers was that it required only a few months of additional training, readily available in summer vacations or in night classes. Teachers also had the social polish and middle-class decorum that offices sought. In some sectors of office work, particularly those in which older women were needed to supervise younger ones, employers found former teachers to be natural recruits. Most important, taking a clerical job did not have to mean a cut in social status.

Some women reversed the direction of this exchange of occupations and went from clerical work to teaching. A woman with a 1913 degree from the Carnegie Institute of Technology in secretarial studies worked in offices for three years and then took up commercial education in 1916: "I like personal contact with the boys and girls," she reported. Many women were still entering teaching with enthusiasm and dedication, and part-time clerical work might earn them money so they could obtain teacher training. A 1913 Goucher College graduate who worked as a secretary at Mt. Vernon

High School returned to school and took a master's degree at the Columbia Teacher's College in 1922. She returned to Mt. Vernon as a teacher and dean. Clerical work proved to be a financial boon for a former Chicago wrapper in a neckwear factory. She became an office worker in a mail order house, increased her stenographer's salary to $20 a week, went to college, and became a teacher.[55]

The two-way street between office work and teaching was one proof that teachers and office workers were often from similar class backgrounds and viewed their occupations as equivalents. The kind of comment made by a California clerk, that "a half-educated teacher is asked everywhere, while a cultured secretary has to win her way," was rare.[56] Secretaries and teachers mingled in women's professional and business clubs, and office work was considered suitable for the middle-class woman as long as she found the right office job. Machine work, typing, and stenography were not considered suitable. A 1926-27 study of the "occupational interests" of about fourteen thousand National Federation of Business and Professional Women's Clubs members, nearly six thousand of whom were white-collar workers and three thousand of whom were teachers, indicates just how important job title distinctions were to middle-class women. Women who filled out the questionnaires had, on average, more college education than working women in general. The sample was also an older one, with a median age of nearly thirty-eight years.[57] These women could be assumed to be largely self-supporting or married and in the work force more or less permanently. They were keenly interested in such matters as job titles, career prospects, and occupational respectability.

Asked to indicate the intensity of like and dislike for 160 different occupations, teachers and clerical workers shared remarkably similar affinities. Teachers, secretaries, and stenographers all listed secretarial work as the most preferred job in office work. Despite its more clear professional status, they put accounting relatively far down on their lists. Bookkeepers and office managers, who held less feminine stereotyped jobs in the office and also had some experience with financial records, were more receptive to accounting. Clerical workers were favorably disposed toward such middle-class occupations as social worker, librarian, lawyer, and musician; they disliked the occupations of factory worker and telephone operator. Teachers expressed an affinity for the occupations of clerical worker, secretary, business manager, executive, librarian, social worker, and professor, but they expressed dislike for factory worker, file clerk, retail saleswoman, stenographer, telephone operator, and waitress. The lumping of these "dislike" categories by teachers indicates that in their minds only certain jobs were appropriate for them and other middle-class women. Stenography was not, but secretarial work was.[58]

The College Woman in Office Work

With only about 3 percent of all young adult women in college in 1900, nearly all of whom became teachers, college graduates were not much of a presence in the business world at the turn of the century.[59] College women continued to be outnumbered by a ballooning population of high school-educated women. But college women began to be more visible with the expansion of college enrollment and the explosion of occupational opportunities in offices for middle-class women during World War I. A 1931-32 Women's Bureau study found that 2.2 percent of all clerks were college graduates and that some training beyond high school in a normal school, college, or university was true of another 8.1 percent.[60]

The college woman, defined here as a woman with a year of more of higher education in a college or university, encountered a mixed reception from both co-workers and employers. She was likely to be resented by her co-workers and was often too opinionated and particular for her bosses. The college woman was expected to accommodate herself to a work environment in which she was likely to be far outnumbered by less educated and often less well-to-do co-workers. She also had to reconcile her actual working situation with the professionally and culturally stimulating life she had been promised as an undergraduate.

Overall, her economic expectations were mixed. Length of experience was the best predictor of salary in clerical work, but college women did tend to make more money than women with less education when years of experience were held constant (Table 10). One study of women office workers who had spent fifteen years or more in the work force showed that a grammar school-educated woman office worker made, on average, $1,549 a year in 1927, or about $30 a week. But she was paid less than the comparable college-educated woman, who made $2,034, or $39 a week. High school-educated women, while they earned more than grammar school-educated women, were also at a disadvantage compared to college-educated women.[61] On the other hand, all women with college degrees, especially those who entered clerical work, were at an extraordinary disadvantage when compared with men who had been

Table 10.
Years of Experience, Education, and Salaries
of Clerical Workers, 1931–32

| Years in Office Work | Grammar School | Median Monthly Salary | | Advanced Education |
| | | High School | | |
		Incomplete	Complete	
Less than 1	—	$68	$74	$88
1-3	$76	80	88	101
3-5	92	95	104	120
5-10	105	111	124	137
10 and more	130	134	147	172

Source: Ethel L. Erickson, "The Employment of Women in Offices," *Women's Bureau Bulletin* 120 (1934): 12.

to college. They were proportionally more disadvantaged, by far, than were grammar school- and high school-educated women when compared to men with the same levels of education. College men's economic advantage over women with similar educations was startling. One comparison of male and female college graduates in similar occupations indicated that men made approximately $3,000 more a year than women by the time both groups reached forty.[62] College-educated women were not unaware of these differences. Their own testimony indicated that whether they had fallen into clerical work or chosen it as a vocation, they had believed the advice books and their college counselors and expected positions with more prestige and higher salaries.

One problem in obtaining promotions was that college women were often advised to avoid the very kinds of firms where promotions were available and instead were steered toward more genteel environments. A list of offices suitable for college women in 1910 included schools, offices of doctors, lawyers and architects, publishing houses, philanthropic and religious organizations, and, vaguely, "the commercial world." Ten years later, Elizabeth Kemper Adams's list of possible office settings for college women was still decidedly proper: "There are secretaries to executives of educational, social, and governmental organizations and departments; secretaries to professional practitioners—ministers, doctors, lawyers, writers, and so on; so-called 'social' secretaries to persons of wealth and leisure." But Adams had to admit that the best access to careers in personnel or research work might very well come through secretarial jobs in the corporate business world.[63]

College women were more likely than grammar school-educated women to find work in the "right" (i.e., socially acceptable) sort of office. College women were often hired in social welfare agencies and the small professional offices of doctors, lawyers, architects, and college teachers, where they did less routine work and sometimes had important responsibilities. Although many middle-class office workers preferred these kinds of jobs to those in large offices, they were often low-paying and unlikely to lead to anything beyond secretarial work. Promotion possibilities, if there were any, were likely to be found in advertising agencies, banks, large manufacturing firms, and financial institutions, all of which employed college-educated women as stenographers, private secretaries, statisticians, office managers, and personnel workers. Workplaces considered least desirable by most clerical workers, such as mail order houses, department stores, public utilities, and insurance firms, had relatively few college-educated women workers and were usually omitted from the advice literature altogether.[64] Such firms had low numbers of private secretaries, partly because they had installed scientific management office techniques such as stenographic pools and emphasized repetitious machine work. The telephone company in Cleveland, for instance, was said to have "no secretarial positions . . . . All the girls taking dictation are in a central department from which they are sent to any man needing them."[65]

The relatively low number of college-educated women at work in offices with routinized operations was probably due both to the avoidance of these jobs by graduates and to employment managers' belief that women who were too educated or "too intelligent" made poor employees for machine or repetitive work. Turnover studies showed that women with college education were more likely to leave these jobs than grammar school-educated women. The Women's Bureau quoted a manager of a large corporation in New York as a typical response: "College women are not satisfactory for the general run of clerical work; they quickly become dissatisfied, and we have always had high turn-over with such women, so usually do not hire them except for jobs that require special training."[66] The writer of *A Handbook for Beginners* (1933) thought that employers preferred the high school graduate to "the older college girl, in that she will accept a lower salary more willingly and be satisfied with work that is of a more routine nature." Less likely to be adequately instructed in commercial subjects, the college woman "finds herself outclassed in competition," even "though she feels herself superior in background."[67]

If a college woman did initially take a job as a typist, she was more able than the person who did not graduate from high school to move to something else. Mary Schauffler noted that in Cleveland "girls just out of college with no definite vocational objective who have picked up typing and who have no other office skill, frequently take positions as typists until they decide what they want to do." Women who had not graduated from high school were likely to stay in typing jobs more than twice as long as college women, partly because they had fewer financial resources and more trouble switching jobs.[68] While employers said in theory that they preferred not to hire college women, in practice they continued to do so. When Mary Schauffler looked at the statistics of an employment bureau in Cleveland she found that college women could find jobs more easily than girls with no high school training. They were, however, "more difficult to satisfy."[69] The heightened ambition and social elitism of the college-educated clerical worker may have made her a more contentious and restless employee than the impressionable young high school-educated woman. It was also true that in a market where clerical workers with good English skills were in demand, these drawbacks of temperament were likely to be overlooked.

Both advice writers and experienced office workers warned the college woman to avoid preconceived notions about soaring to the top in her first job. She might, in fact, have to begin at the bottom. Embedded in these texts was the assumption that college women might find routine clerical work both demeaning and boring. If so, the best course was to forget pretension and roll up one's sleeves. "Employers pay salaries not to bask in culture," warned one advice book, "but to get certain work done."[70] Employers echoed this refrain and argued that college women were often too self-important to make good workers. Mary Schauffler reported that "most employers had had no experience with college graduates but those who had, did not seem to consider the training as an asset. They all raised the same objection . . . . the unwillingness of a college graduate to adapt herself and her feeling that she is too highly trained for many of the tasks that come to her."[71] A 1930 article on opportunities in Buffalo warned that college women sometimes mistakenly demanded higher salaries than women with high school educations. They had a "somewhat distorted idea of the commercial value of their college degree," believed "that they were entitled to special dispensations and consideration, and that advancement should follow closely upon their initial appointment."[72]

College graduates found there was little to do except wait out the early years in stenography. A college woman with extra business training from Katharine Gibbs reported to the BVI: "I take the trouble to return this blank thinking you might be interested to know that most college graduates spend their first year out as stenographers . . . . At present I am still back in the ranks." A Chicago clerk with college training sounded the same theme: "The college girl cannot expect to capitalize upon her education until she has some experience. Until then she must cope with the uneducated girl who has been in the field for a longer time. It makes it difficult for the college girl, for, naturally, she expects to have her college work count for something from the start. That very feeling often handicaps her in getting a position which might lead to very interesting work."[73]

The college woman's relatively new but eye-catching presence in the office triggered resentment from women who had been unable to go to college but were performing similar work. Some women without college degrees thought they would always be at a disadvantage. "Four years college training," said one secretary, "would be a great asset, not so much for *what* one earns but because of the mental habits one acquires."[74] A stenographer agreed: "Being a noncollege woman, my experience has been that a college education is essential to success in the business world. It probably gives the possessor a feeling of assurance, and it most certainly gives to her an immediate prestige which naturally tends to promote self-assurance."[75] Women who lacked college educations resented the implication, whether explicit or inferred, that college women were superior in intellect and social position. One clerk, described by her BVI interviewer as "a self-made woman . . . forced by circumstances to leave school early," had nonetheless become the secretary to the commissioner of the Bureau of the Interior in Washington, D.C. She said that "she had been snubbed a number of times by college-trained people." An older woman who left high school without graduating in 1899 had similar experiences. She thought that "the fullest education possible would always prove helpful provided the person receiving it is intelligent enough to realize that . . . [it] does not mean that the recipient is the possessor of all possible knowledge and in no further need of training. This attitude I have noted as a decided handicap to many college graduates of limited intelligence, who might have proved very useful if they could have been disabused of the opinion that their college degree had made them omniscient." A high school graduate who had been at work for seventeen years thought college women were generally incompetent and were responsible for undermining the integrity of the secretary: "The demand for college women and the efficiency given by such in New York City is a farce . . . . Practical experience is what counts."[76] Behind criticisms like these lay a subtext of real animosity toward college women, who were accused of aristocratic pretension, laziness, and the "college girl attitude" elaborated upon by Miriam Leuck in 1929:

> There is, for instance, the case of a certain college girl. She obtained her place through an employment bureau and seemed the ideal person for the work. She was attractive, charming, a leader in college activities, and a good student; and the head of the bureau felt every justification in recommending her. A month later she met the employer and asked how her charge was progressing. The man exploded. After a dozen incoherent sentences, the facts began to emerge.
>
> The girl had been dismissed at the end of a week, as guilty of gross incompetence. From beginning to end she was nothing but a bluff. She never finished a thing she started, considered inaccuracy a joke, lost her sweet disposition when a critical suggestion was made, and made no real effort to learn thoroughly any process of the work. She showed herself an adept at making excuses, at placing blame for mistakes on some other member of the staff, and at passing her work on for other people to do.[77]

Secretaries who were college graduates verified both the resentment other office workers sometimes directed at them and their own sense of social distance from less educated women. A Smith graduate felt the "lack of companionship of girls who have been to college" in her job, and a University of Nebraska alumna agreed: "a college girl is very apt to be lacking in companionship in large offices." A successful secretary in the advertising department of a manufacturing firm, who had degrees from both Radcliffe and Simmons, "would never let anyone in [the] department know she has gone to college. [She] says that they are extremely antagonistic against college women in this company." But her own sense of superiority was evident: "when anybody wants an opinion on something he is trying to work out, he comes to her. She feels that she is a general adviser for the department, and attributes it to the fact that she has had a college education while none of the others have." High school-educated women in general, she charged, were less serious than college women and undermined the wage system: "there are a great number of inexperienced girls with very little education who are living at home with their families, and who are willing to do anything and accept a very low salary, which makes competition very keen. In this concern it seems they would rather have three girls of this sort than one capable well trained person who could do the work of these three."[78]

Despite her snobbery, the college woman's education and class background also gave her a healthy dose of self-confidence and a purposeful intent to find the "right job." Some of the criticisms directed at college women were not corroborated by evidence. While it was often claimed that college women were unreliable and frequently changed jobs, the Bureau of Vocational Information study in 1925 showed that their quit rates were not much different than those of high school-educated women. When she did move, the college woman was likely to better her position.[79] Once she found a job she thought tolerable she was a longer-term worker compared to other women and more likely to make important personal and family decisions on the basis of her paid work. In the first two decades of the twentieth century, college graduates were more likely to remain single than women with less education. By the 1920s college women who married tended to continue working until they had children, if they had them. An intriguing study of Mt. Holyoke graduates shows that while their average age at marriage and average fertility rates both fell in the 1920s, their employed-while-married rates rose. Married 1920s' graduates of Mt. Holyoke were more likely not to have children at all or to postpone child-bearing to a later age than earlier cohorts of graduates. When they did have children, they had fewer of them. With fewer children, they were in a better position to return to work. Almost half of the married women of the Mt. Holyoke classes of 1922-24 eventually returned to work after child-bearing.[80] The appearance of relatively well-paying jobs, an expansion of jobs for middle-class women, and an erratic relaxation of discriminatory hiring policies against married women almost certainly accounted for the possibility of these personal choices.

The Professional Secretary

Whether long- or short-term employees, college-educated women in office jobs thought they were entitled to both interesting work and a professional identity. While women with less elaborate educations were certainly often as ambitious as college women, they did not seem to feel they deserved promotions and enhanced responsibilities by virtue of their education alone. College women had been led to expect these things as a result of their college degrees. College women were, perhaps, more vulnerable than most office workers to the expectation that secretarial work was a springboard to more responsible positions.

Sometimes these expectations came true. Jean Aiken Reinke, a 1907 graduate of Wellesley and a widow with two children, returned to the workplace in 1920 as a secretary and office manager in a lawyer's office. She had been able to arrange her hours so that she could work in the afternoon and attend Fordham Law School in the morning. "This came about," she said, "from the fact that I felt I could not progress much farther in my present position, and yet enjoyed law work." She expected to go into partnership with her boss once she was admitted to the bar. Bertha Ives found fulfilling work as the executive secretary for the Republican Women's Committee of New York: "I came here as my first venture with no special secretarial training other than the foundation of a college course and the special training in organization and politics which was gained through work in suffrage. I have been seemingly successful and have enjoyed the work. I have one secretary who is a stenographer under me in my special department . . . . I come and go as the work requires and am out of town and attending meetings in the city a good deal."[81] Both Ives and Reinke had obtained what their college advisors had promised that secretarial work might deliver; interesting, independent work, freedom to arrange their work day as they sought fit, a chance for self-improvement, and a setting appropriate to middle-class women. In these circumstances it was enormously tempting to label the private secretary or office manager a "professional," especially if she had a college degree.

But these experiences were atypical. As reality set in and the grim awareness that talent, hard work, and college education would do little to crack discrimination against women in executive positions, some college women became dismayed and embittered. They had expected careers, not just jobs. Louise Nail, who had a 1923 business degree from the University of Chicago, expressed outrage over her disappointments. Fired from her last job because "she bawled out the vice president," she had gone to work as a secretary at a garment factory. Within months the employer let go the male credit manager making $75 a week and added his duties to hers; she was currently making $40 a week. "I have . . . deep feelings on the

lack of opportunities for women in business," she wrote, "and especially those who get in the routine office work positions . . . . the
possibilities in secretarial work are so limited that I doubt if I
would list it as an occupation. About four women graduate from
the school of commerce and administration each June, and I hope
you will follow their success, or rather lack of success. They all
change around a number of times until they come to the conclusion
that nowhere will they find an 'opportunity' (that word about
which we have heard too much for four collegiate years) and they
resort themselves to some position such as mine and wait for
anything—matrimony, another equally stupid position, and perhaps a better, more remunerative one."[82]

Money was not the main issue, but rather the right to expect
meaningful and rewarding work as the result of a college education.
Kathryn Martell of Brooklyn echoed similar themes in the letter
she fired off to the BVI in 1925:

> After several years of experience as private secretary . . . it is my hon-
> est opinion that secretarial work at the present time is anything but
> desirable, and so sincere am I in this opinion that I have prevented
> two nieces from entering this field . . . . Even ten years ago a capable
> stenographer was really understudy to some particular individual of
> standing in the larger corporations and . . . later had a prospect of
> working into either an executive position or acting as confidential
> secretary . . . . One has but to glance into the "stenographic depart-
> ments" of these same corporations today. Efficiency . . . but in what
> way differing from clean factory work, and with just about as much
> prospect of a future.[83]

Martell's assumption that there had once been a time when the
secretary (especially the woman secretary) was destined to rise to a
position of importance was not correct. But the hold of the myth
persisted in the advice literature and for individual women. As scientific management techniques took hold, the myth seemed more
and more unattainable. Its failure could also be increasingly pinned
on the working-class clerk, who supposedly undermined the position of the "educated" secretary.

Others were less angry and judgmental, but felt they had strayed
from their original goals and somehow fallen into clerical work and
could not get back out again. A woman who had worked as a clerk
in an architectural firm in Washington decided to get an architectural degree at George Washington University. She had never managed to work in her profession: "Unfortunately, a number of young

women in Washington followed my course, but like myself, were obliged to seek employment elsewhere, because of the inadequate salaries paid and the uncertainty of steady employment . . . . one of these young women is now working on maps for the Geological Survey. I have recently secured a Government position, entering at the very bottom, as a stenographer." A BVI interviewer reported that a Smith graduate claimed there were "very few attractions in this field of work, except that it has given her some inside knowledge to managing of the organization . . . . Does not think secretarial work wears well—becomes boring. Is perhaps too easy. Many positions give no chance of initiative." A former Barnard student ruefully commented that "I might be a more contented secretary if I hadn't gone to college."[84]

Both the advice literature and individual clerks struggled to resolve the dream of individual success with the mundane reality that most women in office work might expect. Women who worked in offices but who wanted to think of themselves as professionals had to find some way of distinguishing themselves from what they perceived to be more ordinary workers. The professional secretary, not to be confused with the order-following "mechanical" stenographer, emerged from most discussions of career work in the office as a model for the aspiring middle-class woman.

The choice of the adjective *professional* to modify secretary indicated the status that much of the middle class coveted. There was considerable confusion, not just among college women, over how to think about American professions after 1900. Most people in the newer professions such as engineering, hospital nursing, personnel management, and accounting worked for salaries paid by institutions and corporations and had relatively little control over their own working conditions. What did, exactly, distinguish these professionals from salaried workers like salesmen and stenographers? While a comptometer operator who worked on a strict schedule for wages on a bonus plan under intensive supervision was clearly not a professional, the college-educated secretary who worked for an important executive and had a variety of tasks to do, many of them requiring writing and managerial skills, did seem to do what many professionals did. On the other hand, defining secretaries by educational levels alone remained problematical. The secretary did not need college training to secure or do her job. Could the secretary with a college degree from Simmons really differentiate herself from an office worker with only two years of high school? And once she got her job, could the secretary, whatever her class or educational background, really hope for the individual responsibility and decision-making powers traditionally associated with the professions? Both the overqualified college woman and the upwardly mobile high school woman found themselves in an occupation that might be done professionally, but that in and of itself would never be a profession.[85]

Elizabeth Kemper Adams agreed that the temptation to label a secretary a professional was overpowering, but she advised that doing so was stretching the use of the term. She described ordinary clerical work as "stereotyped, monotonous, . . . humanly deadening and exhausting," and warned that with newer systems of business training in place, "secretarial work ceases to be an exclusive or preferred line of advancement for either men or women." While the secretary had "a trained mind, an acquaintance with sources of information, and a knowledge of the operations of the business with which she is connected," she remained an "intermediary without final responsibility and with limited independence . . . . Her opportunities even for intellectual development depend largely upon the personality of her employer; and she lacks the stimulus of sharing in the working out of group plans of action. Her position is somewhat like that of the bedside nurse." Adams's solution to this dilemma was again to make the class boundaries clearer between kinds of clerical workers. If one could differentiate between the stenographer and the secretary precisely, then it might be possible "to establish the professional character of the secretarial worker."[86]

The Bureau of Vocational Information put Adams's suggestion into practice when it interviewed two thousand office workers in 1925 and began its list of in-depth questions with the chief differences between stenographic and secretarial work. The possibility of settling the issue now seems impossible, but its centrality to the 1925 study reveals the mind set of an earlier generation. It remained critical before 1930 to middle-class women to confine the term *secretary* to those who did secretarial work and to distinguish secretaries from those who allegedly did assembly-line work like stenography.

The answers of the BVI respondents demonstrated the passion with which many secretaries delineated the boundaries between stenographic and secretarial work and the realism with which others analyzed them. Most in the survey agreed that while the stenographer was a "dictating machine, taking and transcribing notes," there was "more elasticity to a secretarial position—a wider scope, a variety of duties—the feeling that one is part of an organization;

there is no monotony about the work; greater opportunity for self-expression."[87]

Others observed that in real practice the duties of the stenographer and secretary usually overlapped, and job titles were often the only actual difference between the two occupations. A 1915 graduate of Wellesley who had been at work since 1917 claimed there was "no difference at all" between secretaries and stenographers. The secretary was a "high sounding name which some stenographers assume." She had noticed that some stenographers actually doing secretarial work were stuck with stenographer job titles because they worked for "a parsimonious company" seeking to avoid the payment of "high salaries."[88] Anna Raymond, supervisor of a large stenographic department, agreed that "the line of demarcation between secretaries and stenographers is often very negligible" but also believed it was very important to many women's sense of self-worth. "I know most excellent stenographers who while called stenographers are really secretaries," she commented, "and I have known secretaries who were merely clerks who scorned stenographers, yet the latter commanded a higher salary than the so-called secretaries .... I must interview many applicants and I have noticed a certain sneer at the term stenographer with the remark, 'I am looking for a secretarial position.'"[89] "Because of the gum chewing stenographer of newspaper jokes and cartoons," continued another secretary, "many people look down upon stenographers, but the greatest disadvantage is the low salary usually paid. A stenographer is expected to dress well, have a knowledge of English and a more professional knowledge that requires brains and money to acquire. They should be more adequately rewarded." A 1923 high school graduate with six months of training in business college who had already left five jobs, including one where dictaphones had been installed, agreed that "individuals do treat 'secretaries' with more respect than a typist, store clerk, waitress, etc., regarding them more as a co-worker than someone who is doing a service for them."[90]

Some women who worked as secretaries decided that secretarial work was not a real profession. They argued that "a real professional" originated and took responsibility for her or his own work and, most importantly, was never confused with a stenographer. The disdain felt for office work by some women who passed through it on their way to bigger and better things emerged in a lengthy BVI interview with "Miss H." Unable to afford college, she had taken commercial training and then a position with a law firm in California. She managed to save enough to study law at Stanford; with her "finances again at low ebb" in 1920 she became secretary to a prominent California attorney and also did much of his legal work. Having finished her law degree and passed the bar examinations in Kentucky and California, she was currently a law clerk in New York, where she hoped to be admitted to the bar. Miss H. described her own history in strictly individualistic terms. She thought most secretaries remained secretaries because "they hesitate to take on responsibility and in this way waste the time of their employers." For herself, she could never envision returning to secretarial work, which now "looks very small, . . . almost menial. It's like being married," she said; "you have always to adapt yourself to someone else's mood . . . . You feel almost as though you prostitute (that may be too strong a word) yourself to making money—for you must sacrifice yourself and approach everything through the point of view of your employer."[91] H's allusion to prostitution grappled with the ever-present dichotomy of the private secretary's (or the stenographer's) job. She was supposed to do her job independently and resourcefully, but she was also supposed, if not to provide sexual services to her employer, then to give him the services of her gender: domesticity, passivity, charm, and endless patience.

It became easier and easier for middle-class women to fall into clerical work, at least temporarily. As office jobs expanded during the war and through the 1920s, well-educated clerical workers with middle-class manners were in demand in towns and cities throughout the country. For women whose parents could not or would not send them to college, clerical work was often the only reasonable choice of employment. Turned away from most of the well-paying professions and no longer willing to settle for teaching, many college graduates decided to break into office work and were enthusiastically advised to do so by their college counselors. Some would rise to important positions within the office or go on to managerial positions, especially in personnel work. A few would be able to use their office job contacts and earnings to secure further professional training and become part of the tiny percentage of women competing in the male-dominated professions.

With office jobs available for the asking, clerical work did become the way in which middle-class women enacted fantasies of their future lives. Mothers' or grandmothers' advice that girls should take typing in high school so they would have "something to fall back on" was not so misguided; women used clerking jobs to support themselves as students, to finance careers as artists and writers, to bide their time until something better came along.

Take, as a final example, the case of the Herbst sisters, Josephine and Helen, who were high school students in Sioux City in 1910 and dreamed about becoming writers. The Herbst parents had fallen on hard times and could not afford college educations for their children. Josephine spent two years in a mediocre midwestern college and worked in her father's store, where she saved enough money to attend the University of Iowa for a year. She secured a job teaching seventh and eighth grade. Helen was unable to attend college at all, at least for the moment, and went straight from high school to teach in a one-room schoolhouse in a country town. Both sisters disliked their teaching positions, and Josephine left hers in 1914 to return to Sioux City, where she studied shorthand, took a job in a lawyer's office, and lived at home. By 1915 she had saved enough money to finish college on the West Coast; Helen had saved enough to attend the University of Wisconsin for a year. Over the next four years Josephine held a series of stenographic positions in the Bay area of California while she got a start in writing. By World War I Helen had married a handsome young farmer and become the society reporter at a newspaper office in Sioux City; Josephine headed to New York to the radical writers' community of Greenwich Village. Both women became pregnant but feared the disruption babies would create in their fledgling careers. They both had abortions, but Helen died of complications in Sioux City. Only Josephine lived on to fulfill the sisters' ambitions, supported in her early years as a writer in New York by secretarial and editing jobs, longing still for Helen's companionship.[92]

The Herbst sisters may have appeared as statistics in overall aggregates of teachers and clerical workers in twentieth-century census figures. On one level they were simply two of countless numbers of women who ended up in predictable women's occupations. But teaching and clerking were never the jobs they wanted, they were the jobs they could get, and therein lay not only, as in Helen's case, the rub of woman's condition, but, as in Josephine's, the possibility of salvation.

Gender Frontiers: Career Women of the 1920s

Women who rose to positions of secretary, office manager, bookkeeper, or personnel manager—by definition middle class—were not always very sympathetic with the work culture of the office or with women clerical workers in general. These "career women" sometimes saw themselves as a different breed, not tempted by the frivolities that ensnared so many women and distracted them from what they often thought should be the main business at hand: getting ahead and proving to a skeptical world the qualifications of women for better positions. Successful women often blamed the degrading conditions of clerical work on clerical workers themselves. Sometimes it was the working-class non-high school graduate who received the blame, sometimes the youthful stenographer, sometimes the woman who left the work force to marry, sometimes the woman who married and tried to work.

The faith that women's success was dependent on women's determination was remarkably strong in the 1920s. It coexisted, as contradictions often do, alongside the perception that women faced discrimination at every turn. We would expect successful women to perceive the reality that men, not women, were likely to receive high salaries, to be promoted, and to wield real authority, even though many women had improved their original positions. What is more interesting is why they held to their faith in women's success. A sense that a critical moment in women's history was at hand pervaded women's discussions of ambition and success in the 1920s. Everyone agreed that World War I and the decade that followed represented a litmus test for women's future in the world of work. The onus of such a responsibility was often terrifying, particularly when the demands being made of women were so unclear. Did the advances of some mean that all women had been given a golden opportunity to sink or swim? Would the chances for betterment be withdrawn if women did not prove themselves? What did such proving mean? To what extent was this a test to see if women could think of jobs as careers instead of as a transition between the homes of parents and the homes of husbands? Could ordinary women be counted upon to uphold feminist goals of putting the whole sex in a better light?

In some ways this generation of career women was ill-prepared to openly confront the ongoing hostility to women they faced in the workplace. Many had succeeded in so much so quickly that it seemed a misperception to argue that women could not make real gains in office work; some obviously had. Others had struggled and sacrificed so much to get where they were that they wanted to view their success as evidence of their own exceptionalism. Women who had succeeded in clerical work were, perhaps, personally invested in the notion of individual success, more believing in the possibility of obtaining it, and therefore more defensive about their own failure to obtain positions beyond the upper reaches of clerical work. The ways in which occupations were both open to a few and closed to most created further confusion and misreadings of reality. The winning of the suffrage and the expectation of further gains gave many women a rosy vision of the future, which made it difficult to see that women might continue to be denied jobs, good salaries, and promotions, not because of flaws in their training, their "attitude," their class attributes, or their marital status, but because they were women.

Conquering inequality through ambition, proper training, and devotion to a job had been a resonant theme in the musings of successful office workers and professional advice workers for many years. A single woman who had entered office work in 1912 was convinced by 1925 that "if only the girls who decide on business as their career, would thoroughly train themselves for the work on which they hope to concentrate, we would soon have better paid, more efficient workers."[93] A former school teacher from Everett, Washington, who had become a stenographer in 1906, moved to Los Angeles and became one of the first women in the city to do credit work. She was single but lived with relatives whom she helped to support. She had been instrumental in forming a professional group of women in the local credit association. Her interviewer noted that "she believes that most business and professional women of today have won success because of stern necessity—because they were forced to work and work hard to support themselves and others."[94] A statistican at the Henry L. Doherty Company thought most women were not up to the demands of success: "I believe that if a woman can display the same qualities that make up a good business man, in most places she will meet with no opposition whatever, but will stand on an equal footing with men. I think, however, that such women are not overnumerous. And it is the average woman, who gets so far and no further, on whom a firm will base its methods of treatment of women."[95]

When women succeeded in gaining access to higher levels in the office hierarchy they often tried to suggest that they had proven themselves in some sort of objective way to be superior; the reverse of this argument was that the failure of other women lay in their own faults or miscalculations. "The opposition from some men," Eleanor Gilbert claimed, "is not an insurmountable obstacle to the able woman, trained and ambitious for executive responsibility. More than anything else, lack of preparation and lack of desire for a high commercial goal has kept women from executive posts."[96] In this context Gilbert's choice of the word *desire* as the ultimate characteristic of the successful woman was revealing. It suggested that woman's progress was a product of her single-mindedness, her inner compulsions, her getting stuck a result of her diffused intent, her own lethargy. The journalist Adelaide A. Lyons said of Caroline Wylie, the successful New York accountant, that "she has always picked herself up when she was down, and always prepared herself for a bigger job than the one she was in. This is the secret of Mrs. Wylie's success."[97] And in choosing these interpretations, successful women and their chroniclers tended to cut themselves off from other women office workers and to highlight the notion that advancement in business required giving up a normal life. The notion that women had to work harder, stay later, and devote themselves single-mindedly to their occupations made slackers out of not just the flapper stenographer but of the average woman as well.

The alleged failings of the unsuccessful included not only a lack of ambition and dedication but also of a future vision. Gilbert thought that two kinds of office workers did not make suitable executives: young woman waiting to be rescued by husbands, and older women whose life plans were too limited to save them from drudgery. Her sentiments were echoed by the anxiety-ridden Edith M. Miller, who was interviewed by the BVI in 1921 for a study of statistical workers. A graduate of Ohio Wesleyan, Miller had first worked in the Ohio Bureau of Labor Statistics, then for the Ohio State Industrial Commission. During the war she became a statistician at the National Bank of Commerce in New York, and by 1921 managed a large department of both women and men. Although she thought the women in her department were as capable as the men, "the normal woman gets married and stops working and only the extremely able or the incapable are left." Miller considered herself, obviously, one of the former, and, unlike most of the weak sisters in her charge, able and willing to work a fourteen-hour day. Yet she wistfully reported that since the male executives who worked at the bank took lunch at the Bankers Club, which was closed to women, she often missed out on "the informal discussions which men have freer access to than women," which were "extremely valuable in developing business information and judgment." Her own future was unclear; the bank was increasingly hiring younger men trained in business at Princeton and the Harvard Business School for new executive positions.[98]

Women like Edith Miller sometimes joined organizations such as the Business and Professional Women's Club (BPW) or the New York Women's City Club to substitute for their exclusion from male groups and to find other working women like themselves. These clubs were dominated by older women who were more financially successful in their occupations than the norm.[99] Private secretaries and office managers were members in far larger proportions than their usual contingents in offices, although the largest single group of clerical workers in the BPW were stenographers.[100]

While it is doubtful that all the women who joined such clubs were originally middle class in background, they certainly were ascribing to a middle-class set of working women's values by the time they enrolled. An emphasis on education, success, and the removal of discriminatory barriers to working women's progress was the theme of these groups, where women professionals, clerical workers, and business proprietors seemed to mingle with each other amicably. The Woman's City Club of New York, for instance, founded in 1916 to promote suffrage and women's citizenship activities, had expanded by the mid-twenties to a membership of several thousand, with teachers and secretaries the most dominant groups of working women in the membership.[101] BPW groups were composed of the same occupational proportions. The slogan of the National Federation of Business and Professional Women's Clubs was "at least a high school education for every business girl." While there was no doubt that high school education could contribute to success in office work, concern over graduation as a criterion may have reflected BPW women's fears that more and more working-class women were coming into the office. Separation from factory workers or youthful clerical workers without high school educations, that is, working-class women, was something these women sought to maintain.[102]

Although it was not necessary to hold a certain kind of occupation to enter the Woman's City Club, hefty membership fees and a temporary ban on women who were not native-born guaranteed that most women who joined would be Yankee and middle class. Some women who joined YWCA and BPW clubs may have been in search of a genteel, homosocial alternative to the dance halls and "cheap amusements" of working-class clerks. Ruth Shonle Cavan cited the case in her study of Chicago business girls of a woman who had "made friends at the girls' club where she lives . . . . She has not sought friendships at the office where she works because they go to public dance halls, which she regards as wrong."[103] In suggesting that the working woman away from home and in search of friends and leisure-time activities seek out YWCA groups, churches, and "clubs for business and professional women" instead of dance halls and movie theaters, one advice-giver suggested that working women were creating new social groups for themselves with middle-class respectabilities and a career-woman mentality: through "sheer charm and ability" they were winning "enviable positions in society . . . . They are pioneers, blazing new trails for the millions of clever and ambitious women crowding the marketplace." "In the near . . . future, a woman who goes out into the world to earn a livelihood will be received on the same basis as a man. If she is a member of a good family; if she succeeds in her work; if she is clever and charming and attractive . . . her pay envelope will rear no barrier against her social progress as all too frequently has been the case in the past."[104] However elitist these working women's clubs were, they were instrumental in helping some women create a new identity as self-made individuals separate from family, church, and ethnic representations.

In addition to joining groups such as the BPW, career women might also support political measures like the equal rights amendment. The abstract clarity of "equal pay for equal work" and other such feminist slogans seemed to be one solution to the messiness of most women's actual lives and the prejudicial climate they often encountered. A woman in a high-level position at one firm complained that "executives refuse to have a woman at Board Meetings, because they cannot tell their little stories," and they would not "talk over policies with her because they feel that she being a woman would not understand it." Her reaction to these exclusions was to believe "completely in the Alice Paul program of equality between sexes."[105] BPW clubs supported the rights of married working women, although most club members were single.

Marion Bills was adored by many long-term women employees at Aetna Insurance because she championed the promotion of women on an equal basis with men to mid-level positions. She refused to ride the back elevator, to which the president had consigned all women. Bills's statistical work on the life insurance industry had a clear subtext: women made much more responsible employees, even if married, than popular sentiment gave them credit for being, and promoting women on the basis of intelligence and performance would be advantageous to both women and business. But Bills herself did everything she could to establish her own seriousness and to distance herself from the Hartford working-class women who staffed many positions at Aetna. She never married, dressed in sensible clothes and shoes, wore her hair in a bun, and hired the services of a cook and housekeeper to manage her home. She was a member of Hartford's BPW club. Mary Gilson, who shared her home with another woman, made similar choices in dress and life-style.[106] Gilson and Bills were challenging the dictum that women needed to be married and to have children to be full-fledged adults. They were creating an alternative life-style built on homosocial relationships. Perhaps everything about these women's lives made them understandably suspicious of the woman who married and gave up—or was forced to give up—on paid work.

Beneath much of the successful women's advice to and condemnation of what they perceived to be frivolous working women was another agenda: to convince more women not to marry so that they could pursue both clerical work and professional careers with determination, or if they did marry, to think of careers in lengthier terms. Then the entire class of working women would not be "shamed" by the defection of these converts to love, marriage, and the nursery. Although career woman often criticized the marriage bar and argued that it was inherently unfair, they also seemed to be arguing that while it was in effect, women should remain single as long as possible or even rule out marriage altogether. Elizabeth Cook, a bond salesperson at a Wall Street firm, told an audience of women at the New York University Business School that "The obstacle which looms largest in the minds of men as a reason why women don't get further in business is the temporary aspect of their work. You go and talk with them about a position and they say 'oh, well, but you will marry,' and they have had some experience in that line and have reason to say that." And while Cook did not openly say that women should not marry, women who did marry were, in her view, clearly turncoats: "Another thing that will help you very much if you really mean to get ahead is to take a long view of things. If you have in mind that you are . . . going to do it for years, perhaps all your life, you will be more likely to succeed . . . and then if the lover crosses your path and you go off with him, that is your affair, if you have done your best while you were there."[107]

Some career women thought fewer women would marry in the future as they took up more serious work. A teacher of business, whom the BVI interviewed in 1919, argued that "women should accept vocations with permanent intention. There will be less and less marriage," she maintained, "as we grow less and less materially minded."[108] These women might gain intellectual solace from someone like Charlotte Perkins Gilman, who lectured in the same

1915 New York University series with Cook and whose book, *Women and Economics*, was widely read in feminist circles. She too had argued that traditional "marriage" was an outmoded concept and that a new seriousness of intention could liberate women to do meaningful work, even if they chose a male companion.[109]

Another side of this debate was surfacing in the 1920s as younger women saw a more complex attitude emerge toward married working women. The percentage of married women who worked and the years they stayed in the work force were both increasing. Here and there the marriage bar was lifting. The concept of the working wife, and even of the working mother, had begun to enter the popular consciousness. Married women and women with children were managing to find clerical jobs and to think of themselves as reliable and permanent employees. Many firms quietly overlooked the marriages of women they considered to be valuable. Others hired widowed or divorced women with children and did not find their performances lackluster. None of these developments did much, however, to secure top-level management jobs for women.

Some commentators understood that there was no single solution to the discrimination and psychic dismissal awaiting women in office work and that deep-seated cultural forms as well as economic exploitation underlay these. They conceded that most women could not be expected to give up marriage or family for a long-term career, and that when professional women held themselves up as different in some ways from "ordinary" clerical workers they were likely to be seen more as tokens than as pioneers for a new group of women. Elizabeth Kemper Adams pondered these issues as the twenties began and aptly described the dilemmas to be faced by working women in the professions and office work:

There is considerable reaction from the professional hospitalities extended during the war; and women who worked shoulder to shoulder with men are discovering that the masculine shoulder may again be coldly turned .... They will have special problems of their own to meet and solve, such as the basic problem of combining a professional career with marriage and parenthood .....they will have to forge ahead for some time to come against a professional psychology which forgets all about them even more frequently than it objects to them, and is prone to include all women in sweeping generalizations:—that the prospect of marriage makes them a shifting and undependable labor supply; .... that they lack group spirit and group standards; that they are detail-minded; that they are more appropriately assistants and substitutes than directors and organizers—a sort of innately secretarial sex.[110]

What many career-minded women had really failed to perceive was that the new vistas of scientific management, of corporate organization, of high finance, were adventures not so much closed to undedicated women as they were adventures reserved for men. The marriage bar became the smokescreen behind which the perpetuation of women's otherness was maintained, an otherness necessary to justify women's by-and-large exclusion from the world beyond menial work. The anonymous author of a brief pamphlet on women and the war effort put out by the Alexander Hamilton Institute in New York made clear in 1918 that token women could never be equivalent to men, and that women would, because of their sex, have to be excluded from the higher levels of business indefinitely. In this analysis, biology merged with gender and became an inescapable destiny:

> Right here seems to be the *fundamental and eternal cause which may forever prevent women* from reaching the positions of high skill and responsibility which require long periods of apprenticeship and training . . . . There are women who never intend to marry, and some who actually do not marry. But you can never depend upon your woman in this respect. The most adamant, the homeliest, the unlikeliest do marry and they do quit work . . . . . We would not have it otherwise, for we believe the average woman is worth more to society as a builder of men and women of character than she is as a maker of steel. So long as conditions remain as they are, men will hold the highest positions. Employers know they will stay if they are properly rewarded; they know with greater certainty that women will not. Granted, there are many, many exceptions. Most businessmen will not care to risk finding the exception . . . . All this is hard on the woman who does want to stay in the game. It is not her fault. It lies in the nature of things as they are.[111]

The impossibility of refuting this logic, circular and primitive as it was, was demonstrated to women again and again. Mary Gilson presented an interesting case of it in her autobiography, when she described the visit of the dean of the Harvard Graduate School of Business Administration to the Clothcraft factory in Cleveland:

> We were training more and more women for supervisory positions . . . . I was eager to send a couple of our promising young college women apprentices to the newly founded Harvard Graduate School of Business Administration. When Dean Wallace B. Donham visited

our factory I thought my chance to put this through had come. No, he said, they were not admitting any women. I took him through our plant and showed him the responsible work some of our women supervisors were doing, and suggested that the graduate school would not suffer by admitting a few well-qualified women. He grew irritated. Sarcastically, and with a would-be "humorous" touch, he said, "Well, to be candid, we are not interested in training women, for if they are attractive they get married, and we don't wish to take on unattractive ones."[112]

Donham's remark was not as frivolous or as eccentric as it might seem; it was the consequence of a man pushed to reveal his ultimate prejudice. The implications of it were enough to bring women to tears, for it represented the classic double bind of the ambitious office woman, whether college-trained or not. If unmarried she was a freak of nature and therefore doomed to be a social pariah, and if married, socially acceptable but a reaffirming demonstration of the inherent weakness of woman and the folly of wasting good positions or special training on her. It was no wonder that many career women found it difficult to confront the sheer hopelessness of this double bind and instead tended to blame their condition on less serious-minded women.

NOTES

1. Interview with R. S. by Gail Sansbury, Nov. 6, 1982, Rhode Island Working Women Oral History Project [RIWW], Special Collections, University of Rhode Island Library, Kingston.

2. Bureau of Vocational Information Survey of Secretaries and Stenographers, [BVIWS] 425 (200), California, Schlesinger Library, Radcliffe College.

3. Ruth Shonle Cavan, *Business Girls: A Study of Their Problems* (Chicago: Religious Education Association, 1929), 26.

4. I have assumed that the range of those who might be defined as middle class in the early twentieth century must be fairly wide; daughters of clerks, teachers, merchants, and professionals are obvious inclusions, but so might be native-born families, many of them on farms, who sought education for their children and to set themselves apart from factory workers and immigrants, even though their incomes were relatively low. I face the usual dilemma of using income, life-style, or self-perception to indicate economic class in American society. For a helpful discussion of middle-class formation, see Stuart M. Blumin, "The Hypothesis of Middle-Class Formation in Nineteenth-Century America: A Critique and Some Proposals," *American Historical Review* 90 (April 1985): 299-38. On the num-

bers of "women adrift" seeking work in major American cities, see Joanne J. Meyerowitz, *Women Adrift: Independent Wage Earners in Chicago, 1880-1930* (Chicago: University of Chicago Press, 1988), 31-32.

5. Edith Johnson, *To Women of the Business World* (Philadelphia: J. B. Lippincott, 1923), 40-41.

6. For an important discussion of why some middle-class women may have avoided competition with men, see Elizabeth Nottingham, "Toward an Analysis of Two World Wars on the Role and Status of Middle-Class Women in the English-Speaking World," *American Sociological Review* 12 (Dec. 1947): 670.

7. Miriam Simons Leuck, *Fields of Work for Women* (New York: D. Appleton, 1929), 59.

8. Ethel L. Erickson, "The Employment of Women in Offices", *Women's Bureau Bulletin* 120 (1934): 6 and 20; M. C. Elmer, "A Study of Women in Clerical and Secretarial Work in Minneapolis, Minn." (Minneapolis: Woman's Occupational Bureau, 1925), 9. The implications of the Minneapolis study are discussed by Sophonisba P. Breckinridge, *Women in the Twentieth Century: A Study of Their Political, Social and Economic Activities* (New York: McGraw-Hill, 1933), 179.

9. Eleanor Gilbert (Anne Rosenblatt), *The Ambitious Woman in Business* (New York: Funk and Wagnalls, 1916), 227-78.

10. Agnes F. Perkins, *Vocations for the Trained Woman: Opportunities Other than Teaching* (New York: Longmans, Green, 1910), 201, 208.

11. Leuck, *Fields of Work for Women*, 50.

12. Edward A. Filene, *Next Steps Forward in Retailing* (New York: Harper and Brothers, 1937), 538-39.

13. Perkins, *Vocations for the Trained Woman*, 203-4.

14. Dorothy Dunbar Bromley, "Are Women a Success in Business?" *Harpers*, Feb. 28, 1928, 300.

15. BVIWS 915 (444), Georgia.

16. BVIWS 285 (1816), New York; 132 (1845), New York; and (21305), New York.

17. The exact date of these interviews is unclear, but they were probably conducted in 1929 or 1930 as data for the author's 1932 doctoral thesis, completed at Bryn Mawr. Anne Hendry Morrison, *Women and Their Careers: A Study of 306 Women in Business and the Professions* (New York: National Federation of Business and Professional Women's Clubs, 1934), 28.

18. Grace L. Coyle, "Women in the Clerical Occupations," *Annals* 143 (May 1929): 180-87.

19. Erickson, "The Employment of Women in Offices," 14; Mary Schauffler, "Impressions on Secretarial Work, Cleveland, Ohio, April 20-May 15, [1925]," BVI, folder 494; Coyle, "Women in the Clerical Occupations," 185; Breckinridge, *Women in the Twentieth Century*, 175.

20. Thomas Woody, *A History of Women's Education in the United*

States (New York: Octagon Books, 1966), 2: 137-303; Mabel Newcomer, *A Century of Higher Education for American Women* (New York: Harper and Brothers, 1959), 35-51; Barbara Solomon, *In the Company of Educated Women: A History of Women and Higher Education in America* (New Haven: Yale University Press, 1985), 43-61; Patricia Albjerg Graham, "Expansion and Exclusion: A History of Women in Higher Education," *Signs* 3 (Summer, 1978): 759-61.

21. Woody, *History of Women's Education*, 2: 323. James Burt Miner's survey of students at the University of Minnesota showed most women there were enrolled in the College of Arts and Sciences, but two-thirds were "planning to teach for a livelihood in case of necessity." "A Vocational Census of College Students," *Educational Review* 50 (Sept. 1915): 156-60. Mary van Kleeck's study of sixteen thousand women college graduates at work in 1915 showed that 83.5 percent of them were teachers. Solomon, *In the Company of Educated Women*, 127.

22. Chase Going Woodhouse and Ruth Yeomans Schiffman, "Occupations, Earnings, Familes and Some Undergraduate Problems," Institute of Women's Professional Relations, Bulletin no. 4 (May 1932): pt. 1, 5, 18-20. The proportions observed by Woodhouse and Schiffman declined only gradually before 1960; see Newcomer, *A Century of Higher Education*, 176-77.

23. Miner's study of undergraduate men in the College of Arts and Sciences at the University of Minnesota showed that nearly 40 percent intended to enter professions related to finance, business, and engineering; another 26 percent intended to enter law and medicine. "A Vocational Census of College Students," 158-59. Figures have been extracted from categories Miner presents in a somewhat different way.

24. Newcomer, *A Century of Higher Education*, 177, 182-83.

25. Solomon, *In the Company of Educated Women*, 147-49. Paula Fass disagrees with Solomon, claiming that most students who worked did so for pocket money, Paula S. Fass, *The Damned and the Beautiful: American Youth in the 1920's* (New York: Oxford University Press, 1977), 134-35. The importance of part-time work for college students surely varied according to class. About 15 percent of women attending private women's colleges worked while attending, but Woodhouse and Schiffman found that about 53 percent of a large sample of those in land grant colleges from 1919 to 1922 were contributing to their own support. "Occupations, Earnings, Familes and Some Undergraduate Problems," 9.

26. Mary E. Cookingham, "Combining Marriage, Motherhood and Jobs Before World War II: Women College Graduates, Classes of 1905-1935," *Journal of Family History* 9(Summer 1984): 180-84; Fass, *The Damned and the Beautiful*, 63-71.

27. Solomon, *In the Company of Educated Women*, 150.

28. "Women in Business," *BVI News Bulletin* [*BVINB*], Sept. 1, 1923, 1.

29. "Round-Table Conferences: Secretarial Training in Schools of Business," *Journal of Business of the University of Chicago* 3 (Oct. 1930): 60.

30. "Women in Business," 6.

31. Elizabeth Kemper Adams, *Women Professional Workers: A Study Made for the Women's Educational and Industrial Union* (Chautauqua: Chautauqua Press, 1921), 223.

32. By 1925, eleven of these bureaus were still in existence. Mary Ross Potter, "Chicago Collegiate Bureau of Occupations," *BVINB*, Dec. 1925, 92.

33. Julia Searing Leacraft and Mary L. Bush, "The College Alumna's Work," *Columbia University Quarterly* (March 1917): 145-56; and "Notes on the History of the Bureau of Vocational Information," BVI, folder 1.

34. The Bureau of Vocational Information," *BVINB*, Aug. 15, 1923, 1-3.

35. Bureau of Vocational Information, *Training for the Professions and Allied Occupations* (New York: Bureau of Vocational Information, 1924). Adams's readable work, *Women Professional Workers*, introduced women to dozens of jobs that had recently been opened as a result of the war. Catharine Filene's book of edited essays, *Careers for Women*, was a crossover work that combined many of the assumptions of the popular advice literature with college vocational guidance techniques. It included such curiosities as dairy farmer, map-maker, cafeteria manager, and chemical engineer. Beatrice Doerschuk claimed that Filene had begun her work at the BVI and then set up the Institute of Women's Professions in competition. "Notes on the History of the Bureau of Vocational Information."

36. "Bureau of Vocational Information," 2, 6.

37. Nancy F. Cott, *The Grounding of Modern Feminism* (New Haven: Yale University Press, 1987), 90.

38. Woodhouse and Schiffman, "Occupations, Earnings, Familes and Some Undergraduate Problems," 34; also see Nottingham, "Toward an Analysis of the Effects of Two World Wars," 667-68.

39. Leacraft and Bush, "The College Alumna's Work," 153.

40. By 1924 it was estimated that about a hundred thousand teachers a year, or 16 percent of the total, were leaving teaching, and that fewer than 5 percent of the teachers of the country had been teaching for twenty years or more. Charyl Williams, "The Position of Women in the Public Schools," *Annals* 143 (May 1929): 163.

41. Free responses of 141 former teachers polled by the BVI in 1924 and 1925 are given here. Some gave more than one reason for leaving teaching, so there were 152 total responses: did not care for teaching, thirty-seven; teaching too stressful, put strain on health, eighteen; teaching pays too little, thirteen; left teaching for a better position, thirteen; lack of opportunity in teaching, one; no reason or other reason not listed, seventy.

42. Morrison, *Women and their Careers*, 26-27. Of seventy clerical workers in the study, thirteen, or 18 percent, began as teachers, about the same proportions as in the BVI study.

43. Williams, "The Position of Women in the Public Schools," 156-59. On women in school administration, see Willystine Goodsell, "The Educational Opportunities of American Women—Theoretical and Actual," *Annals* 143 (May 1929): 8-10.

44. On teacher training, see Walter S. Monroe, *Teaching-Learning Theory and Teacher Education, 1890-1950* (1952, repr. New York: Greenwood Press, 1969), 193-94; Geraldine Joncich Clifford and James W. Guthrie, *Ed School: A Brief for Professional Education* (Chicago: University of Chicago Press, 1988), 57-64; Newcomer, *A Century of Higher Education for American Women*, 88-89; Solomon, *In the Company of Educated Women*, 46-47; and Dorothy M. Brown, *Setting a Course: American Women in the 1920s* (Boston: Twayne Publishers, 1987), 152-54. Newcomer estimates that at the turn of the century more than half of all the women in higher education were in normal schools and teacher colleges and that most of these institutions did not require a four-year degree.

45. Williams, "The Position of Women in the Public Schools," 156-59.

46. Margaret Elliott and Grace E. Manson, "Earnings of Women in Business and the Professions," *Michigan Business Studies* 3 (Sept. 1930): 77. A survey of more than six thousand matriculants from land grant colleges—those who had attended school between 1899 and 1922—found that of the 3,521 at work, earnings for teachers ranged from $1,554 to $2,750; for those in occupations other than teaching, $1,596 to $1,999; for those in "all business" (including clerical work), $1,457 to 1,923; and for those in "executive positions" in business (accounting, advertising, auditing, and personnel management), $1,909 to $2,333. While 3.6 percent of the teachers earned $3,000 or more, 7.4 percent of those in occupations other than teaching did, and 18.5 percent of the business executives did. It must also be kept in mind that because most of these women had four-year college degrees, those in teaching had secured the better positions in the profession and therefore earned higher salaries than the norm: 9.4 percent taught in colleges, 67.1 percent in high schools, and only 18.2 percent in elementary schools. Woodhouse and Schiffman, "Occupations, Earnings, Families and Some Undergraduate Problems," 7, 18-19, 51.

47. A poll of more than 1,500 cities by the National Education Association in 1928 showed that in most, married women would not be hired and teachers who married on the job were fired in about half. Williams, "Position of Women in the Public Schools," 163-64. As Cookingham emphasizes, however, conditions for married teachers in the teens and twenties were improved over both earlier conditions and the wave of discrimination against married women teachers that set in during the depression. "Combining Marriage, Motherhood and Jobs Before WWII," 191-92.

48. BVIWS 405 (65), California.

49. BVIWS 154 (1646), New York.

50. See Williams, "The Position of Women in the Public Schools," 164, for reference to teachers' periodic nervous breakdowns.

51. These quotes by former teachers are from BVIWS 711 (569), Illinois; 302 (147), California; and 724 (435), Georgia.

52. A young teacher in Sinclair Lewis's novel *Main Street*, for example, is forced to quit her job and leave town after she attends a dance with one of her students. Sinclair Lewis, *Main Street* (1920, repr. New York: Signet Classics, 1961), ch. 32. On the new urban heterosocial leisure, see Meyerowitz, *Women Adrift*, and Kathy Peiss, *Cheap Amusements: Working Women and Leisure in Turn-of-the-Century New York* (Philadelphia: Temple University Press, 1986).

53. Robert S. and Helen Merrill Lynd commented on the lackluster lives of teachers in *Middletown: A Study in American Culture* (1929, repr. New York: Harcourt, Brace and World, 1956), 209.

54. BVIWS 61 (1817), New York.

55. BVIWS 37 (2004), New York; 893 (2256), Pennsylvania; 724 (435), Georgia; and 325 (128), California.

56. BVIWS 325 (128), California.

57. Grace E. Manson, "Occupational Interests and Personality Requirements of Women in Business and the Professions," *Michigan Business Studies* 3 (April 1931): 281-347. Nearly six thousand of the group were clerical workers, another three thousand were teachers, and about 1,400 were in sales and publicity. Other occupations included 866 women in health care, 601 in finance, 316 in welfare, and 204 in library work. The bulk of the clerical workers were high school-educated (67 percent), nearly 60 percent of the teachers had attended some years of college, and sales workers had the lowest levels of education; about 21 percent of them had attended only grade school.

58. Manson, "Occupational Interests and Personality Requirements." While the teachers tended to think of clerical work as a reasonable alternative to their current occupation, clerks did not feel the same way about teaching; they disliked teaching except for the occupation of business education teacher. The clerical workers' dislike for both teaching and accounting may have reflected the realization that extended education would have been required for these jobs, whereas it was possible to go from teaching to clerking with relatively little new training.

59. For example, in secretarial work in Boston, Perkins found negligible numbers of college-trained women who had more than five years of experience, indicating that college women were just beginning to enter clerical work in that city after 1910. *Vocations for the Trained Woman*, 129.

60. Erickson, "The Employment of Women in Offices," 12.

61. Ibid.; Elliott and Manson, "Earnings of Women in Business and the Professions," 86-87.

62. At the age of forty, high school-educated men made about $900 more than high school-educated women, and grammar school-educated

men made about $150 more than grammar school-educated women. Elliott and Manson, "Earnings of Women in Business and the Professions," 51-54, 70-73.

63. Helen M. Kelsey, "Clerical and Secretarial Work," in Perkins, *Vocations for the Trained Woman*, 206; Adams, *Women Professional Workers*, 230.

64. See Erickson's breakdown of type of firm in New York City correlated with education, "The Employment of Women in Offices," 23. Some of these large corporations, run on scientific management, hired women college graduates in other capacities, especially as personnel workers, statisticians, and research and planning workers.

65. Schauffler, "Impressions on Secretarial Work in Cleveland," 2.

66. Erickson, "The Employment of Women in Offices," 30.

67. Esther Eberstadt Brooke, *The Girl and Her Job: A Handbook for Beginners* (New York: D. Appleton, 1933), 19-20; also see Gilbert, *The Ambitious Woman in Business*, 216.

68. Mary Schauffler, "A Study of Three Clerical Occupations for Women: Stenography, Typing, Bookkeeping," M.A. thesis, Western Reserve University, May, 1927, 13, 16.

69. Schauffler, "A Study of Three Clerical Occupations," 16.

70. Leuck, *Fields of Work for Women*, 23-24.

71. Schauffler, "Impressions on Secretarial Work in Cleveland," 5.

72. Helen E. Fairburn, "Opportunities for College Women: A Study of Occupations Other than Teaching Held by College Women in Buffalo," *University of Buffalo Studies* 8 (Aug. 1920): 149.

73. BVIWS 456 (1627), New York, and 741 (530), Illinois.

74. Letter from Margaret H. Fairlam to Emma P. Hirth, July 17, 1925, BVI, folder 471.

75. BVIWS 106 (1595), New York.

76. BVIWS 741 (530), Illinois; 946 (2246), Pennsylvania; and 477 (1662), New York.

77. Leuck, *Fields of Work for Women*, 16-17, 19-20, 23.

78. BVIWS 65 (1801), New York, and 88 (1804), New York.

79. Beatrice Doerschuk, "The Woman Secretary," typewritten manuscript with handwritten notes and corrections, unpaged, section on "Reasons for Leaving," BVI, folder 505; Florence E. Boebmer, "Staying in the Job: A Study of Vocational Continuity of College Women," Institute of Women's Professional Relations, Bulletin no. 4 (May 1932): pt. 2, 178-82.

80. "Combining Marriage, Motherhood and Jobs Before World War II," 178-95. Cookingham's work begins to substantiate the possibility that both lower age at marriage and lower fertility rates in the 1920s may have been economically motivated or due to what she calls the "opportunity cost of marriage and childbearing." As more jobs for married women appeared, along with birth control, some couples married at younger ages than had been the case but delayed having children or had fewer children so

the wife could work. See Fass, *The Damned and the Beautiful*, 68-71, and Chase Going Woodhouse, "Married College Women in Business and the Professions," *Annals* 143 (May 1929): 325-28. Woodhouse found that 43 percent of the women in her sample worked for "financial reasons," and about 22 percent worked for "love of work" or for a "career." She thought the economic motives somehow undermined the purposefulness of her subjects' work, but from a more modern perspective the responses seem to be both realistic and reasonable.

81. BVIWS 531 (2022), New York; and Bertha S. Ives to Emma P. Hirth, July 15, 1925, BVI, folder 471.

82. BVIWS 662 (584), Illinois.

83. Kathryn Martell to Emma P. Hirth, July 28, 1925, BVI, folder 472.

84. BVIWS 238 (314), Washington, D.C.; 65 (1801), New York; and 159 (1475), New York.

85. A parallel discussion of the same issues took place in nursing. See Barbara Melosh, *"The Physician's Hand": Work Culture and Conflict in American Nursing* (Philadelphia: Temple University Press, 1982), 15-20.

86. Adams, *Women Professional Workers*, 227-29.

87. BVIWS 634 (308), California, and 86 (1899), New York.

88. BVIWS 41 (1917), New York.

89. Anna A. Raymond, Philadelphia, July 17, 1925 to Emma Hirth, BVI, folder 471.

90. BVIWS 102 (1508), New York, and 360 (212), California.

91. BVIWS (2504), California.

92. Elinor Langer, *Josephine Herbst* (New York: Warner Books, 1985), 30-74.

93. BVIWS 601 (529), Illinois.

94. BVIWS 375 (231), California.

95. BVI, folder 337.

96. Gilbert, *The Ambitious Woman in Business*, 352.

97. Adelaide A. Lyons, "Caroline D. Wylie, Expert Accountant," unidentified newspaper clipping, BVI, folder 511.

98. Handwritten notes, "Interview with Edith Miller," BVI, folder 339.

99. The National Federation of Women's Clubs distributed questionnaires to more than forty-six thousand of its members and obtained 14,073 usable replies, about 42 percent of which were filled out by clerical workers. Elliott and Manson's analysis of the questionnaires of clerical workers showed a median age of 37.7 years and a median experience of 13.7 years. Only 10.7 percent of the entire sample was between the ages of 18 and 24.9. About 86 percent of the group was single (including divorced and widowed women). Elliott and Manson, "Earnings of Women in Business and the Professions," 7-9.

100. Elliott and Manson turned up 285 office managers, 534 private secretaries, 1,027 bookkeepers, bookkeeper-cashiers, and cashiers, 1,152 stenographers and stenographer-clerks, and 352 clerks in a total of 5,862

clerical workers. Only twenty-six women said they were typists, whereas more than a thousand claimed to be secretaries. Ibid., 22.

101. Elisabeth Israels Perry, "Training for Public Life: Eleanor Roosevelt and Women's Political Networks," in *Without Precedent: The Life and Career of Eleanor Roosevelt*, ed. Joan Hoff-Wilson and Marjorie Lightman (Bloomington: Indiana University Press, 1984), 32. Perry found the City Club had 194 teachers, 145 secretaries, 86 social workers, 36 editors, 35 office managers, 33 nurses, 27 physicians, 24 advertising agents, 23 lawyers, and lesser numbers of librarians, lecturers, artists, interior decorators, buyers, musicians, managers, inspectors, insurance brokers, bankers, dieticians, personnel mangers, designers, psychologists, actresses, architects, dentists, engineeers, sculptors, real estate agents, saleswomen, office workers, researchers, importers, statisticians, printers, accountants, professional shoppers, and photographers.

102. On the National Federation of Business and Professional Women's Clubs, see Cott, *The Grounding of Modern Feminism*, 89-90.

103. Cavan, *Business Girls*, 40.

104. Johnson, *To Women of the Business World*, 130-31.

105. BVIWS 87 (1803), New York.

106. Priscilla Murolo has investigated the life of Marion Bills most thoroughly, and this biographical information comes from her paper, "White Collar Women," 28-30. Most of Bills's work on office management and hiring in the insurance industry has been previously cited. Toward the end of Millicent Pond's tenure at Scovill Manufacturing, she and Bills collaborated on a lengthy article, "Intelligence and Clerical Jobs: Two Studies of Relation of Test Score to Job Held," *Personnel Journal* 12, no. 1 (1933): 41-56. The study demonstrated that those who scored the highest on intelligence tests were most likely to be promoted, regardless of sex, but that men with lower intelligence scores did better in promotions than did comparable women. The authors make no policy recommendations at all; the reader must extrapolate the "feminist" conclusions from the evidence with no help from the authors.

107. Typewritten transcript of lecture by Elizabeth E. Cook, "Finance and Banking," April 11, 1916, 22, 28, BVI, folder 23.

108. "Brief Investigations of Girls in Commercial Work," handwritten notes, Oct. 1919, BVI, folder 72.

109. Typewritten transcript of lecture by Charlotte Perkins Gilman, "Women and Vocations," Oct. 4, 1915, BVI, folder 3. Gilman summarized the ideas of *Women and Economics* in her lecture.

110. Adams, *Women Professional Workers*, 18.

111. *Women in Industry* (New York: Alexander Hamilton Institute, 1918), 18.

112. Mary Barnett Gilson, *What's Past Is Prologue: Reflections on My Industrial Experience* (New York: Harper and Brothers, 1940), 123.

8

Flappers and Feminists: Women's Office Work Culture in the 1920s

By 1930, THE GENDER and class hierarchy of the office was securely in place. Both working- and middle-class women were present in the office in large numbers. Although not a strict rule, mechanized and routinized jobs were likely to be held by working-class women, and many private secretaries and employment managers were middle class. I saw the Hollywood film *Working Girl* while I was writing this book, and I was struck by the way in which the movie, set in a Wall Street firm in the 1980s, portrayed what I had found in an earlier period. Although many secretaries are now working class, women office workers still share a combination of womanly ambition, sisterly solidarity and class conflict. There is still confusion between dressing for success or sexual display, and male executives hold the power to determine women's place. The title *Working Girl* implies the ambiguity of the woman clerk's situation, then and now. Is she a worker, a sex object, or both? Can a working-class woman find fame and fortune in the office, and if so, will it be her sexual availability or her performance that gets her to the top?

A computer clerk from Staten Island, Tess McGill first moves before the camera on her way to work, attired in "working girl" costume—short, tight skirt, lots of makeup, flashy jewelry, and a teased hairdo. In the crowded main office, Tess takes orders from a number of men and is the butt of sexist behavior. But the audience has been mislead. The heroine's nemesis in the film will not be a man, but another woman: Katherine Parker, an ambitious, well-tailored, aristocratic-mannered graduate of a private women's college, recently hired because she is reputed to be good at mergers and acquisitions. Tess receives a promotion and is assigned to be Katherine's new secretary. Tess finds that, if anything, women make more exploitative bosses than men. Anxious to succeed in the "man's world" of executive privilege, Katherine works harder and stays later, which means more work for the secretary. Katherine pretends to form a sisterly alliance with Tess. She promises to teach her the business and help her get ahead; if she's successful, she'll take her secretary along with her. But Katherine's patronizing manner begins to grate, and her real attitude is revealed when she steals one of Tess's ideas and presents it as her own. She's not only a snob at heart, but she also could really care less about sisterhood, and she will happily step on her secretary's back in her climb to the top.

In a twist of fate that could only happen in Hollywood, the heroine gets a chance to turn the tables. Katherine has an accident and puts Tess in charge while she recuperates. Tess begins to impersonate her boss over the telephone and then with clients outside the office. The impersonation requires a new wardrobe and cosmetics, conveniently available in Katherine's apartment. Tess can, it seems, step into Katherine's shoes, both literally and figuratively. Her combination of the right clothes, quick thinking, sexual vulnerability, and raw ambition brings her to the verge of closing a deal that will ensure her not only fame and fortune, but also Katherine's boyfriend.

Because the heroine remains sympathetic with her sister workers on the office floor and has a healthy dose of romantic and sexual sensibility, the film seems to say, she deserves both personal and workplace success. Unlike her aristocratic boss, she has not sacrificed her womanliness for her career. In a final confrontation in front of an audience of powerful men, the two women are forced to fight until one can be eliminated. Katherine, faced with the terrible truth that she cannot even keep her boyfriend, fails to prove her case and is humiliated in every way. Tess proves her mettle, however. She has not only gone to night school, but she also reads the New York City tabloids, where she discovers a vital clue that proves she triggered the big idea. Her old friends cheer, and the film ends with Tess ensconced in an office of her own, guarded by a woman secretary. Katherine has simply disappeared.

Working Girl evokes the gender and class ordering of the office hierarchy that came into being in the early twentieth century. The sexual objectification of women—as well as the requirement that women be complicit in that sexual objectification—was integral to office work culture. Women office workers were divided (or segmented) according to educational levels and class origins, and, of course, race. Ambition—women's ambition—was present in the lowliest of employees as well as the highest. Separating performance from sexuality remained difficult, and the rise of women supervisors often depended on the performance of her female underlings. Yet distinctions among women were also bound up in a common workplace culture that nearly all women shared: navigating city amusements on limited salaries, finding the right clothing and hairdos, and negotiating a workplace dominated by male privilege.

In this final chapter I turn to the terrain of the office itself, where the kinds of power relationships and workplace culture evoked in *Working Girl* play themselves out. Descriptions of women office workers in the twentieth century have not looked carefully at the segmentation of women office workers according to job category, age, education, marital status and class. The predominance in clerical work at any one time of young women, most native-born, white, and unmarried, has, perhaps, along with the assumptions that women's work is more or less all of a piece, blinded analysts to the fact that the segmentation of women workers might be a significant factor in office workplace culture.[1] Differences among women office workers structured the way in which they perceived their position in the office, their possibilities for advancement, and their attitudes toward work. These differences—generally those of class, age, marital status, and sexual-social orientation—probably undermined the likelihood of devising cooperative strategies for attacking discrimination and exploitation, organizing into unions, and, in general, perceiving common ground with other workers.

The Office and Its Culture: "Working Downtown"

Important differences segmented women's clerical work along lines of age and class before 1930. But there were ways in which common experiences created a workplace culture that all women office workers shared. They were participants in a heterosocial environment but enjoyed homosocial companionship. They were sexual objects in a workplace increasingly conscious of the female body and the need to both contain and display it. Women clerks also built networks of female friendship and with their girlfriends explored urban streets full of consumerist and leisure-time activities.

The display of the female body in the office proved to be problematical for employers and workers alike. As a result, all women office workers were continually presented with the struggle of how to look and what to wear. Supervisors and women workers found hair and dress styles to be contested terrain. Short hair and short dresses, often made of thin, clinging, or even transparent materials, heightened women's sexuality and, some employers thought, distracted male employees. Some managers tried to outlaw bobbed hair during World War I when short hair first began to appear, but the style, which was easy to care for and also associated with independent movie stars and a more glamorous appearance, inexorably made its way into the workplace. Although a clerk recalled two "strict" rules at the bank she worked for in the 1920s—"If you got married, you had to leave, and you couldn't have your hair bobbed" —only the first was really enforceable: "A friend of mine eloped, . . . and she had to quit her job, . . . [but] another friend of mine who had long hair went out and had her hair bobbed, and she got away with it. And I think maybe after that, they weren't quite so strict about bobbing your hair."[2]

Choosing clothes to wear to work was no easy matter. The clerical worker was expected to dress for the office, and stockings, shoes, dresses, and hats made up a costly part of her budget. Keeping an eye out for bargains and sales during lunchtime shopping was crucial to workers on a limited budget. Beatrice Reed, who worked as a secretary for a judge in Garden City, Kansas, lived away from home in a boardinghouse and had to watch her expenses carefully; she bought dresses on sale once a year at a local women's clothing store that specialized in "better" dresses for office workers and teachers.[3]

The clerical worker was supposed to be attractive, but not too sexy. She was not supposed to dress drably, but she also had to avoid flashiness. She should "look like a woman" but not attract untoward attention by her appearance. Jessie R. Wilson, who had worked as a personnel manager for the Curtis Publishing Company in the teens and for the Pennsylvania Railroad in the 1920s, tried to explain the dress code and its importance. Women had been barred from wearing the "peek-a-boo" shirtwaist at Curtis because the revealing blouses "invited very unwelcome advances from some of their men associates as well as the disapproval of supervisors and other girls with whom they worked." On the other hand, she "also dealt with the question of girls in general office work dressing like men. . . . I tried to point out that no successful business man ever attempted to dress like a woman." But she could not be very specific on how, exactly, a woman should dress for the office. The point was to avoid "eccentricity and informality," and she urged young women to use fashion sections in popular magazines as inspiration for their clothing styles. Eleanor Gilbert hinted at the same problem in her advice to the ambitious woman in business:

> Gone are the days when a striped blouse, a stiff, mannish collar, a four-in-hand tie, an ugly rainy-day skirt, were considered the only proper regalia for the business woman. But are we advancing when we adopt in their stead the cold-inviting, transparent flimsies in blouse and hose, and the high-healed unhygenic pumps? It is quite possible to look neat and well-drest in business by wearing simply made opaque blouses of good material or several one-piece gowns with low collars and sleeves reaching slightly below the elbow for comfort, which will always look dignified and keep neater than the blouse and skirt.[4]

A middle-aged private secretary echoed the advice books when she gave the following description of suitable clothing for the office: "Dress should should be up-to-date. Have fewer clothes if necessary, but let them be of best quality, neat, harmonious, consistently good."[5]

Hinted at in this kind of advice may have been the old fear of working women bringing prostitution in the office via seductive and indecent attire. At the same time the advice acknowledged that young working women could hardly be expected to dress like spinster schoolmarms. One advice book warned "the young woman who presides over the typewriter, the adding machine, or the switchboard" to complete her toilet at home instead of on the streetcar and to avoid lurid colors such as scarlet or orange.[6] The bank where May worked had an explicit rule against wearing see-through blouses; she generally wore a blouse and a skirt or a jersey dress to work. At one point the bank insisted the women clerks wear smocks over their clothing, but that met with resistance; "everybody would look all alike."[7] Women used dress to express their individuality and heighten their attractiveness. This was, moreover, no casual matter; their success at work and in attracting future partners might depend on their looks.

The problem of choosing proper clothing suggested the difficulty of keeping a proper balance between two competing demands; women office workers were expected to contribute to an atmosphere of heightened sexuality but not be explicitly sexual. The aura of flirtatious romance, nonetheless, hovered over the workplace. Heterosexual interaction took a variety of forms. Male and female clerks began with flirtation, took up dating, and sometimes married. At the insurance company where Rose worked, male and female clerks often met and fell in love. May met her husband at the bank where she worked as an information clerk and he as a teller.[8] In large Chicago offices, women clerks used the workplace as a way of arranging casual dates. Sometimes the most fleeting exchanges might lead to something: a young switchboard operator, for instance, made a date with a man who had called up her boss.[9]

Some young women had trouble meeting men at work. The preference of employers for married men often meant there weren't enough eligible young single men to go around. In that event, dance halls, parks, and even elevated trains might prove to be suitable places for meeting the opposite sex. A young office worker in Chicago dated a neighborhood boy for about three years but eventually threw him over because he embarassed her by drinking too much at parties. She began to use public entertainment spots to find men. On a skating trip to the park with her sister she met another young man, "who helped them when they fell down." Another encounter at a public dance hall led to the dispensation of her telephone number and then an engagement to be married. A second Chicago clerk picked up men on the train, in elevators, and public dance halls, "but the friendships did not last long."[10] As many disapproving parents had suspected, both the office and its urban location provided women clerks with opportunities for unsupervised and casual adventures with men.

There were other dangers in the modern office. The office hierarchy virtually guaranteed that young office workers would be in some kind of submissive power relationship with an older man. Bosses could choose private secretaries and stenographers on the basis of appearance. Single women and married men could have illicit love affairs. Women clerks might receive unwelcome sexual advances. The possibility of the man using his power to gain sexual advantage—or, perhaps of the young woman using sexual attraction to gain a supervisor's attention—was clearly present. Clerks who worked in all-female departments were probably shielded from what might be defined today as sexual harassment, but many women encountered sexual advances from men for whom they worked. A young Cleveland clerk complained about an employer who "put his arm around her every time he came to ask her anything about her notes." Some men pretended not to be married men in order to take advantage of inexperienced young stenographers. One clerk "went with a man from the office and later discovered he was married." She decided to give up dating men at the office. When May became information clerk at Rhode Island Hospital Trust Bank she was "told not to date any of the men who might approach her there," but the man who gave her the warning, she later learned, "was a philanderer himself."[11]

Women's networks in the office were helpful in alerting newcomers to sexual predators. A Cleveland woman warned her employment service not to send any more job candidates to her former employer because he "had been most insulting in his familiarity." A young Brooklyn clerk quit her job when her sister learned that the "employer was not a suitable person to employ a young girl." Sexual advances, although rarely spoken of explicitly, were common knowledge among women clerks who had worked for any length of time. A woman who had worked for fifteen years explained the motive which often lay behind quitting for "personal reasons": "Of course, a woman frequently has to guard against attentions from the men or man where or by whom she is employed. This experience was the reason for the writer's leaving the most interesting position she has had. Others have had similar experiences."[12]

Some women were very clear in their own minds about what constituted unwelcome sexual advances, but it was also likely to be the case that others did not quite know how to respond to such attentions. Should the woman be flattered? Was this appropriate office behavior? After all, this person was her employer and didn't he know best? Wasn't he able to spend money on her and make her feel important? The confusion strewn by bosses who acted on their physical attraction to clerical workers emerged in a Bureau of Vocational Information summary of an interview with a New York secretary who had attended college for two years and then joined Western Electric as a stenographer in 1923. After a year, she was suddenly transferred to the treasurer's office. "Why she was chosen to become secretary to the treasurer is not clear," commented her interviewer, but "she is an exceedingly beautiful girl," and she "intimated that the treasurer took a strong personal liking to her." The interviewer hinted at the possibility of a sexual liaison at worst and at something fishy at best. The secretary preferred her previous job in the personnel department but "believed it decidedly to her advantage to remain in her present position." Her typing and stenography skills were not put to much use; she produced only five to ten letters a week. Instead she kept her boss's personal accounts, greeted people who came to his office, employed his servants, arranged for his car repairs, and made certain he had a lunch appointment every day. Her continued success, she thought, depended "on her continuing to anticipate and satisfy [her] employer's whims and wishes."[13]

Many women clerks worked all day alongside other women and rarely interacted with men. Whatever their work or leisure-time relationships with men, the important friendships that most women clerks shared with other women provided important strategies for coping with workplace demands and navigating urban amusements. Some employers provided special facilities, clubs, and athletic programs for women clerical workers that allowed for both the pursuit of homosocial friendships at work and their shaping around "healthy" activities after working hours. A clerk at Rhode Island Hospital Trust Bank in Providence was a member of the bank's club for employees. Through the club she bowled downtown once a week, attended dances, and used "the nice little room upstairs where they had their club meetings, quite often."[14] These welfare programs might be especially elaborate at large manufacturing plants, which were often on self-contained sites remote from the downtowns accessible to bank, public utility, and department store workers.

Scovill Manufacturing provided a Scovill Girls' Club for employees at its Waterbury plant; workers used it for wedding showers, birthday and going-away parties, sewing groups, bridge games, and club meetings. Members elected sister workers as club officers, and the club did charitable work, offered swimming lessons, put on annual variety shows, organized basketball and bowling teams, and planned dinner dances and country outings. Such company-sponsored programs were popular with many Scovill workers, who used them for leisure-time activities and the pursuit of both homosocial and heterosocial relationships. In 1918, for example, the cost office at Scovill staged a dinner dance for men and women in the company cafeteria, at which "everyone on the force loosened up." But in 1930 only women from the main office "motored to Black Rock and the Wigwam Reservoir where they enjoyed a broiled steak dinner," and the *Scovill Bulletin* announced that "the girls have planned a series of these Saturday afternoon trips."[15]

Employers often relied on young women's friendships with each other to create productive work habits. More experienced workers instructed newcomers on how to do jobs, taught them the office ropes, and initiated work discipline. A manager of a firm in a small town in the Northwest had to recruit office workers from young women who had held summer jobs in the local cannery, where they could "chatter and gossip" as they worked. They had to be broken of habits like gabbing endlessly on the telephone and calling each other by their first names. This employer relied on more experienced women and the homosocial culture of which they were a part to "break in" the newly hired. "As much at sea in an office as a plumber would be at the court of St. James," he observed, "the thing to do is to turn the girl over to the girl at the next desk, who may have come to work only last week, but who knows what's necessary, . . . and she'll explain it." The Scovill Girls' Club proved to be a useful way for management to foster a sense of company loyalty among its women employees. President E. O. Goss addressed the club's annual banquet in 1930 and coyly assured his audience that they were indispensible to the company's production efforts: "What would we at Scovill's do if we had not our secretaries to run our business for us? I can see Miss Ella Patchen winking at me now!"[16]

But women's friendships also created supervision problems in the office. Battles against talking while working were constantly fought and usually lost by management; most office workers were spirited young women looking for peer relationships and social interaction. A memo to office workers at Scovill in 1922 reminded them not to "skip, jump or run in the office and hallways," and to forego "loud talking across desks," "unnecessary conversation," and "visits" to the desks of others.[17] Rose recalled the sporadic attempts of management at her insurance company to impose discipline: "Every once in a while they'd make a rule—pass a paper 'round that you couldn't talk to each other. . . . And then there was one spell that they . . . said you should call each other 'Miss,' instead of by your first name, but that didn't last very long." Rose, who supervised the card department, recalled that a misplaced card could throw the department into turmoil. But when workers went to the file, "they would take the card out and then talk to their friends and the card didn't get back in the right place."[18]

Office workers' peer activities spilled out of the office and into the street. Because most offices were in big cities, they gave women clericals, along with other "city girls" like saleswomen and waitresses, access to downtown and its panoply of stimulating activities. In Providence, Rhode Island, where a spate of office building accompanied the city's emergence as a reinvigorated regional commercial center at the turn of the century, banks, a telephone company, a newspaper, department stores, public utilities, and insurance companies provided thousands of jobs for women clerical workers. Along with the office buildings came elaborate theaters, a public library, and a YWCA. Department stores, dime stores, restaurants, movie theaters, and dance halls provided both lunchtime and early evening entertainment and an excuse to roam the streets.

The opportunity clerical workers had for working downtown made for an interesting breakdown of the boundaries between inside and outside the workplace.[19] Workplace relationships were carried out into the city, and urban activities influenced new ways of interacting. Both homosocial and heterosocial relationships could be enhanced by the city's amusements, and even the most respectable middle-class woman wanted to explore downtown, often with a girlfriend. Edith, who was the only woman clerk in the branch office of a car dealer, did not eat lunch with the two salesmen or the bookkeeper at her firm. Instead she met her friend, a secretary from another establishment. "We had a favorite place," she remembered. "We got a very nice lunch for fifteen cents and on Fridays they had special lobster salad."[20]

Many large employers provided their own lunchrooms, especially if their offices were on manufacturing sites or were inaccessible to commercial eateries. Employers probably hoped lunchrooms in urban firms would deter clerks from leaving the premises and extending the lunch hour to shop or stroll city streets. Some employment managers claimed that women were apt to skip lunch to save money for clothes, or wolf down a soda and a sandwich at a lunch counter; providing healthy meals, either free or at cost, ensured more energetic clerks.[21] Whether or not they ate in company cafeterias, exploration of the city in the company of girlfriends was a common theme among women who had worked as clerks.

Sometimes lunch involved high adventure. Florence, who worked at Brown and Sharpe in the teens, visited "Pie Alley" one day with her friends, an establishment alleged to have the best food in town but also off-limits for "proper young ladies." On their way back to work, "they spotted a fellow male office worker" and hid until he had returned to work. Reprimanded for coming in late, "they never returned to Pie Alley."[22] May, who worked at a big bank as an information clerk in the mid-twenties, ate lunch with her friends in the company cafeteria but would then "get up and go uptown" for a second "lunch." Although her supervisor was a stickler for being on time in the morning, she allowed May to take an extended lunch hour if she had "extra shopping" to do.

These lunches were important factors in a network of homosocial activites that cemented friendships and perhaps broke down, at least to some extent, class barriers as well. "There was a variety of backgrounds," recalled May, "but we didn't seem to . . . make any comparisons. . . . Some girls came from very humble circumstances, but they were all polite. . . . [We] might go out for lunch together and might go out to do an errand. . . . We always went up to the city, . . . and well, we used to have all the nice shops and stores."[23] Common styles of dress, manners, and workplace-centered activities helped to create an office culture that influenced women's lives even after they left their jobs; women sometimes kept in touch with their girlfriends from work for years.[24]

Ruth Shonle Cavan perceptively commented on just how significant urban expeditions and peer-based work culture in Chicago might be; they hastened young women's separation from their ethnic and family ties and drew them into an Americanized life-style based on shared leisure and workplace activities. The stores and entertainments surrounding urban offices tempted young women to cut into their salaries and spend money on themselves instead of contributing all or most of their earnings to the family. Who was to say whether a new pair of shoes was a necessity for the office or a consumerist indulgence? Conflicts over Americanization, Cavan thought, were particularly acute in immigrant families because parents expected daughters to form social ties within their own ethnic group, perceived the protection of their daughters' sexuality as one of their primary duties, and wanted their daughters to spend leisure time at home:

In cities especially, where lunch is eaten near the place of work and where new friendships are formed which may be contrary to national lines, the separation tends to be complete between the day-time life of the girl with its American customs and the evening and weekend life among her family and friends. As the girl makes friends at work or in evening clubs she becomes more and more an American; . . . she tends to dress, talk and act like the girls she meets while her attitudes and interests undergo a similar shift. The usual story is that the mother disapproves and is perhaps shocked at the things her daughter does and says. The daughter is placed under considerable strain, not only because of her attachment to her mother but also because she shares in her mother's attitudes and is often confused and uncertain regarding which course to follow.[25]

Whether Yankees or daughters of immigrants, women clerks were carving out a place for themselves in the American work force. They prided themselves on the education, competence, and mastery that their jobs demanded. They sometimes left their parents' households to live in the city and more frequently used the urban transportation system of trolleys, trains, and buses to get downtown. In the office middle-class and working-class women rubbed elbows, and married men and single women worked in the same spaces. Office manners and business English provided important character acquisitions that could be transported to new jobs and new positions. The workplace and the streets provided women clerks with opportunities for peer relationships and romantic attachments that excited them and disturbed their parents. Clerical workers dressed like movie stars and shopped on white-collar salaries, but their appearance should not deceive us; they were determined to make a mark for themselves in the world of business, and they did.

Women and the Question of Ambition

Some historians and social scientists have argued that youthful women saw their jobs as inherently different than male workers did. Women workers, these scholars argue, purposely sought out relatively undemanding jobs that would not interfere with their ultimate goal of finding a marriage partner and establishing a domestic life. Women workers supposedly found it difficult to extract themselves from the context of the family and make any significant investment in a workplace identity. In an extreme version of this view, one economist argues that women took up "unrewarding" occupations like clerical work because, unlike men, they were "not only unqualified but also uninterested" in seeking better jobs. While "men vied with each other" for good jobs, women were, in general, inherently uninterested in "self-advancement." Focused on "feminine goals" instead, a woman saw demanding jobs as "burdens that would interfere with her life work of caring for her family. The success, power, recognition and self which they would give to her were not what she sought—they were masculine by definition."[26]

This approach assumes, first, that there is only one kind of woman worker and only one woman worker identity. It also supposes that women's work attitudes were based on lack—lack of interest and ambition in particular—and that feminine goals are unlikely to include a self-identity based on pride in work and workplace roles. It assumes that all women share similar life-cyles based on the great divide of marriage and raises invidious possibilities for justifying the continued refusal to take women workers seriously.[27]

The idea that most women's intention to marry kept them focused on "feminine goals" having little to do with the workplace can be criticized in several ways. Like human capital theory, it tends to ignore discrimination in the work force and instead makes psychological motivation based on gender identity the chief predictor of behavior. We need not say that most women's life-cycles tend to be different than men's to claim that a single-minded conception of workplace culture is both reductionist and insulting to women. A series of simple questions highlights the reasons why. Were all men ambitious and all women unambitious? Did the simple desire for promotion automatically guarantee it, regardless of sex, class, and race? How could women enter "rewarding" occupations if their sex made them ineligible for them? How could women ask for promotions to jobs for which they were not "promotable"? Could women not be sexy and ambitious too? Couldn't women focus on their work and take up a domestic life as well? Was choosing clerical work irrational when clerical jobs offered limited mobility and rewards to the ambitious?

There is a danger here of falling into another set of false assumptions. In exploding the myth of a working women's culture based on lack, we would not want to argue that just because women had ambition and a sense of pride and mastery in work meant that women and men could enter the work force on the same terms. There were powerful ways in which sex discrimination, sexual stereotyping of jobs, and the cultural framing of men's and women's participation in the work force limited women's choices; ambition, in the face of these forces, could carry women only so far. Any analysis of the woman clerk's view of her own position must incorporate the reality that women's willpower (or agency) existed but was limited by the constraints of gender in the workplace and in American culture at large.[28]

The youthful woman clerk should be placed within a dynamic process where human agency abrades the constraints of the gender system but also struggles to transform it. Her sex and age severely limited her options. She was still likely to be in some kind of childlike relationship with her parents. Unless a "woman-identified" woman (a lesbian or a woman who lived with or preferred the company of women) she most likely expected to be married at some point. Whether heterosexually or homosocially inclined, the youthful woman clerk, defined in part by others as worker, sexual object, and dependent daughter, had to take in and integrate these definitions of herself in the heterosocial milieu of office life. She was likely to come to the workplace with a number of agendas: to fulfill her parents' expectations, to succeed in her job, to earn an adequate living, to demonstrate her attractiveness to men, and to pursue friendships with other women.

Ruth S. Cavan's 1927 study of business girls younger than thirty-one who attended YWCA clubs and summer camps in Chicago and other midwestern cities provides some intriguing glimpses of these aspects of youthful office women's work culture: ambition, connectedness to parents, and the working out of the confusing demands of workplace sexuality. Most of Cavan's subjects were seventeen or eighteen when they obtained their first clerical jobs. Although most lived at home, some resided in apartment houses and residential clubs for women. Many of those living away from home had traveled to Chicago from rural towns or smaller cities; they were often homesick and missed their mothers, to whom they wrote frequently.[29]

Whether living at home or not, nearly all contributed part of their salaries to their families, although there were some middle-class women whose parents did not expect them to do much more than bide time until they married. Most of these young middle-class women did not earn enough money to support themselves independently and so lived at home, but were thus free to spend all or most of the money they made upon themselves. Most clerks, however, faced the real demands of partially supporting themselves or members of their families. Some were daughters whose married siblings expected them to provide for parents because they were still single and living at home. Mildred, who had two married siblings, helped support a widowed mother and was saving money to help her open a dressmaking shop; the mother had supported herself and her three children in earlier years by sewing. Another young woman whose mother had "slaved for us children" while her "father was too lazy to work" was "working hard to repay my mother for all she has done for me."[30]

Despite their devotion to their mothers, many of these young women were making a sharp break with parents' ideas about respectable leisure-time activities and friendships. Even if their mothers supervised the spending of their incomes, Cavan found, many of the daughters carried on "their social activities with entire independence and perhaps along lines contrary to their mothers' wishes." These often included the new "cheap amusements" around which young people built activities: dancing, movies, nightclubs, amusement parks and eating in restaurants. These activities cemented both homosocial and heterosexual relationships. When asked which activities "hold you and your girl chum together," the YWCA women listed dancing, music, and shows first, then sports and clubs. Church and school followed, with work nearly at the bottom. Most of these women had begun to date men, and more than half said they had two or more dates a week.[31]

When asked to list their "chief problems," Cavan's young women revealed their youthful anxieties about physical appearance, personal qualities, and social relationships: "lack of self confidence" and "self-conciousness" drew the largest number of responses, and other "personal" attributes (like "not good-looking," "feeling of inferiority") also drew a fair number. Of those problems that might be grouped together as peer relationships and social activities—"lack of men friends," "not enough social life," "need of better clothes," "problems of sex conduct," "lack of girl friends," and "left out of parties, lonely,"—all made an appearance. Some listed the "smoking, drinking" and "unconventional behavior" of women they knew as a problem; not all young women were able to commit themselves to being flappers. Problems with housekeeping arrangements were fairly low on the list but included "how much to help parents financially," "health of parents," "homesickness," "quarrels at home," "too much supervision of parents," and "not appreciated at home." These young women were solving typical problems of teenagers and young adults: separating from their parents and becoming independent adults, negotiating relationships with peers, and exploring their sexuality. They were also doing their jobs at the same time.[32]

Cavan thought that youthful workers' emphasis on peer culture meant they were not very devoted to their jobs. For the very young women clerical worker, Cavan argued, "the job is an economic necessity, a burden filling the day with which she would dispense, if she could." Cavan saw the break between the "younger" and the "older" clerical worker as a definitive one. The woman approaching her late twenties was likely to develop a new seriousness around her job: "She faces a future in which she knows office work will be the dominant occupation. The temporary aspect of office work . . . has gone. . . . in all probability she will never marry. . . . It is then through her work that the older girl expects to realize whatever ambition of service and status she hopes for."[33]

Yet Cavan's assessment was surely too dichotomous. Her own analysis of the daydreams and problems of young business women showed that they cared about their work and were anxious to succeed. When asked to list "what kind of daydreams you repeatedly have," young women said they most often had fantasies of marriage and a home of their own, but these were closely followed in frequency by dreams of business or professional success. When asked to list "what things have happened since you began to work have given you the most happiness," success at work was listed nearly twice as frequently as meeting new friends. Cavan's findings corroborated those of the psychologist Lorine Pruette, whose work on daydreams of the adolescent girl revealed similar fantasies about enjoying both marriage and success at work as a part of adult life. Not yet at the point where they felt forced to choose between these fantasies, young women continued to have them both. Neither Cavan or Pruette felt very comfortable with what they saw as an apparent contradiction and warned of the "reality" yet to come. In Pruette's own words, "these figures . . . suggest a considerable maladjustment between desire and actuality, and . . . we see potentialities of disappointment and emotional conflict."[34] But by looking at these dreams in a less judgmental way we can underscore the essentially "modernist" point of view of the younger generation of the 1920s. Most young women had, eventually, to adjust to the realities of the marriage bar and the demands of young families, but their inner lives showed that they did not do so without a sense of loss. They were entirely capable of being flappers and responsible—and ambitious—working women at the same time.

Concerns about work were important themes in these women's lives. Cavan's study listed the two most frequently cited problems of young clerks: "not enough advance in work" and "lack of money." About one in three women in Cavan's survey cited these as problems. About midway down the list came "overwork" and "disagreements with fellow employees." Near the bottom were "domineering people at work" and "women employees or supervisors." The list demonstrated that most young women recognized the crux of their exploitation as workers; they were confined to low-paying jobs with little chance of promotion and were frequently asked to work too hard. Supervisors in general, and women supervisors in particular, while the source of some irritation, were not the main cause of their dissatisfaction at work. Instead, lack of appreciation for the effort they put in and inadequate monetary rewards loomed largest in most women's complaints. They thought of themselves as competent workers deserving proper rewards.

Satisfaction with the work they did and enjoyment of a period of relative independence—from parents, from husbands—crept into older women's accounts of their lives as young clerical workers. Some women at least toyed with the idea of not marrying at all. Elaine, who worked as an office manager in Rhode Island until her marriage in 1926 at the age of twenty-eight, smiled when her granddaughter asked if she had been worried about being an old maid. "She replied that she was doing just fine the way she was. She worked at a job that she enjoyed and brought home a good salary every week. She was well off for a single girl and could support herself, without the help of a husband." Josephine lived in a city apartment and sent money home to her parents. "They . . . knew I considered remaining single. . . . I liked working in the business world and I was very good at my job." Many of Edna's friends wondered "if she was ever going to marry," and although she "liked the thought of one day marrying, . . . she liked to work also."[35]

Women were initially hired for office work partly because the marriage bar could be applied to them and thus prevent them from exercising ambition. Women continued to harbor ambition anyway, however, but in a context that reflected the limitations placed on their gender by the sexual division of labor. The nexus of complaint, satisfaction, ambition, and sexual objectification that characterized the work of many women in their jobs showed up in the account of a young stenographer who was about twenty-three in 1925. She had been hired to take legal dictation at a law firm despite her lack of a high school diploma. She fitted her employer's requirements in other ways, for she understood "that the girls must be young, and that they [must] have never worked before. . . . He wants to train them himself. Personal appearance is important here." She found her job to be "very strenuous" and over the preceding year had done extra work on a long case in addition to her regular job. She did not think it fair for her employer to send a bill for stenographic services to the client for $500 while she was paid nothing extra for putting in overtime. "At night [she] would cry . . . because of the severe nervous strain." A $100 bonus at the end of the year had compensated somewhat, and in general she liked her job because she was "pretty much her own boss." Her employer allowed her time off when she needed it, and she "feels that her employer is very proud of her ability, for she has got on as far with much less education than the other secretaries whom he has had previously."[36] Ambition, mastery, and pride in work were clearly in evidence here, but they would never end the patronizing relationship that most clerical workers had with their employers, nor result in the kinds of rewards in promotion and responsibility that men could envision.

The Labor Segmentation of Women in Office Work

In the office world of the 1920s, the woman clerical worker was most often engaged in comparing herself with other women. It was true that some women held responsible and highly paid positions (especially in comparison to other women). The women's rights movement endorsed women's access to these positions and also made optimistic promises about the changing nature of women's position in society. In moderate political circles, anyway, the 1920s were optimistic times, and the juxtaposition of hopeful ambition and the frequent discouragement of discrimination of women workers posed a bewildering array of exciting questions. Lack of individual progress might easily be attributed to personal failure. Discrimination in employment might be difficult to recognize; self-blame or blame of one's co-workers might seem more rational an explanation than the recognition that, contrary to all the upbeat evidence, there were deep and abiding prejudices against giving most women better jobs. There were fierce debates in the 1920s over whether or not married women or mothers should work, whether ambition in a woman was unbecoming, or whether differences between the sexes were biologically rooted or merely the product of socialization. These issues made their way into clerical workers' thoughts about their work, their self-identity, and their lives.

Employers both contributed to and capitalized on the confusion of the situation by maintaining a maze of seemingly impenetrable rules, spoken and unspoken, about women's employment. A tangle of job duties, titles, and salaries varied both within firms and among firms. While many employers refused to hire or retain married women, the fact that others sometimes did so made for inconsistency and unpredictability. Unmarried workers sometimes resented married ones, who supposedly had husbands to support them. Older women, whom the culture at large suggested were unattractive and unappealing, might be resentful of the flattering attention paid to younger women. By placing older women in charge of younger ones, employers tended to make different generations of women the targets of each others' workplace resentment rather than the system itself. Or women might blame their lack of mobility on themselves for somehow picking the wrong kind of education, the wrong occupational field, or the wrong job. Age, class, marital status, and individual competition might all pit clerical workers against each other.

Class difference was surely among the most important ways of segmenting office workers. While evidence of middle-class resentment of working-class women appears in the advice literature and in personal accounts (chapter 7), the importance of class difference and its effect on conflict or cooperation among women in the office remains difficult to assess precisely. Levels of education are really the only available aggregate indication of the class status of clerical workers, but it remains a rough measure. College-educated women were certainly middle class, and most younger grammar school-educated women working class, but proportions of both of these segments in office work were relatively small by 1930. In fact, a smaller proportion than ever of women entering clerical work had only grammar school educations.[37] The growing tendency was for both working-class and middle-class women to attend high school; about 75 percent of Ethel Erickson's 1931-32 nationwide sample of large offices had some years of secondary schooling.[38]

Because more and more working-class children were attending high school, secondary education alone was not indicative of class. High school education was, to some extent, a force that eased class distinction because it enabled working-class women to gain entree to workplaces with middle-class environs and manners. Although I can only speculate on the idea, it seems likely that in accommodating themselves to middle-class manners working-class women in clerical work tended to lose their hold on a working-class identity. Ambivalence about class identity probably muted union activity and created conflicting loyalties. In no other significant occupation for women were the English-speaking working class and the middle class so likely to rub shoulders in the same workplaces.

Some aspects of class position in the office workplace can be pinned down more precisely. Levels of education were positively correlated with the kind of clerical job a woman had and the salary she earned. Vocational guidance experts claimed that women who left school before graduating from high school fared poorly in the office and that the grammar school-educated were especially likely to fail. The truth of the matter, however, was that women who left school before graduating usually improved their salaries and their positions over time, although most continued to enter clerical work as machine operators or typists instead of as stenographers or secretaries. A sample of women seeking work as typists in Cleveland showed that more than half had not graduated from high school. The less education the Cleveland typist had, the longer she was likely to remain a typist; high school and college graduates had greater mobility out of typing and into stenography or bookkeeping.[39] However, working-class women with limited educations were able, over time, to move into better clerical positions. A woman who left high school in 1906 first worked as a saleswoman for $6 a week, moved on to stenography in department stores, and then to the stenographic department of Western Electric in 1916 at $18 a week. She took "advanced English" at the corporation's evening school and eventually became secretary to a vice president; her salary in 1924 was $45 a week. A former factory worker who had a grammar school education and attended business college began as a stenographer at $6 a week at the turn of the century. After holding her position for four years, she changed to another job at a higher salary, and then in 1909 moved to her present job. By 1926, after seventeen years, she made about $190 a month, a salary that put her in the upper ranks of clerical wage earners.[40]

The middle-aged woman with a college education was especially likely to do well in office work. But age (or, more precisely, longevity on the job) was a more significant predictor of salary than education, even college education. Up to a point, the older the woman, the higher her salary. While a woman with an incomplete high school education in New York with one to three years of experience made $80 a month, $8 less than a high school graduate and $13 less than a college graduate with similar experience, by the time she had five to nine years of experience she had increased her monthly salary by $31 to $111.[41] Over time, years of experience tended to override lack of education, and the majority of clerical workers with some high school education found themselves in roughly the same salary categories (Table 10).

Although most clerical workers shared the common experience of attending some high school, they were becoming more differentiated by age. The majority were twenty-five and under, and clerical workers were, on average, younger than workers in other occupations like manufacturing and domestic service. But during the 1920s the proportion of women over twenty-five at work in offices increased, and those under twenty declined. By 1930 the average woman clerical worker was twenty to twenty-four years old. However, those twenty-five to forty and older were a significant category; they made up as much as 43 percent of the total. As a general rule, these "older" women held the best jobs.[42]

Categorizing workers according to age, education, and class helped employers to prevent women workers from finding common ground. It need not be argued that these practices were entirely conspiratorial or even very self-conscious to claim that they worked nonetheless. One of the reasons they were so effective was that when combined with the marriage bar and ideas about women's sexuality, they reflected deep-seated ideas about how women's participation in the work force should be constructed. The marriage bar was not only a rational economic device for making women clerks into "temporarily permanent" workers; it was also a cultural symbol that heightened women's difference from men, women's differences from each other, and diverted attention from women's real position in the office work force.

Marriage: The Great Divide?

The marriage bar not only resulted in the firing of many women upon marriage, but it also rationalized lower wages for women and their exclusion from prestigious positions. Whatever the importance of the marriage bar as an economic principle, it was being applied more erratically after World War I. By 1930 more women who were married or had been married worked in offices than ever before; roughly 20 percent of all office workers were married by 1930, whereas only about 10 percent had been in 1910.[43] There were many reasons for this change. In an expansive economy, social attitudes toward working wives were being transformed, with much public discussion of the topic in every conceivable forum. Although working mothers of young children were probably rare in most of the middle class in the 1920s, shorter work days and changes in household technology made it possible to envision the daring role of working mother. Not all wives had children. Some women were childless; others were obviously using birth control, delaying childbirth, or limiting the size of their families. Divorces were on the rise, adding divorced women to widows and the never-married in the total number of women heads of households in need of financial support.[44]

Proscriptions against the employment of married women were in flux. Ethel Erickson's 1931 study showed that about half of the firms surveyed in New York, Chicago, and Atlanta said they would hire married women as new employees, and about 75 percent claimed they allowed women who married while on the job to stay at work.[45] Shortages of experienced clerical labor probably motivated some of these more liberal policies, but some firms with more progressive personnel management policies had also begun to see married women as a pool of experienced workers whose long-term employment would be beneficial to company interests. When the Henry Doherty Company modernized its personnel policies and eliminated the marriage bar, it found women to be more stable employees. "Women in business get married," claimed the personnel manager, "but they do not necessarily resign afterward." At Aetna Insurance Company, personnel director Marion Bills claimed that there was "no rule precluding women from working after marriage," but she did not evidently champion the employment of married women as new hires.[46]

Despite these more liberal but erratically applied policies, married women continued to disguise their marital status in order to obtain new jobs or to keep the ones they had. One Bureau of Vocational Information respondent noted that "although I am married, it is not known at the office. After my marriage, I did not work for a year. I decided to go back to work, and found it almost impossible to find a position when I admitted that I was married. Finally I used my maiden name, and found work without any trouble. I think I am justified in this. Most firms refuse to employ married women if they can get an unmarried one to do the work." A University of Wisconsin graduate ruefully reported that she had been fired from her stenography job at International Harvester, even though the firm did not officially refuse to employ married women: "It became necessary to reduce the staff during the depression following postwar prosperity, and, to quote, since 'I was married' they felt I ought to be the person to leave. Confidentially, they also said to my employer they believed a woman's place is 'in the home or behind the typewriter.'"[47]

Banks and insurance companies remained relatively inflexible on the issue of hiring married women workers, which observers in Hartford, for instance, thought had a dampening effect on the city's wages paid to women.[48] Public utilities, mail order houses, and direct mail establishments, which, coincidently had large amounts of machine work and paid the lowest wages, were more likely to employ married women. At the Public Service Electric and Gas Company of Newark, one efficiency expert reported that nearly one-third of the women workers in the billing department were married, and that married women earned the highest efficiency bonuses. The expert claimed that "married employees approach their work with a feeling of responsibility and earnestness which results favorably both for the employees and for management."[49] Employers preferred to hire married men according to the same rationale. Frank Rowland, a life insurance employment expert, predicted in 1929 that there would be "an increasing tendency toward the utilization of married women in office work."[50] With apartment living and the sale of electrical appliances on the rise, he thought young married women's domestic duties were minimal, and at least part-time employment of married women might be an option. The telephone company experimented with employing married women workers as temporary employees in the 1920s while it was converting to the dial system so the company would have more flexibility in firings once the conversion had been made.[51] For those who chose to do so, ignoring the marriage bar in certain situations might provide real economic gains.

How individual clerical workers were affected by the marriage bar can be seen in the sample of Rhode Island women clerical workers, all of whom married in their twenties. A few accepted the bar as a moral imperative but most expressed ambivalence, and some experienced a profound sense of loss as they left their jobs or were fired. When Ellen was married in 1929 she left her job at the telephone company and later told her interviewer that it would be all right for "a woman to work if it's necessary but if possible she should stay home with her family." Edith left the main office of the Davis Motor Car Company in 1915 to be married. She claimed that she had considered going out to look for another position, but had been dissuaded by the disapproval of her mother-in-law. May left her job at the Rhode Island Hospital Trust Bank in 1930 to marry, but later found that she missed both her job and her workplace friends. "When I was married . . . I would walk downtown," she recalled. "Oh, I wanted to go into the bank the worst way and see if I couldn't get a position. But women didn't work after they were married then. . . . It wasn't allowed."[52]

Gertrude, who had worked as a typist and filer at an insurance firm since 1915, was fired when she married in 1923. Although she understood there to be a rule—"the women had to be single; once you got married, you lost your jobs"—she felt ambivalent about leaving her position. She had plenty of work to do at home but thought she and her husband could have used her salary. Martha Ashness Doyle was fired by the Rhode Island Insurance Company when she was married in 1924, but suspected she had somehow alienated her boss. She knew a few married women who were working at the firm and would have liked to have been one of them. A year later she had a child and then suffered a nervous breakdown. In the 1930s she returned to part-time work in a department store after her husband lost his small trucking business and suffered a heart attack. Harriet planned to keep her job at the telephone company when she married in 1923, but the company refused to take her back after a strike in the same year because, she thought, she had been active in the union. Alice, who worked at a large bank, recalled that clerks "felt it was . . . unnecessary to leave because you got married. But that was the rule and everybody just took it."[53]

Despite their marriages, nearly a third of these Rhode Island women kept their jobs or found other ones. Rose, who remained childless, had the lengthiest continuous work history, stretching from 1920 to 1955, with thirty years of that time spent at Amica Insurance. Amica allowed women who married to keep their jobs unless their husbands were also employed by the firm. Because many couples met at work, Rose recalled, newly married women were frequently unable to keep working. Grace had to leave her comptometer operative job at Brown and Sharpe when she married a co-worker there in the teens, but she didn't have children for awhile and was "tired of being home without any work." She easily found another job through the comptometer bureau, but when the firm went under in the slump of 1920, she stayed at home and began her family. Rachel, who was considered to be indispensible in her job as bookkeeper and secretary in a small firm, kept her job until her second child was born; Josephine, a private secretary in a textile mill, worked until her first baby arrived.[54] An extreme example of this sort emerged in the BVI study of 1925: A woman with an eighth-grade education worked for a law firm as a bookkeeper and kept her job after her marriage in 1917. She remained at work at the "insistence of [a] senior partner" when she became pregnant. She was only out of the office for three or four months, worked on the books at home, and had her mother watch the baby when she returned.[55]

Employers who were opposed to hiring married women gave a variety of explanations, many of which focused on the transference of the married woman's allegiance from job and employer to home and husband. Employers seemed to feel that a married woman would not be as devoted a clerk because husband and household duties might diffuse her interest, or they anticipated that she might suddenly become pregnant and leave. Such comments often centered around private secretaries or stenographers, whose spousal relationships with bosses or dictators were well known. The office wife should not be in a potentially bigamous situation. If married, said one boss, "her interests are divided. She will not stay late because she must get her husband's meals." He had been particularly outraged by a married secretary whose husband called for her at night; "I couldn't stand that," he reported.[56]

The difference marriage seemed to imply in women's sexual availability was part of this employer's discomfort. Both the complaints of some secretaries that they felt "married" to their jobs and the declarations by others that total devotion to an employer was a requisite of the good secretary developed into cultural iconography: the secretary as a dutiful wife, willing and able to work overtime if necessary, putting her employer's needs before her own. Her physical appearance and attitude toward men seemed to undergo a mysterious change once the clerk "belonged" to another man. The manager of one employment service defined the difficulty in placing married women: "A man wants an unmarried woman of attractive appearance. He wants her to add to the general attractiveness of his office. . . . a married woman's attitude toward men who come to the office is not the same as that of an unmarried woman. They are far more indifferent and casual than the married women. They do not make them want to come again!" But the sexual dynamics between employer and secretary were equally important: "the employer usually prefers the attitude of the unmarried woman toward himself."[57]

Other critiques of the married woman focused on her economic independence. Her husband's employment, theoretically, made it possible for her to quit and find another job or to laze the day away, secure in the knowledge that her husband could support her. One employer interviewed by the BVI thought the married woman did not have the same "economic necessity . . . to work . . . therefore she has not the same incentive to 'make good' on the job."[58] Mary Schauffler, an astute sociologist, thought there was some truth to the greater independence and indifference of married working women, especially those who held jobs not just from "economic necessity, but to keep themselves comfortably busy." It was this group, she thought, "that makes the trouble for the married woman who has to work. Employers say they are too independent in their attitude, they are apt frequently to be absent and late, that they often cause jealousy among the girls in the office because of their better clothes and that they leave abruptly." Occasionally a married woman expressed ideas about work that confirmed these views: "At present I am married (and thank heaven! supported) and freelancing. . . . A married woman who is a secretary can usually get a temporary job at any time. The work is not as nerve-wracking as canvassing or selling, but the main disadvantage, I believe, is the fact that employers usually feel that they can keep a secretary overtime at their convenience."[59] The ideal woman clerk was captive in her job and vulnerable to whatever working conditions her employer sought to impose.

Employers of the 1920s used the idea of the marriage bar to structure women's position in the office but were ambivalent about the actual presence of married women. Women workers were also ambivalent. When women stenographers and secretaries interviewed by the BVI in 1924 were asked what they thought about the suitability of married women at work in the office, many single women declared their disapproval. The reasons given frequently echoed those given by employers. A secretary who had left high school in 1906 was "prejudiced against married women because of their attitude of independence. If not self-supporting, they do not feel the pressure of the need to work and for that reason are apt not to be so dependable." A single woman who had been working since 1911 did not think a woman should work if her husband could support her: "I think most married women holding such a position do so for a love of fine clothes, etc." Another single woman had "a strong prejudice against married women working" because "women who keep house are not as alert on the job as single women."[60]

The most frequent complaint of single women was that married women took positions away from women who were truly dependent upon their salaries for supporting not only themselves, but also, frequently, parents and siblings. Many single women thought that the temporary interest of some married women in their work and the supplemental nature of others' incomes brought wages below those required for independent living. "I do not believe," said one single woman, "that married women should continue in the business field—and, particularly, they should not be permitted to occupy the better positions, taking them from single girls."[61] The circumstances of many married women seemed to allow them to be less interested than single women in their work, in promotion, and in fair wages. The result might be damaging to the single woman's efforts to improve herself. One single woman summarized the fears of many: "If a woman is living with her husband and he also is earning, secretarial work is a splendid field . . . , as her salary combined with that of her husband would make a more comfortable living. This fact is causing some consternation among single women because the number of married women in this field is increasing every year, and because she can or does work for a more or less low wage, it is lowering the salaries of all secretaries."[62]

When women who were married and worked in offices talked about their decision to stay on the job, boredom with housework, the need to earn an income, and the desire for meaningful work all surfaced as motives. One young married woman who worked in a doctor's office found that "as far as I can judge neither my home or my work have suffered. It seems to be an ideal combination for me with only a husband and a two room apartment."[63] An employee at a Los Angeles high school had a variety of reasons for working:

> I enjoy work and find it keeps me from fretting about trivial household matters. It keeps my mind active and interested in other things besides the price of butter and the comings and goings of my neighbors. The money I am making is helping buy a home and get a good start in life. Of course it does not leave much time for household duties, but in my position I find plenty of time to prepare three meals a day at home, and do all my work except the heavy washing, and find it has not impaired my health in the slightest. Of course I do not intend to work indefinitely, but only until we get a good start.[64]

Some married women with children stressed the role that work played in their sense of self-worth and their ability to adjust to domesticity and motherhood. A 1900 high school graduate had been married twice and taken some time off after each wedding, but returned to work even though she had a child. She moved up by examination through the ranks of the Chicago civil service to be secretary to the superintendent of the Board of Education. She saw "no reason why a married woman who has a housekeeper should not continue in her position as secretary. . . . the mental inactivity of housework after regular work outside the home is very difficult to bear."[65] A woman with a college education who left the work force in 1923 to have a second child quickly returned to work. She found the full-time work schedule too rigid, however, and had since combined substitute stenography work by the day with a successful public stenography business in her home. She thought working gave her "an opportunity to keep in touch with outside affairs and thinking people" and freed her from the "drudgery of housework, because of an ability to earn twice as much per hour as is necessary to pay someone to do the housework. I see more of my husband," she claimed, "than when I am not working."[66]

The marriage question not only produced important divisions between married and unmarried workers doing the same jobs, it was also a double-edged sword in the workplace, undermining the full participation of both single and married women. It had as negative an effect on women who did not marry as on those who eventually did. The logic of the marriage bar was that all "ordinary" women eventually married and left the work force. That made the older single woman an aberration; she was, theoretically, by the age of twenty-five or thirty, supposed to be safely tucked away in a man's house. Not only was her presence in the work force vaguely illegitimate, but she also suffered directly from the idea that women could not be promoted because they married, that low wages for women would do because women never had to support themselves for very long. As time went on her salary was likely to stagnate, and she was rarely able to move beyond the upper limits of office supervisor, secretary, or head bookkeeper.

The effects of the expectation that all women eventually married was particularly invidious for the older single woman clerk, who was especially vulnerable to economic need. It was most likely true that she had access to a smaller family wage than the woman who was married and worked or the younger woman who continued to live at home with her parents.[67] Some single women were supporting dependents at home: parents, siblings, and if divorced or widowed, children of their own. Although it is impossible to know how many, some of these single women were surely not heterosocially or heterosexually inclined; they may have been lesbians or women who were single and who lived with another woman or who spent most of their time with other women. Elise Leisring went to work as a clerk at Scovill Manufacturing in 1918 and retired in 1943, when it was reported that "she and her sister have devoted much time to developing their lovely old house into a very attractive, comfy abode. She loves to entertain her friends there around the outdoor fireplace in the backyard where they roast frankfurters and corn ears and have a jolly time."[68] By the time they reached the age of thirty-five, nearly half of a sample of 795 BVI respondents did not live with either a husband, their parents, or relatives (Table 11). Elliott and Manson's study of business and professional women, about 42 percent of whom were office workers and most of whom were older than thirty-five, found that about half of all those who were single lived on their own, most in their own apartments or homes.[69] To many women in this age group the critical indicator of a working woman's identity was not her marital status, but her role as a breadwinner. Nearly any woman who discussed the marriage question agreed that the married woman in need of support should be allowed to work, but single woman wanted incomes to reflect their financial needs as well.

Working-class women clericals faced a particularly thorny dilemma in sorting out their views on the issue of married women holding jobs. They were less likely to have high school and college educations than middle-class women, and more likely to have the lowest-paying jobs. They were less likely to have parents or other relatives who could cushion the effect of their low wages. All of these factors might be presumed to push them toward negative views on the issue of married women's work, but these were also the women who might be most likely to want to continue working

Table 11.
Household Status of Bureau of Vocational Information
Respondents According to Age

Ages of Respondents (Total N = 795)	17-24 180	25-34 409	35 and up 206
Percent living alone	8.0	18.6	28.0
Percent living with parents or other relatives	75.5	56.0	46.0
Percent living with husband	8.0	11.4	7.0
Percent living with friends	7.3	11.0	14.0
Other	1.2	3.0	5.0

Source: Questionnaires filled out by stenographers and secretaries for the Bureau of Vocational Information, 1924-25. BVI Collection, Schlesinger Library, Radcliffe College.

due to economic necessity. During the 1930s, when unemployment for everyone reached crisis proportions, the firing of married women, especially from better jobs, was considered by nearly everyone to be a partial solution to the problem of mass unemployment for men and single women. These sentiments had appeared even earlier. One essay writer of the 1920s cited the "amusing incident" of a telelphone employees council that asked the management to "demote all married women supervisors, whose husbands could support them, asserting that they tended to remain longer with the company, thus decreasing chances of promotion for those lower down."[70]

Lively debates took place in union and socialist periodicals in the 1920s over the issue of married women's employment. While most traditional male trade unionists were opposed to it, growing numbers of married women workers articulated a self-consciously feminist point-of-view and demanded the right to paid employment outside the home. As the historian Maureen Greenwald demonstrates, they were claiming a space for work not only because their families needed the money but also because they thought women had the right to seek meaningful work beyond the sphere of domesticity. Nonetheless, what Greenwald calls the "moral economy" of the working-class was always in the background; during times of grave unemployment, work should be spread around to as many families as possible.[71]

Just how powerful this sentiment could be emerged in a debate launched by union workers at the Long Island Railroad (LIRR) in 1928. The railroads had run far more smoothly under consolidated government management during the war than under the prewar system of chaotic duplication and competition. Once returned to private control, railroad managements built on the centralizing effects of government management by promoting streamlining, mergers, and cuts in operating costs. But the railroads were in for some tough times. Declines in both passenger and freight traffic due to the popularity of automobiles, the growth of trucking companies, and a national highway system cut severely into profits. Some roads went under and others faced serious cutbacks. These developments created depressionlike conditions for railroad workers well before the collapse of the stock market in 1929; thousands of railway employees were fired between 1920 and 1930. Women in particular were targets of these firings, partly because strong unions tried to protect the jobs of men. Nonetheless, large numbers of women continued to work in railroad offices. Between 1920 and

1926 the large railroads, according to the Women's Bureau, fired thirty thousand women; about fifty-one thousand women clerks remained.[72]

In 1928 employee representatives of the LIRR, whose ranks had already faced two years of department consolidations and firings, asked that the company adopt a new policy regarding the employment of married women. Married women should be fired, the only exceptions being those whose husbands were permanently disabled.[73] The LIRR, a subsidiary of the Pennsylvania Railroad, tentatively agreed to the request and in so doing unleashed a flurry of editorial-writing in major city newspapers. These editorials almost all took a progressive view, arguing that many married women needed their incomes, that there was no evidence they made less able employees, that many had years of seniority, and that one of the logical consequences of women's voting rights was the right to be employed, whatever one's marital status.[74] The Atlantic City Business and Professional Women's Club, which was said to have included many married women who were "active in business and the professions," resolved to oppose "such discrimination." It "branded the railroad's action as 'un-American and not conducive to the best interests of women in business,'" and argued that firing married women would undermine the seniority rights of all workers.[75] In the face of such adverse publicity, the Pennsylvania Railroad claimed by 1929 that the clerks had withdrawn their request.[76]

But the Pennsylvania Railroad continued to receive communications from disgruntled employees and stockholders over the employment of married women as firings continued and the country slipped into the depression. In 1931 Marion Mixner, who had worked in the accounting department for seven years, was laid off indefinitely. "Being an orphan and entirely dependent on my own resources," she complained, "I have seriously felt the loss of my position." She was irate that she had been let go when there were married women in her department who might have been laid off instead, even though they had held their positions longer: "Simply because we were not born a few years sooner are we to be deprived of making a living, while girls with a few more years of service to their credit, with husbands, continue to gratify all of their selfish desires for luxuries?" She claimed to know "at least a dozen of these couples" in the accounting department.[77]

Evidently appeals like Mixner's had some effect. While few railroads openly admitted to discriminating against married women already in their employ, a protest distributed to railroad executives by the National Federation of Business and Professional Women's Clubs in 1933 revealed that "where it was ascertained . . . that married women . . . did not need their salaries to enable them to live in comfort, they had been temporarily relieved from duty in order that their positions might be given to persons whose need was considered greater."[78]

When thinking about conflicts between single women and married women it should be kept in mind that people are probably more likely to air complaints than satisfactions, and that positive relationships are usually taken for granted and rarely discussed. Most married and single women probably worked alongside each other happily and cooperatively. But the Pennsylvania Railroad case revealed how tenuous the married woman's legitimacy in the office was once unemployment and declining wages began to cut into men's and single women's opportunities for earning a living. In any event, getting workers to focus on the marital status of individual women rather than on the marriage bar itself was always a victory for management.

Flappers and Matrons: Age Segmentation in Office Work

Women clerical workers might be divided from each other because of their marital status. Age segmentation also fed on and reenforced marital status difference. Most clerical workers were "young"—that is, twenty-five and younger. But as many as 40 percent of all women clerical workers were "older"—over the age of twenty-five. Important differences separated the two groups. Younger women were most likely to be the typists, stenographers, and machine workers. Older women were more likely than younger women to be senior stenographers, clerks, bookkeepers, secretaries, and office managers. Younger women found that it paid to change jobs; older women had to be far more careful about the circumstances under which they moved in order to maintain equivalent salaries and positions.

Younger women, unless confirmedly homosocial or lesbian, were still likely to be operating under the assumption that they would someday marry. They might assume they would be leaving the work force permanently, or at least for some years, in order to have children. Their own paid work was not the only way in which they envisioned earning a household living, nor clerk the only definition of themselves they envisioned in the future. Most of them lived at home and did not yet face significant demands on their incomes. They were likely to be part of a youth culture that stressed romance, dating, and peer friendships.

Younger and older women usually worked in close contact. Younger women were most likely to be supervised by older women; older women supervisors frequently found that governing younger women was as high as they could go in the office hierarchy. If planning on marriage, young women might be likely to view older single women as "old maids," reminiscent of the public school teachers they had perhaps suffered under in high school. Older women might view younger ones as undisciplined, frivolous, and overly interested in men.

Many women who worked after age twenty-five were not only unmarried but perhaps also purposefully thought of themselves as single women or career women. Some shared homes and apartments with other women. This difference in marital status and sexual identification was not a minor one; women who were interested in men and who intended to marry might be likely to view unmarried older women as a different breed. And the tendency of some employers and co-workers to evaluate women on the basis of their age and appearance added to resentments and confusions on both sides of the sexual orientation difference.

Whether married or not, older women were more likely to view themselves as primarily and permanently workers. For nearly all women thirty and over, issues like promotion, higher salaries, and a more professional identity for clerical workers were of real concern. With their intimate relationships in fairly stable order, they were relatively disinterested in dating and romance and had more time for leisure activities like women's clubs. They wanted to set themselves off from younger women in ways that indicated their "career woman" status.

The irony was that the woman over thirty, despite her greater experience and career commitment, was at a distinct disadvantage in the workplace. After thirty "it is increasingly difficult to place her," said one New York City employment agency director, "except in a few instances where her work is more executive in nature. But most of these positions are filled either by promotion within the concern or people are secured through employees already employed—not by the agencies." Another agency manager corroborated this view: "A high school graduate reaches her maximum after six or seven years experience in one job. [She] is equally difficult to place as is the woman who has held a large number of positions in this time; for in the first case employers fear that she is set in her ways, and in the latter that she is unstable." She claimed that it was difficult to place the thirty-year-old woman, and thirty-five years of age was the "outer limit." Another agency agreed that "almost all women over thirty are barred, a few accepted up to thirty-five, provided she does not show her age."[79]

The sexual objectification of the youthful clerk in both the workplace and in American popular culture was part of the perception that made women over thirty "too old." Employment agencies reiterated how important physical appearance and youth were for the women they tried to place. The ideal candidate for the more responsible positions in clerical work, they agreed, was a single, attractive woman in her twenties. Some employers were explicit about the characteristics they expected clerical workers to have. One placement bureau manager thought appearance was "100% important before all other qualifications." Her clients wanted "the white skinned girls with thin and straight mouth. The prettier they are, the better their chances." One executive who was interviewed said that the secretary "must be attractive and add to the general appearance of the office." After observing the clerical workers in his firm, the interviewer concluded the executive was "not alone in this desire—all are young and attractive to look at—and certainly appearance must be quite heavily weighted in the selection of secretaries in this concern."[80]

Feminist social scientists found discrimination against older women in the office to be nearly universal. There were, of course, ways in which hiring younger women saved management money. Youthful employees were assumed to be living at home, thus justifying low wages, while older women (at least until the depression) had to be paid some kind of periodic minimal increase in line with their greater experience and self-supporting status. Employers in New York State told one investigator that accident insurance was higher for older women than for younger ones, and that potential pension costs of older women were ones they did not want to assume. But the investigator concluded that these objections to the hiring of women were easily dismissed and that the chief objection to hiring older women was "psychological rather than ... practical."[81]

There were some niches in the office where women over thirty could find better hope of employment not based so emphatically on the youthful ideal. The Equitable Employment Service thought age and marriage restrictions did not count as much in accounting, statistical work, and bookkeeping as in stenography and secretarial work. In Cleveland, for example, the point seemed to be verified; bookkeepers were, on average, older and less likely to be single than typists and stenographers. Older college-educated women, who sometimes had specialized skills in foreign languages, mathematics, or statistics, were considered candidates for more technical work or positions in personnel management and were thought to be easier to place. Professional offices, colleges, and small firms were said to be not as likely to bar older or married women. Civil services, with their generally more straightforward classification and examination systems, allowed some older women to achieve upward mobility. There were occasional employers who seemed to prefer older women, and widows were sometimes considered to be especially good candidates.[82]

Interest in hiring widows confirmed, in fact, the reason employers "preferred" single women; the employer wanted a "husbandless" woman, not necessarily one without children, who would be devoted to her work and dependent on it for a living. Gussie O. Edwards had been widowed in Philadelphia in 1912 and left with three small children to support. She headed west for California and joined the Los Angeles County Civil Service Commission in 1913, making steady progress through the system by taking examinations and compiling a good work record. She was appointed chief examiner of the Los Angeles County Civil Service Commission after her boss, to whom she had been secretary, died in 1925. A BVI interviewer noted with approval that one of her children was now in college, her other two were nearly through high school, and she owned her own home and car.[83]

Despite the example of Edwards's success, it was entirely possible for older women, especially those forty and older, to end up in fairly miserable circumstances in their last years of employment. Many women did not work at firms with pension benefits, and even if they did, these were pitiably small. If a woman had no children, relatives, or friends to fall back upon, she faced diminishing chances of ever leaving the work force. The physical skills required for most kinds of clerical work—good eyesight and hearing, dexterity, and speed—might be beginning to fail her. Studies of clerical worker wages showed that after a woman was fifty, her wages leveled off or even dropped.[84]

Many women still at work had managed to carve out a fairly secure position for themselves by their fifties and sixties. But there was a terrible precariousness to these women's lives because their security was usually based on a personal relationship with a boss, the ongoing profitability of their place of employment, or their own good health and ability to work. Annie Galhouse, a former stenographer who began work in the early twentieth century, married, had two children, and was widowed in 1917. She found it easy to secure work in Washington during the war and afterward was contented with her job as a secretary at the Federal Reserve Bank in Atlanta. But the office staff was reduced in 1925 due to new centralized clerical services, and she and her boss both lost their jobs. She took a position with "one of the leading firms in the city," but complained that her work was "strictly *stenographic*, and the salary is *only* $140 [a month], with much harder work and longer hours than I have ever had." She thought there were no real chances for her to improve her situation. "From this you will see," she wrote, "that for the time being I am rather pessimistic and feel that my previous experience and years of work mean nothing."[85]

Far more dreadful possibilities could befall older women clericals. A woman who left high school in 1886 worked for sixteen years and then married, only to have "cocaine break up my home in 1911." She had been forced to accept stressful and demanding work as a stenographer in a hospital because "56 year-old employees are in the discard—they could not get a younger woman to fill the jobs here—so they rely on 'age,' and 'age' had to accept, because the different positions are not obtainable except by 'youth.'"[86] A "Miss Wheeler" who went to work at the age of fourteen in 1892 had four different jobs in her first eighteen years of work, but then settled in at a firm in 1910 where "at first she was advanced steadily in responsibility." What she enjoyed most about her job was her manager: "He was a man of high ideals, who held his workers up to his own standards, but who at the same time was always ready to devote time and energy . . . to any of his employees." But the old manager died, and he was replaced by "a self-made man, crude and . . . assertive . . . [and] opposed to the advancement of women." Wheeler's salary had been frozen, but "at her age" she could not risk leaving her job, especially since she had, until recently, been supporting her mother as well as herself.[87]

Women over thirty sometimes felt employers' preferences for youth keenly. Younger women became the scapegoats for their sense of rejection and rage. A woman from Nova Scotia who had been the private secretary to Alexander Graham Bell for thirteen years had to seek work in an advertising firm in Chicago in 1923.

She did not feel free to leave her job as a receptionist and secretary because she lived alone and was also helping to support her mother. She disliked dealing with the "gruff and discourteous" men who called at the office and the petty personal demands of her employer, who insisted that she take his watch in for repair, order his horse for an afternoon ride, and edit his books and articles. She felt competent to move to an executive position but despaired of ever doing so. Her age, she felt, was definitely a factor in her being stuck where she was. "Men," she said, "seemed to prefer pretty, empty-headed, young girls with stenography and typing to really capable, dependable women."[88]

Another Chicago secretary with fifteen years' experience expanded on the same theme and astutely observed how the representation of the "ideal secretary" in popular culture reenforced older women's disadvantage. Youth and physical attractiveness, combined in the person of "the pretty girl," were powerful icons, and might lead to invidious comparisons with more "plain folk":

> An outstanding asset.... must ever be—*the pretty girl*. Given a pretty face and ... the race *is* won! ... Even the stage stresses this advantage—that mistakes made by a pretty stenographer or secretary never seem quite so outrageously gratuitous as those committed by the plain folk! There should be some way of giving the plain folk some slight advantage in receiving offers of positions.... So with those past, or *just* beyond, the usual age for easy employment offers. Why not stress the very distinct advantages that inhere in the middle-aged woman? ... They care far less for outside distractions—have themselves better in hand—are more likely to stay overtime cheerfully—have more poise, and frequently more reserve and dignity and distaste for the cheap flirtations that in every place rise to the surface.... At the moment the country has gone mad on *youth.* ... Again and again I have seen the young and dimpled and marcelled getting off for extra days, whimpering at overtime, clamoring for release when extra work was required—AND some older worker delegated to complete the undertaking required![89]

The notion that the typical youthful stenographer failed to carry her own weight was also developed by Justine Mansfield, an office employment specialist, in a 1926 magazine article. Mansfield claimed the youthful clerk not only had no ambition, but lived a life that undermined all women's prospects at the office. Her semidependent status at home meant she had no sense of the importance of earning a living. In describing the youthful stenographer's daily routine, Mansfield harped on her frivolous life-style, made possible by indulgent parents. The stenographer was awakened in the morning by "a doting mother" and "handed" her breakfast; en route to the office she rarely read a newspaper, preferring "one of those picturesque scandal sheets" instead. She did as little work as possible in the morning, went out to lingerie shops at lunchtime, returned to the office, "dolled up for the afternoon session," during which she produced a few letters, and went home to mother's dinner or out for an evening with her boyfriend. She might do the dishes, but was usually off to the movies, the theater, or the dancehall and was lucky if she "got to bed at 3 or 4 in the morning." The clothing the stenographer wore reenforced her lack of intent: "Why the incongruity of a ball gown to an office? The high-heeled slippers with rhinestone buckles? The perfectly marcelled hair? The short sleeves and low necks?" The only things the stenographer took seriously, Mansfield argued, were her love affairs.[90]

In a spirited letter to the editor in a following issue, Katherine Redfern defended all but some of the "very young . . . women in business." Redfern made the interesting observation that marcelling was a way of keeping bobbed hair neat, not just a silly vanity. Although some of Mansfield's complaints might be true of the youngest workers, Redfern said, most women clerks were serious workers, despite their bobbed hair and flapper clothing: "when a woman has attained the age where she is capable of holding positions of trust and responsibility she has gotten beyond the stage where she is waiting for 'five o-clock' to come. . . . other wise she would not be retained in her position. I reiterate that I am speaking of the hundreds of women holding responsible positions to whom your article is an injustice."[91]

Discord between younger and older clerical workers in the workplace was prevalent enough to be noticed by employers. Some managers interviewed by Johanna Lobsenz insisted that older women were often "moody and irritable" and less adaptable to instruction or new methods of work. Younger people were alleged to "look brighter and fresher" as well. Employers claimed that "younger people and older people in the same office, at similar work and at approximately the same salary, do not get on well together. The younger person is likely to feel contempt for the older woman who has not advanced past her; and the older woman is likely to be envious of a younger person who, in spite of youth, has caught up with her in salary and position." Such assessments revealed the real predicament of older women in office work. Their position was undermined by the culture's contempt for the "old maid" and the string of qualities—all negative—she was assumed to have. Unless she had become an office manager, supervisor, or private secretary, she was likely to be pushed to the periphery of office social life and viewed as a kind of elderly pariah. At the same time, this and other aspects of her employment probably did make her resentful and unhappy at least some of the time.[92]

The Legacy of Women's Ambition and the Labor Segmentation of Office Work

The film *Working Girl*, a discussion of which began this chapter, clearly drew on the continued existence of a lively workplace culture in its depiction of a Staten Island heroine and her office in the 1980s. The film is a reminder that the legacy of women's ambition remains complex. Powerful women in office work often took an individualist approach to the problems of women workers. They stood up for women's right to compete for new jobs. They questioned the rigidity of sex-segregated work and the exclusion of women from management. They believed that jobs should be assigned on the basis of education, intelligence, and performance. They usually supported the right of married women to work, even though most of them remained single and opted out of the distractions of heterosexual marriage and children. But they were also firm advocates of scientific management and the faith that efficiency was a higher good.

The years after 1960 evoked new versions of the ambitious woman's feminism. Women were sometimes urged to postpone marriage and children for their careers, and when they did acquire domestic relations, to make sure they did not interfere with work. Women who refused to take their careers as seriously as the prototypical "successful woman" were sometimes deemed as "sell-outs" to the claim that women could do it all. With more women graduating from college and entering the professions, middle-class women were frequently able to escape clerical work. Many of the political goals of the feminist movement, like affirmative action, had the most impact on the professions and other middle-class occupations to which middle-class women aspired. The "secretary" was now often the epitome of what the individualist woman hoped to avoid, yet the reality is that clerical work is still the employment that most women have.

The ethos of the modern office, rooted as it is in a hierarchy of class, gender, and race distinctions, and a mythology that says merit determines rank, can readily absorb women who graduate from the nation's best business schools, engineering colleges, and personnel management programs without upsetting traditional economic and social relationships of class. Whether women or people of color will ever be admitted to the real inner sancta of white masculine power elites remains to be seen. Old arguments in new theoretical disguises—the "mommy track"—jeopardize further gains. But while complaints about women being closed out of top managerial ranks continue, there is no doubt that some women have achieved salaries and positions of power of which their grandmothers could have only dreamed. The presence of women in the upper levels of management has done little, however, to temper the ongoing effects of scientific management. Without a consciousness of class and race, feminism in corporate offices has allowed some women (mostly middle class and college educated) to escape the grind of routinized office work but left countless others (often working-class women and women of color) to entry-level jobs that are more boring and de-humanizing than ever. As in the years before 1930, however, the fact that many women escape these jobs into better positions by taking classes, earning college degrees, and proving their indispensability to management helps to keep individual ambition alive as a cross-class phenomenon.

Office worker culture remains vibrant and has the potential for posing the problems faced by office workers in a somewhat differ-ent way. The end of the marriage bar as a method of labor segmenta-tion was, I would argue, imperative to a more unified office worker culture and the ability to make organized demands. Part of the rea-son may be simply that when women are workers for most of their lives, they can organize the workplace more successfully because they are in it much longer. But the main effect of the end of the marriage bar was that a major obstacle to office worker solidarity was finally removed. Differences that segmented clerical workers so effectively in the 1920s—sex and age—might, once the mar-riage bar was gone, add diversity rather than distraction.

The future promises that women will continue to be divided by class and race in the office. Women in office work, whatever their class or race, face common problems: sex discrimination, gender stereotyping, sexual harassment, homophobia, lack of day-care, and a long work day that robs parents of important time with their children. But differences among women in salary and power mean that women clerks and their women bosses have vastly different re-sources for solving these problems.[93] Office work production continues to rely on the "light manufacturing" of working-class women clerical workers. Unionism and feminism offer strategies for solving the problems of women clerical workers, but women managers and women clerks, despite their common workplace problems, may find themselves increasingly at odds over the implementation of these strategies.

NOTES

1. The tautological and rather incomprehensible dismissal of women workers by Gordon, Edwards, and Reich is all too typical: "Occupational segregation meant that most employed women had not yet been affected by the job differentiation among different ethnic and racial groups that was beginning to develop throughout the corporate capitalist sector. Women were employed in female occupations, whereas male workers felt the principle impact of the process of homogenization and the new corporate strategies." That "women were employed in female occupations" explains everything necessary to know about women's employment is an oxymoronic notion. While I would agree that "it was precisely the weak bargaining power of women, and their neglect by male unions, that helped contribute to the ability of corporations to isolate women," I would not then conclude that it enabled management to "continue to manage female labor with relatively traditional techniques." Rather, this isolation may have enabled management, in the case of clerical work anyway, to use the new personnel management techniques most effectively on women. David M. Gordon, Richard Edwards, and Michael Reich, *Segmented Work, Divided Workers: The Historical Transformation of Labor in the United States* (Cambridge: Cambridge University Press, 1982), 151-52.

2. Interview with L. P. by Gail Sansbury, Nov. 8, 1972, Rhode Island Working Women Oral History Project [RIWW], Special Collections, University of Rhode Island Library, Kingston. Names of RIWW interviewees have been replaced with pseudonyms.

3. Interview with Beatrice Reed Anderson by Sharon Hartman Strom, July, 1989.

4. Jessie R. Wilson to E. H. Enochs, June 28, 1940, Pennsylvania Railroad Records, Hagley Library Wilmington, Delaware; Eleanor Gilbert (Anne Rosenblatt), *The Ambitious Woman in Business* (New York: Funk and Wagnalls, 1916), 147-48.

5. Bureau of Vocational Information Survey of Women Secretaries and Stenographers [BVIWS], 342 (131), California.

6. Edith Johnson, *To Women of the Business World* (Philadelphia: J. B. Lippincott, 1923), 43-47.

7. Interview with M. C. by Valerie Raleigh Yow, Oct. 25, 1982, RIWW.

8. Interviews with R. S. by Gail Sansbury, Nov. 6, 1982, and with M. C. by Valerie Raleigh Yow, RIWW.

9. Ruth Shonle Cavan, *Business Girls: A Study of Their Problems* (Chicago: Religious Education Association, 1929), 46.

10. Cavan, *Business Girls*, 46.

11. Jeanette Eaton and Bertha M. Stevens, *Commercial Work and Training for Girls* (New York: Macmillan, 1915), 247; Cavan, *Business Girls*, 45; interview with M. C. by Valerie Raleigh Yow.

12. Eaton and Stevens, *Commercial Work and Training for Girls*, 247; BVIWS 173 (1956), New York; BVIWS 47 (1937), New York.

13. BVIWS 284 (1924), New York.

14. Interview with L. P. by Gail Sansbury.

15. *Scovill Bulletin* [*SB*], Nov. 1918, 6, June 1930, 12.

16. *SB*, June 1930, 13; Willis Brindley, "What We Have Learned about Handling Women Employees in a Small Town," *Office Economist* [*OE*] 7 (July-Aug. 1925): 10-11. Although the Scovill Girls' Club was originally available to both factory and clerical workers, it seems to have fallen more and more under the aegis of office workers by the 1920s. For accounts of the activities of the Scovill Girls' Club see the *SB*, 1919-1930.

17. Typewritten memo from E. R. DeTamble (comptroller's office), June 15, 1922. Scovill Manufacturing Papers, case 34, Harvard Business School Library.

18. Interview with R. S. by Gail Sansbury.

19. The phrase "working downtown" and its special importance for clerical workers was suggested to me by Gail Gregory Sansbury, "Working Downtown: A Survey of Women Office Workers in the Working Environment in Providence, R.I., 1867-1978," unpublished paper, University of Rhode Island, April 1983.

The first skyscraper was built in Rhode Island in 1896. It was followed by the Providence Public Library in 1900, the Union Trust Bank in 1901, the YWCA in 1906, the Turk's Head Office Building in 1913, the Union and Strand theaters in 1916, the telephone company building and Shubert's Majestic Theatre in 1917, the Biltmore Hotel in 1922, the Providence Gas Company Building in 1925, and the Industrial National Bank in 1928. For descriptions of these and a complete inventory of buildings in downtown Providence, see Rhode Isand Historical Preservation Commission, *Downtown Providence: Statewide Historical Preservation Report*, P-P-5 (Providence: Rhode Island Historical Preservation Commission, 1970).

20. Interview with E. B. by Valerie Raleigh Yow, Jan. 8, 1983, RIWW.

21. Edith Padelford Cochrane, "Welfare Work for Women Office Employees," *OE* 7 (May 1925): 7.

22. Rhode Island Women's Biography Project [RIWBP], 281, Special Collections, University of Rhode Island, Kingston.

23. Interview with M. C. by Valerie Raleigh Yow.

24. See, for example, interview with G. M. by Gail Sansbury, Feb. 6, 1983, RIWW.

25. Cavan, *Business Girls*, 29.

26. Julie A. Mattahei, *An Economic History of Women in America: Women's Work, the Sexual Division of Labor, and the Development of Capitalism* (New York: Schocken Books, 1982), 220. For an earlier version of the notion that women's roles as wives and mothers created radically different job expectations in women than in men, see Leslie Woodcock Tentler, *Wage-Earning Women: Industrial Work and Family Life in the United States, 1900-1930* (New York: Oxford University Press, 1979).

27. For an important critique of the notion that a unified "women's culture" can explain women's economic choices and behavior, see Susan Levine, "Labors in the Field: Reviewing Women's Cultural History," *Radical History Review* 35 (April 1986): 49-57.

28. While Alice Kessler-Harris argues that "among women, a common ideological bond puts them in a relation to the labor force that has historically differed from that of men," she develops the idea that women's self-identity within the work force changes over time and may be connected to race and class. I would argue that sexual orientation and marital status should also be added as categories. Alice Kessler-Harris, "Independence and Virtue in the Lives and Wage-Earning Women in the United States, 1870-1930," in *Women in Culture and Politics: A Century of Change*, ed. Judith Friedlander (Bloomington: University of Indiana Press, 1986), 3-15.

29. It should be emphasized that Cavan's study is impressionistic and anecdotal. It is, however, the only attempt I know of in the 1920s to link gender, sexuality, work, and ambition among young working women. Cavan, *Business Girls*, 59.

30. Ibid., 73, 20, 26-27.

31. Ibid., 39, 43.

32. Ibid., 16. A total of 321 young women filled out forms and marked a total of 1,473 "problems" from a list of 36 categories. The proportions of those checking responses ranged from 42.3 percent at the top ("lack of self-confidence") to 3.7 percent at the bottom ("loss of position" and "failures in work undertaken").

33. Ibid., 55.

34. Lorine Pruette, *Women and Leisure: A Study of Social Waste* (New York: E. P. Dutton, 1924), 153-99, 199.

35. RIWBP 476, 564, and 662.

36. BVIWS 84 (1853), New York.

37. Mary Schauffler, "A Study of Three Clerical Occupations for Women: Stenography, Typing, Bookkeeping," M.A. thesis, Western Reserve University, 1927, 13-14, 32. Nearly 73 percent of 155 employers interviewed in Minneapolis in 1924-25 said that they preferred to hire women with high school education. Only .6 percent preferred grammar school education, and about 7.1 percent preferred college education. M. C. Elmer, *A Study of Women in Clerical and Secretarial Work in Minneapolis, Minn.* (Minneapolis; Woman's Occupational Bureau, 1925), 28.

38. Ethel Erickson's study found that although 33 percent of women clericals over forty had only grammar school educations, only 13 percent of those under twenty-five had not completed some high school. In New York City, nearly 30 percent of the entire sample had graduated from high school, and another 43 percent had attended high school for some period. "The Employment of Women in Offices," *Women's Bureau Bulletin* [WBB] 120 (1934): 23.

39. For an especially careful exploration of education as a factor in salary, see Schauffler, "A Study of Three Clerical Occupations," 11-14.

40. BVIWS 666 (534), Illinois; Anne Hendry Morrison, *Women and Their Careers: A Study of 306 Women in Business and the Professions* (New York: National Federation of Business and Professional Women's Clubs, 1934), 90.

41. Erickson, "Employment of Women in Offices," 11-12.

42. Erickson's study showed "little variation in age distribution" in offices in St. Louis, Philadelphia, Chicago, New York, Atlanta, Hartford, and Des Moines, "The Employment of Women in Offices," 10: under twenty, 9.2 percent; twenty but under twenty-five, 40.5 percent; twenty-five but under thirty, 24 percent; thirty but under forty, 18.8 percent; forty and older, 7.5 percent.

Schauffler, "A Study of Three Clerical Occupations," 7-8, shows age breakdowns very similar to those of Erickson. A large firm in New York City, presumably a department store, gave Johanna Lobsenz its age breakdown according to sex for the year 1927. Of 842 clerical workers, 263 (31 percent) were under twenty-one; 309 (37 percent) were twenty-one to thirty-four; 195 (23 percent) were thirty-five to forty-four; and seventy-five (9 percent) were forty-five and older. Johanna Lobsenz, *The Older Woman in Industry* (New York: Charles Scribner's Sons, 1929), 161. Looking at typists and stenographers alone gives the impression that clerical work was overwhelmingly dominated by the youthful, but as chapter 4 documents, these positions made up a minority of all clerical jobs. For a discussion of the census figures on clerical work and age distribution see Elyce Jean Rotella, "Women's Labor Force Participation and the Growth of Clerical Employment in the United States, 1870-1930," Ph.D. diss., University of Pennsylvania, 1977, 183-84.

43. The census figures of 1910 showed that 5.34 percent of all women clerical workers were married. By 1920 this figure had risen to 8.93 percent and by 1930 to 18.231 percent. Rotella, *Women's Labor Force Participation*, 193. As usual, census figures should be used with caution. Ethel Erickson's 1931 study of clerical workers for the Women's Bureau found that 11.8 percent were married and 3.4 percent were widowed, separated, or divorced. Schauffler found an average of 10.6 percent married clericals in Cleveland, "A Study of Three Clerical Occupations," 9. As both Erickson and Grace Coyle observed, the discrepancy between the census figures and employment figures was probably due to women's underreporting of mar-

riage to employers to escape the marriage bar. Grace L. Coyle, "Women in the Clerical Occupations," *Annals* 143(May 1929): 183, and Erickson, "Employment of Women in Offices," 12-13; also see Lois Scharf, *To Work and to Wed: Female Employment, Feminism and the Great Depression* (Westport: Greenwood Press, 1980), 103-7. Some of the kinds of offices which appeared in Erickson's study—notably large offices and insurance companies—were most widely known for enforcing the marriage bar, which may also have made her estimates of married clericals low. Smaller offices appear to have restricted the employment of married clerical workers the least.

44. For discussions of the issue of working wives and mothers in this period, see Nancy F. Cott, *The Grounding of Modern Feminism* (New Haven: Yale University Press, 1987), 180-211; Winifred D. Wandersee, *Women's Work and Family Values, 1920-1940* (Cambridge: Harvard University Press, 1981), 67-83; and Lynn Y. Wiener, *From Working Girl to Working Mother: The Female Labor Force in the United States* (Chapel Hill: University of North Carolina Press, 1985), 98-110, 133-34. On birth control, see Mary E. Cookingham, "Combining Marriage, Motherhood and Jobs Before World War II: Women College Graduates, Classes of 1905-1935," *Journal of Family History* 9 (Summer 1984): 178-95, and Warren S. Thompson and P. K. Whelpton, "The Population of the Nation," in Report of the President's Research Committee on Social Trends, *Recent Social Trends* (New York: McGraw-Hill, 1934), 41-46. A particularly helpful analysis of birthrates and their consequences for a decline in the relative proportion of young people can be found in Paula S. Fass, *The Damned and the Beautiful: American Youth in the 1920's* (New York: Oxford University Press, 1977), 57-71. Both Fass and Cookingham argue that new contraceptive measures available in the 1920s probably increased the marriage rate and also allowed couples to marry younger.

45. Employers probably exaggerated these figures because they were being interviewed by the Women's Bureau and knew their reports would become a matter of the public record. Erickson, "Employment of Women in Offices," 29, 46, 84-85. For similar findings, see Beatrice Doerschuk, "The Woman Secretary," typewritten manuscript (1926), section beginning "Secretarial Work as an Occupation for Married Women," BVI, folder 506.

46. Harold B. Bergen, "Stability of Men and Women Office Workers," *Personnel Journal* 5 (July 1926): 72; Marion A. Bills, "Relative Permanency of Men and Women Office Workers," *Journal of Personnel Research* 5 (Feb. 1927): 208; also see Priscilla Murolo, "White-Collar Women: The Feminization of Aetna Life Insurance Company," unpublished paper, Yale University, June 8, 1982, 31-32.

47. BVIWS 415 (45), California.

48. The Business and Professional Women's Club of Hartford, which attempted to place women in "high-grade" positions, complained that "Hartford is most conservative about married women's work. Almost uni-

versal prejudice against it. Lowers the whole standard of women's work in the city." Comments by Employment Agents or Agencies, 1925, BVI, folder 500.

49. John L. Conover, "Management as Applied to Public Utility Billing Problems," American Management *Office Executive Series* 43 (1929): 15.

50. Rowland is quoted by John H. MacDonald, *Office Management* (New York: Prentice-Hall, 1942), 17.

51. On temporary married telephone workers, see Ethel H. Best, "The Change from Manual to Dial Operation in the Telephone Industry," *WBB* 110 (1933): 5. Best saw AT&T's plan for a transition to the dial system as "progressive" because it prevented the laying off of large numbers of permanent workers. N. R. Danielian, on the other hand, saw both the introduction of the dial system and steady speed-ups for dial system operators in a more sinister light. By 1929 about half of the total system had been converted to the dial system, and by 1935, when the system was complete, as many as twenty-thousand operators had lost their jobs. Hour loads of calls per operator had increased from about 100 in 1920 to 173 by 1935. In this instance, married women seem to have been used much like strike-breakers, brought in to defuse discontent by decreasing the number of full-time workers the company would have to hire and then fired once the transition to direct dial had been made. *A.T.&T.: The Story of Industrial Conquest* (New York: Vanguard Press, 1939), 209-12. For effects of the dial system on telephone workers, see Stephen H. Norwood, *Labor's Flaming Youth: Telephone Operators and Worker Militancy, 1878-1923* (Urbana: University of Illinois Press, 1990), 262-65, 307-9.

For comments on the feasibility of hiring married women for part-time work in the telephone company, see the comments of Mr. Frank in "Business school (?) Interviews—Brief Investigation of Girls in Commercial Work," (handwritten notes, circa 1919), BVI, folder 72. Frank claimed that "the Traffic Dept. [in New York City], has tried part-time work, using married women, former employees. . . . They were very irregular, did unsatisfactory work and prejudiced the company against part-time workers." The office manager in question thought the failure could be explained by "the fact that a certain mental mechanism for defence against the strain of telephone work had broken down and was not readily set up again in part-time workers."

52. RIWBP 24; interview with E. B. by Valerie Raleigh Yow, Jan. 8, 1983; interview with M.C. by Valerie Raleigh Yow, RIWW.

53. RIWBP 303; interview with M. D. by Sharon Hartman Strom, June 5, 1986; RIWBP 324; interview with L. P. by Gail Sansbury, RIWW.

54. Interviews with R. S. and G. M. by Gail Sansbury; RIWBP 635 and 564.

55. BVIWS 180 (1912), New York.

56. BVI interview with Mr. Linke on Married Women's Work, Dec. 31, 1924, BVI, folder 499.

57. Interview with Miss M. Fish of Executive Supply, BVI, folder 499; interview with Mr. Stevenson of the Equitable Employment Service and with Mrs. Laird of the National Employment Agency, BVI, folder 500.

58. Interview with Mr. Linke, BVI, folder 499.

59. Schauffler, "A Study of Three Clerical Occupations," 10; BVIWS 102 (1508), New York.

60. BVIWS 765 (606), 716 (476), 747 (609), all Illinois.

61. BVIWS 601 (529), Illinois.

62. BVIWS 47 (1937), New York. Nancy Cott surveyed the BVI respondents' attitudes toward married women in the office and found, as might be expected, mixed results. About 64 percent of the single women seemed to think combining marriage and work was a real possibility. Cott, *Grounding of Modern Feminism*, 190, 344, fn. 21. Some married women made a special case for their own employment but generally condemned that of other marrieds. A woman who married in 1906 was still working in 1925 because her husband had been chronically ill, but she hired a housekeeper and only worked part-time. She did not think any woman should work fulltime who also had "home duties." BVIWS 040 (1954), New York.

63. BVIWS 452 (1643), New York.

64. BVIWS 415 (45), California.

65. BVIWS 773 (610), Illinois.

66. BVIWS 316 (197), California. This respondent had taken the commercial course in high school, worked off and on until 1915, then enrolled in Stanford and earned a bachelor's degree in English and foreign language. She then worked as a business manager for the *Palo Alto News* until 1917, when she left for Washington to work in both the Food and Fuel Administrations during the war. Her college training, evidently, made it possible for her to type academic manuscripts at home.

67. The term *family wage* refers to the total amount of wages made by wage earners in a family or household. For analyses of salaries required to live away from parents, see Elmer, "A Study of Women in Clerical and Secretarial Work," 41-42; and Dorothy W. Douglas, "The Cost of Living for Working Women: A Criticism of Current Theories," *Quarterly Journal of Economics* 34 (1920): 225-41. For a helpful discussion of women on their own in these years, see Joanne J. Meyerowitz, *Women Adrift: Independent Wage Earners in Chicago, 1880-1930* (Chicago: University of Chicago Press, 1988), especially 31-38, 89-125. Meyerowitz emphasizes that while alarm over women living away from parents in these years increased, so did the number of women doing so; by the 1920s it had become socially acceptable for middle-class as well as working-class women to live in boardinghouses and apartments. Clerical workers were more able to afford living apart from families than factory or department store workers. Also see Gary Cross and Peter Shergold, "'We Think We Are of the Oppressed': Gender, White Collar Work, and Grievances of Late Nineteenth-Century Women," *Labor History* 28 (Winter 1987): 31.

68. *SB*, Oct. 4, 1943, 6.

69. Margaret Elliott and Grace E. Manson, "Earnings of Women in Business and the Professions," *Michigan Business Studies* 3 (Sept. 1930): 108-10. Of 946 BVI respondents, 91 said they were currently married and living with their husbands. Of the remaining 855, 526 lived with parents, 192 lived alone, and 111 lived with friends, one lived with "other," and 25 did not indicate their household situation. A surprising 88 of the total provided full economic support for one and up to as many as four dependents, and another 252 partially supported dependents, mostly parents and younger siblings. Some of the married women had husbands who were ill or disabled; widows and divorced women were trying to support children on one income. When the 795 who gave the years they left high school (used to determine age) are divided into groups according to age, the likelihood of living with others than parents or living alone increased (Table 11).

70. Marguerite B. Benson, "Labor Turnover of Working Women," *Annals* 143 (May 1929): 118-19.

71. Maureen Wiener Greenwald, "Working Class Feminism and the Family Wage Ideal," *Journal of American History* 76 (June 1989): 118-50.

72. George Soule, *Prosperity Decade: From War to Depression: 1917-1929* (New York: Rinehart, 1947), 158-62; "Railroad Women Decrease 30,000," *New York Commercial*, Dec. 24, 1926.

73. Maury Klein of the University of Rhode Island generously shared this example with me, discovered in his research of the Pennsylvania Railroad Records, [PR], Hagley Library, Wilmington, Delaware. Pennsylvania Railroad, "For the Information of the Public," Sept. 13, 1928, 2 pp. typewritten memorandum.

74. "Wage-Earning Wives," *New York Herald Tribune*, Sept. 15, 1928; "Problem of the Married Woman in Industry," *Philadelphia Inquirer*, Sept. 18, 1928; "Married Women and Employment," *Houston Post-Dispatch*, Sept. 17, 1928; also see Mary Phlegar Smith, "Legal and Administrative Restrictions Affecting the Rights of Married Women to Work," *Annals* 143 (May 1929): 262-63.

75. "Railroad Rebuked by Women's Club," *Philadelphia Inquirer*, Sept. 15, 1928.

76. G. Boutillier to R. V. Massey, Feb. 5, 1929, PR, Hagley Library.

77. Marion Mixner to R. V. Massey, Aug. 6, 1931, PR, Hagley Library.

78. "Wives Keep Jobs on 17 Railroads," *New York Times*, April 16, 1933. By 1930 the number of women holding jobs in the railroad industry had declined by 52 percent. Avis Lobell, "Railroad Work for Women," in *Careers for Women: New Ideas, New Methods, New Opportunities—to Fit a New World*, ed. Catharine Filene (Boston: Houghton Mifflin, 1934), 605. Lobell reported that nearly all openings for women in railroads were still in clerical work, but that the supply of potential employees far exceeded the demand for their services.

79. Interviews with Mrs. Laird of the National Employment Agency, Mrs. Lower, and Miss Hamilton, BVI, folder 500.

80. Interview with Mr. Linke, Dec. 31, 1924, BVI, folder 499.

81. See Lobsenz, *The Older Woman in Industry*, 145-56, quote on 166. Ethel Erickson reported that of thirty-five New York City firms who answered her request for pension information in 1931, eighteen had pension schemes which, presumably, covered women as well as men. "Employment of Women in Offices," 33.

82. Comments by employment agencies, BVI, folders 499-500; Schauffler, "A Study of Three Clerical Occupations," 8.

83. BVIWS 368 (227), California, with typewritten note of BVI interviewer attached to newspaper clipping describing Edwards's appointment, *Los Angeles Herald*, June 22, 1925.

84. Elliott and Manson, "Earnings of Women in Business," 25.

85. BVIWS 922 (420), Georgia, with letter from Annie H. Galhouse to BVI, Sept. 15, 1925.

86. BVIWS (212010).

87. Morrison, *Women and their Careers*, 93.

88. BVIWS 737 (1903), Illinois.

89. BVIWS 769 (601), Illinois.

90. Justine Mansfield, "I Believe Women Have a Future in the Office," *OE* 8 (Jan. 1926): 5-6, 13.

91. Katharine Redfern, "Defending the Women in Business," *Office Economist* 8 (March 1926): 10, 14.

92. Lobsenz, *Older Woman in Industry*, 94-95.

93. On this point see Linda Blum and Vicki Smith, "Women's Mobility in the Corporation: A Critique of the Politics of Optimism," *Signs* 13, no. 31 (1987): 38-39.

Index

About the Author

Sharon Hartman Strom did graduate work in American social and intellectual history at Cornell University, where she received a Ph.D. in 1969. She is professor of history and women's studies at the University of Rhode Island and teaches courses in social history and gender studies. She has previously published work on the American suffrage movement, clerical worker unions in the CIO, and the history of office work. She is now at work on a biography of Florence Luscomb.

Books in the Series
Women in American History